AMERICA'S FIRST GENERAL STAFF

AMERICA'S FIRST GENERAL STAFF

A Short History of the Rise and Fall of the General Board of the Navy, 1900–1950

JOHN T. KUEHN

Naval Institute Press
Annapolis, Maryland

Naval Institute Press
291 Wood Road
Annapolis, MD 21402

© 2017 by John T. Kuehn
All rights reserved. No part of this book may be reproduced or utilized in any form or by any means, electronic or mechanical, including photocopying and recording, or by any information storage and retrieval system, without permission in writing from the publisher.

Names: Kuehn, John T., author.
Title: America's first general staff : a short history of the rise and fall of the General Board of the Navy, 1900–1950 / John T. Kuehn.
Other titles: Short history of the rise and fall of the General Board of the Navy, 1900–1950
Description: Annapolis, Maryland : Naval Institute Press, [2017] | Includes bibliographical references and index.
Identifiers: LCCN 2017031226| ISBN 9781682471913 (hard cover : alk. paper) | ISBN 9781682471920 (mobi)
Subjects: LCSH: United States. Navy. General Board—History. | United States. Navy—History—20th century. | Naval strategy—United States.
Classification: LCC VA58 .K843 2017 | DDC 359.40973/09041—dc23 LC record available at https://lccn.loc.gov/2017031226

Caribbean map created by Chris Robinson.
War Plan Orange map courtesy of the U.S. Naval Institute map archive.

♾ Print editions meet the requirements of ANSI/NISO z39.48–1992 (Permanence of Paper).
Printed in the United States of America.

25 24 23 22 21 20 19 18 17   9 8 7 6 5 4 3 2 1
First printing

CONTENTS

List of Illustrations — vii
Preface and Acknowledgments — ix
List of Abbreviations — xi

Chapter 1. What Was the General Board of the Navy? — 1
Chapter 2. The Naval Reform Movement and the Creation of the General Board — 9
Chapter 3. In the Shadows of Nelson and Scharnhorst, 1900–1904 — 33
Chapter 4. From Taylor to Fiske: The General Board, 1904–13 — 61
Chapter 5. The General Board in Peace and War, 1913–18 — 88
Chapter 6. The Challenges of Peace: From Versailles to Washington, 1918–22 — 114
Chapter 7. The Heyday of the General Board: From Washington to London and After, 1922–31 — 139
Chapter 8. Innovation and Decline, 1932–41 — 172
Chapter 9. Phoenix or Icarus? The Resurgence and Death of the General Board, 1941–51 — 196
Epilogue. America's First General Staff — 221

Appendix 1. General Orders Relating to the Establishment and Reorganization of the General Board of the Navy — 225
Appendix 2. Secretaries of the Navy, 1900–1951 — 227
Appendix 3. General Board Studies Produced in 1901 — 229

Notes 231
Selected Bibliography 279
Index 291

ILLUSTRATIONS

Images

Meeting of the General Board of the Navy, c. 1900	3
The General Board in a meeting at the Navy Department, 1932	6
RADM Stephen B. Luce	15
Alfred Thayer Mahan	25
RADM Henry C. Taylor	29
ADM George Dewey	35
RADM Charles J. Badger and RADM Bradley A. Fiske	83
Secretary of the Navy Josephus Daniels and Chief of Naval Operations ADM William S. Benson ADM	94
Hilary P. Jones on the deck of the battleship USS *Pennsylvania*	177
VADM William V. Pratt	183
ADM John Towers	199
The rejuvenated General Board with ADM Towers as its chairman, 1947	210

Maps

Map 1. The Caribbean and Culebra area	50
Map 2. War Plan Orange	70

PREFACE AND ACKNOWLEDGMENTS

During my research for my doctoral dissertation in 2007, I ran across an organization known as the General Board of the Navy. My work linking naval arms limitation treaties to military innovation, both deliberate and serendipitous, revealed that the General Board was not only an important organization but also one whose influence had not been studied in a systematic or comprehensive way. Some scholars, especially Norman Friedman, Thomas Hone, Mark Mandeles, Robert W. Love Jr., and George Baer, had woven the General Board into their work, but no one monograph, including any unpublished graduate thesis, had dealt singularly with the board over the entire span of its organizational history.[1] This led to my first published work on the board in 2008, *Agents of Innovation: The General Board and the Design of the Fleet that Defeated the Japanese Navy*. That work was never intended as the first or last word on the board; rather, it was intended as an examination of its influence on naval innovation during the period between World War I and World War II. It did, however, inspire me to contemplate a more comprehensive work.

After completing *Agents*, I continued my investigation of the General Board, and this led me to conclude that it can claim pride of place as the United States' first permanent, peacetime general staff. The research for that effort has been integrated and included in portions of this book as part of a larger narrative built around the idea of the board as the nation's first general staff and, on balance, as a comprehensive case study of a generally successful and innovative organization. My inclination to complete the work was spurred by various people, mostly historians. First and foremost is Jeff Barlow, longtime historian at the Naval Historical Center, now known as the Naval History and Heritage Command (NHHC). The General Board is too complex and interesting to be contained by just one volume. That said, Jeff

Barlow advised me to go with a shorter narrative work of synthesis first, and I decided to follow his sage advice and leave a multivolume effort for my golden years. In addition to Jeff, Al Nofi provided further impetus because his wonderful monograph about the fleet battle problems between World War I and World War II included mention of the need for a complete history of the General Board.[2] Jonathan M. House also gets special mention for his insightful comments and proofreading of the entire manuscript as well as his encouragement to simply finish the project.

I also thank the many students I have supervised for their master's theses at the U.S. Army Command and General Staff College (CGSC) over the years whose research also contributed to this book: LCDR Jason H. Davis, LCDR Jeffrey K. Juergens, LCDR Christopher J. Mergen, LCDR Jeremy P. Schaub, and LCDR Mark W. Wever. I hope they all got promoted to higher rank and command. The Navy needs their brains. William "Kirk" Petrovic has been especially supportive in forwarding materials to both myself and my students. Other supporters include (in no particular order) CAPT Peter Swartz (Ret.), John Maurer, Christopher Bell, Sadao Asada, Corbin Williamson, Bob Keane, Larrie Ferreiro, CDR B. J. Armstrong, Randy Papadopoulos, D. M. Giangreco, Michael Crawford, and the folks at NHHC, especially its former chief, CAPT Jerry Hendrix (Ret.), whose support of my scholarship was critical. Jerry's book on Theodore Roosevelt's diplomacy helped fill critical gaps in my own scholarship.

Jim Willbanks, director of the Department of Military History at CGSC and currently its George C. Marshall Professor of Military History, urged me to apply for the Major General William Stofft historical research chair, a sinecure that allowed me more time to think and write. Thanks go to longtime naval historians Norman Friedman, Tom C. Hone, and Mark Mandeles, who share my interest in the General Board and have continued to provide critical advice and inspiration. Finally, in my first book I thanked my wonderful wife and collaborator, Kimberlee, first. For this book I will instead have her come last, giving her all the credit for not giving me too many "to do list" items during the government shutdown in 2013 (and after) and thus allowing me time to think, write, and finish this self-imposed labor of love. Thank you, Kimberlee!

ABBREVIATIONS

ABSD	Advanced base sectional dock
ACNO	Assistant Chief of Naval Operations
AF	U.S. Asiatic Fleet
ARD	Auxiliary (floating) repair dock
BB	Battleship
BOC	Board on Construction
BuAer	Bureau of Aeronautics (U.S. Navy)
BuC&R	Bureau of Construction and Repair
BuEng	Bureau of Engineering
BuEquip	Bureau of Equipment
BuMed	Bureau of Medicine and Surgery
BuNav	Bureau of Navigation
BuOrd	Bureau of Ordnance
BuPers	Bureau of Personnel
BuShips	Bureau of Ships (created in 1940 by the consolidation of BuEng and BuC&R)
CA	Heavy cruiser (originally armored cruiser)
CB	Battlecruiser
CF	Flight deck cruiser (also designated CLV)
CINCAF	Commander in chief, U.S. Asiatic Fleet
CINCUS	Commander in chief, U.S. Fleet (before 1942)
CL	Light cruiser
CNO	Chief of Naval Operations
COMINCH	Commander in chief, U.S. Fleet (after 1942)
CV	Aircraft carrier

CVL	Light aircraft carrier
DNI	Director of Naval Intelligence
EXOS	Executive Office of the Secretary of the Navy
GB	General Board of the U.S. Navy
JCS	Joint Chiefs of Staff
NARA	National Archives and Records Administration
NavyRegs	U.S. Navy Regulations
NHC	Naval Historical Center (today the Naval History and Heritage Command)
NHHC	Naval History and Heritage Command
NM	Nautical mile
NTS	Naval Transportation Service
NWC	Naval War College
ONI	Office of Naval Intelligence
OpNav	Office of the Chief of Naval Operations
PBY	Refers to the consolidated PBY Catalina patrol aircraft/seaplane
PHGB	Proceedings and Hearings of the General Board
RAF	Royal Air Force
RN	Royal Navy
SCB	Ship Characteristics Board
SecDef	Secretary of Defense
SecNav	Secretary of the Navy
SecState	Secretary of State
USA	U.S. Army
USMC	U.S. Marine Corps
USN	U.S. Navy
USNI	United States Naval Institute

AMERICA'S
═ FIRST ═
GENERAL
═ STAFF ═

CHAPTER 1

What Was the General Board of the Navy?

Hence it is that all governmental organizations, especially those charged with the problems of national defense, must be guided by sound judgment and administered by master hands. . . . Herein lies the vital value of the Board to the Navy and the nation.
    —Jarvis Butler, secretary to the Joint Army and Navy Board, 1930

The biological name for our species is *Homo sapiens*, translated variously as "man the wise" or "man the sentient." My father has said it should be "man the toolmaker" (*Homo fabricus*). All of these characterizations have their limitations, although "man the sentient" seems to fit reasonably well. However, I propose our collective name should instead be "man the problem solver." It makes no difference that man creates most of his own problems to solve; one cannot deny man's fundamental activity of solving problems for the span his life here on earth. This book is about a group of men who solved problems. Their collective and uniquely American approach to what they deemed to be the strategic and naval challenges of their day has much to teach us. In particular, their activities addressed the solution of problems of the first magnitude concerning the security and prosperity—as viewed in their day—of the United States in the first half of the twentieth century.

The General Board of the United States Navy was a uniquely American strategic planning organization with few analogs at the time of its establishment, except perhaps the various components of the Admiralty in Great Britain.[1] Jarvis Butler's article on the General Board, which appeared in *Proceedings* so many years ago, shed light on the role and influence of the board for the audience of that day, perhaps because its deliberations and studies were kept tightly secret, unlike the leaks and transparent strategies of today. Then, as now, confusion reigned over what sort of fleet to design and how to build it. The General Board served as the "balance wheel," or nexus, for bringing together coherent strategy and fleet design.[2] The board, the United States' first modern general staff in peacetime, emerged from the trends and developments of the Progressive Era of the late nineteenth and early twentieth centuries. Its creation was very much a reflection of the reformist spirit of the times, which also gave birth to the Army War College, the Army General Staff, and the Chief of Naval Operations (CNO).[3]

The General Board reflected a uniquely American attempt to reconcile the primacy of civilian control with the new requirements of the modern age, which seemed to dictate a more formal military and naval planning establishment and associated processes and methods. Thus its name reflected corporate America as well as a longstanding naval tradition in which challenges and problems were met with special, temporary boards. The General Board, however, differed from these temporary boards due to its longevity. By the 1920s it had become a permanent feature of the Navy and was regarded as the premier strategic "think tank" for advice to the Secretary of the Navy (SecNav). The following overview provides the master narrative around which the subsequent and more detailed chapters are structured. It might be regarded as presenting both my primary claim—that the General Board was America's first peacetime general staff—as well as a number of secondary claims about the innovative character and influence of the General Board and how it changed from 1900 to 1950.

As with most military innovations, the General Board was born out of an honest study of the lessons learned from a recent war. They were learned the hard way, from a conflict that had been poorly managed by both the Army and, to a lesser degree, the Navy—the Spanish-American War.[4] One of the few bright spots in its conduct at the strategic level was the establishment by Secretary of the Navy John D. Long of the Naval War Board of 1898, whose members included Alfred Thayer Mahan, Assistant Secretary of the Navy Theodore Roosevelt, and several senior Navy captains. This experience with a wartime strategy organization seemed to validate a longstanding effort by naval officers, dating back to the Civil War, to establish a standing organization to provide planning and direction for naval operations.[5]

Secretary Long acknowledged that he lacked "professional experience and the Navy being without a General Staff, it was necessary that he should have the assistance of such a Board." Based on these factors, and at

Meeting of the General Board of the Navy, c. 1900, shortly after its establishment. Admiral of the Fleet George Dewey is at the head of the table, and CAPT Henry Taylor, his right-hand man, is fifth from the left. Notice the maps and planning papers tacked to the walls as well as the civilian attire required for wear in the District of Columbia (this did not change until World War II). *Naval History and Heritage Command*

the urging of the chief of the Bureau of Navigation (BuNav), ADM Henry C. Taylor, Long issued General Order 544 on 13 March 1900, establishing the General Board of the Navy. Its purpose was "to insure efficient preparation of the fleet in case of war and for the naval defense of the coast."[6] Taylor dominated the board's first years of organizational existence and its president, the hero of the Battle of Manila Bay—Admiral of the Navy George Dewey. Dewey served in this capacity until his death in January 1917. Its charter was as broad or as narrow as the Secretary of the Navy chose to make it, since he determined the agenda. The position of the board was always precarious, since its creation had not been the result of congressional legislation but of executive fiat as an "experiment."[7]

Nonetheless, the longer the General Board survived as an organizational entity, the more it came to be recognized as an institutional authority on large strategic issues within the cognizance of the Navy, including in the language of congressional legislation. Despite Taylor's death in 1904, the board continued. The longer it remained in existence, the better its chance of survival, especially when Long was followed by a series of Navy secretaries, none of whom saw fit to cancel his "experiment." It was in this slow, evolutionary manner that the General Board became more than a temporary organization and developed into a bona fide institutional component atop the Navy hierarchy. In metaphorical language it became part of the Navy's "brain"— its frontal lobe, if you will. Until 1909, the board was overwhelmingly concerned with fulfilling its role as a strategic and operational war-planning entity, as envisaged by ADM Taylor and others.[8]

During the bureaucratic conflict over the United States' first dreadnought battleship designs in 1908–9, the General Board became preeminent in fleet design. Up to that point, the process had been dominated by the often-bickering and semiautonomous naval bureaus: Engineering (BuEng), Ordinance (BuOrd), and Construction and Repair (BuC&R). A conference convened at the Naval War College (NWC) in 1908 by President Theodore Roosevelt set out to resolve this problem. Participants concluded that line officers should be more involved in the process of warship design, and they decided that the General Board could fulfill this function. This decision had the force of a presidential order.[9] U.S. Navy Regulations later formalized it, so that by 1930 it read, "When the designs are to be prepared for a new ship, the General Board shall submit to the Secretary of the Navy a recommendation as to the military characteristics to be embodied therein." By this process the General Board became the final arbiter in the design of warships and, by extension, the fleet.[10]

Once the precedent for this expansion of the General Board's authority had been established, its influence over the structure of the fleet gradually increased. The establishment of the Office of the Chief of Naval Operations (OpNav) by congressional legislation in 1915 and 1916 has been regarded by some historians as the beginning of the end of the influence of the board.[11] Although OpNav replaced the General Board as the principal *operational* war-planning entity in the Navy, the board retained its authority over fleet-building policy—in effect, retaining a strategic-resource veto over operational matters. Its role was to connect strategy and operations, since it was still required to remain cognizant of the war plans produced by OpNav: "The General Board shall be furnished, *for information*, [emphasis added] with the approved war plans, including cooperation with the Army and employment of the elements of naval defense."[12] Simply put, the Chief of Naval Operations was only in charge of the Navy's operational-level planning staff. The General Board, always small, devoted its fewer human resources and clout to what today might be termed strategic planning and high-level policy formulation and advice, something like the original conception for today's National Security Council. In this sense, the president, and later chairman, of the General Board served as a de facto *maritime* national security adviser to the Secretary of the Navy. Recall, too, that the Secretary of the Navy, like the secretary of war, served as a co-secretary of defense to the president prior to 1947.[13]

By 1922 the Washington Naval Treaty limiting naval armaments of the five great naval powers—the United States, Britain, Japan, France, and Italy—had been signed. The execution of its terms was delegated to the General Board, which promptly issued the naval policy of 1922. This policy, issued in handbill fashion to the entire fleet, furnished the "Building and Maintenance Policy," which formalized a system of warship design. Practically speaking, this development resulted in the annual production of building-policy studies by the board, which established construction priority recommendations for legislation and funding. The board's processes during the period between the world wars were dominated by design hearings on every class of ship—from battleships to submarines.[14] Because of the constraints imposed by the Washington and London naval treaties, the board influenced every major design decision during the period due to its oversight of the treaty

The General Board in a meeting at the Navy Department, Washington, D.C., 1932, on the eve of ADM William V. Pratt's structural changes to its membership. *Seated left to right*: RADM Mark L. Bristol, RADM Charles B. McVay Jr., CAPT John W. Greenslade, CDR Theodore S. Wilkinson (secretary), RADM Jehu V. Chase, and CAPT Cyrus W. Cole. *Standing left to right*: LtCol Lewis C. Lucas, USMC (Ret.), and CDR Edgar M. Williams. The number over the door in left center is 2748, indicating that this office was located on the second deck of the Main Navy Building. *Naval History and Heritage Command*

terms. At the same time, the General Board routinely brought in OpNav planners to testify during its design hearings on the suitability or shortfalls in the fleet regarding capabilities required for existing war plans—especially War Plan Orange, the contingency plan for war with the Empire of Japan.[15]

During this time, the CNO, the president of the Naval War College, the director of the Office of Naval Intelligence, and the commandant of the Marine Corps all served as ex officio permanent members of the General Board, lending a collaborative element to its hearings and proceedings. Although there was no longer a board president, its senior member was usually an officer coming from command of a fleet—either commander in chief (CINC), U.S. Fleet or CINC, Asiatic Fleet—both four-star billets. This officer was neither the CNO's subordinate nor his superior, although he usually outranked the serving CNO in terms of date of rank. Ironically, the accession of ADM William V. Pratt, fleet commander, former War College president, and longtime member of the board, to CNO in 1930 proved both the high point and beginning of the board's slow decline in influence.[16]

In a move probably designed to *increase* the independence of the board vis-à-vis the influence of the CNO, ADM Pratt eliminated all the ex officio memberships in 1932. Nonetheless, he did not eliminate the collaboration of OpNav, the Naval War College, or the bureaus with the board. In fact, he encouraged it. This collaboration continued until World War II, with the General Board continuing to draft its yearly building policies under the enlightened leadership of admirals such as Mark Bristol, Thomas Hart, Ernest King, and, during World War II, A. J. Hepburn.[17]

The global naval war and the towering presence of Ernest King as both CINC, U.S. Fleet (which he abbreviated as COMINCH) and CNO proved to be the agents that undermined the General Board's role and influence within the Navy. During and after the war, the board diminished in influence, becoming almost a "leper colony" of discredited, out-of-favor admirals or those serving their twilight tours, including J. O. Richardson, Thomas Hart (serving for a second time), Frank Jack Fletcher, and Robert Ghormley. The board may have further hastened its demise when member RADM Frederick Horne wrote a 1941 study advocating a Joint General Staff. Although this proposal went nowhere with President Franklin D. Roosevelt's administration or with the Navy, it found support within the Army and with Chief of

Staff GEN George C. Marshall. The idea became a major element in national security reform after the war, which resulted in the creation of the Joint Staff under a chairman of the Joint Chiefs of Staff (CJCS).[18]

The fortunes of the General Board appeared to wax again during the unification battles—efforts to combine the services under one new super-secretary, the secretary of defense (SecDef)—leading to the passage of the National Security Act of 1947. An earlier attempt at unification, in part spurred on by Billy Mitchell, had been defeated in 1925 by the Morrow Board.[19] However, the unification effort after World War II succeeded. Secretary of the Navy James Forrestal (later the first secretary of defense) and Secretary of the Navy John Sullivan attempted to reestablish the power and influence of the General Board in an atmosphere of bitter service rivalries and parochialism generated by the creation of a single secretary of defense and the U.S. Air Force. ADM John Towers, one of the organizational architects of victory in World War II, replaced VADM Frank Jack Fletcher as chairman of the General Board; and talented younger officers such as VADM Charles H. McMorris and CAPT Arleigh Burke also joined the board.[20]

This proved to be too little, too late, however. The long-term damage had been done, and in the wake of the "Revolt of the Admirals," which almost resulted in the elimination of naval aviation, the General Board eventually became a casualty. There was no place for a "competing" and independent advisory staff in the new national security structure dominated by the second secretary of defense, Louis Johnson, the Joint Chiefs of Staff, and the powerful new Department of the Air Force. The General Board seemed a relic of a bygone age, and its fleet-design function migrated to the Bureau of Ships (the combined bureaus of Construction and Repair and Engineering) within OpNav. The board had done such a good job of integrating fleet design with strategy and war plans that it put itself out of a job when no peer competitor remained at the end of World War II—excepting, of course, the U.S. Air Force and defense reform and reorganization.[21]

That, in a nutshell, is an overview of the General Board. Let us now return to a day and age when the U.S. Navy was not even big enough to constitute a proper coast guard, when there were no general staffs, and when the idea of the United States as the foremost naval power in the world seemed very remote indeed.

CHAPTER 2

The Naval Reform Movement and the Creation of the General Board

The experience of the war with Spain showed the need of a general staff.

—John D. Long, Secretary of the Navy

The factors that contributed to the founding of the General Board reflected the ongoing professionalization of the officer corps of the U.S. Navy. This professionalism often advanced under the banner of reform. Naval professionalism in turn became a component of a larger "martial spirit" that had come to grip the United States in the late nineteenth century, although in many respects it prefigured a general trend toward a more military-friendly attitude by the American political elites and population at large. The period of these changes—1880 to 1900—was an age of reform and innovation that both prefigured and predated the better-known and more extensively written about "Dreadnought Revolution," engineered by Sir John "Jacky" Fisher in Britain's Royal Navy (RN) in the early twentieth century.[1]

At the time of the General Board's establishment, there were no permanent general staffs in the United States. This was a direct reflection of the antimilitary heritage of the United States, derived from Great Britain's own experience and distaste for standing armies and military dictators (such as Oliver Cromwell) as well as the young Republic's own experience as a mistreated British colony at the hands of military men.[2] The Constitution of the United States specifically enjoined against the raising of armies for more than two years, and in the Bill of Rights, Amendments 2 and 3 enshrine a militia and eschew military quartering, respectively. However, the Constitution permitted the establishment and maintenance of a Navy—without codicils.[3] When a Prussian-style war college and the precursor of a professional general staff emerged in the United States in the last half of the nineteenth century and the first year of the twentieth, they emerged in the Navy Department, not in the War Department or U.S. Army. This result should not, therefore, surprise anyone.

In 1931 American journalist Walter Millis published *The Martial Spirit*, a revisionist and critical account of the events leading up to and through the Spanish-American War in 1898. Millis' important book on the martial spirit reflected a thoughtful reappraisal of the development of a uniquely American form of militarism tied to the United States' expansionist foreign policy. Millis found that the two phenomena were interrelated and interdependent. Often touted as "jingoism" for foreign policy and "navalism" when applied to the policies and writings of Theodore Roosevelt and A. T. Mahan, this spirit encompassed those tendencies. Other observers, both contemporary and subsequently, have also identified these emerging attitudes.[4] "Navalism," in particular, is a term that came to have a pejorative meaning. After World War I, conventional wisdom identified the prewar naval arms race as one of the major causes of that conflict's origins.[5] It is against this larger background of a transformation in the civic attitudes of the American polity and public that the naval reforms leading establishment of the General Board of the Navy must be examined.

The establishment of an organization to help the Secretary of the Navy plan for war also had its roots in the trends and developments of the Progressive Era of the late nineteenth and early twentieth centuries. The formation of a General Board was very much a reflection of the reformist spirit of the times.[6] Another trend that contributed to the establishment of a general staff that predates Millis' martial spirit has to do with American naval officers' long history of desiring a greater role in the planning and use of the fleet.[7] As with most reform, the impetus came from recent experience, lessons learned "the hard way" in a war.[8] For example, out of the mismanagement of the War of 1812, Congress authorized the Board of Navy Commissioners in 1815, composed of three post captains. This marks, to some degree, the tradition of the establishment of special boards by the Navy Department to solve specific problems. The results of this board did give the officer corps what it wanted, since the scope for this board was administrative and not operational. Operational employment of the fleet remained firmly in civilian hands. This initiative, however, was a foot in the door that in 1842 led to the establishment of the Navy bureau system. However, the fundamental purpose of the bureaus remained administrative and reflected the attitude that "no special experience or knowledge was required for the direction of the fleet." The reformers wanted seven bureaus but got only five: Yards and Docks, Construction Equipment and Repairs, Provisions and Clothing, Ordinance and Hydrography, and Medicine. Professional knowledge was only really needed for building and maintaining the fleet and the health of its crews.[9]

During the Civil War, further operational reform occurred, but only on the civilian side. Abraham Lincoln and Secretary of the Navy Gideon Welles soon recognized the need for naval expertise and created what might be called operational control by civilian proxy when they established the position of the assistant secretary of the Navy. In this new office, they placed the former naval officer Gustavus Vasa Fox. Most naval historians characterize Fox's actions as those of a de facto if not de jure Chief of Naval Operations. Under Fox's competent leadership, the seed kernel for a planning organization was created using the expansion of the bureau system from five to eight during the war, including the significant creation of a Bureau of Navigation.[10] Meanwhile, the bureaus developed into powerful bureaucracies in their own right, and they came to impede the reformers' desire for an operational and even strategic voice at the highest policy levels. The Civil War's conclusion (and perhaps Lincoln's death) nullified many of these gains as they pertained to the establishment of an operational planning organization composed of active-duty officers. The position of assistant secretary of the Navy was abolished (1869) and ADM David Farragut's efforts to establish a Board of Admiralty along British lines were also defeated in Congress. The Navy went from being the second largest fleet in the world to the smallest among the major powers.[11] Historian Frederick Jackson Turner's "frontiers" did not yet include command of the seas, and the naval martial spirit would have to find expression at some later date.[12]

The First Phase of Reform, 1879–98

Reform came to the United States Navy, but not all at once. The years of reconstruction and the taming of Jackson Turner's "frontier" took several decades. Despite the years of seeming stasis between 1865 and 1881, events and personalities were casting the mold of the shapes of things to come. David Dixon Porter, the Civil War–era admiral, worked against a backdrop of neglect and infighting between line and staff officers (the latter included engineers) using the hero of the famous *Merrimac-Monitor* encounter, COMMO John Worden, superintendent of the U.S. Naval Academy, as his "front man."[13] In 1873 Worden and several other naval officers founded a professional association—the United States Naval Institute (USNI), reputedly the third stage in the professionalization of a group. This organization was formed for "the advancement of professional, literary, and scientific knowledge in the naval and maritime services, and the advancement of the knowledge of sea power."[14]

Early in 1879, winds of change could be discerned when founding USNI member RADM Daniel Ammen authored a significant essay titled "The Purposes of a Navy, and the Best Methods of Rendering it Efficient." Ammen, a boyhood friend of President U. S. Grant from Ohio, had served with distinction in the Civil War at the battle of Port Royal (1861) and both assaults on Fort Fisher (1864).[15] Ammen articulated the long-held opinion of naval officers in favor of education, but his remarks at the essay's end also pointed to the need for preparation for war by planning while at peace:

> It seems worth while for us neither to be fixed in the idea that we have reached a state of comparative permanency, nor on the other hand to expect to rely upon supposititious and untried developments of naval strength. *The time of peace, however, is the time to design and test whatever seems calculated to make naval warfare formidable, destructive and economic*, remembering that nothing is economic that is not effective.... Courage is a natural quality, far more common than many suppose,—at least sufficient courage to do a recognized duty; but *that alone will not suffice* [emphases added].[16]

That same year, the *Record* (later the *Proceedings*) of the Naval Institute began quarterly publication and established an annual prize essay competition, in part due to the lobbying of several board members, including CDR A. T. Mahan. The USNI chose "Naval education" as the first topic for this new annual competition. Mahan was now head of the Ordnance Department at the Naval Academy (co-located with offices of the USNI). His own essay on naval education won third prize, but it was his first article and a visible portent of the move toward a more intellectual track by the officer corps of the Navy. In it, Mahan argued for a broader educational approach as opposed to narrow "scientific" and "materialist" approaches to educating an officer corps for a modern (but not yet modernized) navy.[17]

Significantly, the second-prize essay, by LCDR C. F. Goodrich, reflected the real awareness by the officer corps (at least those involved with the institute) of the problems facing naval reform and modernization in the face of the traditional American attitude toward the military. Goodrich wrote, "The American people, as a natural deduction from their keen love of liberty, have ever cherished an equally keen antipathy to a large standing army and navy." All three prize-winning essays were discussed at Annapolis at the 10 April 1879 meeting of the Naval Institute, with J. Russell Soley, whose significance will soon be apparent, as chairman.[18]

In the 1880s the reformist spirit within the Navy found practical expression in two ways—organizationally and in the construction of a new generation of modern steam warships. These initiatives were catalyzed via the mechanism of another temporary naval board. The Naval Advisory Board, established by Secretary of the Navy William Hunt in 1881, unofficially became known as the Rodgers Board, named after RADM John Rodgers, who presided over it.[19] The building of modern steam and steel warships, which encompassed the so-called ABCD ships during the Chester Arthur administration, has been discussed adequately elsewhere in the literature. Only three of these ships can properly be termed warships. One of them, the cruiser *Chicago*, was later commanded by Mahan. The organizational group of improvements recommended by the Rodgers Board proved more significant and included the ongoing professionalization and modernization of the officer corps via the agency of military education (as advocated by Mahan, Ammen, and others). These nonmaterial improvements also included organizational innovations by and within the bureaus.[20]

The organizational reforms enacted during the 1880s proved to be more profound than the technological advances of the ABCD ships. They show the agency of several reformist officers at work, sponsored in part by the towering figure of ADM Porter. The Rodgers Board's recommendations led to the language in approved congressional legislation (1882) that provided for two seemingly short-term initiatives. The first allowed the Secretary of the Navy to create a second Naval Advisory Board to continue to meet and recommend more reforms. The second established the Board of Inspection and Survey, created to examine new construction ships as well as the retention of older vessels. By now the dynamic William E. Chandler had become Secretary of the Navy, and a cabal of reformers was emerging to advocate a system modeled on that of the Germans with their Kriegsakademie (War

College) and Grosser Generalstab (Great General Staff). In addition to Porter and Rodgers, the reformers comprised a younger group of officers that included CAPT John G. Walker (chief of the Bureau of Navigation), COMMO Stephen B. Luce, CDR Henry C. Taylor, and, of course, CDR A. T. Mahan. Of these officers, Luce was the most adamant in advocating the establishment of a professional school along German lines—a war college. All these officers shared a conviction that the study of military and naval history could best establish sound strategic judgment. Interestingly, officers like Luce and Taylor had derived their knowledge about the German system from their counterparts in the U.S. Army—Luce from GEN Emory Upton, when he had met that officer while serving on the faculty at Fort Monroe's Artillery School. Upton had made a firm study of the German system during an extended visit to Europe in the 1870s and published a book, *The Armies of Asia and Europe*, that extolled the German system for its superior merits in studying war systematically. Taylor, on the other hand, probably got much of his initial exposure from his fellow faculty member at the soon-to-be-established Naval War College, LT Tasker Bliss.[21]

At the Bureau of Navigation, Captain Walker had taken advantage of the spirit of the times in 1882 to act on existing guidance from 1869 to establish an intelligence office inside his bureau "for the purpose of collecting and recording such naval information as may be useful to the Department in time of war, as well as in peace."[22] This organization became known as the Office of Naval Intelligence (ONI). At the same time, a mechanism for the collection of information and intelligence abroad occurred with the dispatch of the first naval attachés on overseas assignments. The Navy Department library was attached to ONI by the same Navy general order, with the purpose of assisting the ONI in its research and nascent war-planning function. J. Russell Solely, an activist member of the institute and soon a lecturer at the Naval War College, became librarian with appropriations for the purchase and production of books. Among these books was a three-volume set on the operations of the Navy during the Civil War published by Charles Scribner's Sons: Soley authored the first volume, A. T. Mahan wrote the second, and ADM Ammen wrote the third.[23] To some degree, then, Soley had subtly transformed the departmental library into a historical research section to support a war-planning function inside the ONI.

Concurrently with these developments, the second Naval Advisory Board was established in 1884 by Chandler, this time with Commodore

RADM Stephen B. Luce was the founder of the Naval War College and a key advocate for a naval general staff along the lines of the German General Staff in Imperial Germany. *Naval History and Heritage Command*

Luce as president with specific direction to investigate the establishment of the Naval War College. Meeting from May to October, Luce's board, not unsurprisingly, found that a naval college was indeed in the best interests of the nation and the service. With this favorable report, Chandler issued an order forming a college under the Bureau of Navigation at Coaster's Harbor Island in Newport, Rhode Island, next to the Naval Torpedo Station there. There was no money for its operation until 1885, so the Naval War College did not formally open until that year. It was intended to be "combined" ("joint" in today's language) with active Navy, Army (LT Tasker Bliss), and civilian professors (such as Soley) lecturing. Luce had barely begun operations when he was ordered back to sea. One of his incoming history lecturers, A. T. Mahan, succeeded him as president.[24]

Under Mahan's leadership, the Naval War College grew in stature and came to include a war-planning function. However, the college closed for two years in the late 1880s as it became a source of contention between the powerful Bureau of Ordnance and Bureau of Navigation. Mahan was actually sent to Puget Sound while it was closed. In 1889 Porter and Mahan managed to convince the Secretary of the Navy to reopen the college.[25] In 1890, with the reestablishment of the office of the assistant secretary of the Navy, which had been disestablished after the Civil War, and the appointment of Soley to that position, the war-planning functions of both the college and ONI moved from Navigation into Soley's control at the Navy Library, located at the Washington Navy Yard.[26] A pattern seemed to be emerging wherein these war-planning organizations and functions moved under the authority of whoever would make best use of them. However, officers such as Taylor still longed for a more permanent general staff organization to coordinate unified planning.

One must remember, too, that these accomplishments could be undone with the stroke of a secretarial pen. One reason Mahan refused to publish his lectures in the U.S. Naval Institute *Proceedings* and instead published them in book form had to do with this organizational fragility—for both the ONI and Naval War College. He argued, correctly, that his opponents, such as ADM Ramsay, might point to the availability of his lectures in *Proceedings* as another reason to get rid of the War College. Officers could simply read these lectures on their own time and not waste time in some shore-bound college. In fact, Mahan's next assignment to sea duty resulted in a poor fitness report and one of the most famous quotations about him. Ramsay had Mahan installed as captain of the USS *Chicago*, which also turned out to be the flagship for RADM Henry Erben, station commander in the Mediterranean. Mahan was to be under his thumb for the entire time. He wrote of Mahan in his fitness report, "He is not at all observant regarding officers tending to the ship's general welfare or appearance, nor does he inspire or suggest anything in this connection. In fact, the first few weeks of the cruise she was positively discreditable. In fact, Capt. Mahan's interests lie wholly in the direction of literary work, and in no way connected with the service." Nonetheless, the Naval War College survived and, as we shall see, thrived—perhaps in part because Ramsay and his confederates were too busy focusing on professionally abusing Mahan.[27]

It is worth reviewing and discussing these events. The decade from 1880 to 1890 had seen a pace of organizational and structural change and modernization like no other in the Navy's history to that point. It could be argued that a period of comparable reform has not occurred since. The Navy leadership had embarked on a highly technical modernization of its fleet while establishing the first postgraduate-level institution to study war in the United States. These reformers had included a war-planning "shop" inside the Office of Naval Intelligence as well as instituting a system to collect human intelligence overseas. At the same time, they created a historical section using the department's library and sponsored, or had written themselves, several scholarly and operational works culminating in the most influential book about sea power of all time. The Navy had embraced the new technologies of warship design, although not without some stops and starts, while using the Board of Inspection and Survey to streamline the fleet (eventually the Board of Construction).

However, the preferred organizational solution—a naval general staff—did not come to fruition. The war-planning function was shared by two sub-organizations, the Naval War College and the Office of Naval Intelligence, with the Navy Library sometimes attached. Mahan and the later historian, Henry P. Beers, both noted how a reactionary or antireform chief of Navigation could muck up the system. Such occurred when Francis Ramsay succeeded the more enlightened Walker at Navigation and provides an example of why organizational stability was needed. The arrival of the dynamic reformer Soley as the reconstituted assistant secretary of the Navy resulted in his bringing all these pieces back under his authority, to some degree reminiscent of the Chief of Naval Operations—and similar to the actions of Gus Fox during the Civil War, except this time with a more lasting infrastructure in place.[28]

Enlightened Interregnum

From 1891 to 1898, with Mahan, Goodrich, and Henry Taylor all serving various stints at the Naval War College in Newport and Soley as assistant secretary of the Navy, the Navy's new approach to education and planning for war became relatively stable. As a result, it thrived. This period provided time for consolidation of the reforms and consideration of ways to continue to build on a promising start. It was during this period that Mahan's fame and that of the Naval War College were often conflated. Mahan pointed out to Luce that his success as a writer was not nearly as important as the education of officers for war at Newport.[29] Sometimes success has the unintended consequence of obscuring important original objectives. To what purpose was the new American fleet, now acquiring battleships like every other navy and studying war in a serious and systematic fashion, to be put?

Writers on innovation have emphasized that the more evolutionary and lasting changes often occur within organizational and institutional contexts when leaders build on the foundations laid by others by getting what is now known as a "buy-in" by the larger institutional constituency. This is very much what took place in the officer corps of the Navy during the 1890s.[30] It was also during this time frame that naval leaders laid the groundwork for a second phase of reform. Captain Taylor, a faculty member at the college even before Mahan, emerged during this period as a key agent for reform.[31] Taylor was not alone in his efforts; however, as a member of the Naval Institute and from his perch as chief of BuNav and later as president of the Naval War College, he was ideally positioned to both proclaim the gospel of organizational reform leading to a general staff as well as support others whose vision was congruent with his. A fine example of him doing both occurred in 1894, when another of the reformers, CDR French E. Chadwick, presented his paper on "Naval Department Organization" to the Naval Institute at Annapolis. Chadwick, it should be noted, was both a confidant and friend of Mahan's as well as having the distinction of being the first (and for a time the only) of the naval attachés (in London) created to support the ONI when it was first constituted by Walker. Chadwick had seen much of the world and brought an intimate knowledge of other nations' organizational structures to the paper he presented. He later became president of the college during the first three years of the General Board's existence, from 1900 to 1903. At the time he presented the paper, he was a chief in his own right at the Bureau of Equipment.[32] Taylor was in attendance and at the time serving as the president of the Naval War College.

The main purpose for Chadwick's paper was to argue for a much-simplified structure for the department. The paper remains valuable for its concise organizational history of the Navy to its current condition at the time Chadwick wrote it. He refers to Fox, the former assistant secretary of the Navy, as a "Chief of Staff" and emphasized Fox's experience as a naval officer. He then reviewed the current organizational state of the Navy as promulgated by the 1891 law that had reestablished the office of the assistant secretary. In his review, he noted, "An Office of Naval Intelligence has been established . . . but does not exist by mandate of law, [and] was formed as a necessity. Elsewhere it is regarded *as an essential part of a general staff* [emphasis added], and it would at once drop into its proper place in the event of a war, necessity bringing a result in our case which is arrived at elsewhere by foresight bred of the imminency [*sic*] of war." He then criticized in strenuous terms the authors of the law as creating an organization of "unsurpassed crudity" and of thoughtlessness due to no systematic study of "administrative systems." The point here, of course, is that the reformers were by no means satisfied and realized that what had been done could be undone by the same political winds and processes that had blown after the Civil War.[33]

Chadwick advocated reorganizing the system of bureaus and offices into four main sub-organizations underneath the authority of the Secretary of the Navy: a General Staff, a Bureau of Personnel, a Bureau of Pay and Accounts, and then an extremely large organization under a "Superintendent of Material."[34] This last organization would cover the functions of Ordnance, Construction, Steam Engineering, Equipment, General Stores, Provisions and Clothing, and Public Works. The main effort of the paper was a discussion of this new super-sub-organization for material and the higher level relationships and lines of authority between them all. Chadwick provided detailed sketches of both the British and French naval organizations, clearly favoring the British template. In addition to the major four organizations, he advocated two additional independent boards, one of inspection and another "on Construction." These two bodies were to have watchdog functions and thus independence. Above all this and integrating it all at the policy level with the Secretary of the Navy, he recommended a body composed of all the heads of these organizations to be called "The Naval Council," which would also include the most senior admiral not afloat. In his codicil to his annotation for the Naval Council on his line diagram, he wrote: "If matters not military be discussed the officer in the Navy Department representing each corps affected by the discussion to be a temporary member." Henry Taylor took this all in; in it, we see both a vision of the future in the final makeup of the General Board as well as an attempt to decrease the power of the existing bureaus by making them third-tier organizations under the four superbureaus.[35]

As for the future form of the General Board, the codicil discussed above about the council bears a very strong resemblance to the final mature form that the later hearings of the General Board eventually took, including the attendance of the SecNav and assistant secretaries at meetings.[36] As for the General Staff, the relatively small amount of space devoted in the paper to its discussion is instructive by the absence of an existential argument. A naval general staff was simply taken for granted in Chadwick's diagram and given primacy of place in the sketch directly under the Secretary of the Navy (with no assistant in between) and with the Naval Council description directly underneath it. Position matters. Chadwick assumed his audience was of the same mind as he about the necessity for it, given his introductory history of the dysfunction of the Navy in lacking for one. It is worth restating his short description of it here in his overall description of his proposal for a general staff:

> The movements of the fleet; inspection of ships [in commission]; *preparation of plan of campaign;* [emphasis added] the Intelligence Office; naval attaches; the receipt and sending out of all communications from and to ships in commission; all orders to officers affecting ships in commission to pass through the General Staff; all correspondence from ships necessary to go to the Superintendent of Material to be forwarded to the General Staff.[37]

Clearly the outline of the future functions and form of the office of the Chief of Naval Operations can be seen in this description, although it took twenty years to get there. However, as a blueprint for the fleet, most of these functions, with the significant exception of the subordination of the bureaus, came about with the creation first of the General Board (the Naval Council) and then the office of the Chief of Naval Operations.

The comments by the members at this meeting on the paper are as illustrative of the zeitgeist in the officer corps as the paper itself. In these Naval Institute sessions, the sitting chairman always spoke first and Taylor lauded Chadwick's paper as "excellent," "methodized and systematic." He then presumed to speak for all present, announcing, "I think we all recognize a great loss of effective power in a departmental system which, while dividing the work among the various . . . bureaus . . . does not provide for their conjoint united effectiveness." He then essentially reiterated Chadwick's points about the effectiveness of Fox before addressing his first mild criticism. Significantly, Chadwick had left out a discussion of where the Naval War College fit into his scheme. Since it currently resided with the ONI under the assistant secretary of the Navy, Chadwick left it out inadvertently, and his comments about the ONI applied equally to the college. He acknowledged as much in his final response after the others had commented. Taylor simply stated that "it might be well to insert the Naval War College, which in conjunction with the Office of Naval Intelligence, will, it is hoped, in the future do much toward the efficiency of the General Staff."[38]

The other comments on the paper focused mostly on the idea of a super-chief of material and the various smaller proposals underneath it for improvements to the functions of the existing bureaus that would be subsumed by such. Significantly, Naval Constructors David W. Taylor and Francis T. Bowles were dissenting voices on this point. Taylor acknowledged that a "full discussion" was needed and that the paper was valuable. He found the idea of the Naval Council "superfluous" and emphasized the authority and flexibility of navy secretaries to consult whomever they wished whenever they wished. Taylor presented an articulate defense of the bureau system, but with improvements. His opinion on a general staff probably falls under the rule of silence is consent, either that or he did not consider himself qualified to venture an opinion. Given David Taylor's stature and importance, the former is probably a more correct assessment of his position. Bowles brought up the issue of the civil-military relationship and favored the status quo with an activist and involved assistant secretary.[39] As to the remainder of the comments about the idea of the General Staff, this was the one area where consensus for its creation was universal, at least at that particular session of the Naval Institute.[40]

Chadwick received the last word, and he emphasized that he had expected more discussion of what he called the "military phase of the scheme" and highlighted that it was "the primal question in any proper scheme of naval administration. That the establishment of the military part . . . into a General Staff and a Bureau of Personnel . . . is in full accord with the consensus of all opinion . . . within the last ten or twelve years, and in accord with the practice of at least four of the most important military nations."[41] It may seem here that Chadwick and Henry Taylor were "preaching to the choir," but often individuals and groups, once they have declared themselves publicly, gain a deeper commitment to a particular reform. In this case the issue of the General Staff appears to be assuming the character of a sine qua non for any further naval reorganization. What was needed now was a catalyst. Just as forecast in Chadwick's paper, that catalyst for further reform was a war—in this case, one with Spain.

Taylor's time at the Naval War College proved important to the mission of the institution. He came to regard what he was doing there as involving general staff activities as much as the education of naval officers. In 1894 Taylor instituted a program for looking at the "problems of naval campaigns."[42] This initiative occurred against the backdrop of the first Sino-Japanese War (1894–95) and the actual execution of a combined army-navy campaign in Korea and northern China by the Empire of Japan. Taylor also oversaw the drafting of contingency plans for war with Spain over Cuba at this time by the classes of 1894 and 1895.[43] Taylor later wrote to his friend Luce that the Secretary of the Navy "is now . . . using me and the College as [a] General Staff and me as the Chief of same with considerable powers but wouldn't move in the direction of making a permanent general staff without his chief advisers [sic] consent."[44]

If Mahan's geopolitical suppositions regarding the importance of trade routes and geographic position were correct, then it seems no accident that the mid-1890s gave meaning, purpose, and validation to the naval reforms of the 1880s.[45] It was during this second decade that U.S. foreign policy pronouncements became more strident and even bombastic. The first such incident involved the government of Chile and provided a preview of Chadwick's claim that the "imminency of war" would result in reform. The crew of the USS *Baltimore* had been attacked by a mob at Valparaiso on 16 October 1891.[46] Secretary of the Navy Benjamin Tracy had come to rely on Mahan for advice, in part through the good offices of the ailing ADM Porter. When the *Baltimore* incident occurred, Tracy called Mahan to Washington and in concert with Soley and Chadwick began planning for war with Chile using the ad hoc Naval Strategy Board. By January 1892 the Chileans had apologized, and the board, now augmented by bureau chiefs Ramsay (Mahan's nemesis) and William Folger, was disbanded. No permanent war-planning system was established, but on the positive side the precedent of recognizing that the expertise was to be obtained through the ONI and the college had been demonstrated. These were the de facto repositories for war-planning expertise. Mahan, in his important December 1891 letter to Luce, emphasized that more than himself was needed, that there was a "necessity of gathering a group of officers who may cover the whole ground." In the same letter, Mahan emphasized the need to appoint another president in his absence while the "the work" (planning) took place in Washington, not knowing how soon the incident would be resolved.[47]

On the larger stage, Great Britain was in a period of strategic transformation—in today's language we would say that its "strategic threat assessment" had changed. The long Pax Britannica at sea had been challenged, tactically and culturally, by the Jeune École movement involving the torpedo, torpedo boat, and, soon, the "submarine boat" technologies.[48] Geopolitically, Britain's hegemony at sea was also being challenged by the emergence of new naval powers such as the German Reich, Empire of Japan, and the United States, and internally in Britain by reformers as well as by pacifists.[49] Even the "pacific" Cleveland administration in the United States could display a rather Mahanian maritime martial spirit in its diplomatic language when conflict arose in 1895 with Britain over a boundary dispute with Venezuela:

> The United States is practically sovereign on this continent and its fiat is law upon the subjects to which it confines its interposition. Why? It is not because of the pure friendship or good-will for it. It is not simply by reason of its high character as a civilized state, nor because wisdom and equity are the invariable characteristics of the dealings of the United States. It is because in addition to all other grounds its infinite resources combined with its isolated position render it master of the situation and practically invulnerable against any and all other powers.

Lest the maritime threat inherent in this synthesis of the Melian Dialogue and Mahan not be apparent, President Cleveland referred to his secretary of state's missive as "Olney's twenty-inch gun."[50] It seems that now the United States had the means and the will, prior even to the Roosevelt Corollary, to bluster enforcement of the Monroe Doctrine across the seas, at least when

British and American interests diverged. Developments such as these caused the British to rethink their entire strategic approach for the new century.

By the time the McKinley administration was firmly in the saddle, with Mahan's pen pal Theodore Roosevelt as assistant secretary of the Navy, all the pieces seemed to be in place for reform. The catalyzing event of war had yet to occur. With the explosion of the USS *Maine* and the martial spirit animated, this now happened.[51] Even so, reform may not have come so quickly since Secretary John D. Long had all but relinquished his every duty to his young and dynamic historian-assistant. Roosevelt's actions were indeed dynamic enough to honor the memory of Fox and even garner the praise of Millis.[52] However, Roosevelt, not to be denied the opportunity for patriotic glory, and perhaps to atone for his father's failure to serve in the Civil War, abdicated his post as chief of a nascent naval general staff and left a planning vacuum in his wake. This event ironically advanced the cause of the reformers. Long formed the Naval War Board from an existing ad hoc board constituted prior to hostilities and composed of the commander in chief of the North Atlantic Fleet (RADM Montgomery Sicard), the heads of BuNav and BuOrd, personnel from the NWC, and the chief intelligence officer. As all the talent of the naval officer corps went to sea, the War College closed for a period of seven months during the war, reopening that November—eliminating the option of using its students and faculty as a planning staff. Roosevelt and two others soon departed, at which point Long ordered Mahan, now retired, to service on the board on 9 May 1898.[53]

The very next day Mahan wrote Long, recommending that the "'Board of War' be abolished, and that in place of it . . . there be appointed a single officer, to be known by such title as may seem convenient to designate his duties." Chief of staff, perhaps? He further proposed that this officer pick his own "assistants." Here Mahan's dedication to the Jominian virtue of unity of command as well as his dislike of councils of war and consensus decision making is firmly on display.[54] Long ignored this advice but retained Mahan, although with doubts about this icon's efficacy. By this time the board consisted of just Sicard, CAPT Arent S. Crowninshield of BuNav, Mahan, and a secretary. Shortly after the Battle of Manila Bay, Luce vented his frustration that the war had not led to the establishment of a general staff to his friend Senator Henry Cabot Lodge: "Our Navy Department is not organized for a state of war. . . . The Secretary of the Navy needs . . . a General Staff with the best officer of that rank that can be found for the Chief of

Staff."[55] Luce then went on to recommend RADM Walker, one of his fellow reformers, for that position. Lodge responded in kind: "I quite agree with you that there ought to be a chief of staff in the Navy Department. . . . In justice to the [War] Board it ought to be said they are giving the Admirals in command no inconvenience now and are not hampering them at all."[56] Lodge's response is born out by more recent scholarship that supports the effectiveness of the War Board. Although Luce bore the board's members no ill will, it was the ad hoc organizational approach that so irritated him. In the event, Long acted faithfully on the board's recommendations —which were operational and did not interfere with commanders at the tactical level (as attested by Lodge).[57]

Alfred Thayer Mahan, sea power theorist extraordinaire and naval reformer. Mahan, like his friend Luce, was an untiring advocate for a naval general staff. He was not satisfied with the General Board, although he felt it better than no general staff at all. *Naval History and Heritage Command*

After the war was over, Long disestablished the Naval War Board. Mahan later recalled the work of the board in a memorandum to the General Board of the Navy. In that document, his ill will toward the process of its creation is apparent; however, his judgment as to its purpose and effectiveness is less harsh. He specifically mentioned that Long subsequently said he needed it because he lacked a "General Staff" and that "the authority of a General Staff designate exactly that exercised by the body . . . in its *relations* to the head of the Navy Department." Throughout the lengthy memorandum, he emphasized that the board performed as efficiently and effectively as it did primarily due to the members' knowledge "of the leading principles of war" and, here Mahan again takes to task the lack of a standing general staff, "without previous mature considerations of the effect of this or that disposition on the whole theater of war,—of the relations of the parts to the whole." He closed by estimating that the United States was lucky the war was short and the enemy less efficient, implying that had it not been so, "there could not but be mistakes, which careful previous study would have prevented." It is a lawyerly document, defending his and the board's work while at the same time criticizing the process and the organizational foundations for it. Mahan also avoided the topic of the Naval War College serving as a sort of peacetime, stealth general staff as Taylor had written in 1896. Mahan did so in order to avoid giving opponents of the idea of a more formal general staff any ammunition with which they might oppose further reform or even undo more recent changes.[58]

One must give due credit to John D. Long's willingness to give a general staff–like organization a try. The war with Spain had made him amenable to further reform. Again the indefatigable Henry Taylor can be found upon the center stage of reform. After serving at the Naval War College, Taylor had gone on to command the new battleship *Indiana* through the period of the war. In 1899 Long offered him appointment as superintendent of the U.S. Naval Academy, but Taylor turned down the job, informing Long that he wanted a "less demanding" position so he could advocate for the development of a general staff. Long eventually gave Taylor the opportunity that officer had hoped for and asked him to summarize his thoughts about a general staff and submit them to him.[59] Taylor proceeded to write one of the more hard-hitting and persuasive memoranda ever received by a Secretary of the Navy. Although only eight pages in length, he reviewed the genesis for the memo, the justification based on the example of the "effectiveness," "efficiency," and success of the German General Staff, the purposes for such a staff in peace and in war, and, finally, the rocky experience of the United States in trying to mimic such an organization without creating something permanent. During the course of his discussion, he betrayed his own familiarity with the work of "General von Clausewitz, himself a veteran chief of staff," although whether Long had ever heard of Clausewitz at that point is not known.[60]

In addition to his command of the history of the German General Staff and knowledge of the lack of such an institution in U.S. history, Taylor betrayed a talent for bureaucratic button pushing in the way he closed out his argument. First, prior to his final declarative recommendations, he intimated that "the Secretary for War . . . has in view a General Staff for the army, under the name and form of a War College." In other words, the Army had seen the light and might beat the Navy to the punch in establishing the basis for a more efficient general staff organization. Taylor's prescience about the forthcoming Elihu Root reforms is rather astonishing at this early date, although he might have been getting inside information from his old friend Tasker Bliss, who was later appointed as the first president of the Army War College in 1903. At any rate, he appealed to the inherent parochialism of the Secretary of the Navy not to be outdone by his cabinet rival, the secretary of war.[61]

Taylor cataloged that most of the components for a functional general staff *system* already existed. The ONI encompassed what might regarded as the research section of the general staff, including the Navy Library, which later gave birth to the Naval Historical Center, analog to the historical section of the German General Staff.[62] The other component involved education, and that function, including a nascent war-planning function, as discussed above, already resided in Newport at the NWC. Recent experience, though, in the war with Spain militated for a more formal general staff organization. Taylor then listed his major recommendations. He repackaged (or perhaps plagiarized) French Chadwick's recommendation for a naval council composed of the major bureau heads and commander in chief of the United States' fleet (CINCUS). Taylor's "permanent board" would be composed of the NWC president and ONI director and their assistants plus the chief of the Bureau of Navigation, who would act as the chief of the general staff, with the NWC and ONI remaining organizationally underneath him. The officers at the NWC would include at least ten non-Navy personnel, including

Revenue Cutter Service (later the Coast Guard), Marine, Army, Reserve, and militia officers. These officers would spend half their time in studies at NWC and then spend the other half analyzing intelligence and planning at ONI, with a swap occurring after four months. At the end of the course of instruction, the most suitable of these graduates would go on to serve as faculty or staff at the Naval War College or ONI "whenever sea duty permits." This last set of proposals were among the most progressive and innovative concepts in the memorandum.[63]

Finally, in rather vague language Taylor argued for a formal board that would meet annually in November to consider the work of the general staff and include the standing council listed above plus the senior officer of the Navy (ADM George Dewey) as well as the commander of the North Atlantic Fleet along with their chiefs of staff. During this month they would review the war plans developed by the general staff within the Bureau of Navigation.[64] The inclusion of these two senior officers was meant to appeal to reformers (e.g., Mahan and Taylor) who wanted officers with recent seagoing experience to judge the work of the planners as well as to provide a position of authority for ADM Dewey, the hero of Manila Bay, who had been appointed Admiral of the Navy with "lifetime tenure" by a grateful Congress.[65]

"An Experiment"

Taylor was to be disappointed in Long's response to his memorandum, which was an incremental synthesis of Taylor's recommendations and his own problem of what to do with Dewey. He essentially adopted Taylor's idea for larger, second board and placed Dewey in charge as president. Long promulgated General Order 544 on 13 March 1900 and established this organization as the General Board of the Navy. Nonetheless, he worried that the establishment of a naval general staff would create a direct line from the chief of the general staff to the president, telling Taylor that he was establishing the board "as an experiment." To avoid this problem, Long restricted the statutory powers of the new planning organization. In particular, ADM Dewey had no authority over either the administrative bureaus or the fleet. His authority would be entirely informal, a "superadvisor" with a limited staff of line officers. Thus installed, Long could use Dewey's fame and institutional authority to influence events. The board's "mission" was to draft advice on a range of topics provided by the Secretary of the Navy "to insure efficient preparation of the fleet in case of war and for the naval defense of the coast."[66] The reformers were also disappointed in their long-held goal of having this organization established by Congress in formal legislation.

The membership consisted of the admiral of the Navy (Dewey), the chief of the Bureau of Navigation (RADM A. C. Crowninshield, previously a member of the war board), the chief intelligence officer and his principal assistant, the president of the Naval War College (CAPT C. H. Stockton) and his principal assistant, and three other officers above the rank of lieutenant commander. The Navigation, War College, and Intelligence positions were considered ex officio positions that changed with their occupancy. The remainder of the members were picked by Long (on Taylor's advice) and included two above the three allowed for in the establishing instruction

RADM Henry C. Taylor, c. 1900. Taylor, the "American Moltke," was the brains behind the creation and early years of the General Board, although he did not live to see how successful it eventually became. *Courtesy of Captain E. S. Kellogg, January 1931, Naval History and Heritage Command*

written by Taylor: CAPT Charles E. Clark, French Chadwick (now a captain), CAPT Robley D. "Fighting Bob" Evans, Taylor himself, and—significantly and at Taylor's insistence—Col George C. Reid of the U.S. Marine Corps. Also included was LT H. H. Ward as secretary.[67] Almost to a man these officers can be considered as members of the reform faction of the Navy, although historian George Baer has nicknamed them "Mahanians."[68]

Long used the board's creation to answer those reformers who wanted a planning body, yet its initial mandate remained to advise the secretary only. As such, the General Board reflected incremental rather than radical military reform of that era in the naval sphere. Nonetheless, the establishment of the General Board can be categorized as organizational innovation, meant to increase the efficiency of the Navy as a whole as well as to provide civilian administrations with formal policy and planning advice.

Such was the path that led to the establishment of the General Board of the Navy. As a way of suggesting larger themes and conclusions, this compares and coincides with a similar process that occurred nearly simultaneously in the Royal Navy. The British story, generally referred to as the "Dreadnought Revolution" or "Fisher Revolution," is better known and has been the occasion of much discussion.[69] First, one must define the word "revolution" in a naval or military context. In colloquial terms, revolution equates to significant change across a broad range of areas in a short space of time and usually preceded by more profound changes of an evolutionary form—"under-the-radar coverage," as it were. Much of the process that resulted in the General Board can be categorized as evolutionary. However, the end result proved measurably, evenly radically, different from the situation at the end of the Civil War.

One observer identifies four ingredients in Sir "Jacky" Fisher's stewardship of the Royal Navy as First Sea Lord: "the adaptation of existing technologies" to produce new types of warships, the reorganization of stations and commands to serve a new strategy, the reduction of antiquated inventory, and the "recasting of officer education."[70] In the American case, all these elements are mirrored, if not exactly, then closely enough to invite comment. Often the technological piece gets first billing, and this chapter acknowledged but did not belabor the modernization efforts during the 1880s with the ABCD fleet and then the larger predreadnought battle fleet authorized in 1890–91 by Congress.[71] Navy officers used the arrival of modern weaponry and warships in their arguments for the organizational reforms that they held to be most important. Naval technology had become complex, and the implications of steam power, torpedoes, and other developments demanded a more modern organization founded along the lines of the leading military powers in Europe.

These organizational reforms matched the changing strategic situation of the United States, and it took more than twenty years to approximate a general staff as reflected by the establishment of the General Board. In Great Britain, strategic change had impelled revolutionary changes over a shorter period. In the United States, it was not so much strategic change as strategic deficit (as made clear in the testimony of the naval officers of the day), a lack of strategic organization to deal with the expanding geopolitical responsibilities of the United States. From ADM Ammen in 1879 to Commander Chadwick 1894, U.S. naval officers foresaw a need to match organization to need a priori to an actual expansion of foreign policy imperatives. Ammen, as we saw, identified the complexity and observed accordingly that "a Navy cannot be improvised."[72] Chadwick made a similar point fifteen years later, adding that other "powers dealing with the subject on a much larger scale and under much greater pressure of [the] ... prospect of war" had developed proven administrative systems like general staffs to meet their strategic requirements.[73]

In addition to organizing more efficiently to meet the needs of strategy, the officer corps, especially via the mechanism of the U.S. Naval Institute, encouraged intellectual development. This development revolved around the bedrock belief that naval warfare adhered to the general principles of the art of war and that these were best learned through a "critical" study of military history. The result was not just a method (which already existed) but a treatise offering a theory of sea power with a historical narrative to illustrate its main points. Mahan provided the model upon which his fellow professionals could begin their study.[74] He never meant it to be the final word on sea power, but rather the beginning. He later noted that "so far as they stand the test, my own lectures, form a desirable preparation for works such as those of [Sir Julian] Corbett."[75]

Concurrently with modernization and reorganization, the various boards of inspection accomplished the third element of reducing a legacy inventory of aging and obsolete warships—weeding out the deadwood prior to the modern steel and steam fleet. Officer professional education, or professional military education as it is known today, is perhaps more striking in the American case, since it provided both the vehicle and the continuity for greater strategic and operational reorganization while fulfilling the need for a broader professional, and ironically less technically focused, higher education for the Navy's officer corps. The Naval War College also preceded development of similar institutions in the Royal Navy and U.S. Army by more than a decade. Whereas the British experience had strong elements of a "cult of personality" centered on Fisher, that in the United States was more group oriented and driven by a collective desire for reform, beginning modestly with the establishment of an intellectual and professional framework with the U.S. Naval Institute. As is so often the case, there was no one "hero" but many. Often the focus is on just Mahan, just Luce, or just Dewey. However, group dynamics and a strong desire to be efficient drove the effort by the Navy officers of the late nineteenth century to lift themselves up by their collective bootstraps. This martial and intellectual spirit—naval style led to a U.S. Navy, led by the General Board, that within a generation that became "second to none."[76]

CHAPTER 3

In the Shadows of Nelson and Scharnhorst, 1900–1904

The first years of the General Board reflected the secretarial ambivalence, and congressional hostility, surrounding its establishment. By simply surviving as an organization, the board secured a more authoritative role for itself in the future of Navy policy. There were many factors influencing the evolution of the General Board from an experimental organization working directly for the Secretary of the Navy to an organization recognized by Congress as speaking on behalf of the Department of the Navy in matters of policy and strategy. Foremost to the board's survival after its anticlimactic genesis were two individuals whose influence proved decisive, one well known and the other more opaque to history: George Dewey and Henry Clay Taylor.

Admiral Lord Horatio Nelson and General Gerhard von Scharnhorst, chief of what became the German General Staff, offer comparative personality metaphors as a means to understand this dynamic duo. Dewey more closely matches the ethos of Nelson, whereas Taylor is more like Scharnhorst. The shadows suggested by these personality metaphors shaped the General Board for the next four years. Certainly, these two were not the only personalities involved in the evolution of the board from an experiment to an authoritative organization with significant, albeit informal, power. However, they represent the key leaders involved and thus serve as a framework with which to examine how the other players, factors, and agencies interacted. Dewey, and especially Taylor, established a basis for a permanence that came later via a process of evolution rather than revolution. However, when Taylor died unexpectedly in 1904, it seemed that his goal of a congressionally mandated *American* naval general staff remained as elusive as ever.

George Dewey, a native of Montpelier, Vermont, served in the American Civil War, most famously under RADM David Dixon Porter at the Battle of Fort Fisher. There Dewey had volunteered to lead one of the naval assaults along with another young officer, Robley Evans. After the war he remained with the Navy through its lean years of downsizing from one of the largest fleets in the world into the small navy that naval reformers attempted to expand, painfully, in the 1870s and 1880s.[1] Until the Spanish-American War, however, it was really Dewey's combat experience as a junior officer, his ability to maintain his health in seagoing billets, and his practical Yankee good sense that resulted in his moving up the ladder of command to the U.S. Navy's Far Eastern Squadron. Dewey's astonishing victory at the Battle of Manila Bay in 1898 catapulted him into the national limelight, and he emerged as the most famous contemporary hero of the Spanish-American War. He became the only admiral of the Navy (essentially a six-star admiral) in American history. However, the gunnery at Manila Bay, as Dewey well knew, had been abysmal, and he agreed with Mahan that the Navy needed more work if it was to ever face one of the major naval powers, including the other two "new kids on the block," the navies of Imperial Germany and Imperial Japan.[2] Dewey, despite his age (sixty-three), turned out to be a fortuitous choice for establishing and shepherding the General Board through its inaugural years as a naval "experiment."[3]

Dewey can be characterized as *Nelsonian* in its commonly understood sense, that is, as the advocate of the major fleet engagement, the heroic naval commander and leader who, like Nelson, brought his seagoing experience and fame to bear on matters of naval strategy and policy. Dewey often referred to himself "as an 'old sea dog,'" thus highlighting his identity as being more aligned with Nelson.[4] Unlike Nelson, though, Dewey did not seek the spotlight, and this was to be one of the keys to his, and the General Board's, longevity.[5] Dewey has been criticized by historians for his lack of intellect and, as he got older, lack of the energy, purpose, and drive—qualities the younger reformers wanted in their leadership.[6] These characteristics, somewhat unfair on the latter score for a man in his sixties, are decidedly un-Nelsonian. Dewey's leadership of the board was more like the leadership of Marshal Gebhard von Blücher—another man not noted for his intellectual reputation but his charismatic leadership at an advanced age. Bradley Fiske, who reported to the board in 1910, found that Dewey, now

ADM George Dewey, president of the General Board. Dewey served as the first and only president of the General Board until his death in 1917. His longevity probably secured the long-term survival of the board in the face of its critics. *Estate of Lieutenant C. J. Dutreaux, Naval History and Heritage Command*

seventy-two, handled the goings-on of the board with "exceeding skill."[7] Dewey's great talent was his ability to recognize talent, including intellect, in others—for example, Taylor, Sims, and Fiske—and then to put those men into positions where they could be of most use while further developing the higher-level executive skills needed by their nation.

In the role as Dewey's Scharnhorst, we have Henry Clay Taylor, a former president of the Naval War College, naval intellectual, and significant member of the naval reform faction inside the Navy. He also had key operational experience, but unlike Dewey he was more overtly committed to a rational and systematic approach to planning, preparing, and conducting war. Taylor's methods reflected the influence of the Prusso-Germans he admired—typified by the leader of the Prussian military reform movement, Gerhard von Scharnhorst.[8] He often referred to the Germans in his arguments for a naval general staff that had preceded the establishment of the General Board and in the arguments he made later to establish it more formally in congressional legislation.[9] Dewey and Taylor, each in his own way, "pushed the cart down the track" toward the common objective of a powerful and professional U.S. Navy served by rational staff planning organization. Dewey was the Nelsonian commander, the front man, with Taylor as the chief of staff, always seeking to demonstrate the efficacy of a general staff system as reflected by the newly created General Board.

How the General Board Functioned in Its Early Years

Before proceeding to the early years and activity of the General Board, one must examine how it operated *as an organization*. RADM Bradley Fiske was one of the few officers to share an "inside view" of its membership and proceedings. Of Dewey, he perceptively wrote that he "was the paramount figure on the board; in fact, without his prestige the board could not have survived. ADM Dewey handled the board with exceeding skill, keeping himself in the background . . . but nevertheless keeping a tight rein, which all of us felt though none of us saw." Of the board in general, Fiske wrote, "It was most . . . interesting . . . and I found that it was carried on with the most remarkable absence of anything like personal self-seeking. . . . The aim of every man seemed merely to be to find out and urge whatever was best for the navy, and it was considered a virtue in a man to be willing to say that he had made a mistake and to change his opinion on proper evidence. Nothing was considered more deplorable than pride of opinion."[10] Thus collegiality and collaboration, and the muting of personality and "self-seeking," became innovative hallmarks of the board, such that by 1910, when Fiske reported on board, they had been institutionalized.[11] Dewey and Taylor deserve equal credit for this critical early accomplishment in setting the quiet professional tone for the organization. Because the board remained small, it managed to avoid the bureaucratic offshoots that undermined this collectivist spirit.

The board operated as a pure democracy, one man and one vote for appointed members. Dewey did not have "veto power" over decisions and sometimes was in the minority view on issues. Finalized decisions were then committed in writing to formal studies and the result provided to the Secretary of the Navy. On occasion, admirals ready to retire would be assigned to the board prior to leaving the Navy. If not named members, they could express their opinion but were not allowed to vote.[12] Dewey and Taylor divided the board's work by committees, with an "executive committee" that was composed of both of them, the chief of Bureau of Navigation, the Naval War College president, and the chief intelligence officer.[13] There is some evidence that RADM Crowninshield, the chief of BuNav, had attempted to keep Taylor off the executive committee but that Dewey personally penciled his name in on 11 April 1900, several days before the board's first full meeting.[14]

Until 1902, other committees were formed to work on an ad hoc basis. For instance, committees were created to work on war plans and the study of the acquisition of bases in the West Indies and the Philippines (these last two directed by Secretary of the Navy Long). The reports of these committees, for example, work by the ONI, were at first added as appendices to the formal minutes. The executive committee usually met daily, which meant that the president of the War College had to be in Washington when the board was in session. The entire General Board, at least during these early years, did not meet as frequently. Its inaugural meetings occurred on 16 and 17 April, and then it did not meet again as a full body until 21 May.[15]

However, more formality and structure came with time. The board rapidly realized that it needed more structure in the written policy advice it provided the Secretary of the Navy, and by late June it had instituted the "serial" report system, which tracked and cataloged the studies it produced on various topics. Not surprisingly, given the guidance of Long, the very first study produced that June was titled "Naval Base in the Philippines" and cataloged by year and number as "01–00."[16] By 1902 the ad hoc committee system had been replaced by two standing committees. The First Committee oversaw studies on organization, "combined operations with the Army, mobilization plans, and analyses of foreign fleets."[17] The Second Committee had oversight of war plans, sealift, and "naval militia affairs." This last represented a longstanding effort by the reformers to promote a bona fide naval reserve, and the Second Committee provided them a platform with which to do so. Long's initial worries about limiting the General Board's scope of responsibility seem to have been overcome, as he colluded, sometimes passively, in all these moves by Dewey and Taylor that expanded the scope of the board's responsibilities.[18]

Another salient feature that emerges as one examines the genesis of the board and its functioning was its meticulous effort in keeping written records of everything, from meetings to its analytic work, as reflected in its studies. By its third meeting in May, it had adopted an indexed "card system" to track and catalog the work it had produced and the work that was ongoing.[19] It seemed to have a real sense of its own history and identity, however tentative those must have seemed at the time; and again we must probably assign the credit for implanting these organizational habits to both Dewey and Taylor—especially Taylor, the studious former president of the Naval War College. Dewey provided the top cover and "firepower" for Taylor's initiatives and plans, much like Field Marshal Blücher did for his chief of staff Scharnhorst.[20]

One final element of this early board structure deserves particular mention: the role of the chief of BuNav. The Bureau of Navigation controlled ship movements, the War College, and ONI prior to the creation of the General Board. Its chief was the Navy's primary liaison to the Navy secretary and had long been used to being treated as a "military advisor" for that civilian leader. With the advent of the board and BuNav representation on it, all those general staff functions executed by Navigation became available to Dewey and the General Board. They could use BuNav to actually execute policy as a bureau chief. Also, because Navigation controlled officer assignments, it gave the General Board a way to influence the career assignments of line officers. As it was, Dewey had absolute control over who was assigned to the General Board, but through BuNav his reach was even greater and more comprehensive in channeling talent to where the board thought it needed to go in the Navy. BuNav was not absolutely obligated to act in the board's interests, but by putting him on the board, Taylor and Dewey co-opted this powerful organization even more to their purposes. With the promotion of Taylor to rear admiral and chief of BuNav in 1902, this mechanism only became stronger.[21]

The Taylor Years

In 1900 CAPT Henry Taylor was a man on a mission—and had been for some time. Born in Washington, D.C., on 4 March 1845, he received an appointment to the United States Naval Academy in September 1860. Four years later, he, like Mahan, was serving on blockading duty and was later involved in the hunt for the Confederate raider *Shenandoah*. RADM Robley D. "Fighting Bob" Evans, another Navy reformer, was Taylor's brother-in-law.[22] Taylor was one of Luce's bright young protégés and served on the original faculty of the NWC in 1885, before even Mahan.[23] Taylor commanded the battleship USS *Indiana* during the Spanish-American War, being involved with the bombardment of San Juan, Puerto Rico, in May 1898. As captain of the *Indiana*, his achievements also included an early form of information warfare. This involved his severing the oceanic telegraph cables by which Cuba communicated with higher authority in Spain. He had twice served as chief of staff for ADM Dewey and was his de facto chief of staff on the General Board and one of the officers closest to Dewey, both professionally and personally, until his "untimely death" in 1904.[24]

Although there was no single leader of the Navy reform faction, Taylor was definitely among its first rank, which included Luce, Mahan, Chadwick, Robley, and Goodrich. Taylor was especially instrumental in advancing the careers of younger reformers such as Bradley Fiske, whom he sent in 1896 to the faculty of the Naval War College, a platform from which Fiske could continue to write and advance his innovative ideas among other naval officers. Similarly, once Taylor became head of the Bureau of Navigation in 1902, he engineered the assignment of the fiery young William Sims as inspector of target practice in order to effect badly needed gunnery reform in the Navy.[25] Taylor and all these proselytes and fellow travelers shared a burning desire to establish a naval general staff on the Prussian model.

Taylor now had his "general staff," but he had to figure out how to make it more influential while at the same time not appearing to do so. He had to accomplish this in the face of opponents both inside and outside the Navy. His main internal opponents were the powerful bureaus, especially the so-called staff bureaus, jealous of their prerogatives and unwilling to cede authority to this new "board." Staff bureaus such as Yards and Docks (BuY&D) and Construction and Repair also wielded considerable clout because of congressional patronage in key districts containing bases—such as Philadelphia, Brooklyn, and Norfolk—shipyards, and construction contracts. As far as the bureau chiefs were concerned, the General Board was just another temporary board created to quiet the reformers, make some decisions, and then be disestablished by the Secretary of the Navy, even though none of them had formally objected to Long's proposal when he consulted them.[26] Outside the Navy, Taylor faced the opposition of powerful members in Congress who worried about creeping militarism and the encroachment of civilian control of the military as enshrined in the Constitution. Foremost among these was Senator Eugene Hale of Maine, who chaired the Naval Affairs Committee. Hale and the bureaus had "bitterly" opposed Long's establishment of the board, so its position remained precarious. This was probably another reason Dewey was appointed as president, since disestablishing an organization with this venerated naval hero at the helm might reflect poorly on the politicians who attempted it.[27]

The General Board began its work without much fanfare or even publicity. This low profile was probably deliberate. As mentioned, not all the reformers were happy with the compromise the General Board seemed to represent as opposed to their real wish for a much more authoritative and powerful naval general staff. Among these officers was CDR Richard Wainwright, who thought that once Taylor and Dewey left, the board would become a "useless appendage." Wainwright later changed his mind about the board once he became a member of it.[28] Dewey, on the other hand, was optimistic about the future and utility of the board in correspondence with Taylor and his good friend ADM Luce. Luce's attitude tended toward that of the "maximists" like Wainwright. He had written on the issue as early as 1898 to Mahan at the time of the Naval War Board that it mattered not what one called the "General Staff, or any other title," it only mattered that one existed and that it be established on a "permanent" basis.[29]

The board's first formal meeting occurred on 16 April 1900, as noted, and in addition to the creation of the executive committee and other organizational initiatives, it committed itself almost immediately to Long's primary purpose for it, as a war-planning entity. The chief focus of these first efforts focused on Germany, which had joined European colonization of the globe late. Germany was aggressively pursuing bases and possessions overseas, ironically in accordance with how its Kaiser had interpreted the writings of Mahan.[30] Ever since German actions during the Spanish-American War, Dewey's views about the primacy of the threat of the German fleet informed the views of the General Board. He presciently wrote in 1899, "The German policy is to prevent other powers from obtaining what she cannot accept herself.... Our next war will be with Germany."[31] It was, therefore, no surprise that Taylor proposed three contingency studies for the following situations: an attempt by Germany to seize Puerto Rico, war with Germany over some issue in South America, and a war with England over the Panama Canal. The board also decided to develop studies on coast defense, logistics, mobilization, force requirements, base requirements, and disposition of the fleet.[32]

After the initial frenzy of activity that April, the board did not meet again until late May.[33] Much had been produced in the way of papers and studies, as the executive committee shouldered the bulk of the work involving the contingency studies on bases that seemed the most urgent task. Meeting three consecutive days, the board made several significant decisions that had a long-term impact, both on how the board operated and on its style of war planning. The board was packed with former faculty of the Naval War College in addition to the current president and his assistant (Chadwick, soon to be the president), which gave it probably the greatest concentration of war-planning talent in the Navy. CAPT Charles Stockton had written war plans at Newport in the 1880s and 1890s for use against Spain, and Taylor as president had guided the classes of both 1894 and 1895 in constructing contingency plans in case of war with Great Britain. However, as noted, the main target of board planning efforts was Germany.[34] At the close of the session the board decided to switch to the now-famous color-coded system for war plans instead of using the actual names of the threat countries being considered. The second decision it made as it adjourned was to meet again in Newport at the War College on 26 June. It even listed the precise hour as "2 P.M.," which was done in order to take the draft plans already produced up to the college and then take advantage of the summer session and use the students and faculty in the planning and wargaming sessions with a view to obtaining a "plan of campaign." In today's language, they intended to "leverage the human capital" at their disposal in Newport. This "battle rhythm" of going to spend the summers in Newport remained in place until after World War I started. Additionally, this move institutionalized the system of addressing key "general problems" of interest to the board. These "summer problems" remained a feature of the Naval War College until World War II.[35] Such ideas, which constitute organizational innovation, came directly out of the first two months' work of the General Board.

Promptly at 2 p.m. on 26 June, the entire General Board convened at the Naval War College to begin work for its "long meeting."[36] However, the tone had changed. Reality had intruded upon the speculative planning processes of the board, especially in China. The so-called Boxer Uprising had erupted in June 1900, and the foreign legations of all the great powers were under siege by the "rebels" inside Peking (Beijing). The empire of China subsequently sided with the rebels and declared war on the United States and the major powers. The board was caught without a contingency plan. At the same time, the Philippine insurgency continued and it too intruded in board calculations, the board fearing that Germany would attempt to exploit the situation by seizing an island or two while the Americans were heavily engaged ashore against Filipino nationalists. This explains why, given the chaotic situation in China, the first study approved by the board addressed a "Naval Base in the Philippines."[37] The board flexibly changed course to address Asiatic matters, with the result that the first seven studies it prepared focused on "Asiatic Bases," coaling issues, and even operations vis-à-vis China and the Philippines. This course was wise, and it gave the board practice in crafting effective policy advice for the Secretary of the Navy during a crisis. This does not mean the board neglected the German challenge, but it simply recognized that Asia had priority in its calculations ahead of the Caribbean. Germany, too, was focused more on its Chinese concessions in Shandong and for the moment had little time or resources to make trouble in the Western Hemisphere. The board wanted to be prepared should the locus of a likely conflict with Germany instead move to the Western Pacific.[38]

Much of the remainder of the work that summer revolved around contingency planning for the Boxer War in northern China. Taylor put together and briefed three different proposals for naval bases north of the Philippines, and on 29 June the board forwarded the number one choice, Sam-Sa Bay, a location not far from Hong Kong, to Secretary Long should he and the president decide to deploy major portions of the fleet to China. As for direct orders to the operational commander of the Asiatic Squadron, the board limited itself to forwarding intelligence analyses and studies, usually conducted by the ONI, for information only.[39] It was only in late August that the board then convened as a whole again, primarily to share and "brief back" all the work that had been going on throughout the summer. By this time the siege of the Peking legations was over and the Boxers had been defeated, but the board now realized that the Pacific needed as much, if not more, intellectual effort than home waters. These briefs took several days and covered everything from coaling stations in the Pacific to establishment of a naval reserve and the issue of "Eastern Alliances," in particular, an earlier suggestion from Captain Stockton that the United States avoid an alliance with Japan.[40] This last point was soon moot because Japan was more interested in an alliance with Great Britain, which was concluded in 1901 and formally announced in 1902. Finally, the board made the important decision to share its war plans with the other bureaus pursuant to "their cooperation ... in providing materials and facilities."[41]

When the board reconvened that October in Washington, it underwent its first personnel changes as the leadership of the NWC changed hands, with Chadwick replacing Stockton and a commensurate change in their principal assistants. The main areas of discussion focused on the issue of creation of a naval reserve, which eventually became the first non-Asian-focused study promulgated by the board, and the development of bases in the Aleutians to support quicker fleet transits on great circle routes to Northeast Asia, presumably to support American interests should the Chinese situation deteriorate again.[42] From these modest beginnings inside the General Board, along with the existent Open Door policy of the United States with regard to commercial activity in China, would develop the American riverine "China Patrol" with gunboats inside Chinese territorial waters.[43] The remainder of the General Board's work for 1900 is reflected, again, by the studies it produced for war plans. However, by December, as China seemed to resume a semblance of stability, three more studies were produced that reflected concerns of a German attack on Haiti and how to meet it along with another study on Cuban naval bases at Guantanamo and Cienfuegos. The remainder of the studies, of the twenty overall produced from April to December, reflected logistical matters.[44]

Despite this solid record of achievement, Taylor remained concerned about resentment against the General Board inside the Navy. He tried to assuage the staff bureaus' concerns in a letter to the editor to the *Army-Navy Journal* in June 1900, writing, "The 'General Board' shall confine itself to [war plans] and avoid all questions of material or personnel which ... are already cared for intelligently ... by the able Chiefs of Bureau."[45] It seemed, too, that despite its record of hard work, the activity of the General Board remained opaque to much of the rest of the officer corps, or at least that component of the officer corps engaged in the ongoing debates over administration in the pages of the Naval Institute's *Proceedings*. A March 1901 prize essay by LT John Hood titled "Naval Administration" bemoaned the lack of a general staff, which the author referred to as "this most important of subdivisions of personnel." Although Hood acknowledged the roles of the ONI and NWC in accomplishing this function, he did not mention either ADM Dewey or the General Board.[46]

Interestingly, Captain Chadwick, who served on the General Board, gave the first response and had mentioned his support for a general staff in 1894 (see chapter 2). However, he added that he had a "change of view on the subject" that he forwarded, presumably to the Secretary of the Navy, in 1899. Chadwick went on to state his admiration for the British system of a First Sea Lord, but he also mentioned nothing about the General Board— an odd omission, given his involvement in its activity the previous year.[47] Chadwick's comments were followed by those of fellow reformer CAPT C. F. Goodrich, who showed more agreement with Hood on the issue of the lack of a formal general staff. However, Goodrich reminded those at the meeting and *Proceedings*' readers about the General Board, writing, "Of the General Board much was expected and by it much may have been accomplished." He then opined that a "smaller body of advisors" co-located with the secretary and meeting "frequently" might yield more "good fruit" as a "balance wheel upon undue real or self-centered projects."[48] This is the first reference to the term "balance wheel" and General Board in the same sentence in the records of this period.

At the same time, it must have become apparent to Dewey and Taylor that some change was necessary in the membership of the General Board. The work of the previous year had highlighted the absence of leadership of the War College during much of the year (except in the summer) due to mandatory membership on the executive committee, which often met daily when in session in Washington, D.C. Accordingly, precisely one year after the board's establishment, Long issued another general order modifying the statutory membership of the board. It eliminated the NWC and ONI assistants and allowed the secretary to designate as many members in the grade of lieutenant commander or higher as he deemed necessary. Since the board rendered its advice based on a simple majority in all cases, this gave the secretary quite a bit more control and power over the board, although Dewey naturally served as a counterweight since he (and Taylor, soon to be chief of BuNav) still selected who these "extra" members might be. In any case, this change did not modify the inner workings of the board. Taylor also tried to get more junior officer representation on the board but had to wait until Long's departure and his own promotion to rear admiral and assignment as BuNav chief to achieve this goal.[49] However, Long stymied Taylor's and Dewey's effort to get the General Board formalized in law by congressional legislation in 1901 with a specific proposal that they put "the general staff in the Bureau of Navigation." Long emphasized in the same letter the "continued good work of the Board."[50]

Captain Chadwick's neglect of the General Board disappeared in his opening address to the new NWC class of 1901 that June. For the students, he defined what he saw as the "triune organization" encompassing the general staff of the Navy: the General Board, ONI, and War College. His emphasis on the college's role in this structure consisted of its "studies in general staff work, with which of course summer's work on the general problem is in line."[51] This emphasizes that the General Board was regarded by Navy leaders of the period as only one component in a larger general staff organization that also included NWC and ONI. Later that August, another member was added to the General Board at the direction of the Secretary of the Navy, the chief of the Bureau of Equipment (BuEquip), RADM R. B. Bradford, whom the SecNav had temporarily attached to the board during its deliberations the previous year at Newport. This move constituted another incremental step to co-opt the bureau system in favor of the board's authority and influence because Bradford had initially refused to confer with the board on the issues of coaling stations.[52]

At this point the reader may be wondering why so much time has been spent on the first year of the General Board's existence. But the first year of any new organization, like the first year of a human life, is often the most important. This is especially true for organizations that prove effective, and by doing so survive and become part of the fabric of the larger institution. The decisions made, the habits ingrained, tend to become more solid, every decision having the weight of precedence in these early periods of organizational gestation. Many an organization has foundered in this respect, and not just an organization whose creation was termed "an experiment" by its founder. Taylor perhaps saw clearly that by just getting his stealthy general staff through one entire year of work, and productive work at that, turned out to be a major accomplishment.

For the remainder of 1901, the General Board almost doubled its output of studies, producing thirty-five as opposed to the twenty it had issued the year before. The sheer expanse of the topics covered by the General Board can be found in appendix 3 and emphasizes that its scope of interest had broadened beyond war plans and that it interpreted its mandates in the various establishing orders of the Secretary of the Navy as broadly as possible. Since Long was made aware of all these activities (all studies were produced effectively for his review), he could not have been unaware of this "mission creep" in the activities of the board and so countenanced it either deliberately or by passive acquiescence.

In addition to the topics the board had already established regarding basing in the Pacific and war plans, it began to broach a new concept it termed "Advanced Bases," initially with respect to the Pacific. A later report buttressed this concept by addressing the organization of "Marine Companies for Expeditionary Field Service," almost certainly a byproduct of Taylor's insistence on having Col G. C. Reid, USMC, serve on the board. One of the last studies of 1901 addressed "Preparedness of the Marine Corps for War."[53] These studies foreshadowed the later development of the Marine Advanced Base Force as a shipborne "fire brigade" for use to counter the Germans or in any other crisis where troops might be needed to secure sites ashore for a naval campaign. This almost certainly reflects Taylor's vision of the U.S. Navy and Marine Corps as a combined-arms team, under the control of a general staff, and a portent of the Marine Expeditionary Units, which were created during the Cold War. Taylor's work in the mid-1890s in war planning at NWC had emphasized naval campaigns, and under his tutelage, faculty member Capt Richard Wallach, USMC, had produced a study of the Japanese army and navy that included combined amphibious operations during the Sino-Japanese War of 1894-95.[54]

Another report reflected Taylor's ongoing concern for the lack of congressional recognition of board, as well as the majority opinion of the board.[55] He must have remembered how the NWC had only narrowly averted such an ignominious end in 1890 under Mahan, these memories being fresh when he had begun serving as president of the college in 1894.[56] Perhaps the biggest development of 1901, however, occurred in the political arena with the accession of the navalist Theodore Roosevelt to the presidency in September after William McKinley was assassinated.[57] It remained to be seen, however, if the new president could be won over to assist Taylor in his quest for formal recognition of the General Board by Congress or the goal of the more radical reformers—the "maximists"—to create a large and nearly autonomous naval general staff.

The General Board Goes to Sea

1902 brought more change and real-world events that influenced the activity of the board. Organizationally the most important development was Taylor's promotion to rear admiral and appointment as BuNav chief in April, replacing Crowninshield, a former member of the War Board and chief of BuNav since 1897.[58] Crowninshield might also be characterized as a "plank owner" of the General Board, a naval term that is only applied to the first crew members of any unit or vessel. Taylor had now become chief of staff to Dewey in name as well as in fact by assuming this all-important portfolio. His appointment also demonstrated Dewey's power, and no doubt Dewey meant to keep Taylor in this job as long as he possibly could and perhaps he meant for Taylor to succeed him. However, the elevation, as we shall see, was something of a "poisoned pill." It added to the heavy workload that Taylor had already created for himself as the agenda-setting "go-to guy" for Dewey, the executive committee, and the larger board. It would, in fact, probably contribute to his untimely death in 1904 due to stress and overwork as he traveled through Canada on his way to the summer session of the General Board in Newport.[59]

In addition to Taylor's promotion, April also brought a new Secretary of the Navy in William H. Moody. Moody, like Long, had no background in naval affairs and was a lawyer from an "old Massachusetts family." President Roosevelt had probably chosen him because of his "pugnacity and virility," which would soon be tested. Moody turned out to be a sympathetic secretary when it came to Taylor's attempts to legislatively establish the authority of the board. He only served two years and set the pattern for secretarial instability under Roosevelt that both helped the board's survival as an organization and hindered the reformers' desire for a congressionally recognized equivalent of a general staff.[60]

The General Board produced seven studies in 1902 prior to Taylor's elevation to BuNav and Moody's appointment as SecNav. One examined "Proposed Joint Maneuvers with [the U.S.] Army and Militia." This reflected Taylor's ongoing interest in combined operations with ground forces and would culminate in the following year with Taylor's proposal to create the Joint Army and Navy Board.[61] However, all the work of the board came to a screeching halt as the specter of Germany, and violation of the Monroe Doctrine, reared its ugly head off the coast of Venezuela in 1902. This crisis had its genesis in the default by that nation's government on loans owed to several of the Great Powers. Great Britain, Germany, and Italy all deployed warships to the Caribbean to effect a blockade of Venezuela in order to coerce repayment of these loans. A German warship had started mapping the waters around the Venezuelan port of Margarita as early as May 1901, something the General Board was actively concerned with and probably apprised of at the time by the ONI.[62]

Certainly, German activity was a major reason the board continued its efforts to develop Culebra, an island just east of Puerto Rico, as a base in its studies of 1901 as well as its April 1901 study of the same Margarita area that interested the Germans.[63] The General Board had studied the problem closely, which was one of the reasons RADM Bradford had been directed to join the board. It estimated that it would take ninety-seven colliers to support the German fleet without a base. This explains the great concern over acquisition of a German base in the Caribbean. Such fears were not groundless. Germany refused to recognize the Monroe Doctrine, its naval leadership seeing the U.S. Navy as its most likely principal opponent, and even had plans—no matter how unrealistic—for such an eventuality.[64]

These factors caused the General Board to produce its first study recommending the size of the fleet to accomplish a defense of the Monroe Doctrine against a consortium of European naval powers. In 1901, Germany, France, and Great Britain had a combined total of more than fifty predreadnought battleships, without counting the navies of other powers such as the Italians and the Japanese. The United States only had ten battleships in commission at this time. Even though such a coalition was unlikely, by 1903 the General Board eventually settled on forty-eight as the number of battleships the United States needed to defend its interests. It was from these circumstances that the General Board's building policy proposals (later the 420 series), first broached in a study dated October 1901, came into being and later became an annual policy study provided by the board to secretaries of the Navy. Another idea the board had examined involved concentrating and "combining" the fleet for maneuvers somewhere, but various squadron commanders had resisted this initiative.[65]

Against this backdrop, President Roosevelt made the decision, abetted by Dewey and Taylor, to engage in "naval diplomacy." The General Board had been agitating via the mechanism of its studies to conduct large fleet maneuvers while working on the problems of actually executing them at sea during a real-world crisis.[66] Maneuvers of this kind might demonstrate the value of a strong U.S. Navy to Congress and assist in continuing a program of robust naval construction, especially battleships. Finally, Taylor also knew the fleet maneuvers could be used to demonstrate the efficacy of the General Board as a naval general staff. In other words, the Venezuelan Crisis seemed tailor-made to highlight and support their various agendas vis-à-vis the U.S. Navy.

Moody placed his yacht USS *Dolphin*, the D of the ABCD fleet, under Dewey's control as a command ship on 24 April 1902 for anticipated fleet maneuvers at the end of the year in the Caribbean. Taylor, newly promoted to admiral and chief of BuNav, was named as his seagoing chief of staff as well, although it was likely that this had been agreed to ahead of time; if Dewey went to sea he had every intention of taking "Harry" Taylor with him.[67] Later that June, Dewey was formally apprised by Moody that he would command the "combined" fleet, composed of the Caribbean, Atlantic, and European squadrons, for the winter fleet maneuvers. These ended up being framed around war planning that postulated a German attempt to establish a naval base in the Caribbean or attack an American one. The Blue (U.S.) fleet based out of Culebra would oppose a White (enemy) fleet built around one of the other U.S. squadrons.[68] In July 1902 Moody ordered naval assets to survey the Venezuelan coast, no doubt on the advice of Dewey and Taylor, who had studied this eventuality the year before. Moody also advised all the bureaus to support Dewey's mobilization of the fleet in the Caribbean.[69]

President Roosevelt provided Dewey and his staff with the presidential yacht USS *Mayflower* the next month as the flagship for the combined fleet maneuvers. By September, Dewey had Moody appoint his flag aide, CDR Nathan Sargent, as a voting member of the General Board; thus, when Dewey went to sea later that year, he had two members of the General Board

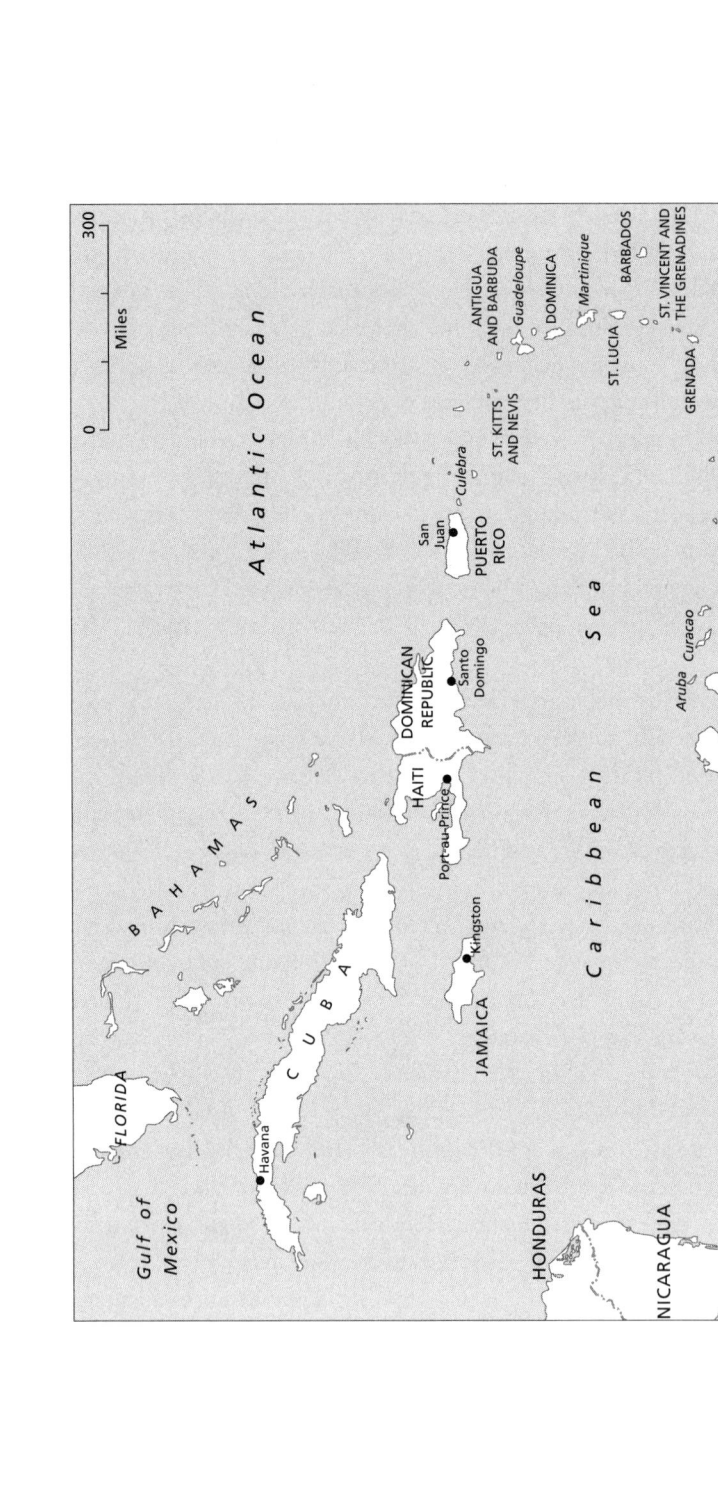

Map 1. The Caribbean and Culebra area

with him. Meanwhile, all studies by the General Board had come to a halt as the principal members made ready to go to sea while they advised the president. Production of the studies did not resume until late September, and when they did, they addressed fueling stations and their fortification.[70] However, all these moves were not as well received inside the Navy as one might imagine. Crowninshield, in command of the European Station Squadron and recently second in seniority on the General Board only to Dewey, was reportedly considering retirement. He had been notified, apparently, to join the combined fleet, where he would serve in a role subordinate to RADM Francis J. Higginson of the North Atlantic Squadron in the winter maneuvers. He and Higginson had had a falling out, and this may have been one source of his irritation and his reputed threat to retire rather than serve in a subordinate position.[71] The attitude from some in the fleet, as reflected in Bradley Fiske's memoir, was a bit different. Fiske suggested that the problem might actually lie in a dispute between Taylor and Crowninshield, possibly going back to their days on the General Board together. Fiske reported that "Taylor had also ordered to the [fleet maneuvers] the battle-ships in Europe, under the command of Rear-Admiral Crowninshield."[72] This order to join the fleet originated with Taylor, and thus potentially broadened the scope of Crowninshield's animosity since Taylor was still junior by date of rank to Crowninshield. It also highlights who was really directing the overall operational framework for these maneuvers, Dewey's trusty chief of staff.

Taylor was not only orchestrating the fleet maneuvers for Dewey but also serving as a virtual national security adviser to the president prior to his and Dewey's departure. Taylor sent a memorandum to Roosevelt that November emphasizing that all Venezuela had to offer Germany was territory, thus potentially establishing a "foothold" for what Taylor and Dewey regarded as the primary and most likely enemy in the United States' watery backyard. Additionally, a Marine battalion under command of Capt Smedley Butler, USMC, was dispatched on USS *Prairie* to establish a practice defensive base at Culebra for the fleet maneuvers by the united Atlantic and Caribbean squadrons of Higginson and RADM Joseph Coghlan. No doubt the work of Col Reid, USMC, whom Taylor had insisted on being on the General Board, was paying dividends with this move. By the end of the month the crisis had intensified, with Germany and Great Britain formally announcing a peaceful blockade of Venezuela. This began almost two weeks later, on 7 December.[73]

With a potential war looming on the horizon, the president personally saw Dewey and Taylor off at Washington Navy Yard as they embarked on the *Mayflower*. Dewey and Roosevelt spoke briefly, but neither one ever shared what was said for posterity. However, given all the contingency planning that had been done, and Dewey's noted distaste for Germany—his wife feared for Dewey's life in a third war—Dewey left with the understanding that his training mission could turn "real world" at any moment. Venezuela did not bow to European demands, and on 7 December 1902 the "peaceful" blockade began. Violence soon erupted and resulted in the seizure of the small Venezuelan navy shortly after by British and German naval forces. The Venezuelan government requested arbitration of the crisis by the United States at the new international court at The Hague. Germany rejected arbitration outright, whereas the British remained aloof.[74]

On 8 December, Dewey and his staff arrived to command of the combined fleet at Culebra. Bradley Fiske, serving as the executive officer of the battleship *Massachusetts*, noted the arrival as follows:

> While we were at Culebra, however, our tactical drills were displaced... when the *Dolphin* [it was actually the *Mayflower*] arrived there, carrying the four-starred flag of Admiral Dewey ... with Rear Admiral Henry C. Taylor as his chief of staff. Fortunately for the navy, Taylor had been made chief of [BuNav], and had already formed what was a very, very mild kind of *general staff* by securing the establishment of the General Board, with Admiral Dewey at its head, and *persuading* Admiral Dewey to take personal charge of the [fleet maneuvers] of the Atlantic Fleet, first at Culebra and afterward near Narragansett Bay [emphases added].[75]

Fiske's characterization of the General Board as a "very, very mild kind of general staff" reflects his thinking years later, after legislation creating the Chief of Naval Operations, not necessarily at the time. Fiske emphasized how the entire atmosphere in the fleet changed with the arrival of Dewey and Taylor and that only later did the fleet learn that the deployment had had to do with the Venezuelan crisis, which shows how closely Dewey and Taylor kept knowledge of their instructions from Roosevelt limited.[76]

From 9 to 18 December, Dewey and Taylor conducted the fleet maneuvers as they waited for events to play out. They turned the exercise into a cover for bringing the fleet up to fighting trim in case war with Germany broke out. At the same time the combined fleet conducted rigorous gunnery practice using the new system LDCR William Sims had learned from Percy Scott in Great Britain. It seemed that all the accomplishments of the reformers were now on full display for all to see against the backdrop of an international naval crisis. Throughout the crisis, Moody, Dewey, and Taylor went to extra lengths to maintain communication by boat courier to the undersea telegraph terminus in San Juan, Puerto Rico. Taylor was charged primarily with the flow of urgent information through this means while Dewey recalled all the ambulatory sick from the hospitals ashore to return to their ships and man their stations. One historian has argued that this presents "clear" proof that Dewey and Taylor expected, and had been advised by Roosevelt to expect, hostilities with Germany, if not all the European powers enforcing the blockade. Finally, the two men requested that Moody countermand the plan to disperse the fleet for the Christmas holidays and Moody gladly complied.[77]

This earlier version of the Cuban Missile Crisis was defused in a similar manner; at the last moment, the European powers "blinked." The British acquiesced to the American offer of arbitration on 18 December. Germany found herself isolated diplomatically and had to back down in the face of the overwhelming naval power the Americans had ready to hand under their famous admiral. Germany simply could not go it alone against the United States in these distant waters. Britain saw that her true interests lay in maintaining good relations with the United States, not underwriting German adventurism, which could result in a naval base as dangerous to its interests as to those of the United States at some later time.[78]

Moody gladly reversed his previous orders and sent a message to the fleet to disperse for the holidays as previously planned. All this activity had strained the old sea dog Dewey, who had planned to continue commanding his "splendid fleet" into 1903. However, he soon gave orders for *Mayflower* to proceed at best speed "for home," returning by early January. At the height of the crisis, Dewey and Taylor—the very model of a Prussian command team—had commanded more than fifty-four ships of the four squadrons in the Atlantic. It was later stated that "never before had a full American admiral commanded a fleet at sea; never before had such a powerful concentration of American naval force been assembled."[79] It might be added that never before had an American general staff existed in peacetime that was used so quickly after its creation as a seagoing staff prepared at a moment's notice for war. The General Board of the Navy, with its versions of Nelson and Scharnhorst at the head, claims that honor and remains the only peacetime staff to have ever done so in American history.

In a coda to these events, a short story in the *New York Times* that March reported, "Rear Admiral Arent S. Crowninshield . . . has asked for immediate retirement from the navy. Admiral Crowninshield is now in command of the European Station. It is known that he was dissatisfied because he was deprived of the battleship *Illinois* and given the cruiser *Chicago* for his flagship." Crowninshield had been demoted to serve under men he thought his subordinates while in command at sea.[80] Fiske declared in his memoirs that "a strenuous effort was made to let Crowninshield's ships go back to the comfortable European cruising that had formerly been carried on; but Taylor was strong enough to prevent it. This was a more important victory for the navy than many appreciate. . . . It committed the navy to the policy of organized effectiveness, and set the official seal of disapproval on the idea of division of force so firmly that our fleet has ever since been kept together." Fiske's explanation rings a bit truer, since it seems to clarify that Crowninshield only decided to retire after he was informed that the fleet would remain in the west to exercise that summer off Newport. It also suggests that Crowninshield had been against uniting the fleet in the Caribbean as well.[81]

Based on the lessons learned from the crisis, the General Board presented its famous "2 battleship" program in October 1903 to Secretary Moody for relay to Congress. By authorizing the construction of an additional two battleships (as well as thirteen smaller warships) per annum, it hoped to have forty-eight battleships to overmatch the expected size of the German navy by 1919. This remained the General Board's fleet design, with few modifications, until after the outbreak of World War I, although Dewey would die mere months before the United States finally went to war with what he perceived as the nation's most likely naval opponent.[82]

The 1902–3 maneuvers also foreshadowed the mature process for tactical and operational innovation in subsequent years, especially those in the period between the coming world wars. The General Board (and later OpNav/CNO) produced war plans and identified specific tactical or logistical problems (e.g., basing).[83] These issues would then get worked as a general problem or problems in the summer at Newport. Following this, fleet maneuvers occurred in the autumn or winter, often with free play, wherein solutions were tested and other issues identified. This process first occurred in 1902–3 against the backdrop of the Venezuelan Crisis, and the General

Board can claim credit for having demonstrated its worth. In reality, Taylor et al. had simply adapted the German general staff process for land warfare to the naval domain. That this occurred simultaneously with a real-world crisis and resulted in a tangible political result only confirmed its value, both for the existing generation of naval officers and those of the coming generation.

Taylor's Final Struggle and Death

Taylor's goal of getting his de facto general staff (the General Board) recognized in congressional legislation proved to be his final battle. However, it must be understood that the creation of a formal general staff, although his ideal, was "for the present improbable."[84] He had seen how effectively the existing "triune" system of the General Board, NWC, and ONI operated in 1902 and 1903, with the strong leadership of Dewey at its head. His goal was to see that system institutionalized.[85] To that end, his primary fear remained that Congress would intervene and pass a law prohibiting the board or directing the Secretary of the Navy to disestablish it. In Secretary Moody and the new president, he had powerful allies to aid him in his effort to put in place a law that would prevent this.[86]

Once Taylor returned from the Caribbean in 1903, he and Moody immediately began to craft legislation for a bill in Congress that formalized recognition of the board's general staff function. Roosevelt supported them in this initiative. The board continued what Taylor called its "principal" task, "plans of war," against this charged backdrop.[87] Their enemies were many, including some in Congress, others inside the Navy officer corps, and even Assistant Secretary of the Navy Charles H. Darling, who worked counter to his chief's desires.[88] In addition, Representative Alston Dayton (R-WV) of the House Naval Affairs Committee opposed the idea of a naval general staff. Evidently loyalty to the president of one's own party did not count for much with these men. Dayton was supported inside the committee by Democrat John Rixey of Virginia, who was no doubt swayed by his brother who served chief of the Bureau of Medicine and Surgery (BuMed). Inside the Navy there was the aforementioned RADM Bradford of BuEquip, who came from Maine, which explains his close alliance with Hale. Another bureau chief with great animosity toward the board was RADM George Melville from the Bureau of Steam Engineering. The anti-reform faction in the Navy had now become the "anti–general staff" faction and wanted to restrict and constrain the board as much as possible. Taylor's fear of an adverse reaction by Congress was not unfounded due to these alliances.[89]

In the campaign that followed, opponents criticized the board's summer meetings at Newport as government-funded vacations.[90] This criticism came at a very busy time during the board's routine of work, as it prepared to move up to Newport. The minutes of the General Board from late May through July chronicle repeated delays and "special" unscheduled sessions of the board that reflected turbulent machinations in the background.[91] The General Board's recommendation for the formation of naval districts and a naval patrol force had resulted in Moody's issuance of General Order 128, which created them by secretarial fiat. The establishment of the naval districts in particular—something the board had done based on its charter "for the naval defense of the coast"—was probably interpreted by most of the bureaus as another infringement of their authority.[92] At the same time, Taylor and the executive committee were alarmed by the Anglo-Japanese Alliance in the Far East and the likelihood of war between Japan and Russia. The minutes make clear that Taylor was concerned that a potential general war might break out with Japan, Britain, and possibly the United States on one side and Germany, France, and Russia on the other. Contingency plans needed to be developed for this worst-case scenario, and the General Board almost certainly intended to examine these closely in its coming session in Newport in July.[93] That Newport meeting was now at risk, which probably explains why it had nine "special sessions" in June prior to the next scheduled meeting on the twenty-fifth. These were probably conducted to make up for work it anticipated it might not get done in July due to the possibility that the Newport session would be cancelled to avoid giving the critics fresh ammunition against the upcoming legislation.[94]

Taylor's ongoing goal of a formal joint planning relationship with the Army might have been spurred by these war fears. While serving as president of the War College in the mid-1890s, Taylor had become convinced of this necessity, and in 1896 he had enlisted Assistant Secretary of the Navy William McAdoo to achieve this end, but since neither service had a general staff, nothing was developed. With the creation of the General Board, he had accomplished half of the equation, a body from which naval members for a "joint" Army-Navy board could come.[95] Parallel efforts in the Army to achieve a general staff had finally succeeded under the dynamic Secretary of War Elihu Root in 1903—the so-called Root reforms. With legislation for these reforms finally passed, against strong congressional opposition and that of older generals inside the Army, in February 1903, Taylor had his chance.[96] Again with Moody's support, he proposed the formation of a "joint board." Thus it was that during this turbulent period, when the General Board thought it might get some time off, that Taylor revealed, on 20 June 1903, his proposal for a "joint committee of officers of the General Board and of the General Staff of the Army." The Joint Army and Navy Board was subsequently established by General Order 136 on 18 July 1903. Secretary Moody named Dewey, Taylor, CAPT John Pillsbury, and CDR William Barnette, all members of the General Board executive committee, as members of the entity. Dewey, due to his seniority, became its chairman.[97]

Thus Taylor can be seen as the American founder of "jointness" within the U.S. military, although prior to this time the word "combined" had been used to describe synchronized Army and Navy operations. Another advantage involved here was the formal linkage of the General Board to an organization that did exist in congressional legislation, the Army Staff. Disestablishing the General Board would mean changing a formal relationship and possibly even disestablishing the Joint Army and Navy Board. However, Taylor almost certainly did not see it this way, especially since the latter board had not been formally established by legislation. Ironically, it was during this period that the General Board formally decided not to meet that summer Newport, due to a request by Taylor to Dewey because of the criticism mentioned earlier. As a result, many of the General Board's records and some of its members who had already traveled north had to be returned.[98]

Taylor had decided to play the game as cleanly as possible and concluded his best efforts could probably be made inside the Navy with rational persuasion, no matter what the outcome of the proposed legislation. To that end, he roughly outlined two possible courses of action for the proposal in an article in *Proceedings* that December. Modestly in print, he aimed at stimulating consideration of the "question [of a general staff] in its general aspect." However, in all likelihood he was using the bully pulpit as the new president of Naval Institute (yet another "hat" for this overworked man) to reach out to naval officer leadership in the bureaus since many of them would be testifying before the House Naval Affairs Committee once the legislation as forwarded by Moody.[99]

As for the courses of action, the first was that of the "maximists" like Wainwright and Luce, who advocated a full general staff in name and size with control over the bureaus. This goal was to plan "supplies for the fleet necessary to its maintenance and efficiency; of deciding the types of ships to be recommended to the Secretary, their speed and armament; the number of reserve guns needed; the number of men and officers needed for the fleet; the amount of coal required to be stored at different points and the choice of those points; the location of future dry-docks."[100] Under this plan, the General Board would be replaced. The second proposal, the one Moody and Taylor eventually moved forward with, simply provided for recognition of the General Board by Congress and appointment of an officer from the board as "chief of staff" to the Secretary of the Navy. Dewey opposed the term "chief of staff," and it was replaced by "military adviser" to the Secretary of the Navy. This plan left the bureaus' authorities intact.[101] At the same time, President Roosevelt informed Congress in his annual message, "We need the establishment by law of a body of trained officers who shall exercise systematic control of the military affairs of the Navy, and be authorized advisors of the Secretary concerning it."[102]

The House Naval Affairs Committee hearings for the legislation finally got under way in April 1904. They went very badly, even for the modest legislation that was proposed. Moody and Taylor even compromised, willing to restrict the size of the General Board in the legislation to make it more palatable. During the hearings Moody revealed that Dewey would not accept the job of "military adviser" due to his age. It was later admitted by Dewey and Luce that the next choice by Moody was in fact Taylor for the adviser position. This might be seen as an attempt to formalize Taylor's role as Roosevelt's military adviser during the Venezuelan Crisis.[103] Additionally, Moody emphasized that the General Board "will be small" and would not consist of longstanding members that might develop into an "oligarchy."[104]

Roosevelt undermined his own position on this issue by his habit of changing out his Navy secretaries every two years or even less, thus starting the process of educating them about this vital issue anew each time.[105] Stephen Luce highlighted this problem for Taylor shortly after the legislative defeat: "The solution of the General Staff question . . . is part of the 'unfinished business,' and properly belongs to *the outgoing Secretary* [Moody], who is perfectly familiar with the subject and appreciates its importance; rather than by the incoming Secretary who is a fresh hand and would have to study up."[106] Luce then went on, in a surprisingly prophetic tone, to advocate the creation of the general staff in spite of Congress using secretarial fiat, similar to how the ONI, NWC, and the General Board had been established in the first place. He advocated an "Office of Naval Operation" with an "officer of rank" at its head. He would be "the Secretary's adviser on all naval questions of a military nature" with "H. C. Taylor [as] the officer for this place." He was obviously writing a straw man that he wanted Taylor (and possibly Dewey) to comment on first before forwarding it to the outgoing Secretary Moody. The entire tone of the letter is one of "making lemons into lemonade" or, as Luce put it, "converting . . . a pretty bad defeat, into victory."[107]

Taylor responded four days later, one of the last papers, if not the last, he wrote about the General Board. It shows how far he had come in his thinking about the practicalities of trying to get a more permanent basis for his "stealth" general staff: "I think we might get a great deal out of what you suggest, but having gone so far . . . toward General Board methods, I believe the relief . . . would be only temporary. You say plant the seed now and let it grow; that is what I think [the board is] doing. If we plant this other seed you suggest [a new operations office co-located with the Secretary of the Navy], I am afraid the two plants would not grow well together." This foreshadowed what happened later when the aide system was established by executive fiat during the Taft administration. Taylor agreed with Luce that the recent setback as to legislation formally recognizing the General Board as a naval general staff should not be seen as a defeat, but he then went on at length to say new initiatives might result in a "law which would prevent our efforts." He worried the Congress might legislatively disestablish the board "for a long time." Taylor closed the letter by promising to raise the issue with the SecNav but also recommending that they continue on the more moderate path and be patient. Interestingly, he offered that without a permanent naval general staff established by law the United States might be building ships it would only lose to "heroic defeats" in a future war.[108]

The strain of all this effort proved too much for Harry Taylor. His frantic pace since 1902, including the fleet deployment as an operational chief of staff to Dewey in the Caribbean, duties as chief of the Bureau of Navigation, president of the Naval Institute, and leadership of the executive committee of the General Board, to say nothing of personal factors about which we know very little (after all he had six children), proved too stressful. Taylor died less than a month later, on 26 July, while traveling through Canada on his way to the summer 1904 Newport sessions of the board, his goal of getting it established by law unmet. Even his obituary in the U.S. Naval Institute *Proceedings* lamented that he was "overburdened with work."[109]

Taylor had written to his friend Stephen Luce presciently about the General Board more than a year earlier, prior to the Naval Affairs Committee fight: "It is of course a little ragged in its workings as a General Staff . . . but it is gradually being recognized as such, and is used effectively by those who wish to better the Navy. . . . You perceive that there is nothing very triumphant in this statement, and in truth there is not the amount of success for which we make great parade and blow trumpets, but in certain ways I am heartily satisfied with the present results . . . even if I should leave it tomorrow."[110]

CHAPTER 4

From Taylor to Fiske
The General Board, 1904-13

After Taylor's death . . . the General Board achieved a degree of recognition and permanence which it had never enjoyed while he was alive. But without his leadership, the line began to split into two factions: those who favored retaining the board as the principal voice of the seagoing officers; and a group of insurgents who still saw it as an evolutionary mutation in the growth towards an all powerful general staff.

—CDR Daniel J. Costello

The words of CDR Costello remain germane to the early history of the General Board. Recent scholarship has not discovered much to change his analysis of the period after Taylor's death. However, Dewey's role in providing continuity as the board gained power and influence, a role that was well understood by contemporaries, seems to have been slighted in subsequent understandings of this period. The naval insurgents used the General Board as a platform to continue to agitate for their reforms, and when the secretarial instability of the Roosevelt years ended in 1909, a perceived "solution" was implemented. This solution reflected Taylor's concerns that the General Board, and the new special naval "aide for operations," who now advised the Secretary of the Navy, might not be "growing well together." But this solution worked well enough until the election of a new president, who then appointed a pacifist SecNav in 1913.[1]

Dewey believed in the value of the work of the board just as Secretary of the Navy Moody had tried to have the board recognized in legislation. Although this goal had not been accomplished, Taylor's fear that agitation for congressional recognition might cause a legislative backlash disestablishing the board had not occurred either. Taylor, Dewey, Chadwick, and Goodrich were incrementalists. However, the leaders who came after Taylor—Richard Wainwright, William Sims, Albert Key, and Bradley Fiske—were not as restrained in their agitation for reform. Egged on by the "revolutionist" Luce, they shaped the activities of the General Board through the next eight years. The only continuity during this period was Admiral of the Fleet Dewey, whose calm, guiding hand and immense informal influence proved so crucial to the survival of the General Board in its first ten years. However, he was growing older, and more infirm, and younger, less-restrained wills longed for the day when he no longer served as president of the board.

Another part of the story of the next eight years revolved around the theme of finding a replacement for the "irreplaceable" Taylor. We might turn again to the example of the German General Staff, where Scharnhorst had mentored several brilliant protégés, including Carl von Clausewitz, should he die or lose influence. This, in fact, occurred. Scharnhorst died of wounds received in battle in 1813, but his patron, Marshal Blücher, survived and Scharnhorst had a ready replacement as chief of the general staff in his close friend and fellow reformer General August von Gneisenau.[2] Dewey still served as president and thus provided continued continuity à la Blücher. However, who would serve as his Gneisenau, as Taylor's replacement? That was the question of the moment as the board began its summer deliberations in Newport that sad summer of 1904.

"Do Not Wait for Congress!"
Roosevelt was still president, and he believed and supported the work of the General Board, so all was not lost. However, his next four years in office after reelection saw secretarial stability only worsen, highlighted especially with the mediocre secretariat of Charles Bonaparte in 1905–6.[3] Roosevelt changed secretaries no fewer than four more times after Moody departed.[4] This instability left continuity in the hands of Dewey and the General Board, who became the proverbial "pros from Dover" on matters of strategy and policy. As discussed earlier, this, along with Dewey's leadership, probably helped the board's continued survival. But it also fed the perception of the insurgents that the status quo was inadequate because no specific authority for the board's work existed in congressional legislation. In fact, the board seemed to have lost ground since it was now reduced to nine members and was further cut to seven by 1906.[5]

Dewey underwrote much of the board's work during Roosevelt's second term; while outside the board, the writings of RADM Luce (Ret.) led the agitation for formal recognition. Inside the board, Dewey was assisted by an officer who had disesteemed the board after it was first established, now-captain Richard Wainwright, who reported to the board a few months after Taylor died.[6] These two men, Luce and Wainwright, helped Dewey in 1909 to get that "second plant" referred to by Taylor, an "aide for operations" who worked directly with the Secretary of the Navy while remaining a statutory member of the General Board. The SecNavs after 1909 had two men they communicated with directly about strategic policy and military operations, Dewey and the aide for operations.

With Taylor's death, the new appointee to BuNav, RADM George A. Converse, joined the General Board in August, second only to Dewey in seniority.[7] Like Dewey, Converse hailed from Vermont and had attended Norwich University before becoming a midshipman at the Naval Academy. He was primarily an engineer and served in the Spanish-American War off Cuba in command of the cruiser USS *Montgomery* with ADM William Sampson's fleet.[8] However, in the fight of the year before, he had taken a neutral position regarding recognition of the board and the appointment of a military adviser to the Secretary of the Navy. He testified that he thought the board "too large" and so was one of those who favored legislation that restricted its size.[9] However, Converse is perhaps best known for his work on the Torpedo Board of the 1890s and then again during his brief stint as chief of the Bureau of Ordnance in 1904 before replacing Taylor. His later design work on destroyers resulted in two ships of this class being named after him.[10]

In the meantime, the board had increased its output of studies, in spite of Taylor's death and the fight in Congress. By the end of 1904 it had produced a whopping forty-three different studies. Of these, nearly one-third were on base and advanced base topics, five were on fleet composition and number, five addressed equipment and ordnance, four focused on Marine Corps issues, and three were on naval tactics.[11] By October of that year, Converse's tepid support of the General Board had changed and he had joined in the incrementalists, stating that the board be recognized in the annual BuNav report, presumably by Congress, as a "permanent element of the Navy Department." Secretary of the Navy Paul Morton, Moody's successor, implemented this advice via the mechanism of the U.S. Navy Regulations (NavyRegs) in June the following year.[12] Converse turned out to be a stabilizing force for the board, continuing to serve on it until May 1907.[13] These changes to the NavyRegs also formalized the board's original scope granted by Secretary of the Navy Long to "consider the number and types of ships proper to constitute the fleet" and so had the effect of giving the General Board the ability to intrude further, as permitted by SecNav, into the business of the staff bureaus and the business of the Board on Construction (BOC).[14]

The BOC had been established in 1889, during the first reform period, and was composed of the chief intelligence officer (established six years earlier) and the chiefs of the BuC&R (as chairman), BuEquip, BuOrd, and BuEng. This gave it organizational seniority over the General Board. Secretary of the Navy Long had later lauded its work in his two-volume history *The New American Navy* as improving coordination between these bureaus. By 1904 it had become a bastion of conservatism and the anathema of the General Board and the insurgents.[15]

One of the unfortunate developments during this time in the evolution of the board was the loss of Marine representation when Colonel Reid, who was its longest serving member to that point next to Dewey, was detached on 15 December 1904 for retirement. He was not replaced, possibly due to the bad blood from a fight the previous year, when the Marine Corps commandant had testified for a mandatory Marine representation on the board. At any rate, Reid's retirement had been announced almost six months before, giving the board and the Corps time to find a replacement, but no one was appointed. Official Marine representation disappeared from the board until just prior to the United States' entry into World War I, when the commandant of the Marine Corps joined the board at the same time as the new Chief of Naval Operations.[16]

Luce continued his efforts to achieve Taylor's vision for a general staff after his death. Writing to the board in March 1905, he appealed to Converse's own efforts in establishing the Torpedo Station as showing how noncongressional activities could lead to the institutionalization of ideas. However, Luce agitated for something more than simple recognition of the status quo in NavyRegs. He still held out hope for a Navy adviser of very high rank: "Looking to the appointment, by the Secretary of the Navy, of an officer of rank to act in the capacity of acting second assistant secretary of the Navy, to hold the office until such time as Congress shall sanction the appointment by legal enactment." Here was a mix of the evolutionary and revolutionary approaches. On one hand, the Secretary of the Navy could create by a general order a secretarial post occupied an active-duty officer (somewhat like Britain's First Sea Lord), and on the other, such a post would only be "acting" until actual congressional sanction. It could then become a second assistant secretary of the navy, presumably for operations. Luce hoped the General Board would endorse and submit this proposal to the new SecNav. He closed out his letter in his typically bravura fashion: "These cases [e.g., Torpedo Station, ONI, NWC], so familiar to the board, are cited simply to show that the Executive has only to take the steps necessary for the completion of the organization . . . in order that Congress may follow with its approval. Should this proposal meet with a favorable consideration of the General Board there seems to be no reason why it should not be carried out at once. In any event, do not wait for Congress!"[17] This became the battle cry of the insurgents.

Charles Bonaparte, a distant relative of both Emperor Napoleon I and III, assumed the mantle of Secretary of the Navy not long after Morton changed the NavyRegs in 1905. Morton believed that his action vis-à-vis NavyRegs had solved the problem of a general staff—the General Board was a general staff in function, along with its component memberships of BuNav, NWC, and ONI, and that was that. A confederate informed Luce that the "General Staff movement was dead." CDR Costello's assessment was instead that the movement "had gone underground."[18]

Luce's correspondence with the board yielded considerable fruit as the underground movement came to reside within the board itself, with General Board members such as CAPT William J. Barnette, CAPT William Swift, and Wainwright. Swift was already serving on the board when Wainwright first arrived in October 1904. Barnette left briefly in June 1904 but came back to serve again on 7 May 1906. Now a captain, Barnette replaced Swift, who detached the same day.[19] Additionally, although the board's size (in August 1905) was now eight voting members, Dewey and Wainwright had already instituted a system of associate members, which were nonvoting officers, usually very junior in rank. By January 1906 the board had expanded to three committees, and these junior officer associates served in these committees. The new third committee was charged with considering "the number and types of ships proper to constitute the fleet," how they were crewed, and the logistics of the fleet, especially supplies of coal. One voting member captain headed each committee, and he was seconded by a nonvoting associate. In January 1906 the committees were manned as follows:

First Committee: CAPT William Swift and LCDR William Andrews
Second Committee: CAPT Richard Wainwright and LT Edward H. Campbell
Third Committee: CAPT William Swinburne and LCDR Albert Key[20]

Andrews and Key can be considered insurgents. Andrews' service on the First Committee made sense, since the First Committee was concerned with organization and what the insurgents wanted was change in overall organization of the general staff function as it currently existed. Andrews had been first attached for additional duty to the board as a lieutenant and nonvoting member shortly after Taylor's death, on 26 September 1904.[21] This hidden structure of the board, with bright officers such as Andrews and Key, explains why it was able to increase its production of studies by almost 50 percent, despite its statutory decrease in size.[22]

William Barnette, while detached between stints on the board, told Luce what he thought needed to be done and hatched "a plot" to replace the entire structure.[23] The many components of his plan centered on the creation, inside BuNav, of a de facto chief of the general staff position by secretarial fiat—a variation of Luce's proposed uniformed assistant to the secretary. The office would reside with a BuNav assistant, who would then get the NWC and ONI under his control, along with war planning, while remaining linked to the General Board. This new schema would then be congressionally sanctioned as innocuous language in a future appropriations bill.[24] Dewey and Taylor had selected Barnette for the Joint Army and Navy Board due to their esteem for him, and Dewey trusted him. Ironically, however, Barnette wrote to Luce in October 1905, "I want to make clear to you again that my plan presumes *the status quo so far as Dewey is concerned (unfortunately)* but when he is unable to perform further duty, (*may that be soon*) then the Chief of BuNav comes into his own. Dewey, so long as he acts, will of course be the President of the G.B. but the chief of BuNav has the power and is therefore the executive head [emphases added]."[25]

RADM Albert Greaves, himself something of an insurgent and later a member of the General Board, produced an edited version of Luce's letters in later years and significantly left this unseemly exchange out.[26] Fortunately, history had its revenge on the fickle Barnette. Dewey went on to live for another thirteen years and continued to control the General Board until the day of his death. However, elements of Barnette's plan, which came to nothing at the time, never went away in the scheming of the insurgent faction. In

May of the following year, Barnette reported to the board, where he joined Wainwright as one of its principal members and continued his plotting. Writing to Luce conspiratorially later that month, he mentioned Andrews in another scheme to use the 1906 naval appropriations bill to make the chief of BuNav (at that time Converse) Dewey's successor.[27]

Meanwhile, the main work of the board, war planning, continued. As French Chadwick had informed the new NWC class in 1902, the charter of the board was to "prepare studies for all eventualities," words that had antagonized the bureaus to no end. On a large scale, despite Admiral Alfred von Tirpitz and the German Naval Staff's preoccupation with the Royal Navy, the board continued to keep Germany the main focus in its war plans.[28] The bulk of the work relating directly to war plans focused on basing and logistic issues in the Caribbean and Philippines. The emphasis on the Philippines might be thought to reflect a concern with Japan. In fact, however, the studies done for it reflect the dual concern posed by Germany's possessions in the Far East, not the least of which was Qingdao, as well as the need to be able to have forces to project naval power in case of more trouble in China vis-à-vis the Open Door. The second study of 1905 looked at "Enforcement of the Neutrality of the Philippines," a reflection of the concern of the board over scares of war between the Great Powers in Europe and the recent Moroccan Crisis. Chadwick had commanded the South Atlantic Squadron during that crisis.[29]

Thus the board's committees produced studies literally for "all eventualities," but the board's ability to implement its advice with the bureaus remained tentative unless given secretarial force. In early 1906, Dewey had been so consternated by these problems in ship design that he told Senator Henry Cabot Lodge that the "navy was going to hell." He subsequently threatened to resign as president of the board. The current secretary, the ineffectual Charles Bonaparte, mollified Dewey but did not solve the problem.[30] As if to emphasize these systemic defects, in April 1906 the battleship USS *Kearsarge* highlighted design flaws in an accident causing injury and death. The accident related to gun turret design—ironically a similar flaw to that in British battlecruisers that would result in catastrophe for the Royal Navy at Jutland almost exactly ten years later.[31]

Dewey wrote to Secretary Bonaparte that May, citing BuC&R chief RADM Charles O'Neil, who had admitted that ship design needed changing. Interestingly, the reformist A. T. Mahan, under whom O'Neil had served when Mahan had commanded USS *Wasp*, was godfather to O'Neil's son Richard. However, the bureaus were loath to cede what they saw as their ultimate authority over these matters to the General Board, NavyRegs notwithstanding, instead turning to the other standing board of the period, the Board on Construction, which they controlled, as the source of ultimate ship-design authority.[32]

It was on Bonaparte's watch, however, that Germany finally had a competitor as the United States' likely naval enemy in a future war. Typically, events drove Bonaparte rather than he driving them. Racist legislation against Asians in the aftermath of the San Francisco earthquake of April 1906 led to strained relations between Japan and the United States. Roosevelt had engineered a peace favorable to Japan the previous year at Portsmouth ending the Russo-Japanese War (and earned him a Nobel Peace Prize). He and Elihu Root assuaged Japanese feelings while gaining immigration concessions.[33] At the same time, Roosevelt directed his secretary, William Loeb, to ask Bonaparte what war plans the General Board had available regarding Japan. Bonaparte relayed this request to the board in October. The board was caught out: it did not have even a draft war plan for Japan. Its earlier work under Taylor had focused on Japan as a neutral power or even an ally, despite the minority opinion of CAPT Charles Stockton. By November it had produced a template for a plan that it passed to CAPT J. P. Morrell, president of the NWC, for further work in the summer problems. This plan went into what was called the "Asiatic War Portfolio" in Newport, which was one of three geographic files maintained by the board (the other two were Atlantic and Eastern Pacific).[34]

When anti-Asian riots broke out on the West Coast in the following year (1907), the Joint Board became involved, as Dewey, the senior member of that organization, directed combined Army-Navy planning to begin. Dewey submitted the General Board's suggestion for sending "the battle fleet . . . to the Orient as soon as practicable." This was based on an earlier study that had looked at sailing the Atlantic Fleet into the Pacific. This was the genesis of the dispatch of the Great White Fleet around the world in 1908-9.[35] By that time period, Japanese-U.S. relations had improved sufficiently to allow the Great White Fleet to conduct its famous visit to Japan, although the fact that this might be regarded as a "proof of concept" for War Plan Orange has been ignored by many naval historians.[36] The Russo-Japanese War had only ended three years previously, and it had become known how pitiful a material state the Russian fleet under ADM Z. P. Rozhestvensky had been in when it blundered into battle at the Tsushima Strait.[37] As long as Dewey was in charge, the main enemy remained Germany, but planning for War Plan Orange—orange being the color code used for Japan—can be dated from 1906.

By December, Bonaparte's lackluster management of the department had allowed infighting between the line and staff to such a degree—represented by the General Board and BOC, respectively—that it caused Dewey to make a special plea in a public Christmas message in the *Washington Times*: "Let us have neither cliques or grudges, but all stand together for the good of the country and the service." In any case, Roosevelt had put Bonaparte, curiously, at the Navy in a sort of "holding pattern" until Moody left the attorney general portfolio for the Supreme Court. This was an odd move for a president who supposedly was under the influence of junior officers like Sims. Another explanation is that Roosevelt was acting as his own SecNav, using Bonaparte and the others as cyphers. If that is the case, then his plan did not work as well as perhaps he thought it did, especially since he could not change the NavyRegs or issue general orders.[38] At the same time Luce continued his own behind-the-scenes campaign, working to get the board more authority, or to replace it completely.

It was during this time frame that Luce first proposed George von Lengerke Meyer for the job as Bonaparte's replacement. He used as an analogy the British practice of a civilian "First Lord of the Admiralty" in recommending von Meyer as a "good business man, who would take an active interest in the navy."[39]

Throughout this period, the war planners marveled at the irony of planning for war with the inventor of modern war planning—Germany. Even with junior officer augmentation and help from the NWC faculty and students, the officers maintaining the portfolios came to the realization that they did not have the types of "off-the-shelf" plans ready for execution on the German model. Additionally, Taylor and Dewey had identified the critical need to ensure that the actual commanders in chief of the squadrons afloat had knowledge of the plans and tried to institute a system of briefings as these men went out to take command. However, keeping current war plans, as immature as they might be, close to hand on board ships at sea proved a daunting challenge, one that is still difficult in today's Internet communications world.[40] Chief among the headaches of the war planners of the General

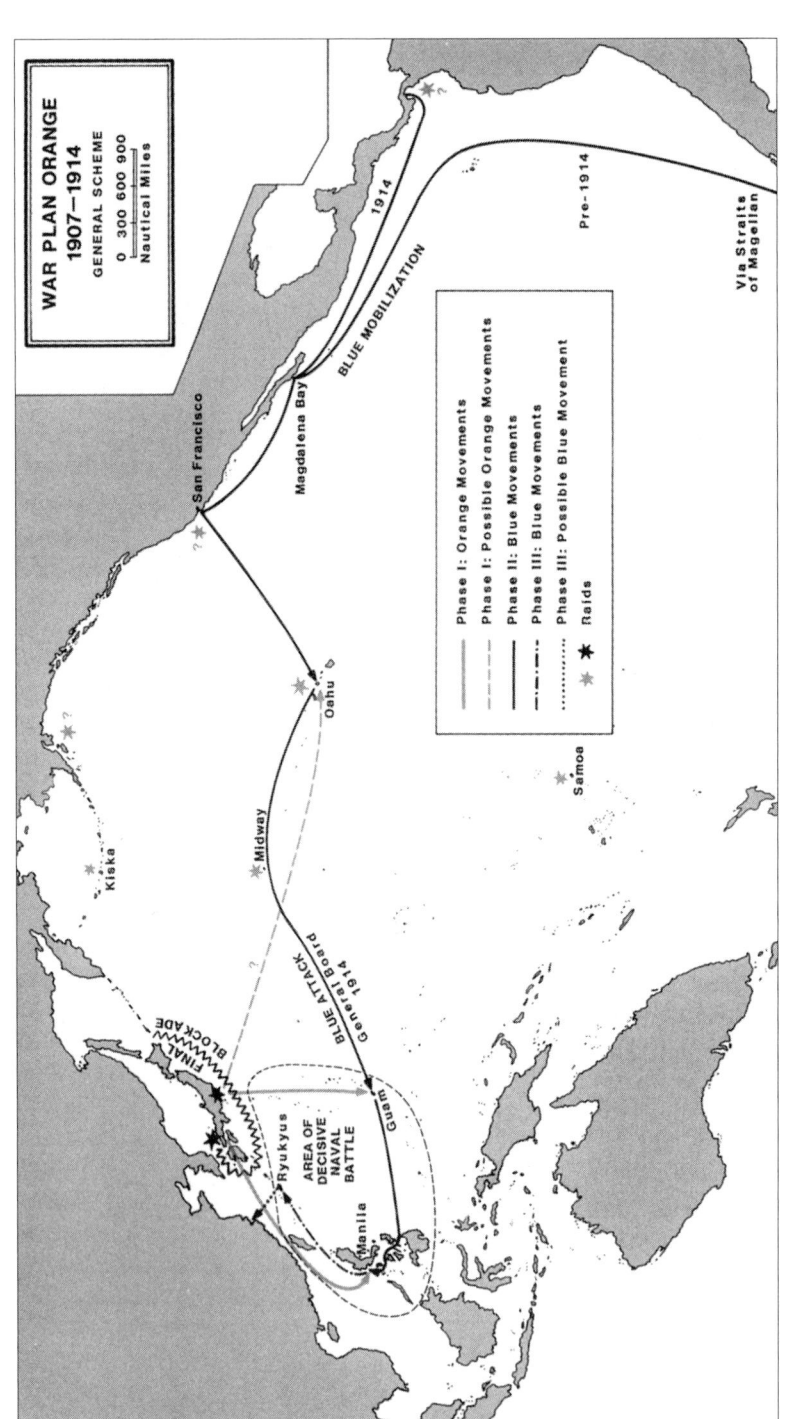

Map 2. War Plan Orange

Board (and NWC) were the logistics challenges of modern naval warfare, especially in the Pacific in an Orange scenario.[41] After all, the German Naval Staff had decided these challenges were too great after the Venezuela Crisis in 1902. One frustrated planner penned that "the condition of the navy as regards war plans must be regarded as deplorable. A safe full of so-called 'war plans' consists really of plans for a landing party seizing ports; and our present organization is such that we can hope for no speedy relief. A committee of three of the General Board is charged with this, as one of numerous other duties."[42] However, CDR Costello, who wrote during a similar planning environment during the Cold War, captured best the true value gained from the process as it existed until after the CNO took over the bulk of the function after World War I: "Nevertheless, the board's development of a system of war planning in peace did much to create within the naval service an awareness of the complexities of modern naval warfare."[43]

The Insurgents, the General Board, and the Advent of the Aide System

By 1907 the insurgents were restless again.[44] The new Secretary of the Navy, Victor Metcalf, another secretary with no experience at sea or association with it, seemed the most antireformist secretary yet, even more than the ineffectual Bonaparte. The former congressman Metcalf (R-CA) was a lawyer and had served on the House Naval Affairs Committee during the Moody-Taylor fight. He had favored building battleships but had not supported recognition of the General Board.[45] Obviously Roosevelt had not taken Luce's advice to employ George L. von Meyer. August found one of the original reformers, C. F. Goodrich, now a rear admiral, proposing yet another means for change through the mechanism of the NavyRegs. He suggested they be changed to allow officers to air in public "service matters not . . . confidential."[46] His goal was to allow officers to go through the press, either firsthand or via proxies—especially officers like Sims, who seemed to have no fear of departmental wrath. In October, Barnette informed Luce privately that the insurgents had decided to go public and use the press to publish articles critical of how the Navy designed and built ships.

In January 1908 the first article sponsored by the insurgents appeared in *McLure's* magazine by Henry Reuterdahl, who claimed the Navy was "unprepared for war" and pinned the blame on the staff bureaus and BOC. Most of Reuterdahl's material was provided by Sims. Sims was protected from a court-martial only because of his close relationship with Roosevelt.[47] On 9 January this action provoked the response that Taylor had most feared, as members of Congress blamed the General Board for fomenting this activity, even though these actions had occurred without the knowledge of Dewey and RADM Brownson, the outgoing BuNav chief. Senator Hale introduced legislation designed to abolish the board, which was not the source of Reuterdahl's information in the first place. Taylor's fears about the reformers overplaying their hand seemed realized. Upon hearing of Hale's action, CDR William Fullam, one of Sims' confederates and another nonvoting officer who had been assigned to the board, called Hale's plan a "traitorous act."[48] The Navy was in a bona fide civil military crisis and something had to give.

Hale began a formal investigation in the Senate Armed Services Committee the month following Reuterdahl's charges. He produced a whitewash of the BOC and the bureaus, especially Construction and Repair. Dewey and his various BuNav chiefs during this period remained above the fray—they were already on the record about the unsatisfactory state of affairs but saw no need to draw further ire against the board. It mattered not, because Hale viewed the board as an icon for all the "troubles" in the Navy since 1900, despite its good work and the esteem of most of the navy secretaries and, of course, the president. Hale soon found, though, that getting legislation to disestablish the board was just as difficult as opposing legislation to formalize it.[49] Taylor's primal fear had been excessive—the longer the board existed, the more sure its continued existence, at least under the current political dynamic.

During these seemingly momentous public events, fundamentally important work was taking place inside the board itself, despite the strife in the Navy Department. In March the board shrank to its smallest formal size, six officers, but because of the NWC and its junior officer augmentation (many of whom had ironically schemed against it), it continued a prodigious output of studies on a wide range of topics in addition to its war-plans work. In 1907 the board produced eighty-four studies, and then, reflecting its smaller size in 1908, it only produced sixty-one—while at the same time continuing its work for two major war plans—Black and Orange. On top of this, it now had its Joint Board responsibilities to fulfill.[50] Motivated by the war planning focused on Japan, in January 1908 the board produced a paper titled "Study of Japanese Language by Naval Officers." As a result, two years later LTJG Fred Rogers and two other junior lieutenants arrived in Tokyo for language training. Naval historian CAPT Steven Maffeo has argued that the seeds of victory in World War II began in 1910 with this modest beginning, which eventually resulted in the Navy's highly effective cryptologic and intelligence organization in place in 1941. However, it appears the board's study of 1908 was the real seed for this initiative, which makes sense given that CAPT Raymond P. Rodgers, the chief intelligence officer representing the ONI, was a member of the board. Rodgers later became the president of the War College, thus maintaining his connection with the General Board.[51]

In the meantime, agitation continued at all levels, both in the open and surreptitiously for a more formal general staff organization. These efforts produced one of the most important milestones in the history of the General Board, its assumption of the critical ship-design oversight to support its war plans. Roosevelt's former naval aide, CDR Albert L. Key, who had served as an associate member of the board in 1906 and helped the board in its war-plan work, wrote to Secretary Metcalf expressing concerns over the design of the new battleship, *North Dakota*. Key proposed using the board session at Newport that summer to hold a conference to resolve the design disagreements between the General Board and the BOC.[52]

Metcalf, suffering health issues, had stepped down, and Truman Newberry, for the past three years the Assistant SecNav, "fleeted up" as acting SecNav. Newberry, in addition to gaining a reputation as a capable administrator under two SecNavs, had experience as a naval officer.[53] On 2 July Newberry directed the board to resolve the design impasse between the bureaus and the line officer community.[54] At the same time Luce wrote to the president informing him of the ongoing controversy, using, of all things, Bonaparte's annual message of 1906 as evidence! Luce suggested that the president take action by giving the General Board the authority at Newport to correct the "defects" identified by Bonaparte two years earlier. Roosevelt wrote a curt response: "That is a very interesting suggestion of yours and I shall carefully consider it. I am not at all contented with the organization of the Navy."[55]

The ship design process that led to the conference highlights several milestones in both the evolution and usefulness of the General Board during this period. We must return to the difficult days of the summer of 1903, when Dewey, Taylor, and the board were prevented from going north for the summer session at Newport. At the time, new developments in technology—increased firing rates for large-caliber guns (11 inch, 12 inch), improvements in fire control and optics for long-range gunnery and its accuracy, and the constant increases in torpedo ranges—mandated that battleship designs had to change to keep up with the times. As discussed, six months earlier Taylor had assigned the fiery young Sims, who had knowledge of the latest gunnery practices and technology, to the new office of inspector of target practice, which he held until 1909.[56]

The officers at the War College, under the enlightened leadership of French Chadwick, had produced studies for the General Board on the efficacy of big-gun battleships versus the current design that mixed calibers. These innovative designs had come from within the Bureau of Construction and Repair. After gaming with these ships, they recommended to the board an all-big-gun battleship design, with smaller guns used only to ward off torpedo boats—a design similar to the later *Dreadnought*. The board submitted this work to the BOC bureaus to determine the feasibility of a 12-inch all-big-gun battleship, which, had it been built quickly, would have preceded ADM Fisher's *Dreadnought*. However, congressional limitations on battleship size and a number of other factors delayed what became the battleships *South Carolina* and *Michigan*, the Navy's first dreadnoughts, from joining the fleet until 1910. Arguments over the design of these ships had highlighted the flawed "take it or leave it" approach of the naval constructor community and BOC. In the heated environment of recrimination in 1908 over the design of a new battleship (*North Dakota*), Sims, Key, and their confederates were bound and determined to make the line officer community more powerful and influential in this process.[57]

Newberry's guidance and Luce's prodding yielded unexpected and significant fruit in response to this dynamic. Newberry ordered the senior members of the BOC to attend the Newport conference, which was packed with General Board members and junior officer insurgents (including Sims, Fullam, and Key), and at the same time Roosevelt embarked on the *Mayflower* to sail north and personally attend the conference, although Dewey did not. The president arrived on 22 July, the opening day designated by Newberry. Outvoted during the meetings and cowed by the personal presence of the commander in chief, the senior members of the BOC were humbled. Despite no legislative confirmation in its aftermath, the conference voted that the General Board should be the clearinghouse for reconciling ship design to war plans in the Navy. This decision had the force of presidential authority and established the precedent for an "iterative" process between the General Board (line) and the staff bureaus, in effect replacing the "take it or leave it" system. This arbiter function in design remained with the General Board until World War II.[58] Some observers have argued that the insurgents were not happy with the results of the Newport Conference and this caused them to view the board as more of an impediment than ally in their reformist efforts. However, the board was satisfied that the young reformers' (their term for them) concerns had been addressed and that a modus vivendi had been reached with the bureaus.

In December, Newberry formerly became Secretary of the Navy in the lame-duck administration of Roosevelt. Dewey had lobbied for his appointment as SecNav in 1905 and had had to settle for Newberry as assistant SecNav in the interim. Continuity in secretarial leadership, albeit at the assistant level, had yielded some progress. More followed. In 1909 Roosevelt, urged on by the indefatigable Sims, directed a joint civilian-military commission to look into establishing a bona fide general staff.[59] Newberry, however, saw the General Board as "the very essence of ... the naval establishment" and testified as much to Congress.[60] Shortly after taking office, Newberry canceled the restrictions in place since 1905 on the board's size, which paved the way for what came next. Newberry's goal was to make the board a "true general staff" by broadening its membership and its mandate via secretarial fiat. His goal was to make Dewey, and in his absence the BuNav chief, a chief of the general staff who would be partnered closely with the civilian assistant SecNav—a true civil-military marriage for the direction of naval policy and strategy.[61] Newberry saw this goal accomplished, but not under his leadership. His plan did not prove to be enough for the insurgents like Sims and Key, as well as newcomer CAPT Bradley Fiske, who joined the board in 1910. These men wanted a general staff with executive authority unencumbered by the bureaus *and* the SecNav. Fiske eventually took over leadership of the insurgent faction from Sims once Sims' direct access to executive power departed with his friend and protector Roosevelt in March 1909.

Roosevelt's last attempt on behalf of Sims et al. occurred on 27 January 1909 with the appointment of the Moody commission meeting in Washington led by the former Secretary of the Navy of the Taylor years.

This delayed Newberry's plan to make the board the de facto general staff. In addition to Moody, the commission included former Secretary Morton, former congressman Alston Dayton, Luce, Mahan, and RADM Robley D. Evans, with Fullam (Sims' heir apparent) as the recorder. This was truly a formidable array of elder statesmen and naval leaders and its officer members included none of the staff officer community.[62]

At the end of February, the commission submitted its final report to the president, which recommended that the department be reorganized along British lines—thus reflecting the influence of Mahan—into five "divisions." The second division of Naval Operations would be led by a chief who would be responsible individually, not collectively like the General Board, for recommendations to the SecNav. This too reflected the influence of Mahan, who believed that leaders must be accountable and that one must have an individual at the top to hold to account—like a Nelson or, more darkly, an ADM Byng.[63] Mahan believed that corporate decision-making bodies were "irresponsible" in the narrow sense that it was difficult to assign responsibility to them.[64] This was nothing new, as Mahan had believed the board a half measure after its creation. Roosevelt submitted the Moody commission's ideas as draft legislation to the U.S. Senate, where no further action occurred.[65] Because of their more radical vision, the insurgents did not get what they wanted, when with Newberry they might have had a more moderate and acceptable general staff as constituted by the General Board, NWC, BuNav, and ONI, seconded by an operationally minded assistant secretary in the mold of Fox or Newberry.

Ironically, the reform movement gained ground rather than losing it after departure of the reformist, navalistic Roosevelt. Roosevelt's handpicked successor, William Howard Taft, appointed Luce's "desirable . . . business man," the very Prussian-sounding George von Lengerke Meyer, as Secretary of the Navy. Kaiser Wilhelm even linked the U.S. naval general staff system to its Prussian intellectual legacy in public comments. Too, the era of secretarial instability ended, and the return of stable leadership was a major factor in the next steps in the evolution of the General Board and the insurgents' push for more reform. For the next twelve years, the board dealt with only two SecNavs (Meyer and Daniels). Meyer gave the board added prestige by attending its meetings, something not done since Secretary Morton.[66]

Taft let Meyer run his department without much interference. Sims' "skip-echelon" connection, at least with the sitting president, was gone.[67] That July, Meyer appointed a special board to look at the question of reform again. At the head of the board he appointed RADM William Swift, a protégé of Taylor's who had served on the board from 1902 to 1906.[68] That October, Swift's board reported out after considering material provided to it by Meyer and the General Board, including the work of the Moody commission. It recommended a modification of the Moody commission's findings, reducing the five divisions to four: Operations, Personnel, Inspections, and Material. The first three were always to be headed by line officers, but the last could be headed by either a line or staff officer. If the Swift board's recommendations had been adopted in toto, the General Board would have been reduced to a weak advisory body, essentially ceding its main war-planning function to a powerful aide for operations. The word "aide" was chosen as a sop to Congress as well as Dewey, who did not like the title "chief of staff." Congress might be moved to act against Meyer if he appointed four new "chiefs," all with executive power over their respective bureaus. The General Board would become a replacement for the BOC, with the Division of Operations and its admiral aide as the general staff and chief of the general staff.[69]

Meyer faced a dilemma. If he adopted the Swift proposal, it was almost certain that Dewey would resign and the motion had little chance of success in Congress. He had been advised by RADM Charles Sperry, a former NWC president and board member at the time of Taylor's death, to keep the board, that "no one officer however intelligent and single minded" could replace the collective and impartial advice of the board.[70] Meyer issued "change 9" to NavyRegs, establishing the "aid [*sic*] system," which was also known as the "Meyer System."[71] The Secretary of the Navy was now augmented by four aides for operations, material, personnel, and inspections; each one of these aides had an officer assigned as an assistant. The aide for operations replaced the BuNav chief as a member on the General Board. Responsibility for the ONI, NWC, and the inspector for target practice and ship movements went to this aide and his new separate office, but he remained on the General Board, essentially becoming Dewey's deputy. He also served as the chief military adviser to the secretary, effectively what Taylor and Luce had attempted to get five years earlier. This marked the decline of BuNav, although not as much as might be thought, since that office retained its detailing function and evolved into the Bureau of Personnel (BuPers), an organization, still in existence today, that has been accused by some of being the real controlling agency in the Navy.[72]

Interestingly, the first four aides were all former or current General Board members and all line officers. Swift became aide for material, perhaps an indication of discipline of the staff bureaus given the work of his board the year before. The current BuNav chief, RADM William Potter, stepped down from that job and became the aide for personnel, and RADM Aaron Ward became aide for inspections.[73] RADM Richard Wainwright served as the powerful first aide for operations. Wainwright might be characterized as standing somewhere between the insurgent faction and the more moderate officers (such as Sperry), having also been a Taylor protégé, serving on the board from 1904 to 1907 as a captain. He was one of the most esteemed line officers in the Navy; like Dewey, he was an advocate for big-gun battleships and represented a subtle and intelligent first pick for the job. Fiske claimed Dewey personally chose Wainwright as the critical inaugural man for this job.[74]

Meyer's action abolished the BOC and replaced it with the General Board, thus institutionalizing the results of the 1908 Newport Conference. Another change included a renaming of the chief intelligence officer as the director of naval intelligence (DNI). The board also increased in size to eleven members, up from an average of seven the year before. These new memberships gave it even more prestige, which was one of Meyer's goals.[75] It seemed that all that Luce had hoped had come to pass, and by the method he had recommended—secretarial fiat. The second part of his prophecy, that Congress would "follow" and support, also seemed borne out by subsequent events. When Hale and his allies in Congress were first presented with Meyer's "fait accompli," it seemed that Taylor's, not Luce's, prediction would come true. However, Hale had learned his lesson the year before; getting legislation to abolish the General Board and override secretarial action was as difficult as the Navy getting legislation to give it official sanction. Too, Dewey had used his political connections to get the favorable appointment of George A. Loud to the House Naval Affairs Committee. This committee and that of the Senate decided to give the aide system a "free and unrestricted trial."[76]

Secretarial stability and wise leadership under Meyer, as well as successful evolutionary reform, resulted in a remarkable period of calm for the Navy during the Taft administration. The insurgents were mollified for the time being. The hated BOC was disestablished, with the General Board performing its function of reconciling war plans to ship and fleet design in an iterative process through the aides with the bureaus. At the same time, the aide for operations now existed and "owned" much of the war-planning apparatus—the NWC and ONI/DNI—as well as the control of day-to-day fleet operations. Indeed, Wainwright's first year in this role caused Meyer to laud the aide system in his 1910 annual report: "The present organization of the navy [*sic*] Department (or so much as concerns the aides), which aimed to place at the disposition of the Secretary expert knowledge information in order that he might keep in touch with what was going on, has now been in operations practically a year. In consequence, the business of the department has been expedited and the Secretary is, without question, better informed on the workings of the department than has been possible under any previous system."[77] Of the aide for operations, Meyer wrote that his reorganization of the fleet, especially the battleships and torpedo vessels, "brought about markedly greater efficiency." He also mentioned that the coordination of the General Board, ONI, and NWC had resulted in better war plans because of the inclusion of experts from the fleet in this process. As for ship design, the aide for material that relieved Swift was another line officer, Frank Friday Fletcher, and Meyer singled out his work with the board in ensuring long-term ship designs matched war plans.[78] Of course, some of this was Meyer justifying his decision, but it did reflect improvement.

However, the relationship between the aide for operations and the General Board was quite different from that of the BuNav chief he replaced. Meyer specifically outlined these differences in a memorandum on "rules for aides" he issued his last year office. First, the aide, although a member of the General Board, could give his opinion directly to the secretary, even if it differed from the board's consensus opinion. Any of the other aides could do this as well, but they had to do so through the aide for operations. This aide was also the titular head of the "council of aides," who met weekly with the secretary, and the conduit, for all information to and from them to the secretary. The General Board submitted its recommendations directly to Meyer but had to relay who the dissenting votes were if the vote was not unanimous (including the member aides). If the General Board needed to communicate with one of the bureaus under the purview of an aide, they had to do it through the aide for operations. Finally, once the secretary had approved or disapproved a General Board recommendation, usually in the form of a study, the aide for operations would communicate that to the board, along with the secretary's reasons for disapproval if that was the case.[79] This concentrated considerable power in the person of the aide for operations, although this power would be wielded with a soft touch until RADM Fiske became aide for operations in 1913.[80]

The later legislation that created the CNO resulted in a similar system, with a CNO in charge of the fleet and the General Board in charge of policy and ship/fleet design. The chief difference involved moving the war-planning function to the CNO and congressional sanction was at last achieved, both for the CNO and General Board.[81] But just like the aide for operations, the CNO continued to serve on the board as an ex officio member, although his power through the other aides of the other bureaus, at least at first, was much less. Shortly after the implementation of the aide system, Meyer upgraded the rank of the president of the NWC from captain to rear admiral, promoting Raymond P. Rodgers, who had been the chief intelligence officer in October 1909. This change marked another incremental change in the General Board's membership, influence, and culture. With the addition of the aides for operation and material, the board now had three admirals as well as Dewey serving by December 1909.[82]

However, as events would show, the system set up by Meyer could all be undone by another secretary at the stroke of a pen with a change to the NavyRegs or a general order disestablishing all these various reorganizations.

Bradley Fiske and the General Board

Bradley Fiske was one of the most dynamic officers in the Navy of the early twentieth century. Due to the machinations of Dewey, he reported from his command of the armored cruiser *Tennessee* to the General Board as a replacement for CAPT Harry S. Knapp, a similarly innovative and ambitious officer. Knapp had recently proposed to the board that the NWC be relocated to Washington so it could work closer with the board and the aide for operations in war planning. But the current NWC president, RADM Raymond Rodgers, endorsed this proposal only if it meant that an "increase [to] the scope of the General Board until it becomes a General Naval Staff of which the War College is to become a branch." However, Rodgers felt compelled to solicit the written advice of previous NWC presidents, including Luce, Mahan, and Chadwick, all of whom thought the idea a bad one. Knapp's initiative quietly died, but it reflects how the reformers were not yet satisfied with the aide system or the General Board.[83]

At the time Fiske reported, it was well known that the General Board was an established path to high command and influence in the Navy. Fiske considered it "an honor to become a member of the General Board."[84] An autodidact, he was an inventor, organizer, reformer, and writer. Fiske inherited Taylor's role of advocating a general staff, but as a replacement for the board, not to augment it. His methods were very aggressive and his goals ambitious.[85]

Taylor's concerns, that the board was not influential enough with the Secretary of the Navy or safe from sudden disestablishment, also became Fiske's concerns. Unlike Dewey, and more like Taylor, he used the Naval Institute *Proceedings* as a forum for his many ideas. One historian claimed that Fiske "was the most prolific writer of any naval officer up to the present [1967]."[86] Whether or not this claim is true, Fiske was a true polymath and, as it turned out, a ferocious bureaucratic infighter. He has been accused of being a part of a clique attempting to subvert the American system of civilian control of the military, in this case the U.S. Navy component, and characterized as a "militarist." There is no doubt that his admiration of the German General Staff drove his efforts to create a more powerful general staff than the one he found in the General Board.[87] Fiske commented that the aide system and the General Board worked "extremely well" together, attributing it to the fact that the aides for operation and material were General Board members, as if this were some sort of accident, when it had been Meyer's and Dewey's sine qua non for the adoption of the aide system.[88]

Despite his laudatory comments in his memoirs about the atmosphere and professionalism of the board, not long after Fiske arrived in August 1910, he decided that it was not the general staff he longed to serve on and eventually lead. His initial assignment was to the First Committee, which addressed design issues—an assignment that makes sense given that Fiske's inventions, like his rangefinder, were on many Navy ships. Not long after, Fiske was moved to the Second Committee, which "dealt with war plans." He recalled his disillusionment with the assignment years later: "I gradually realized, to my disappointment, that the war plans of the General Board were so general in character as hardly to be war plans at all. . . . I found, also, that the work of the General Board was much less influential in guiding the strategy of the navy than I had supposed." He then went on to discuss how he realized how "careful" Dewey had to be in conducting the affairs of the board in order to avoid it being "abolished altogether."[89] The general staff that Fiske wanted is best reflected in his discussion of the German General Staff in his memoir, based on a description of it given to him by CAPT Templin M. Potts, who had served as naval attaché to Germany and then as chief intelligence officer on the General Board:

> Potts told me that the German Naval General Staff, like the Germany Army General Staff, kept a score or more . . . officers at work making war plans. . . . He told me that the General Staff not only made out war plans, but also, as accessory to the war plans, made plans which covered all the tactical and strategical drills and maneuvers of the fleet. . . . Certain members of the General Staff would go out with the fleet as observers, and note how their plans were being carried out, for the double purpose of noting and comparing the degrees of skill of the various officers and of seeing where the drills could be altered and improved.[90]

Fiske's expansion of the power of a general staff would have violated one of the precepts that Dewey (and Mahan) held sacrosanct, the independence of ship and fleet commanders from the kind of staff officer oversight that Fiske proposed.

As might be expected, the output of the board increased, especially now that it had two active war plans, Black and Orange, that required coordination with the Joint Board. Black (Germany) remained Dewey's priority. In addition, Dewey remained committed to using the General Board as much as possible to build the forty-eight all-big-gun battleships he needed for the German threat. He was probably right to build in this fashion, since having what it took to confront Germany at sea would almost certainly be more than enough to deal with Japan. Nonetheless, the board's planners focused more and more of their efforts on the tricky issue of logistics to support both lines of effort, especially the challenges of logistics in the Pacific. As it turned out, the Army and the General Board diverged in their views of how to defend the Philippines, with the Navy wanting to develop Subic Bay (Olongapo) with its easy access to the South China Sea as a naval base and the Army maintaining that the Asiatic Squadron (soon to be fleet) should remain in defense of Manila Bay, the political center of gravity. The General Board stuck to its guns, putting the floating dry dock *Dewey* in Subic Bay in 1910.[91]

RADM Charles J. Badger (*left*), after delivering special instructions from the War Department to RADM Bradley A. Fiske (*right*) in 1914. Fiske later engineered the legislation that created the Chief of Naval Operations in 1915, and Badger became Dewey's successor as the senior officer of the General Board. The new CNO and his staff (OpNav) assumed the war-planning portfolio from the General Board just as the United States entered World War I. *Harris & Ewing Collection, Library of Congress*

By 1909 the board's productivity after the turmoil of 1908 had returned. It produced 147 studies versus the 61 of the previous year. These studies reflected the new role of oversight of ship characteristics by the General Board. For example, study 140–09 of December examined battleship design against a 16,000-ton limit imposed by Congress. Pursuant to this function, the board also produced a study on the "Building Program for 1911," which it had not the previous year (1908). This evolved into the annual building policy 420–2 serials issued every year by the General Board until World War II. Logistical studies highlighted the need for both domestic and overseas dry docks, especially in the Pacific at Pearl Harbor. The board studies also began to face the reality of the inadequacy of crewing such a large Navy with existing active-duty personnel and examined the creation of a naval reserve as well as training naval militias to crew battleships. Finally, new technology represented by submarines, torpedoes, and communications garnered study, especially a very innovative September 1909 report on creating an "advanced base" for submarines using a ship—an idea that later became the submarine tender.[92]

The board maintained this level of output in 1910, the year Fiske first reported as a member. It was at this time, with the first studies of naval aviation, that Fiske's foresight and unique ability to relate technology to strategy and fleet design became apparent. Fiske's self-serving memoir ascribes most of the credit for the General Board's interest in aviation to himself, but the reader must remember that the board operated on a consensus basis, and so the other members of the board at the time also played a role in thinking about how this new and potentially revolutionary technology might be used in the fleet.[93] Fiske's interest in aviation stemmed directly from his work on War Plan Orange. At that time the plan for a war with Japan predicted a Japanese invasion and seizure of the Philippines. According to Fiske, the United States would then respond by sending a "tremendous fleet to fight the Japanese fleet in its home waters, as Russia had done six years before."[94] Historian Edward Miller has named this approach the "thrusting" course of action. Fiske did not like this idea and proposed using naval aviation based at four or more naval air stations around Luzon to sink the vulnerable Japanese landing craft or boats to be used for the invasions in their approach phases to the beaches. Thus Fiske's idea was to use naval aviation at water's edge in an anti-amphibious role. He shared the idea with Dewey and "certain members," but when he proposed it formally to the board, the aide for operations, RADM Richard Wainwright, ridiculed the idea as "wild-cat schemes."

Fiske gives the impression that nothing further occurred in naval aviation development, when in fact as early as October 1910, two months after Fiske had reported to the board, it had already published a study to put an airplane on another of the board's innovative schemes, the scout cruiser USS *Chester*.[95] This lined up with the board's work, in progress since its early days, to give the fleet a scouting force to provide the best possible intelligence on an adversary fleet.[96] The idea of further augmenting the scout capability of these new cruisers (which became light cruisers) with airplanes made its appearance first in 1910. The *Chester*'s sister ship, the scout cruiser USS *Birmingham*, became the demonstration platform for this aviation capability on 14 November of that year with Eugene Ely at the controls, although the Secretary of the Navy emphasized the board's position that the best role for the airplane was embarked on one of its new scout cruisers for reconnaissance purposes.[97]

Perhaps one indicator that Fiske's agitation for aviation had some effect was the assignment of CAPT Washington I. Chambers to BuNav (whose chief was no longer on the board) to oversee aviation developments inside that bureau. Additionally, in 1911, the same month Fiske left the board, the first airplanes were purchased and aviation stations established at Annapolis and North Island, California.[98] The board's other work in 1911, in addition to its war planning, covered many other subjects in addition to Fiske's advocacy of the new airplane technology. Especially of interest was its focus on floating dry docks. One study obsessed over protection of the YFD-2 *Dewey*, now in the Philippines, and another examined building a 35,000-ton floating dry dock, no doubt intended to accommodate the new larger size battleships the General Board was expecting to build with the apparent lifting of the 16,000-ton congressional limit. Meyer duly echoed the recommendation for the larger dry dock in his 1911 annual report. Another area of great interest to the board involved submarines and submarine tenders—it was clear the board was trying to come to grips with fighting a naval war in very distant waters. However, the number of studies actually dropped by almost half in 1911, to seventy-seven.[99] One possible explanation, and Fiske's description of his time on the board supports it, was that the war planning had become more detailed and time consuming. This was not reflected in the serial lists. The other factor that might help explain this drop in the productivity of the board has to do with the increasing size of the fleet, and now the time-consuming communications and memorandum for and from the aides. The studies themselves had to account for steadily increasing amounts of material, ships, and relationships. It is clear that the board focused intently on logistics of a future, distant naval war, and this foresight would pay dividends in the decades to come.

Beginning in 1911, a fleet-wide mobilization took place in the summer in the vicinity of New York City. President Taft attended the one in 1912 and wrote a personal addendum to the 1912 Annual Report of his SecNav describing his (positive) impressions of the event. These ship gatherings were the genesis of Fleet Week, an annual event that still takes place in New York City.[100] The fleet mobilization, an idea that had originally stemmed from Taylor and the early days of the General Board, served two purposes: it exercised the concentration of the fleet as an operational deployment and readiness exercise and it served to show the public how well its tax dollars had been spent (and why they should spend more on their Navy). Taft highlighted how the fleet had increased to thirty-one operating battleships from twenty-four the previous year (1911). Even more important, the Secretary of the Navy's annual report included not just a commentary by the president but also the entire General Board building plan from its study for construction in 1913, the first time this had ever been done. For the first time the board showed great interest in building battle-cruisers to be used as part of its scouting force, but only if that did not lower the rate of building two battleships a year.[101]

One other area of interest during Taft's time in office was his administration's attempt to use scientific management—also known as Taylorism after its founder, Frederick Taylor—to improve the bureaucratic processes and efficiency across the span of the executive branch.[102] Beginning in November 1910, departments had to fill out forms for "The President's Inquiry in Re Economy and Efficiency." These forms found their way to the General Board, which duly filled them in. Because of them we have a better idea of how the board had evolved in its organization. By 1912 the board had four committees. The new fourth committee was charged with studies on the defense of coaling stations and bases but had no personnel assigned that year. It was in these committees that the board put its nonvoting associate members, the "experts" from the fleet mentioned by Meyer in his annual report, who augmented its work. Also present were three civilian clerks, one for each committee. One of these clerks was Jarvis Butler, who later also served as the secretary of the Joint Board after World War I and then chief clerk of the General Board (as a civilian) after World War II.[103]

Fiske remained in charge of the war-planning committee until returning to the fleet in October 1911, when he was promoted to rear admiral in command of the Fifth Battleship Division. Fiske's promotion is another indicator of how the General Board had become an essential component of what officers termed the "Fleet Ladder," key billets that had to be traversed as one proceeded to the rank of admiral.[104] Fiske returned as the powerful aide for operations in February 1913, just one month before Josephus Daniels became Secretary of the Navy. Again, this was almost certainly Dewey's doing.[105] When Fiske rejoined the board, he had solidified his agenda to address the ideas he had had in his earlier stint on the board, aviation and a more German-like naval general staff as opposed to the aide system and the General Board.

After Fiske left active service (see chapter 5) in 1916, he published *The Navy as a Fighting Machine*, a fascinating book—part theory, part management advice, and part strategy—in the Frederick Taylor vein of scientific management. He remained active in the policy debates of the Navy after retirement, especially the fight against the Washington Naval Treaty, serving as president of the U.S. Naval Institute in the 1920s and as a virtual adjunct member of the General Board. The General Board records, especially its studies, include numerous correspondences with him. He lived to see World War II, dying in 1942.[106]

By 1913 the insurgents had managed to place the most extreme advocate for their position, Bradley Fiske, as the aide for operations, the number two man to Dewey, on the General Board. More and more Dewey deferred important decisions to Fiske. Nonetheless, like all radical reformers, the insurgents remained unsatisfied. Ironically, under antimilitarist Secretary of the Navy Josephus Daniels, they would finally achieve their long-sought objective in 1915 with the creation of the Chief of Naval Operations in congressional legislation. At the same time, the General Board remained "in being," evolved, and soon came to play the role in the construct of naval strategy that Fiske had thought it should play when he first joined it as a member in 1910.

CHAPTER 5

The General Board in Peace and War, 1913–18

It has been my opinion for many years that we have in the General Board of the Navy a better general staff than that of the Army. . . . I believe [it] to be of inestimable value as an asset in peace and war.

—ADM George Dewey to Secretary of the Navy
Josephus Daniels, 1915

The role of the General Board of the Navy on the eve of World War I in Europe (and the United States' eventual participation in that conflict) has been overshadowed by a number of factors. These coalesce around three themes that have detracted from the important role played by ADM Dewey and the other members of the General Board in conducting ongoing planning and policy studies for the Wilson administration as well as preparing for the contingency of U.S. involvement in the war. The roles of personality, organizational factors, and operations conspired to make the board's role opaque to history and historians.

Personality, in particular, which naturally appeals to the "great man" approach to history, played a very strong role. Historians have tended to focus on the influence of President Woodrow Wilson and his neutrality policies as executed by his dynamic Secretary of the Navy, Josephus Daniels, and his assistant secretary of the Navy, Franklin D. Roosevelt.[1] The influence of Daniels in the ongoing evolution and even survival of the General Board cannot be overstated. Daniels, who was inimical to the establishment of a formal naval general staff, came to use the General Board and its chief, ADM Dewey, as a response to radical reformers such as Bradley Fiske and Sims, who ached for a general staff in name, approved by Congress, with clear lines of command to both higher (the SecNav or president) and lower levels. Daniels, as discussed below, pointed to the General Board, as if to say, "We already have a general staff that is effective and responsive, the General Board of the Navy led by Admiral of the Navy George Dewey."

Similarly, personality intersects with organizational themes with the installation of ADM William S. Benson as the first CNO. This organizational narrative of reform leading to the creation of the CNO—initiated by Fiske—has also tended to push the role, and even the existence, of the General Board into the shadows.[2] Many historians, in fact, identify the decline of the influence of the board from this time frame, 1915, with the legislation for CNO—or later, in 1917, with the death of ADM Dewey.[3] Another component centers on the legislative narrative that surrounded the passage of Daniels' 1916 Navy Act. This legislation signaled a significant switch from passive neutrality to a heavily armed, Theodore Roosevelt–style posture that went a long way toward preparing the U.S. Navy for entry into World War I the following year. Again, the role of the General Board has been lost in the existing narratives, although a few historians have properly emphasized its role in working with Daniels on naval expansion.[4]

The machinations of Fiske at home and ADM Henry Mayo and others in Mexican waters obscure the board's activity prior to the war in Europe, even though Fiske acted in his capacity as aide for operations and de facto chief of staff of the General Board for Dewey. The entry of the United States and its fleet into the war and subsequent naval operations have played similar roles to those of personality and organizational change. The charismatic (and self-promoting) ADM William S. Sims, Benson, and, again, ADM Mayo commanding the Atlantic Fleet tended to garner all the headlines. Too, Daniels' role has been highlighted in recent scholarship in the debate over Britain's adoption of the convoy. The provision of ready U.S. Navy destroyers was apparently one component that convinced the British to adopt this effective antidote to the lethal crisis created by the German unrestricted submarine warfare campaign. Here, too, the board's role in advocating fleet readiness has been overly marginalized. Thus has the General Board, understandably, been relegated to the shadows in the narratives of the period surrounding World War I.[5]

The Secretary and the Admiral(s)

The officer corps of the Navy had cause to be concerned that a sea change might be coming with the advent of new leadership. Woodrow Wilson, a liberal internationalist, believed more in the diplomatic instrument of power—as wielded by him—than in the military one.[6] The ongoing naval expansion seen during the Republican years might well come to a halt given Wilson's pronouncements on the U.S. role in the world and his stated distaste for war. It was one of the great ironies of his years in office that the Navy grew more under Wilson and his like-minded Secretary of the Navy than at any other time in American history until Daniels' assistant, Franklin Roosevelt, signed the 1940 Naval Act into law as president. Of course, no one in the Navy, much less the members of the General Board, realized that the two men who would create the largest, most powerful Navy ever seen in history were now installed as the civilian leadership of the U.S. Navy.[7] Additionally, the lack of continuity of secretarial leadership that had been a bane in the previous twelve years, especially prior to George L. von Meyer, was now at an end.

Daniels got off to a bad start with the Navy officer corps. At the time he took office in March 1913, Navy officers still maintained "a wine mess" onboard U.S. warships, although the "grog" (rum) ration for enlisted men had been eliminated a number of years earlier. Not only was Daniels a teetotaler, but his egalitarian sense of fairness was offended. Instead of giving back the enlisted rates their rum, he removed the wine mess. The outcry by the officer corps was immediate, with Bradley Fiske claiming it would cause naval officers "increased temptation to use cocaine and other drugs!"[8] Officers subsequently toasted the new secretary, as by tradition they were wont to do, in their messes with coffee rather than wine or port. Thus the proverbial "cup of Joe" was born.[9]

Wilson, however, placed great faith in Daniels and wrote to him prior to his inauguration in 1912, "I know of no one I trust more entirely or affectionately. . . . I cannot spare you from my council table."[10] As a friend and pacifist fellow traveler, Wilson would find no need to move him to other jobs in the administration. This resulted in Daniels serving longer as Secretary of the Navy than anyone before or since—and serving in an age when SecNavs had no secretary of defense between them and the president. The same applied to his assistant SecNav, whom he picked just days after entering office: Franklin D. Roosevelt (FDR). When Daniels told his Republican friend Elihu Root that he wanted FDR for assistant SecNav, Root warned him that "every person named Roosevelt wished to run everything and would try to be Secretary."[11] One measure of Daniels' character is that he picked the young FDR anyway. Roosevelt then served until 1920, almost as long as Daniels did. This kind of continuity has a way of institutionalizing, for good or ill, existing systems, organizations, or new initiatives existent and emergent under the long, stable tenure of the officeholder. The General Board as an authoritative organization benefited from this dynamic. Daniels favored the General Board over the aide system, which he reputedly wanted to eliminate.[12]

The reformers, however, refused to settle for the status quo. The key personality, not surprisingly, was RADM Fiske, newly returned to Washington to serve as the aide for inspections. However, in February 1913, before Wilson and Daniels took office, Secretary Meyer informed Fiske that the current aide for operations, RADM C. E. Vreeland, was having health problems and Fiske instead filled that position. Fiske attested in his memoir three years later: "I did not feel that I was competent to undertake the duties" for what he considered "the most important position in the navy." However, Dewey had asked for Fiske, although he ended up getting more than he bargained for. Fiske thought the Navy "in good condition for times of peace, [but] it was not organized for war."[13]

The day before Fiske reported as aide for operations, Meyer had provided Dewey with his "rules for the Aides," which he assured Dewey "will do much to strengthen the General Board with future secretaries and create even greater cooperation with [in] the Department" (see chapter 4). Meyer directed Dewey to read the rules aloud to the entire General Board at its next meeting. The rules boiled down to empowering the aide for operations to present dissenting opinions directly to the Secretary of the Navy if he or the aide for material were in the minority.[14] These rules had an effect opposite to what Meyer forecast. Fiske began immediately to present his minority positions that the board had voted against, often unanimously. He usually presented these after the SecNav had received the opinion of the board. One wonders if Fiske colluded with Meyer (as he was later to do with Congress) in making sure Dewey understood that Fiske had the SecNav's support, at least until 4 March (inauguration day).[15] Fiske's behavior continued with Secretary of the Navy Josephus Daniels, who did not like the aide system and nearly abolished it while planning to relieve Fiske and send him to be president of the NWC. Dewey dissuaded Daniels from both actions.[16] That Daniels changed his mind in this manner is yet another measure of the esteem he had for Dewey. Still, these shenanigans (there is no other word for them) began the process of estrangement between Dewey and Fiske that finally came to a head in 1915 with the legislation creating the position, and eventually the staff, for the Chief of Naval Operations.

By 1913 Dewey had placed himself on a less arduous schedule and ceded to Fiske leadership of the General Board's summer session at Newport. Fiske claimed in his memoir that it was his idea to go to Newport that summer, but in fact this was the normal routine of the board, as discussed earlier.[17] Daniels admired Dewey and was happy with the General Board arrangement for war planning. Because of his cordial relationship with Dewey, it was an organization he felt he could control. Since the 1910 Naval War College problems and associated games, there had been a division of opinion between the college and the board about priority for planning—Japan (Orange) or Germany (Black). The college wanted to move the bulk of the battle fleet to the Pacific to deter Japan, whereas the board wanted to keep the bulk of the fleet, or at least all of the battleships, in the Atlantic. The fleet mobilizations in 1911 and 1912 around New York reflected this. Prior to the arrival of Daniels in 1913, Meyer had settled in favor of the General Board's position, which was Dewey's position, that Germany was the bigger threat. Therefore, the fleet should not be divided nor the bulk of it concentrated in the Pacific. Thus the 1913 war games held in concert with the board's summer sessions focused on Germany as the most likely enemy.[18] Fiske agreed on this point; he, too, saw Germany as the greater threat because "the Japanese Navy . . . was inferior to ours" but "the German Army and Navy had not been built haphazard, and that they were . . . being operated by mathematical methods." For Fiske, ever the scientific management acolyte, there was no higher compliment than to operate according to "mathematical methods."[19]

Meanwhile, the board was trying to come to terms with two very new technologies—aviation and submarines. We must also remember that the dreadnought battleship and battlecruiser were "new technology," although improvements to the existing ideas of the battle line and cruisers. Fiske was the leading advocate for aviation, as seen with his proposal for using aircraft to attack a Japanese amphibious assault on the Philippines. Fiske was one of the first individuals, if not the first, to see the possibilities of putting the rapidly developing "automobile" torpedo on airplanes, placing a patent on his idea. It would not be until World War II that the capability finally achieved the promise he saw for it in 1912. Fiske as aide for operations was able to beef up the status of nascent naval aviation by moving it away from the Bureau of

Navigation and placing it under him inside the SecNav organization as the Office of Naval Aeronautics, which later became the Bureau of Aeronautics after World War I.[20]

Be it Luce, Taylor, or Dewey, the senior naval leaders of this period knew how to recognize and apportion talent to key jobs. Fiske was no exception, picking CDR Mark Bristol to be the director of the Office of Aeronautics upon his return from a cruise in the Far East. Fiske informed Bristol (in 1913), that he "considered [aeronautics] the most important thing for the navy to take up." Bristol later served as ambassador (while still on active duty) to Turkey after World War I and eventually commanded the Asiatic Fleet during the 1920s warlord period in China. As we shall see, he finished his career as chairman of the executive committee of the General Board.[21] Although some historians have criticized the conservatism of the board with respect to aeronautics, its attitude can be considered more prudent than overly conservative. The technology was simply too immature to devote more effort to it—after all, Fiske's torpedo planes would not come of age until the late 1930s.[22] On 30 August 1913 the board published a study that reported a "dangerous" situation in the United States due to a lack of combat aircraft compared to other nations. It appears that Fiske was behind this report, but it was the majority opinion and so reflects the board's as well as Fiske's position. The board would cite this report after the outbreak of war in Europe to support a major outlay of funds for combat aircraft.[23]

Similarly, and perhaps in spite of the General Board, advances were made in submarines as well. Ironically, because submarines were then perceived as coastal defense weapons, Congress appropriated more money prior to the war for submarines than the General Board desired. The board viewed submarines in the same way but was more concerned about the larger ships of the fleet and the logistical auxiliaries needed to support that fleet over long ranges in the Pacific. Interestingly, LCDR Ridley McLean, assigned as associate member of the General Board in 1911, saw perhaps a larger role for submarines in defense of the Philippines beyond harbor defense as components of the seagoing fleet, an idea still in vogue today with so-called anti-access naval warfare. By April 1914 the board had finally agree that the submarine could become a component of the main fleet, an idea that shaped submarine development during most of the period between the two world wars.[24]

Secretary of the Navy Josephus Daniels (*left*), and Chief of Naval Operations ADM William S. Benson, shown here outside the Ritz Hotel in Paris, late 1918 or early 1919. Benson was appointed by Daniels as the first CNO, which caused Fiske to resign. The two men worked well together, although Daniels also used the General Board and respected Dewey and the work of the board. *Naval History and Heritage Command*

The General Board was progressive when it came to destroyers and cruisers, but Congress, while allocating funds for battleships, was parsimonious with cruisers when it came to the board's recommendations in its annual building-policy studies. Destroyers were a different story, since they were designed to protect the battleships from torpedo boats. Congress approved more of them, although only about half of the 133 the board wanted were built. This would have unintended, albeit positive, consequences in 1917. The board was interested in battlecruisers, but as reflected in the annual reports under both Meyer and Daniels, it recommended building battlecruisers only as long as that building did not slow down the plan to get to forty-eight battleships by 1919.[25]

It was not long before Daniels and Wilson found the fleet that they had inherited of some utility. A civil war in Mexico occurred shortly after Daniels and Wilson took office, which almost immediately forced Daniels to learn, on the job, how to run a global navy engaged in active combat operations.[26] Daniels relied first and foremost on George Dewey and his General Board and eschewed the ideas and advice of his aides, especially Fiske. The Mexican operations emphasized the board's existing approach to current operations, which followed from Mahan. It did not try to micromanage from Washington but strove to ensure that the Secretary of the Navy had the best advice possible—as Long had had with the War Board—and that the on-scene commander, be it Mayo or, later, Charles Badger and Frank Friday Fletcher, had absolute operational command in the theater of operations.[27]

By 1914 both Dewey and the board were established "institutions." However, Dewey's health was becoming ever more precarious by 1914, and it seemed he might soon retire. According to Fiske he suffered a "slight stroke" on 12 June.[28] One historian wrote of the initial establishment of the CNO that "duties not bestowed upon it by law were to accrue to it through necessity and custom in subsequent years." Such was already the case with Dewey and the General Board.[29] Additionally, Dewey wielded immense amounts of what is termed today "informal power," that is, power not stipulated to him by law or regulation but as a result of his prominence and reputation as a national war hero. His correspondence on the eve of World War I is littered with evidence that the Navy, government, and public held him in high regard. Josephus Daniels, in particular, was aware of this widespread public esteem.[30]

However, on the eve of the catastrophe about to unfold in Europe, operations in Mexico continued to occupy Daniels, Dewey, the General

Board, and the U.S. Navy. In June 1914 Dewey wrote ADM Fletcher, congratulating him on his success at Veracruz and for achieving "in one day what General Scott and 18,000 troops with the assistance of the Navy, took more than two weeks to accomplish in 1847." Fletcher had just "fleeted up" to command the Atlantic Fleet, essentially the highest fleet command in the Navy, relieving ADM Charles J. Badger.[31] The intervention in Mexico, from the General's Board perspective, had been as much about counterbalancing German adventurism as about Wilsonian "nation building."

Dewey's views about the primacy of the threat of the German fleet informed the views of the General Board. As he presciently wrote in 1899, "The German policy is to prevent other powers from obtaining what she cannot accept herself.... Our next war will be with Germany."[32] Although the General Board had a contingency war plan for Japan, it continued to place a priority on being able to fight the German High Seas Fleet. Dewey and Fiske were in accord on this issue. That meant countering German diplomatic efforts to obtain influence, let alone bases, in the Western Hemisphere with U.S. naval power. These ends, although perhaps not the means, aligned generally with those of Secretary of the Navy Daniels.[33]

Dewey had handpicked ADM Fletcher's predecessor, Charles J. Badger, to join the General Board in 1914. Badger was coming from command of the Atlantic Fleet, the most senior position afloat in the Navy at that time, with only Dewey senior in rank and influence at the board. It is worth noting Badger's response to Dewey's personal letter of notification, since it emphasizes the high regard officers held about service on the General Board in 1914:

> Your very kind letter of the 18th [June] instant arrived last night and I am glad to know that the Secretary [Daniels] has consented to your request that I be assigned to the General Board when detached from the Command of the Atlantic Fleet. Of course I should like to stay on with the Fleet until the end [of Mexican operations], but that being impossible, *I much prefer the General Board* to any other shore duty and it will be an honor as well as a pleasure to serve under you. By-the-way, it is something of a *coincidence* that I should begin and end my active career in the Navy under your immediate command [emphases added].[34]

It was certainly no "coincidence." In all probability, Dewey had Badger in mind as his eventual successor as president of the board, not the brilliant, mercurial and scheming Fiske, who was acting as Dewey's number two man at this time. Fiske was holding court in Newport as the General Board, without the ailing Dewey, deliberated in the cooler weather in concert with the planners and students at the NWC.[35] Dewey's health was in decline, and the summer and autumn of 1914 saw him essentially take a sabbatical from the board to try to improve his health.[36]

The appointment of Badger turned out to be a significant milestone, since Dewey's health, although making a brief rebound, eventually failed in 1917.[37] Thanks to Dewey's selection of Badger, though, the continuity in the performance of the work of the board did not decline. The General Board would lose its patron saint, but Dewey's seventeen years of wise leadership left a solid organization in place to help the U.S. Navy and the nation meet the challenges of a war like none other it had ever engaged—a total war overseas.

The Outbreak of Global War and Creation of the CNO

As early as May 1914, the General Board had already judged presciently the tense world situation and sent its opinion to the Secretary of the Navy. Under the heading of a study on the implications of the opening of the Panama Canal, the board noted that it believed "it would be wise under the present political and naval situation of the world, and probably for years to come, to have two squadrons of the active fleet in the Atlantic from May to September inclusive; and never be divided [*sic*] that they cannot be concentrated well before war. . . . *At this time*, the squadron in reserve would be best strategically located on the West Coast at San Francisco and Bremerton."[38]

Events, as we now know, moved quickly that July, after the assassination of the Austrian heir Archduke Ferdinand and his wife in Sarajevo, Bosnia. On 1 August, Fiske convened a special session of the board at Newport to address the outbreak of war in Europe. Of note, Great Britain had not yet entered the war on the side of France and Russia. Fiske informed Daniels (and Dewey, who was staying in New York) what the situation in Europe was and suggested preparing the fleet for war immediately. He also recommended moving the General Board immediately back to Washington to better coordinate with the Secretary of the Navy as well as other branches of the government. However, he closed his letter by emphasizing:

> If Great Britain is drawn into war the German fleet will be neutralized as far as any danger from it to our interests in the immediate future is

concerned. If she is not, and if the end of the war should find Germany stronger than ever in her European position and with her fleet practically unimpaired, the temptation will be great to seize the opportunity for obtaining the positon she covets on this side of the ocean. We should prepare now for the situation which would thus be created.[39]

Daniels adhered to Wilson's policy of strict neutrality and vetoed Fiske's recommendations, including moving the General Board back to Washington. Fiske later convinced Daniels to move the board down from Newport to Washington that September "at the usual time."[40]

Against the backdrop of the global crisis that became World War I, the General Board continued intensive contingency planning against the eventuality of war, either on the Allied side or alone against Germany if it won the war while the United States was still neutral. In this sense the General Board planned much in the same way that U.S. planning organizations had with the various "rainbow" plans before World War II.[41] Prior to the United States' entry into World War I, the General Board planned for the worst-case scenario, and its actions as regards the fleet make sense only if this is properly understood. That worst-case scenario was Germany triumphant, possibly with her former enemy, Japan, now an ally against the United States. This last point is essential to understand, since some historians have regarded the General Board and Dewey's actions here as counter, and even detrimental, to the declared neutrality policy of the United States.[42] However, these critics do not understand the nature of contingency planning and have overrated and misunderstood the real desire of naval professionals to be ready to fight the war they might get instead of the one the administration hoped to avoid.

The first important post–August 1914 general study on the matter of preparation for war did not come until November of that year, in the form of a General Board building-policy study for 1916. The study emphasized that the Navy was deficient in its trajectory toward the goal of forty-eight battleships by 1919 by ten battleships based on new ship construction and the retirement of older predreadnoughts. The board had not abandoned, at this early stage, the dreadnought battleship as the paradigm of sea power. Neither had any other navy for that matter. Astonishingly, though, it listed the destroyer as "the warship next in importance to the battleship." This can now be understood in the light of recent scholarship and the importance the Navy attached to protecting the battle fleet with destroyers from torpedo attacks and their potential offensive role in a major fleet action (as Jutland would soon show). It also shows the role of serendipity in war and warship development, in which a platform developed for one mission is well suited to another unforeseen or underappreciated mission. Immediately after destroyers, the study listed "fleet submarines" as next in importance, implying precedence ahead of aircraft, coastal submarines, and scout cruisers. The board stressed that "the value of such a type in war for distant work with the fleet can hardly be overestimated."[43] This language did not address a commerce-raiding role in the manner the Germans were beginning to employ them—which would have shocked Wilson and Daniels. It did reflect the British actions with their experimental submarine force under Roger Keyes as well as the board's continued interest in the submarine as a long-range scout for the battle fleet vis-à-vis War Plan Orange.[44]

The board then cited its previous study from 1913 on the lack of combat aircraft and stated that with the advent of the war, naval aviation situation was "nothing less than deplorable." It saw aircraft as "the eyes of both armies and navies; and it is difficult to place any limit to their offensive possibilities." The study then went on to emphasize the utility of naval aviation in detecting and attacking submarines. It closed with an astonishing request for "an appropriation of at least $5,000,000, to be made available immediately, for the purpose of establishing an efficient air service." This does not sound like a neglect of aviation, as some have complained, and it reflects the profound impact that the first few months of the war already had on the thinking of the General Board. The study closed with a reemphasis of these priorities and a plea to immediately establish a naval reserve and expand the naval militia while filling out the necessary numbers needed by the anticipated expansion of the fleet. The importance of the study was reflected by Dewey's personal signature at the end of the document.[45]

One might think that Secretary Daniels recoiled in horror from these recommendations, but historians forget that they were made confidentially, in a classified format not leaked to the press or Congress. More to the point, they prepared the way for Daniels to have a solid command of naval preparedness for 1915, when the Wilson administration changed its policy to one of armed neutrality—principally by expanding the fleet. Daniels was having problems, however, on another front, with contradictory testimony by Assistant Secretary of the Navy Franklin D. Roosevelt and RADM Fiske to the House Naval Committee. Fiske was the bigger concern because he had implied it would take five years to get the fleet properly ready for war with a major European power. Roosevelt contradicted Fiske in claiming that it would take three months to properly train crews and integrate new personnel. Daniels turned to his favorite resources, George Dewey and the General Board, for their take on the issue. Dewey gave his qualified support to Roosevelt's response of a three-month minimum to get ready (which was what Daniels hoped), writing, "At the present time our fleet except for the shortage of trained personnel is . . . in as efficient condition as that of any European country. To remedy the shortage in personnel and furnish trained crews for the ships in reserve would require some time, but I do not believe five years would be necessary."[46]

It was around this time that Fiske first started meeting with Representative Richmond Hobson (D-AL) on national defense and organizational reform. In addition to being a representative, Hobson was a Navy war hero from the Spanish-American War who had received the rank of rear admiral after his retirement in 1903. He was the ideal ally for Fiske's plans. Fiske's idea was that the United States needed a higher level political-military body, much like Britain's Council of Imperial Defence. He wanted a similar organization for the United States and proposed that it include the secretaries of war and navy and other cabinet officers as well as "certain army and navy officers." No doubt he had in mind at least the aide for operations as one of the Navy officers. This proposal was a foreshadowing of the National Security Council, which was established after World War II, but Daniels would have none of it, and the legislation in Congress introduced by Hobson went nowhere, either.[47]

Fiske, unsatisfied about the preparedness of the Navy for war and convinced the United States would eventually be drawn in, again began to plot for a bona fide general staff. Meeting with Hobson in December, he explained the need for a general staff type of organization, separate from the General Board. He was aided in this effort by a number of other officers on the board, including CAPT John Hood, CAPT Harry Knapp, and CAPT James Oliver (the director of Naval Intelligence). On 3 January 1915, these officers met with Hobson and Fiske along with several junior officers and noted naval officer-historian Dudley Knox. From this meeting came the draft legislation Hobson introduced to create the Chief of Naval Operations and supporting staff.[48]

The bill went through the Congress rather rapidly, but Daniels was allowed to change the wording to make it so that the CNO "shall under the direction of the Secretary . . . be charged with the operations of the fleet, and with the preparations and readiness of plans for its use in war."[49] This language made clear civilian control over the new CNO. The SecNav ensured that Fiske would not head up his creation, instead appointing the relatively junior chief of the Philadelphia Naval Yard, CAPT William S. Benson. Daniels probably believed Benson more pliable and controllable than the fiery and insubordinate Fiske.[50] Indeed, Benson would prove a shrewd and effective choice.

Daniels had also deliberately eliminated a "provision for fifteen naval officers to prepare war plans" in the final legislation. Benson's staff was so small that it was not until August 1916 that he had the resources he needed to begin to supplant the General Board as the Navy's primary war-planning organization.[51] Fiske and the insurgents finally had their general staff, but it shared duties with the General Board and was *an operational level* general staff. Its ability to shape strategy at the higher levels of policy was very limited. In the policy arena and in ship design, therefore, the General Board would remain preeminent in peacetime until World War II.

Daniels expressed his satisfaction with the work of the board on the occasion of a press release on 4 March 1915 in which he commented on the Naval Appropriations Act that had established the position of CNO. ADM Fiske had instigated this announcement in defiance of Daniels and to some degree Dewey. Daniels emphasized to the press his concern that the great resource that Dewey and the board constituted in preparing war plans might be in jeopardy because of this legislation. He stressed that "these plans have for many years been prosecuted with diligence under the able guidance of the Admiral of the Navy, George Dewey. . . . Needless to add that I could not be in sympathy with any measure that would minimize the value of the services of Admiral Dewey to the Navy." Dewey's grateful response is a key to understanding how he, Daniels, and the General Board saw this organization's role in American security: "It has been my opinion for many years that we have in the General Board of the Navy a better general staff than that of the Army. . . . I believe [it] to be of inestimable value as an asset in peace and war."[52]

Creation of the Chief of Naval Operations improved the overall efficiency of the Navy, of that there is no doubt. For example, in January 1914 the General Board took a key step toward war preparedness. It had long argued in its studies that the merchant fleet would be crucial in any war overseas, either as armed auxiliaries or to transport troops and cargo. This remained a "lesson learned" from the Spanish-American War that had not been addressed. The board recommended and Secretary Daniels approved the inspection of merchant vessels for use in war by boards furnished by the Office of Naval Intelligence in cooperation with the existing Board of Inspection for Survey for Ships. The General Board determined the characteristics under which each vessel would be utilized. Until creation of the CNO in 1916, this effort languished somewhat due to lack of unity and conflicting jurisdiction with the War Department. The result was the amalgamation of the Army and Navy efforts in 1916 into a joint inspection board under the CNO's direction. The ONI maintained it records and it became the Joint Merchant Vessel Board in May 1917.[53] This development serves as an example of how the board's ideas often preceded major events and how CNO operationalized the idea into an effective organizational process for maritime readiness. Another welcome outcome of the reorganization caused by the advent of a CNO involved the return of a Marine presence to the General Board with the addition of the commandant, MajGen George Barnett, as an ex officio member in June 1915.[54]

The creation of the Chief of Naval Operations also marked the end of the aide system. Some aspects of the old system remained in place as secretarial assistants, such as material, but the term "aide" was eliminated. The new CNO was an ex officio member of the General Board—just like the former aide for operations—perhaps muddying the waters as to his duties and scope of authority. Benson had already joined the board before becoming CNO and valued his membership on the board. This all changed, of course, with time. But Benson's appointment over Fiske caused that officer to resign that April.[55] Benson was not formally appointed as CNO until May, and he began attending General Board meetings that April, even putting his "chop" (signature) on various board-produced preparedness memos.[56]

The Advent of War and Death of Dewey

Daniels had to walk a fine line between two opposed camps, the peace activists and the war-preparedness faction—the latter led by men such as former president Theodore Roosevelt and GEN Leonard Wood, USA. By employing Dewey actively in war planning and policy inside the government,

Daniels kept the old admiral from being a tool for either group, although it seems clear from correspondence that Dewey favored the preparedness movement. A different view of Daniels also emerges, one of an activist secretary much more interested in national defense and preparedness of the Navy, prior to the sinking of the *Lusitania* that May, but also realistic about the constraints imposed by his commander in chief's neutrality policies.[57]

The year 1915 proved to be a pivotal one in the U.S. Navy's preparation for possible entry into World War I. With the small CNO staff finding its "sea legs" under a relatively unknown quantity in William Benson, preparedness—as advocated "under the radar" by Dewey and the General Board—proceeded apace. A related major issue was that of naval expansion, advocated by the board going back to 1903 studies, which were still being cited by Dewey and Daniels as the basis for the material expansion of the battle fleet and all its supporting warships (and now aircraft). The near war with Germany over unrestricted submarine warfare, reflected in the tragedy of the *Lusitania*, served as a forcing function. The concept of "a navy second to none" emerged, although the General Board termed it a Navy "the equal of any" in its recommendations that summer (1915) to Daniels. This concept program had initially been advocated by Dewey in the early years in response to Germany, and by 1915 it remained an initiative clearly aimed at Germany, with Great Britain's casual disregard of neutral rights hardly mentioned as justification, although the board still viewed Britain's ally, Japan, with great suspicion in the language it used to discuss the issue.[58]

Because the CNO office developed slowly, most of the war planning remained with the General Board during this period, and it was not until 1916 that the CNO really moved to the fore in war planning after Benson's office received the necessary staff augmentation. All the bureaus continued to forward their quarterly readiness reports to the General Board until May 1916, when the General Board authored its last war plan, "Mobilization for a War in the Atlantic," after which it remained on distribution for war planning but no longer retained authorship. Some bureaus continued, however, to forward reports to the General Board even though they were no longer required.[59] Included in the preparedness reports to both the CNO and the General Board was a report from the commandant of the Marine Corps, General George Barnett (from 1914 to 1920), cataloging the table of organization and elements of the Marine Advanced Base Force. This force was a complete combined arms team that by 1916 included organic artillery, aircraft, signal, engineering, and other support troops built around an infantry regiment. It was more than a thousand troops short of its allotted wartime strength by July of that year.[60]

As the General Board and the new CNO worked their way through the transfer of duties involving war planning, the members of the board dealt with the complexities of the expansion of the fleet and its organization against the backdrop of the complex lessons emerging from World War I. It soon realized that between the level of the fleet, which it defined as "the aggregation of the Forces of various classes of vessels in one organization under one command," and that of a squadron there must exist other levels of organization. Pursuant to that end, in an important December 1915 study, it proposed the creation of a new organizational echelon beneath the level of the fleet known as "the force." It decided to use the older term "division" as the basis for this organizational innovation. This usage predates and prefigures the eventual creation of the task forces used as operational components in World War II and is still in use in today's U.S. Navy. Under Dewey's leadership, with the assistance of his heir apparent RADM Charles Badger, the General Board recommended that "these different sub-divisions [of the fleet] be referred to as the Battleship Force; the Scouting Force (including Battle Cruisers, Armored Cruisers, and Scouts); the Cruiser Force (including Gunboats); the Destroyer Force; the Submarine Force; the Mining Force; the Train (Force)."[61]

These forces, as can be seen, were functionally arranged but became the Battle Fleet, Scouting Fleet, Control Force, and Fleet Base Force in the interwar period. The Fleet Base Force consisted of all the logistics and auxiliary vessels and floating dry docks.[62] Nonetheless, this was a major organizational evolution for the Navy and a result of the fleet expansion in great part stimulated by the global crisis and war.

The General Board also paid very close attention to reports of naval combat coming out of the war, as reflected in a May 1915 Office of Naval Intelligence study titled "Fires in Action." This included the most recent intelligence including the battles of the Heligoland Bight (1914), off Coronel (1914), the Falklands (1914), and off the Dogger Bank (1915). Its purpose was to emphasize the danger modern naval combat seemed to pose as to secondary fires on board ships. Especially noteworthy were the U.S. naval attaché's comments about how quickly the Germans began to modify their ships by eliminating combustibles and chipping off all flammable paint from the exposed surfaces of their warships. Thus began the U.S. Navy's path toward modern damage control, which would result, after the war, in its virtual adoption in toto of the German navy's damage-control doctrine.[63]

Although the massive expansion of the Navy had not yet taken place by late 1915, that expansion can be regarded as almost inevitable given the correspondence between the General Board, Dewey, Benson, and Daniels and the preparedness movement's criticisms of the Wilson administration. It was clear that expansion of the Navy could serve as a means to answer the critics without seeming "too warlike" because the case could be made that a larger Navy could protect the nation's neutral rights. Such an argument for an Army was much less convincing, especially considering that Wilson would both expand the Navy and run on a "He Kept Us Out of the War" platform in 1916. The towering figure of Dewey inside the government provided Daniels a way to defer the critics. The argument went this way: "If it is good enough for Dewey and his team of experts on the General Board, then it must be adequate for the security of the United States." The sum total of Dewey's professional correspondence supports this claim from the years 1914 until his death in early 1917. One example from late 1915 in response to a congressman, should suffice to emphasize this dynamic:

> I beg to acknowledge the receipt of your letter . . . asking if I would be willing to give you my views as to what further expenditures this country should make upon its navy.
>
> The Annual Report of the Secretary of the Navy for the year 1915, which will be released for publication on Monday, December 13th, in its appendix contains a carefully prepared Report of the General Board of the Navy to the Secretary, which to my mind covers the question you refer to better than any article I have seen.[64]

Put another way, if preparedness is good enough for the General Board, it is good enough for Dewey!

The year 1916 saw the General Board involved in mobilization planning, which meant primarily two things: expansion of the fleet and the manning of that fleet with competent crews. In this light, then, the General Board's involvement and support for the establishment of a naval reserve and the August 1916 Naval Expansion Act, which approved the construction of 156 ships (including 50 new destroyers), can be seen as positive measures. This act also gave Benson, who still regarded the board as the primary operations planning agent, fifteen more officers who eventually became the OpNav war-planning division. It also provided for an assistant chief of naval operations (ACNO), who served as his chief of staff, a job assigned to CAPT Volney Chase.[65] Some critics have pointed out that this building authorization was "unbalanced" and that the General Board did not properly appreciate the nascent submarine threat. However, the 1916 legislation was passed not to prepare for intervention on the Allied side in Europe so much as to prepare for whatever happened after the war, especially the possibility of a German victory. The implication from the files of the General Board is that it was preparing for a war with either Germany, or Japan, or both after the war concluded and that it considered a German victory just as likely as a British one. That same year, 1916, also saw the board gain the congressional recognition it had long sought. The General Board authored its last official war plan, the May 1916 "Mobilization Plan for a War in the Atlantic," but by congressional legislation in the Naval Expansion Act it was still required to receive and comment, or advise the Secretary, on all the war plans produced by the new CNO organization, OpNav.[66]

After the sinking of the *Lusitania*, it appeared that the German submarine threat had become manageable as the Germans switched—somewhat—to legal "cruiser rules" against Allied commerce. The British did nothing to contradict this rosy picture of a submarine threat contained. Nor did U.S. naval intelligence offer much in the way of contradictory evidence to the British public narrative. In reality, Germany had built more submarines, built new submarine bases in parts of occupied Belgium, and was still doing quite a bit of damage to Allied shipping using legal means of warfare. But all this was unknown to the General Board, Daniels, the CNO, and the Navy at large by the end of 1916.[67]

On 17 January 1917, George Dewey, still on active duty, passed away. Dewey's health had continued to worsen throughout 1916. More and more he deferred his duties to the very capable ADM Charles Badger, whom he had handpicked to succeed him. Interestingly, Badger was already developing RADM Fletcher or RADM Winterhalter to succeed him.[68] Henry Taylor need not have worried about the General Board's existence being tied to Dewey, as it went on in the capacity that Dewey and now Daniels had shaped for it over the years—as the authoritative voice of Navy line officers for general ship characteristics and the annual building policy. With war imminent, Daniels dared not disestablish an organization that he had publicly professed to admire, if in fact he had considered doing that at all. The same applied to the CNO, an organization and position he had publicly gone on the record as not favoring, although his relations with Benson were (initially) cordial.[69] In April 1917 the General Board thus consisted of four ex officio members—the CNO, director of ONI, commandant of the Marine Corps, and president of the NWC. Its senior member was RADM Charles Badger, but he did not assume Dewey's title as president. Instead, the senior member became the chairman of the executive committee or simply the "senior member present." By May 1917, in addition to the senior member and the ex officio members, the board included two other senior admirals (Fletcher and Winterhalter), two captains, and the secretary, who was now a voting member.[70]

Two weeks after Dewey's death, Germany initiated unrestricted warfare against Allied shipping, especially that proceeding to the British Isles (including neutral shipping). In response, the United States broke off diplomatic relations with Germany. War would not come until two months later, but in the interim the U.S. Navy leadership, including the General Board, worked feverishly to bring the fleet up to speed. Meanwhile, Daniels dispatched Sims, who had been serving as president of the Naval War College, that March to London. Once there, Sims learned about the real situation vis-à-vis Britain and the unrestricted submarine offensive, stating that "reports of our Attachés and other professional Americans who have been abroad during the war did not reflect the true situation." With the British revelation of the infamous Zimmermann telegram, Wilson finally asked, and got, a declaration of war on 2 April 1917. Daniels, in part because of the efforts of the General Board to improve readiness and manning, was able to offer thirty-six destroyers as antisubmarine convoy escorts to the British. Admiral Sir Alexander Duff identified this factor as key in convincing the Admiralty to initiate the convoy system that they had believed unworkable due to a paucity of destroyers for escort duty. Nonetheless, the submarine war proved the greatest challenge of the war to the U.S. Navy and to the General Board. It dominated the intellectual efforts of all concerned with its prosecution until the Armistice of November 1918.[71]

Of note, during this extremely busy period, CAPT William V. "Bill" Pratt had started working for Benson in February 1917. Pratt had joined Sims' "band of brothers" at the NWC, where Pratt served as a faculty member from 1911 to 1913. He first met Sims there, who was a student in the new two-year course for more senior officers. He then served as Sims' aide when Sims took command of the Atlantic Torpedo Squadron. In 1916 Pratt was assigned to the Army War College in accordance with Daniels' enlightened instructions that all prospective flag officers attend the other service's war college, but started working before graduation. During duty in Panama prior to his going to Army War College, he had come to appreciate, as had Taylor, the importance of good relations with the Army, especially given the situation in Europe.[72] The insurgents, probably egged on by Fiske, had tried to get Pratt as their "inside" man to help in a "cabal" to "depose" Benson and Daniels. Pratt refused, and about this time he started to diverge in his views from his friend Sims about the leadership of the Navy Department. In June 1917 Pratt took over from Chase, who had died, like Taylor, of "overwork," as ACNO.[73] His biographer mentions Pratt as "being the man in the middle between powerful contending interests" but oddly mentions nothing of the General Board as one of those interests. He worked as an acting ex officio member of the board when Benson was not available, especially after the war, when Benson was in Paris. This implies a good relationship with and, more important, a good opinion of the board, which Pratt later joined in 1921.[74]

Here our story departs from preparedness moves and the General Board's direct impact on events. Sims, Benson, and Mayo (commander of the Atlantic Fleet) now moved to the fore in the Navy's prosecution of its efforts in support of the Allies, both as to the antisubmarine war and the protection of not just merchant ships but also the stream of troopships moving the American Expeditionary Force to France. However, the General Board by no means took the equivalent of a holiday. Two developments highlight the new role of the General Board, as well as its potential future role in wartime, during 1917–19.

The first of these involved ADM Badger's decision to transcribe General Board meetings, called hearings, on specific topic of interest on 14 August 1917. The board had always held hearings, but it had not found the need to keep an exact transcript of them. The first dozen or so transcribed hearings in the archives reflect precisely the emerging lessons of the war the Navy found it had joined, not the one it had planned for through 1916. These hearings addressed two main topics, manning and the submarine threat. The hearings overwhelming emphasized the importance of submarines, destroyers, and, surprisingly, in the third transcribed hearing of the General Board on 20 August, "aeroplanes" and a $45 million appropriation for them and their use against the submarine threat. This indicates a very radical turn of affairs by the General Board. The expert "witness" testifying that day was none other than LT John Towers, who had firsthand knowledge of the state of naval aviation, both in the United States and overseas. It was clear that the board had been holding almost constant hearings since the war began.[75] On 6 September the "testimony" started, with the Navy's chief constructor, RADM David Taylor, and his assistant, Emory Land. It speaks volumes about the focus of the General Board at this critical time and is worth quoting:

> Admiral Badger: *We should stop considering the subject* [unknown but probably submarines] *and look at the future.*
> Admiral Taylor: *We have practically suspended work on the big battleships. We are not pushing them now.*
> Admiral Badger: *It comes under Admiral Winterhalter's section to prepare* [ship] *characteristics and I will ask him to talk to you on this subject.*[76]

The implication to this point was that this hearing intended to address the design of future battleships. However, as the transcript shows, this was not the case at all:

> Admiral Winterhalter: *Where do you want to start?*
> Admiral Badger: *Fleet submarines.*

The remainder of the hearing delves into the weeds of how to design bigger submarines, what engines to use, and the poor habitability of the British submarines and only slightly better habitability of the captured German ones. On page sixteen of the transcript, the board finally gets to battlecruisers but only spends six pages discussing them before moving on to discuss the pressing matter of destroyer design. Also included in the discussion were British seaplane carriers, seaplane design, and kite balloons. This hearing, ostensibly about capital ships, closes with Taylor saying, "We can't have too many destroyers in the present state of the war."[77]

As a result of these hearings, the General Board forwarded to Daniels its "Proposed measures to prevent German submarines from operating against Allied commerce in the Atlantic" on 24 October. Interestingly, this study was (and still is) archived in the war-plans folders of the General Board studies. The study stated, "Obviously the most effective method of combating the submariners is to stop them, if practicable, at their bases. Failing this, to take preventive measure as near these bases as possible before they have had an opportunity to scatter on the trade routes. If none of these measures is practicable, submarines must be hunted down in the open sea by the methods now employed." The study examined various ways of doing the first two items—looking at offensive action by large warships, smaller ones (including submarines attacking the sub bases), and aviation. It decided that none of these offensive means offered much hope given the existing environment and German defenses and minefields and instead recommended establishing barriers (with mines and obstacles) in the North Sea and Dover Strait to contain the German U-boats in concert with the British Admiralty.[78] Of note, the General Board's comment about the third, existing method of hunting them in the "open sea" seems to discount that the best way to kill them was at the convoys themselves, since open-ocean, independent patrolling by the Royal Navy had been a dismal failure to that point.[79] This was another reason why Badger instituted the hearings and established the mechanism of hearing from experts. It was the best way to incorporate the latest lessons learned in order to better develop building policy and naval policy in general. By the time of the Washington Naval Conference, the General Board had become the premier policymaking body in the Navy.[80]

The second development, which predates a General Board study of October 1917 on offensive options against submarines, might be what one could characterize as "homework," as if the General Board was not busy enough already. On 2 August 1917, Daniels issued an all-Navy message, also known as an ALNAV, soliciting from any and every officer in the fleet, "young and old," input "in order that nothing may be left undone by the American Navy to win the war."[81] Daniels directed that any ideas go directly to the CNO. However, as it turned out, the General Board ended up serving as the clearinghouse for this effort, reading hundreds of communications to the CNO on new ideas, from the lowest seaman up through admirals, and then forwarding worthy ideas, with comments, to the appropriate office or bureaus for action. By 24 October the board had gone through the first 156 "papers." Most of them addressed the submarine problem. The board report, signed by Badger, found that most of the ideas had already been broached in one way or another and that none offered "any practicable suggestions for 'Winning the War' which are new or which have not been at one time or another under consideration by those charged with the prosecution of the war." Nevertheless, it forwarded those with promise to the appropriate agency or bureau for "consideration."[82] An example of who wrote these papers can be found in the following submission of papers numbered 157 to 172 and forwarded personally by Daniels to the board. The respondents included mostly junior officers, many of them reservists, but also included a chief electrician's mate and a captain in the new (1915) U.S. Coast Guard as well as retired naval officers. The next batch of twenty papers were forwarded by Benson instead of Daniels—presumably the mail service was no longer delivering them directly to the secretary but instead to the CNO—and it included inputs by three Navy admirals, two of whom were retired.[83]

Among the ideas contained in these responses were many that recommended using naval aviation in an offensive manner against the German submarines bases as well as in "open sea" patrols. Of particular interest among the original 156 papers was one by naval aviation pioneer "Hank" Mustin recommending offensive operations by aircraft that would involve overflights of neutral Holland.[84] Mustin's ideas about aircraft were considered of enough merit to forward to the office of the CNO as well as the proper technical bureaus, presumably to include the newly created Office of Naval Aviation.[85] The ideas about using offensive naval aviation against the submarines found traction and in part resulted in the Navy's creation in 1918 of the Northern Bombing Group, the brainchild of a young naval reserve aviator named Robert Lovett. Lovett later went on to become the assistant secretary of war for air in World War II and served as fourth secretary of defense during the Cold War. Although the promise of the idea to bomb the submarines at their bases did not work out, the latest scholarship, both here and elsewhere, now illustrates the key role of the General Board in the development of these ideas as well as the nascent naval aviation component of the Navy.[86]

Michael Howard famously wrote, "I am tempted indeed to declare dogmatically that whatever doctrine the Armed Forces are working on now, they have got it wrong. I am also tempted to declare that it does not matter that they have got it wrong. What does matter is their capacity to get it right quickly when the moment arrives."[87] Howard had earlier cited this very example of battleships and submarines in World War I. Certainly, in hindsight, most in the U.S. Navy, including the General Board, "got it wrong" vis-à-vis the U-boat menace during the war. They were not alone. So did the Royal Navy. However, the leaders of the Navy and those inside the General Board did quickly "get it right" when the moment arrived, both as to preparation after

July 1914, and helped defeat the threat that might have won the war the United States entered in 1917.

Additionally, it is clear that historians have conflated passage of the 1915 act creating the office of Chief of Naval Operations with the causality and function of Navy policy and planning during the very complex and active period of 1914–18. The creation of CNO did not result in the disestablishment of the General Board, which had come to serve as a kind of strategic general staff and whose processes were well established and mature. It did not even remove its war-planning function until 1916. The fight between Fiske and Daniels, and their associated personalities, has tended to overshadow the fact that the General Board continued to doggedly do its duty during this time.

At the same time, the passage of the 1916 Naval Act can now be seen as something that reflected a conviction by both the General Board and Dewey that the United States needed a navy commensurate with the threats to the nation's security and in recognition of the uncertainty created by global war. Wilson, Daniels, and even Benson have received credit for the "a navy second to none" policy, but credit should also go to the General Board. From this foundation emerged the postwar maritime regime codified at Washington in 1922 by the Washington Naval Treaty—and recognized by all the other major naval powers as such.

Finally, there is the issue of ADM Sims, who as president of the Naval War College was intimately familiar, both before and after the war, with the dynamics and purpose of the General Board. While Sims took command and garnered the attention of scholars for his leadership, coalition warfare savvy, and operations against the U-boats, the General Board remained both busy and undermanned. The great problem of the day was unrestricted submarine warfare and the board's role, now absent Dewey, as a clearinghouse for innovative ideas on how to do so can now be recognized. Of course, it was Daniels' idea to canvass the officer corps, but the execution of this idea he delegated to the "master hands" of the General Board. It was no accident that as war became more complicated, the board began to maintain a permanent record of its hearings in 1917 so that it could best support the nation in the war, and the peace, that was sure to follow.

The board entered a new phase in its evolution from 1913 to 1918. It lost its longtime iconic leader, George Dewey, and its war-planning function to the CNO and his OpNav staff. Had this happened in earlier years, it might have meant the end of the General Board, but the board emerged with a new identity as the Navy's premier concepts-examination organization and ship-fleet-characteristics authority. The latter function was finally recognized by Congress in 1916, but not, as some have claimed, "too late" to save the board from decline. Its most significant achievements, and influence on naval policy, lay in the future.

CHAPTER 6

The Challenges of Peace
From Versailles to Washington, 1918–22

The General Board has aided in keeping alive the spirit of a General Staff and has supplied the need of it as far as its limited authority would permit. With a real General Staff established, a General Board, untrammeled by executive duties, considering and reporting on larger questions of naval policies would be of assistance to any Chief of Staff and would help to protect him from the annoying assaults of Galley Yarns.

—RADM Richard Wainwright USN (Ret.), 1922

The first five chapters of this study focused on the formative years of the General Board, from 1900 to 1918. This period is important because it established the norms and authority of the new structure. Chapters 6 to 8 discuss the heyday of the board, the period between the world wars. During this time frame, the board was the focus for naval policy, maritime strategy, and ship designs to implement that strategy. Inevitably, the surviving documentary record of this era is much more voluminous and has been addressed elsewhere at great length.[1] Rather than confuse and bore the reader with a full discussion of all the events of the interwar period, I have therefore decided to be selective, using a few detailed case studies to illustrate my points concerning the board's preparation for World War II. This chapter serves as a bridge to the period of the General Board's greatest influence, the treaty period between the conclusion of the Washington Naval Conference and World War II.

RADM Wainwright's words in the epigraph above defined the new role the General Board came to play after World War I ended. No longer were there calls for the board's disestablishment, but rather, the naval uniformed leadership had come to see it in a new light as a body of significant influence that could provide "top cover" for a busy CNO while being able to look at the "larger question of naval policies." In short, the General Board became the Navy Department's premier policymaking body, with the proviso that these policy recommendations had no force of law other than what the SecNav gave them. This came about because of the rise of the collective international security movement as a result of the Versailles Peace Conference and the institution afterward by the United States and the other major powers of a naval arms limitations regime during the "treaty period."

World War I had ended, and of the nations that had engaged in it, there were only two real winners, the United States and Japan. ("Winning" is defined here as being better off after the global conflict than before it.) Four large empires that had existed before the war disappeared completely—the Ottoman Empire, tsarist Russia, Imperial Germany, and Hapsburg Austria-Hungary. Every other major power came out of World War I in debt and, in most cases, nearly or actually economically ruined: Great Britain, Italy, France, and a score of lesser powers. Some nations, such as Serbia, disappeared entirely. New ones emerged from the ruins of the four empires; this imperial dissolution and the resulting nation-states spawned problems that still plague us today. Moreover, Japan and the United States had not lost the bulk of an entire generation of their young men, dead or gravely wounded, as had the others.[2]

One may argue that the General Board emerged diminished as well; its powerful war-planning function was now subsumed under the Chief of Naval Operations, who in turn had become the de facto chief of service inside the Navy now that Dewey was dead. This ignores the possibility that both the CNO *and* General Board might gain in power after the war, which is in fact what happened. Although the CNO was a four-star billet, a full admiral, so were the commanders in chief of the Asiatic Fleet and, especially, U.S. Fleet. This last officer, ironically known as CINCUS ("sink U.S."), could lay claim to organizational parity with the CNO, still evolving organizationally inside the Navy Department. And there remained the General Board, most of whose officers, like Badger and Winterhalter, were senior in their date of commissioning to Benson, the first CNO.[3] Too often historians have neglected the concept of seniority and "date of rank" in assessing how admirals back then deferred and worked with each. The highest permanent grade was still two stars, rear admiral; and historians also forget that admirals like Frank Fletcher and Charles Badger had once been themselves four-star admirals and then taken the reduction in rank as their billet assignment changed if they did not retire. Thus the General Board was in fact composed of the most senior admirals on service, among other things—men the CNO had deferred to and even saluted for most of his career. Since World War II this dynamic has changed, and the idea of a four-star admiral reverting to permanent two-star admiral and continuing to serve and wield considerable influence inside an organizational collective is only a dim memory, if that.

It should not, therefore, surprise us that after the war the General Board, with the CNO as a member, resumed its role as the senior decision-making body for policy inside the Navy. History is contingent, so this course was not predetermined, but the aftermath of World War I resulted in several non-violent "engagements" that increased, or rather reclaimed and retrenched, the prewar influence of the General Board. The CNO and OpNav, without a war to fight, lost some of their clout, planning for overseas wars that most Americans preferred to avoid. The three most important events in the postwar period occurred at Versailles in 1919, off Hampton Roads in Chesapeake Bay in 1921, and at Constitutional Hall in Washington, D.C., from November 1921 to February 1922.[4] It is to these events, and the General Board's role in them, that we now turn.

The Naval Battle of Paris

One of the unpleasant realities to dawn on the victorious Allied powers as they gathered at Versailles after the signing of the Armistice with Germany was the fact that one of their war aims, the elimination of ruinous arms races, had not been achieved. A more ruinous naval arms race loomed over the horizon between three of the victors—Imperial Japan, Great Britain, and the United States.[5] The General Board's role in this arms race was not insignificant. It had recommended, prior to the United States' entry into the war, building a navy second to none.[6] The first step toward this goal was the course of the war just ended. Britain, the United States' benchmark for parity, built ships but also lost them, and it eventually built fewer and fewer battleships in favor of other classes such as destroyers (for convoy work) and aircraft carriers (to attack submarine bases).[7] This allowed the United States to play "catch up" with regard to capital shipping until mid-1917, when it too modified its building program to match the actual needs of the war.[8]

The second step was the Naval Act of 1916, which committed the United States to the most expensive single expansion of its military power in peacetime to that point in history.[9] The General Board aimed at nothing less than forty-eight battleships and began a program to build six battlecruisers, which would be faster and more heavily armed than any of that class then afloat. Only two of these had their keels laid (after the war), as the realities of the nature of the war at sea in 1917 dawned on the major decision makers, both inside and outside the Navy. Even so, much of this construction could still be rationalized against a possible war with Japan, nominally an ally of the United States after 1917.[10]

What became known as the "Naval Battle of Paris" occurred in March 1919 against the backdrop of the Versailles Peace Conference, which lasted from December 1918 to July 1919.[11] It resulted because after the war the United States decided to continue to build up its Navy, not as a "second to none" fleet but in a "naked bid for [maritime] supremacy." Although the General Board was not directly involved in this battle as a collective, its ideas were represented through the offices of ADM Benson, an officer who saw himself as much a member of the board as CNO. The goal of this conflict, taking an ends-ways-means approach, was President Wilson's desire to establish a collective security regime via an organization such as the League of Nations (one of his Fourteen Points). With this in place, the United States might not need to build such a large fleet and the naval arms race might end. The General Board backed the construction part of this plan, lending its voice, via Benson as well as its written policy studies, to those of the president and Secretary Daniels for another massive building program to deliver new ships by 1921 and after.[12]

A third step involved Japanese-American relations. These relations, strained off and on since 1907, now came into clearer focus with continued anti-Asian legislation on the U.S. West Coast as well as the German ploy of feeding American fears in their Zimmermann note implying collusion with Japan. Also feeding the animosity was the Mahanian dictate that one must build one's navy based on the most capable opponent, not the most likely. Like it or not, the United States had become the raison d'être for Japanese naval construction, especially the so-called eight-eight plan, for battleships and battlecruisers, of Japan's navy minister, Baron Kato Tomosaburo.[13]

Returning to the Versailles Peace Conference, Wilson and Daniels, if not Benson, were using the stick of continued naval construction as a means to get Great Britain to agree to several things. First and foremost was the League of Nations as a component of the peace treaty, which might then obviate the need to continue with an aggressive naval building program. Another issue was the second of the "Fourteen Points: 'freedom of the seas.'" Britain had won the war in part because it had denied this freedom to Germany by its ability to blockade and did not want to give up this "strategic weapon." Finally, there was the desire to get Britain to agree arms reductions, including naval reductions. To help decide these issues, in January 1919 the Allied powers had created a committee to examine the naval terms of the treaty. The U.S. representative was ADM Benson.[14] Additionally, the United States created its own naval advisory staff at Paris, which included three future members of the General Board—CAPT Frank Schofield, CAPT Luke McNamee, and the current naval attaché in Paris, RADM Andrew T. Long.[15]

Despite the deadlock over these naval issues into March, Britain's civilian leaders advised caution and patience. Their concerns included not only the overall number of capital ships built in the United States but also the expanded size of the U.S. merchant fleet, a direct result of the war. On 25 March, just as Daniels arrived in Paris, First Lord of the Admiralty Walter Long wrote that "threatened competition in merchant shipbuilding is not within the range of practical politics; it is a legitimate inference that agitation for a large Navy will die down." The arrival of Daniels and Wilson in Paris in the last week of March broke this deadlock.[16] Daniels met that night with Benson at his hotel about the deadlock and the issue of "disposition" of the interred German fleet, which was another sticking point for all concerned. On 27 March the president informed Daniels that he wished for him to see both the First Sea Lord, Admiral Sir Rosslyn Wemyss, as well as that officer's civilian master, First Lord of the Admiralty Walter Long.[17]

Events now came to a head in two separate meetings between Daniels and the British naval leadership. On 29 March a stormy conference occurred between Daniels, Benson, and Wemyss. Reputedly, Benson arrived late and found Wemyss badgering Daniels about cancelling the U.S. building program and ceding superiority to the Royal Navy. Benson charged to the rescue and the confrontation nearly degenerated into a shouting match. Daniels clearly appreciated Benson's support, writing in his diary, "Benson talked very straight to Wemyss who wanted us to agree to a larger Navy for G.B. than America should build."[18] The next day Daniels met first with Edward

M. House, Wilson's closest adviser, who advised moderation and the possibility of agreeing to halt naval construction "if others would do likewise." Benson, on the other hand, continued to advise building to reach and maintain parity to avoid giving any one nation "undue weight."[19]

The following day, Daniels finally met Long, with Benson in tow. According to some accounts, this meeting was even stormier and almost resulted in a complete breakdown of the talks. Long maintained that to get the League of Nations the United States would have to stop its naval building program. Benson implied that such a position might cause "war between Great Britain and the United States." Long then reputedly implied they had nothing further to talk about.[20] Daniels' memory of the event was not so charged, and he remembered Long claiming that he "was not fully informed as to Prime Ministers [sic] desire." They agreed to try and meet with Prime Minister Lloyd George the next day (without Benson). This took place over breakfast, with the deadlock now occurring at a higher level between Daniels and Lloyd George over the issue of accepting a subordinate U.S. naval position in exchange for Britain's support for the league. They then met with President Wilson at 11 a.m. Daniels was due to proceed the next day to Italy for further official visits. Lloyd George insisted Daniels cancel the trip in order to settle the issue. Wilson rejected this suggestion in a masterly move that put the entire squabble on hold for a week until Daniels returned on Monday, 7 April 1919. The day before Daniels returned to Paris, Wilson threatened to leave the conference without an agreement, which meant that the United States would continue building come what may.[21]

When Daniels returned the next Monday, the battle resumed, with the secretary first having "a long talk with Benson who feels B[ritain] is trying to dictate naval matters in order to control commerce." Also, Wemyss apparently tried to meet with Daniels at the train station prior to his meeting with Long or Benson. In the upshot, Long and Daniels agreed to a modus vivendi based on Long's thinking that "we might make agreements on principle to stop building and get together on details when I reached England."[22] This turned out to be the mechanism that solved the problem, an understanding to consult each other on naval programs regularly, a promise by Wilson to postpone building pending a future agreement, while pressing ahead with British acquiescence to the League of Nations. No agreement was signed, but in retrospect Wilson had sacrificed "freedom of the seas" and the means to maintain it for the league.

The other issue, the disposition of the German fleet, was solved by the Germans themselves on 21 June 1919 at Scapa Flow, when the caretaker crews of these ships scuttled them. The few ships that remained were divvied out among the allies, with the United States receiving the dreadnought *Ostfriesland*, cruiser *Frankfurt*, and a few other small auxiliaries and submarines.[23] Also, the Anglo-Japanese Naval Treaty referred to by the Naval Advisory Staff during the Paris negotiations remained in force.[24] Its days were numbered, given Britain's severe financial situation and the ability of the United States to build as much as it wished or as little as Wilson promised. There was no signed agreement approved by Congress in force. Throughout these meetings, Benson represented the view of the General Board, serving as a proxy voice, if you will. Moreover, he was a member of the board before formally becoming the Chief of Naval Operations and did not step down from that membership when he became the CNO. This is often forgotten by historians who have tended to criticize Benson's stubbornness in sticking to the stated policy of the General Board of having a navy equal to that of Great Britain.[25] The irony here was that Wilson failed to get congressional approval for the Treaty of Versailles, and Great Britain, not the United States, became a charter member of the League of Nations. Charles Evans Hughes, Wilson's opponent in the 1916 presidential race, would get the naval agreement Wilson and the British sought at Paris at Washington in the winter of 1921–22.

The Pacific "Base"

Wilson's agreement in May 1919 to put the naval expansion program on hold limited the General Board's options.[26] It began to look for other ways to do its twin jobs of recommending policy writ large and overseeing overall ship characteristics. The latter was particularly difficult in a new era in which "peace was breaking out everywhere." The General Board's worldview, expressed in 420-2 policy studies of this era, reflected a conviction that the world was still a dangerous place, a place that required the United States to have a strong and powerful navy. The perceived threat was especially significant in the Pacific vis-à-vis Japan, although relations with Britain were on edge as well.[27] Plan Orange now became the focus; the naval components of the Treaty of Versailles, which essentially limited Germany to a coast guard, had temporarily neutralized the threat of Plan Black.[28]

As discussed, the General Board had disagreed with Army planners about how to defend the Philippines and preferred to fortify Subic Bay rather than develop Manila because of Subic's better access to the sea—easy access being a lesson many had learned from study of the Port Arthur campaign in the Russo-Japanese War. However, by 1910 this idea, although not completely dead, was no longer viable for Navy planners, including the General Board. Attention now switched to the American possession of Guam, especially after Japan was awarded mandate territories by Versailles in the Caroline and Marshall Island groups. Guam, located at the southern end of the Marianas Island chain, was its biggest island, with a deepwater harbor at Apra and significant protected anchorages at Agana and Tamnuning. All of these were on the calm leeward side of Guam, facing west. However, Apra's undeveloped state, inability to host the entire battle fleet, and complete lack of infrastructure constituted real drawbacks.[29] Since the end of the Cold War, Guam's advantages, particularly regarding real estate for airfields, have made it something of the fortified bastion the General Board always wanted it to be—the United States' forward outpost in the Pacific.[30] However, prior to World War I, Guam did not seem worth the effort to turn it into a premier forward naval base.

The board had first recommended Guam as a base during the 1907 war scare, after which the Naval War College studied a board recommendation to fortify the island.[31] With the demise of the Subic option in 1910, a "Guam movement" began to turn it into "a kind of Gibraltar." These last were the words of Mahan, but Bradley Fiske derided the comparison as well as Mahan's other comparison to Malta. Guam controlled no chokepoints.[32] However, Dewey added his voice to Mahan's and thus established the credibility of Guam as a key part of War Plan Orange in 1912, stating, "The possession of Guam under naval control is a vital necessity to our country in engaging in war in the Far East." Of course, Dewey was thinking more of a German raiding squadron than of the Japanese battle fleet, as Graf von Spee's bold cruise in 1914 would validate once World War I began. Accordingly, these thoughts on the "Defense of Guam" were forwarded to the SecNav in December 1912.[33]

Historian Edward Miller has argued that this obsession with Guam as the pillar of Pacific strategy "hobbled" the search for strategic alternatives, although he gives it credit for possibly being an asset with which to threaten Japanese sea lines of communication. He minimizes Guam's importance as part of a more complex scheme involving not just that island but also the capture and fortification of other bases (advanced bases, later mobile bases) as well as the use of emerging technology—that is, the airplane and submarine—to make Guam more effective. With the end of World War I and the deaths of Dewey and Mahan earlier, it seemed the "Guam Lobby" might die out. However, in 1917 the board continued to recommend Guam's improvement, including substantial dredging of Apra Harbor. A new champion also emerged in Benson's replacement in 1919 as CNO, RADM Robert E. Coontz, who had served as the island's governor in 1912.[34] Coontz attached to himself the former insurgent RADM James Oliver, who had served as DNI and on the General Board from 1914 to 1917, and CAPT Harry Yarnell, another up-and-coming naval officer. Under the auspices of the Office of Naval Intelligence, Yarnell teamed up with two other talented officers, LCDR Holloway H. Frost and CDR William Pye, to produce the "Conduct of an Oversea Naval Campaign" study. This document foresaw the need for the seizure of advanced bases and the fortification of existing ones, as well as the importance of recapturing them after the enemy had landed. This paper served as a template for the more famous study on "Advanced Base Operations in Micronesia," written in 1921 by Maj Earl "Pete" Ellis. To improve Guam's capacity, they advocated giant floating dry docks to be towed across the Pacific.[35]

All this work provided ammunition for Coontz to argue that Guam was the key to defense of the Pacific in a war with Japan. Meanwhile, Fiske, now in retirement but still very much in tune with current debates, changed sides on the issue of Guam at some point because of the possibilities of naval aviation being used from air bases located there[36] However, these plans were undermined by a study done by one Coontz's key planners, Clarence S. Williams, who found dredging Apra would not yield enough depth for capital ships or floating dry docks. This seems odd now, because Apra hosted a large floating dry dock from the Vietnam era until 2016 and there were plans under way to dredge it to allow the largest warships—nuclear aircraft carriers—to moor there in 2013. However, what is possible today was almost certainly more difficult or impossible in 1921.[37]

By 1921 the General Board and CNO were in accord about plans for Guam, but because no money had yet been spent on the project, it proved to be low-hanging fruit later that year at the Washington Naval Conference, the results of which caused the Navy to explore other strategic options in the

Pacific. These specific options included the idea of an advanced mobile base, something developed from the existing advanced base idea. This base was to be seized somewhere in the demilitarized Caroline archipelagos, which had formerly belonged to the Germans and had been awarded to Japan under "mandate" status at Versailles.[38]

Against this strategic backdrop, the General Board held intensive hearings in its attempts to understand the "lessons" of the late war and to incorporate them into its building and expansion plans for the Navy.[39] Principal among these were hearings on naval aviation, battleship and battlecruiser designs, submarines, and antisubmarine warfare.[40] Naval aviation was of particular interest due to the shock submarines had administered during the war and the roles naval aviation assumed to counter it. The General Board hearings for much of 1918 had centered on using naval aviation around Dunkirk and Calais in an air offensive to neutralize German submarines.[41] Included in these hearings were aviation considerations for both the Coast Guard and Marines.[42] At the same time, the board found time to educate itself on current geopolitical events with hearings that encompassed briefing by naval attachés who had returned recently from both Germany and Japan.[43] Organizationally the board had renamed its four subcommittees "sections." Associate members still served on the board in December 1918. For example, LtCol L. C. Lucas, USMC, was assigned to the second section, which shows the board had begun augmenting itself with more junior Marine officers since the Marine presence had returned to the board in 1915. For a time Lucas even acted as the secretary for the board. The year 1919 also saw Secretary Daniels and members of the House Naval Affairs Committee attending board meetings as lessons learned from the war were discussed and studied.[44]

The hearings on naval aviation included testimony from Royal Air Force (RAF) officers as well as naval aviation pioneers Hank Mustin, Ernest King, John Towers, Kenneth Whiting, and J. C. Hunsaker.[45] The General Board devoted the bulk of its time in 1919 to the topic of naval aviation, which undermines the claims of those who have accused it of neglecting naval aviation after World War I.[46] Later hearings in early 1921 addressed the topic of using the battlecruiser designs planned for *Lexington* and *Saratoga* as the template for purpose-built aircraft carriers, principally because these ships had electric drive for their turbine propulsion that would allow them to go both forward and backward, the same consideration that made the difference in the picking the coal tender *Jupiter* for conversion to the Navy's first carrier *Langley*.[47] Perhaps the most (in)famous expert witness before the board in 1919 was BG William "Billy" Mitchell.

The Second Naval Battle of Hampton Roads

The U.S. Navy and the General Board faced a domestic challenge,[48] what might be characterized as air-power evangelism unified to, ironically, the isolationists (such as Senator William Borah of Idaho), who wanted to see deep cuts in the Navy building program.[49] Billy Mitchell's arguments that air power practically made warships (and even armies) obsolete found a willing audience, both with Borah and with those intent on cutting naval expenditures—possibly the new Republican administration of Warren G. Harding, which aimed at "normalcy."[50] Mitchell's view of war derived from his own wartime experience and the ideas of men such as Hugh Trenchard and Giulio Douhet, who believed that air power would completely transform warfare, making trench warfare obsolete and navies irrelevant.[51] In the United States, Mitchell personified this new and radical view of warfare.

The son of a U.S. senator from Wisconsin, during World War I Mitchell had essentially become GEN John J. Pershing's air-component commander for the American Expeditionary Force. By 1918 he had planned a comprehensive air campaign to augment the big offensive for 1919. The only problem was that the Germans signed an armistice before Mitchell could show what air power could do. More and more he looked to the writing of Douhet and the organizational example of Britain's RAF as the models for the future of national defense. Air power could win wars all on its own, and quickly, using strategic bombing. Mitchell eventually conflated the two ideas—strategic bombing and an independent air force—to the exclusion of everything else.[52] However, in 1919 his stance was not so fixed, in part because of his evolving view that it was the U.S. Navy and its opposition to a unified military department that was the "real" enemy of the United States. Mitchell favored a ministry of defense along British lines, dominated by a new, independent air force.[53]

The General Board, on the other hand, had been trying to get a handle on air power and how it worked in World War I even before the war ended, holding hearings constantly with experts such as naval air pioneer John Towers to determine the way ahead for the fleet. At a hearing on 27 March 1919, Towers predicted that the "airplane carrier will not last very long," probably due to the idea that land-based bombers could carry more ordnance and attack ships more effectively.[54] The idea for Mitchell to appear before the board had come earlier in March from another naval aviation pioneer, LCDR J. C. Hunsaker. When queried by the board as to other aviation experts they should interview, Hunsaker responded, "I would like to emphasize Brigadier General Mitchell. He has the idea that the Navy['s aviation] should be absorbed by the Army['s aviation] and I would like to hear his views on that."[55]

Mitchell at first had seemed to have gotten along well with the General Board when he and GEN C. T. Menoher (Mitchell's nominal superior) testified before it on 3 April 1919 concerning the implications of air power for sea power. The bad blood between Mitchell and the General Board began because of his testimony that April. Shortly after the so-called Naval Battle of Paris ended in 1919, Mitchell testified to a credulous congressional audience: "We believe that if we are allowed to develop essentially air weapons . . . that we can carry the war to such an extent in the air as *to make navies almost useless* [emphasis added] on the surface of the waters. The Navy General Board, I might say, agree with me on that." This testimony found its way into the records of the General Board, whose members most certainly did not agree with Mitchell. Their protest caused Secretary of War Newton D. Baker to write a letter to the Secretary of the Navy the following October, stating, "A careful perusal of the record of this hearing indicates that General Mitchell was not justified in the conclusion which he reached."[56] It is almost certain that Baker and Pershing were not so circumspect and restrained when they talked with Mitchell about the matter. And so began a feud within a feud, the feud between Mitchell and the General Board that climaxed with the sinking of a German dreadnought.

It is important to understand Mitchell's testimony before the General Board in light of the board's unique hearing process, only recently instituted by the chairman of its executive committee, RADM Charles Badger (see chapter 5). Mitchell's release of information from the hearing should be regarded as a violation of the rules governing classified information of that day. In today's vernacular, he "leaked" what he had said in a public hearing to Congress. Mitchell and Menoher had testified in the presence of several key members of the nascent Directorate of Naval Aviation, whom the General Board had also asked to attend the hearing. These included Towers, Hunsaker, and Whiting. This office was later reorganized into the new Bureau of Aeronautics (BuAer). The rules for these hearings were very liberal for a military organization, a carryover from the ambience set by Dewey and Taylor from the outset and as first observed by Fiske in 1910. The board tolerated a considerable amount of informality and often did not interrupt or contradict a witness in order to get as broad a scope of testimony as possible.[57]

The senior admiral present that day was former fleet commander (1913–14) Charles Badger. Badger deferred the conduct of the meeting to RADM Winterhalter, former commander of the Asiatic Fleet. Mitchell was thus being queried by two former four-star admirals with vast experience in the Pacific and the Atlantic. Winterhalter established a congenial atmosphere and deferred to Mitchell and Menoher, saying, "I have outlined in general what our immediate needs are, and will be very glad if you will, in your own way, handle this subject."[58] The starting point for the discussion was the Navy's acquisition of a number of Sopwith aircraft for training and to test out some concepts. Mitchell's first words were confrontational: "My opinion in regard to the employment of an air service, as a general proposition, is to get what material the people who are using it desire for their work. The airplanes mentioned will be shot down as fast as they go up against an enemy." When Winterhalter stressed that the planes were simply for training, Mitchell remained adamant, firing back, "We would shoot [them] down immediately." This exchange might cause one to conclude that the primary enemy of the United States in Billy Mitchell's mind was its Navy.[59]

Mitchell may have gained the impression that the board agreed with him because it politely listened. The most direct evidence came after about seven pages of testimony, most of it by Mitchell. "My opinion is you can make a direct attack on ships from the air in the future," claimed Mitchell. Winterhalter agreed, but such agreement did not equate to concurrence that navies are "almost useless." Rather, it was a simple recognition that airplanes can attack ships. This line of questioning led to a proposal for some testing. Winterhalter, putting himself in Mitchell's shoes, mused out loud about his own perception of the current vulnerability of ships to attack from the air: "You gentlemen [of the Army Air Corps] ought to feel very much encouraged about the condition of surface vessels at the present time. They are most vulnerable to attack from the air. There is now more weight in vertical armor than in horizontal [i.e., deck] armor."

Mitchell responded immediately by saying, "We can try a good many things out around Chesapeake Bay." At this point Mitchell may have stopped listening and come to his mistaken conclusion that it followed from this discussion that the General Board agreed navies were "almost useless." Winterhalter went on to stress that he agreed that testing was necessary "to find out what your methods of attack are so we can find out how to meet them." The Navy wanted to do the testing to improve its surface vessels' defenses against prospective future enemies, not against the Army Air Corps. However, given this exchange, one can now understand why someone with Mitchell's personality—headstrong and egocentric—might mistake common courtesy with complete agreement. Winterhalter later asked Mitchell if it might not be a good idea for the Army to assign a "liaison" officer to "join our aviators here," that is, at the Directorate for Naval Aviation. Mitchell agreed that this was a good idea.[60] Thus it must have been a bitter surprise to Mitchell to be rebuked by his own service secretary at the instigation of the General Board (and Navy Secretary Josephus Daniels). Lost in all the hype was the board's recommendation to SecNav advocating the further aggressive development of naval aviation ships, planes, and organizations "capable of accompanying and operating with the fleet in all waters of the globe."[61]

In the meantime, other forceful voices lent themselves to the cause of the development of aviation within the Navy. In 1919 ADM William Sims returned from his wartime command of the naval forces deployed to aid the Allies in World War I. He reassumed his duty as NWC president and reopened that institution (closed temporarily during the war) in September. Lost in many histories of this period is Sims' active resumption of his ex officio membership on the General Board. Sims, as we have seen, was a committed "battleship admiral" who was as yet unconvinced of the value of naval aviation. His firm confidence in battleships as the coin of naval power, though, had been shaken by the German submarine campaign in the late war, so he had become more open to questioning even his own positions vis-à-vis sea power. At the NWC he proceeded to rigorously test the use of aircraft in the curriculum at the college during its periodic war games. By January 1921 he had become an advocate for a separate naval air service within the Navy and had even begun to consider aircraft carriers as capital ships that could displace the battleship from its perch as the centerpiece of the fleet.[62]

Another key battleship advocate had become convinced of the value of naval aviation and the need for the Navy to have a strong organization in charge of it: CAPT William Moffett, an officer with political connections and the savvy to use them. In June 1920, while Moffett commanded the battleship *Mississippi*, Towers and Mustin had demonstrated the effectiveness of naval aviation gunnery spotting and converted him to their cause. Moffett had congressional contacts urge Secretary of the Navy Edwin Denby to appoint him to succeed CAPT Thomas Craven as director of Naval Aviation and to recommend that the job be upgraded to a flag billet. In March 1921 Moffett was appointed to the job, and in July the billet was upgraded by Congress to a Navy bureau with accompanying admiral's rank. For an organization to have the status and name of "bureau" was a very big deal in those days; it meant that the institutional Navy believed naval aviation had a promising future.[63]

Ironically, the same month Moffett was appointed to head up the Navy's newest bureau, Mitchell finally got his chance to test out his ideas about aviation making navies "almost useless" against a bona fide dreadnought battleship—the SMS *Ostfriesland*. Few events have been surrounded with so much hype and myth. According to a heroic version of events, Billy Mitchell demonstrated conclusively the obsolescence of battleships, and by extension navies, by sinking a modern dreadnought with his bombers. The opposite view holds that the sinking of a moored vessel of questionable seaworthiness in fine weather with no crew to "fight" her proved nothing about the efficacy of air power against naval power.

As part of the Armistice signed in November 1918, the United States was authorized to take possession of several former High Seas Fleet warships, including the *Ostfriesland*.[64] On 12 July 1921, *Ostfriesland* and the light cruiser *Frankfurt* departed from their moorings in New York Harbor bound for the Lynnhaven Inlet in Chesapeake Bay.[65] Up until March of that year, Mitchell and Secretary Daniels had engaged in a very public debate about the effectiveness of land-based bombers against battleships. Daniels reputedly responded to Mitchell's proposal to test his ideas against the battleship *Iowa* by saying, "I'm so confident that neither Army nor Navy aviators can hit the *Iowa* when she is under way that I would be perfectly willing to be on board her when they bomb her!" Deadlines established by the Allies for destruction of the German vessels after the war and congressional pressure orchestrated by Mitchell resulted in the Harding administration directing Denby to agree to the tests in July 1921.[66]

Mitchell's goals for the test contrasted sharply with those of the Navy. Mitchell meant to prove the concept that battleships could be sunk by airplanes. Once this was accomplished, he hoped it would give his drive to establish an independent air force enough momentum to cause Congress to act. Additionally, in proving that the Navy had no proper appreciation for the potential of air power, he could claim that any naval component for air power properly belonged within the new independent service he hoped to establish. This reflected what the British had done with their Fleet Air Arm, which was controlled, mainly through budgetary means, by the Air Ministry and the Royal Air Force.[67] On the Navy side, the goals were more measured: to study and collect data on the effect of bombs of various sizes on ships of various sizes, to study German warship design, and to take the lessons learned and use them to design less vulnerable warships.[68]

The stage was set and it is no secret that Mitchell prepared his pilots for these tests as if he was preparing for actual combat. For him it was the moral equivalent of war.[69] However, his target was not at all what it was painted in the popular press to be—the latest and greatest in unsinkable dreadnought technology. The *Ostfriesland* was no spring chicken. She had been launched in 1909 as a first-generation German dreadnought, built in response to Sir John "Jacky" Fisher's "dreadnought revolution." *Ostfriesland* managed to survive the Battle of Jutland in 1916 but was almost sunk before reaching port by a British mine. She finished out the war much as the rest of the High Seas Fleet, sitting idle in port with her material condition degrading. She was not at Scapa Flow (where most of the German fleet had scuttled itself) and was turned over to the U.S. Navy in April 1920.[70]

The Navy, as was its habit, assigned an officer of proven experience and competence from BuC&R to take charge of the preparations of the *Ostfriesland* for the test: CDR (later ADM) Alexander Hamilton Van Keuren. He was to inspect the vessel and collect data in order to do what ADM Winterhalter had emphasized to Mitchell two years previously—to figure out how to make warships, especially battleships, less vulnerable to attack from the air. Van Keuren was one of the most innovative officers from BuC&R to collaborate with the General Board during the period between the two world wars, having a hand in just about every major design project from flying deck cruisers to massive mobile floating dry docks.[71] He found the *Ostfriesland* in poor material condition, as expected given her recent history. Many of her watertight hatches and scuttles were damaged so much that they had to be secured with manila ropes for the voyage down to Lynnhaven (to avoid the ship taking on more water). Van Keuren's report clearly indicated she was lower in the water than she should have been and that she contained brackish water in her lower spaces. Too, vents that should have been above the waterline were now at the waterline and secured to prevent even more water from entering the ship.[72]

By the time *Ostfriesland* reached the Virginia Capes, Van Keuren found that the ship had taken on even more water during her transit, which raised real concerns in his mind about the overall integrity of the ship. He wrote that "a slow leakage was taking place which became more serious later on when anchored outside [Lynnhaven inlet] in rough water." On 18 July the ships were towed out to the "Experimental Grounds" test site in Chesapeake Bay. On 20 July, before the first round of bombing, Van Keuren observed that the *Ostfriesland* had settled another foot into the sea, convincing him that she was slowly sinking. Also, her port list was now more pronounced at two degrees.[73]

The first round of bombings prior to 20 July went well. *Frankfurt*, a submarine, and a destroyer had all been sent to the bottom through the cumulative efforts of Navy, Marine, and Army aviators. On 20 July it was *Ostfriesland*'s turn. The big news that day was that *Ostfriesland* remained afloat, despite the delivery of five 1,100-pound bombs in an unauthorized low-level raid by Mitchell's flyers (using compasses supplied by the Navy). The nominal purpose of the tests was to test the effectiveness of level medium- to high-altitude bombing. Mitchell was furious and made the decision to use his specially built 1,800-pound bombs the following day—he needed his big media event. Nonetheless, the 20 July bombing had caused serious damage to *Ostfriesland*. Van Keuren believed that the day's bombing had accelerated the process by which the ship was slowly sinking; she was now down by the stern by more than four feet, with large quantities of water in her engine rooms, "bilges," and "dead pockets." Her port list was now three degrees. He was so concerned she might sink during the night that he had the old battleship *Delaware* stationed alongside. One might assume that Van Keuren meant for *Delaware* to stand by in order to send another party on board to make final observations to better determine how and why the ship sank one more time before she went down.[74]

Mitchell had one more day to prove his point, and his actions immediately prior to the final day of bombing reflect his anxiety: a change in the bomb load and a personal briefing to his pilots. Prior to the Army bombers' arrival, Van Keuren had observed that *Ostfriesland* was now down by her stern by more than eight feet, almost double from the day before, and that she had settled another two feet into the Chesapeake. The first five planes carrying the lighter 1,100-pound bombs went in and scored two hits. The second wave, per the rules when hits were scored, was sent back to Langley, Virginia, while Van Keuren and his team went on board to assess the damage. Van Keuren observed, "There was no free water in any holds or compartments that we entered on the days immediately preceding bombing nor any signs of strained bulkheads. As remarked before, however, I felt sure the ship was slowly taking water all the time from the time she anchored on the experimental grounds, and this may have been spreading slowly to bunkers through the inner bottom or 2nd skin."

Nonetheless, the beat-up German dreadnought remained stubbornly afloat. The Navy leadership was prepared to sink her with the 14-inch guns of the battleship *Pennsylvania* if she remained afloat after flight operations ended. The Army aviators, recalled to allow the inspection per the rules, dumped their bomb loads not far from the Navy ships observing the test in a dangerous fit of juvenile pique. Finally, Van Keuren noted that several of the watertight hatches had been jarred open, but that there was no time to resecure them, probably due to the unexpected arrival of General Mitchell and his bombers for a final bombing run.[75]

This time Mitchell and his aviators ignored the rules and the recall signals after the first hits, delivering 1,800-pound bombs one after the other. Van Keuren and his team were thus denied the opportunity to collect further data. *Ostfriesland* began to settle rapidly by her stern, something the famous photograph of her final moments shows quite clearly—much as the cruiser *Admiral Belgrano* would do in the Falklands War more than sixty years later due to poor damage-control procedures. After twenty-one minutes, *Ostfriesland* disappeared into the water, standing almost on end with her bow in the air. Mitchell sent his final bomber in to drop its load on the bubbling water where she had once been. He then flew a victory pass by the "enemy" warships.[76] A picture is worth a thousand words, and Mitchell had gotten his, despite his violation of the rules and the questionable circumstances surrounding *Ostfriesland*'s demise. Mitchell was exultant, as were those who favored drastic naval disarmament in Congress. Senator Borah trumpeted that the "experiment off the Virginia coast demonstrated ... that the battleship is practically obsolete."[77]

The more sober Van Keuren came away with a different set of conclusions, which he cataloged in a secret report forwarded to the General Board on 30 August 1921. He believed that the test clearly showed that "a crew aboard could have easily kept the ship almost free of water." He also observed, "That but for the initial water in the ship, the damage inflicted by bombs would not have sunk the ship, and that gun fire would have had to be resorted to accomplish this end." These comments, being secret and not meant for public consumption, give us very little reason to believe that Van Keuren was not in fact rendering his best professional opinion as a construction engineer. Van Keuren summarized for the board the following larger conclusions:

- Eliminate and strengthen any areas of contact with the outside sea
- Develop shrapnel-type antiaircraft ordinance
- Develop aircraft carriers with fighters to shoot down bombers
- Develop new tactics and maneuvers to defeat bombers and shoot bombers down before they reach the battle line

As Van Keuren opined in his final sentence, "Since the shots that miss are the shots that count in this new form of warfare, we must see that the least possible number of shots are fired by hostile airplanes and that those that are fired go very wide of their mark." This last opinion perhaps influenced the General Board the most in terms of battleship design. It must have also been gratified to see Van Keuren support its own earlier decision to convert *Jupiter* into the aircraft carrier *Langley*. Clearly the General Board appreciated the potential of naval aviation.[78]

The confrontation with Mitchell and the military aviation technology he claimed as the preserve of his special expertise represented a conceptual challenge for the board and the Navy, which had to plan for the future in the face of new technology. One might characterize the application of air power against sea power as a disruptive technology or innovation. This can be defined as a technology or innovations "that require successful organizations to improve at secondary tasks but not at primary ones."[79] In this case the airplane proved supremely disruptive. It could disrupt many different tasks that a navy saw itself as traditionally performing, both primary and secondary. For example, airplanes, like submarines in World War I, mandated that navies develop special defenses, in this case antiaircraft protection. Not just the fleet, but any surface ship deemed worth protecting, such as oil tankers or troop transports, needed such special defenses.

Before Van Keuren's report arrived, though, the Harding administration had already acted, sending out invitations to a naval disarmament conference to meet that November in Washington, D.C. Harding and Secretary of State Charles Evans Hughes wanted to defuse tensions in the Pacific and halt the postwar naval arms race between Great Britain, Japan, and the United States—the unfinished business of the battle at Paris in 1919. It seemed possible that the battleship would fare poorly and perhaps even be abolished, along with submarines and bombers, as military weapons. Meanwhile, Mitchell had very much overplayed his hand after his great moment. In particular, he alienated air-power advocates inside the Navy that might, under different circumstances, have supported his bid for an independent air force—particularly Moffett and Towers, to say nothing of the General Board. Towers, especially, would prove instrumental in keeping naval aviation inside the Navy during the critical period of the Morrow Board and its report in 1925. Within his own service Mitchell was repudiated by none other than General Pershing in the report of the Joint Board on the tests that characterized the battleship as "still the backbone of the fleet."[80]

The General Board and the Washington Naval Treaty

In the meantime, the General Board prepared for the Washington Naval Conference. The technical experts provided by the active-duty naval officer corps to the conference included Sims' protégé, CAPT William V. Pratt, as well as RADM William L. Rodgers. Both were sitting members of the General Board, and Rodgers was its senior member.[81] The board recommended that Secretary Hughes propose a fleet equal in size to that of the British and twice the size of the Japanese fleet. Hughes rejected the recommendation and instead made sweeping proposals to declare a "Capital Ship Building Holiday" for ten years and fixed tonnage ratios for the three major naval powers. This meant that Great Britain, the United States, and Japan would scrap existing vessels down to around 535,000 tons' displacement at a ratio of 5:5:3, respectively, for all capital ships (i.e., battleships and battlecruisers). Much of what has been written about the Washington Naval Conference has missed that Hughes preempted any discussion of the abolition of all battleships in the seemingly liberal proposal to actually decommission and scrap some battleships. This proposal in fact had been crafted jointly by Chief of Naval Operations Coontz, Captain Pratt, Assistant Secretary of the Navy Theodore Roosevelt Jr., and Hughes. Pratt made the copies of Hughes' opening comments for the U.S. delegation inside the offices of the General Board the day before the conference opened! On 21 November 1921, he used one of these copies to open the conference. Later in the conference, the Americans traded away the right to further develop naval bases in the Philippines and Guam to gain the Japanese agreement to the "inferior position" conferred by the ratio. This fortification restriction was incorporated as Article 19 of the Washington Naval Treaty. In this manner, the idea of Guam as the great Pacific base was set aside for the duration of the treaty.[82]

With this restriction on the construction of naval bases, Coontz, a supporter of the Guam plan, backed out of his support of the Washington Naval Treaty, leaving Pratt as the lone minority voice on the General Board in favor of the treaty. The board's own opinion was best represented by a speech given by former member and retired admiral Harry S. Knapp that April, which found that the critical element of the treaty was not so much its limitations on construction and holiday as Article 19, the nonfortification clause. Knapp was joined in this opinion by both Dudley Knox, now chief of the Naval Historical Center (NHC), and Bradley Fiske. What none of them noted was the fact that in exchange Pratt and Hughes had gotten de facto recognition of the U.S. Navy as "second to none" by the British as well as replaced the Anglo-Japanese Alliance with a new, milder Four-Power Treaty for maintaining the status quo in the Pacific between France, Japan, Britain, and the United States.[83]

Two other articles of the Washington Naval Treaty also resulted from intense negotiations, and both reflected the direct impact of the *Ostfriesland* sinking and Van Keuren's recommendations to the General Board. It is worth emphasizing that a copy of Van Keuren's report was filed specifically in the naval aviation papers categorized as 449, papers used to write General Board studies for the Secretary of the Navy in August 1921 *prior* to the Washington Naval Conference. The importance of aircraft carriers was reflected in Article 9 of the treaty, which made the allowance to convert as many as two battlecruisers targeted for scrapping—up to 33,000 tons—into aircraft carriers. The General Board had already proposed the idea of using the existing battlecruiser hull and propulsion designs as the bases for its first purpose-built aircraft carriers, and here was the opportunity to do just that under the sanction of the Washington Naval Treaty. The treaty also made no mention of the numbers of naval aircraft navies could build to use in concert with their fleets.[84]

A second article emphasized the General Board's actions concerning the battleships retained under the terms of the Washington Naval Treaty. With *Ostfriesland* very much in their minds, the Americans, and possibly the British, ensured the insertion of a special paragraph in Article 20 of the treaty permitting weight increases of up to 3,000 tons to allow the major powers to improve the defenses of battleships "against air and submarine attack." Pratt testified to the General Board after the fact about his own role in the adoption of this proposal at the conference. He told the board that the proposal was initially the idea of the British naval delegates and that its intent was to allow battleships to keep pace with threats by aircraft and submarines, which were not limited under the terms of the treaty. As a member of the General Board he had certainly seen Van Keuren's report. This suggests that the *Ostfriesland* experience, especially the comments regarding near misses and watertight integrity, played a direct role in the drafting of the treaty's "reconstruction clause." It opened the door for the signatory powers, including the U.S. Navy, to continue to improve the survivability of the battleships retained under the treaty and to keep pace with the threat posed by air power. Two years later the first major naval spending program passed in Congress approved the first phase of a battleship modernization program and implemented antiaircraft improvements and internal changes to improve survivability against air and submarine attacks.[85]

Although the General Board opposed the ratification of the Washington Naval Treaty, it made the most of the situation after the treaty system became a reality.[86] It learned that scrapped battleships, especially of the most modern types, make for excellent opportunities to test weapons development and warship design. Pursuant to this, the board lobbied the Secretary of the Navy and President Harding to allow them to scrap some of the newest battleships in much the same manner they had disposed of the German ships, by the deployment of the newest gunnery, aerial, and torpedo weapons against them. The treaty allowed the Navy to dispose of one of the ships scheduled for scrapping as a target each year. Given the experience of the *Ostfriesland*, the Navy was keen on taking advantage of this clause.[87] The battleship *Washington*'s use as an experimental target was immediately proposed. She was the Navy's most modern battleship scheduled for scrapping under the treaty. Someone on the board had broached this issue, because use of the *Washington* for experimentation had been adopted on 22 April 1922 as the board's official policy. ADM Rodgers stated that he knew "of no reason why we cannot destroy the *Washington* by target practice in the period set by the treaty and be in every respect within the terms of the treaty."[88]

The *Washington* was not the first ship to be disposed of in this way. In 1923 the older *Virginia* and *New Jersey* were bombed and sunk by the Army Air Corps. Service feeling over these tests tended to increase, rather than weaken, the Navy's resolve to strengthen the battleship as well as beef up its own fleet aviation.[89] The next ships disposed of were the battleships *North Dakota* and *South Carolina*, which were altered with the proposed conversion designs in mind, especially the *South Carolina*. Their use as targets provided valuable data to test the blister design for the retained coal-burning battleships and their deck protection designs. Useful information was also gathered on shock protection for gun turrets.[90]

President Coolidge approved *Washington*'s use as a target in August 1924. The SecNav emphasized to the president that the tests were experimental and "in the public interest" since the results would be studied "by a board of naval experts" for use in the modernization program.[91] By "board of experts" he meant the General Board as assisted by the indefatigable Van Keuren of BuC&R. The subsequent tests showed that the Navy's design for survivability of the *Tennessee* class were basically sound. The *Washington* tests, which would not have been held if not for the Washington Naval Treaty and the experience of the *Ostfriesland*, established the soundness of the Navy's continued institutional support for the battleship.

These tests did much to defuse the Navy's concern over the near misses that had resulted from the *Ostfriesland* and other level bombing tests while providing the Navy with valuable underwater data to enhance torpedo protection for all ships, not just battleships. *Washington* was eventually sunk by 14-inch gunfire from *Texas*, which further reinforced the Navy's commitment to improve deck protection and lengthen the range of its guns as permitted by the Treaty.[92] Navy leaders' attitudes were both changing and staying the same. Attitudes about the central role of the battleship changed little inside the institutional Navy. Most Navy leaders redoubled their efforts to retain it as the coin of naval power. However, in maintaining this stance, leaders changed their views in other areas, especially regarding the threat of air power and submarines. These nontraditional platforms gained importance in the minds of these men, in part due to their dedication to the idea of the survivable, big-gun battleship.[93]

The tests, particularly on the *Washington*, alleviated many of the concerns the General Board had about the soundness of the design of its most modern battleships, and in the crucible of war these same ship designs held up well against the best that aviation could throw at them. On 7 December 1941, at Pearl Harbor, the *Tennessee, West Virginia,* and *Maryland,* ships whose design and damage control training were based on the experience of the *Washington*, were hit with bombs and torpedoes from Japan's finest naval aviators of Dai Ichi Kido Butai (First Mobile Striking Force). It was a testament, perhaps, to the legacy of the *Ostfriesland*, the General Board, and the Washington Naval Treaty that both *Tennessee* and *Maryland* were easily raised from the shallow bottom of Pearl Harbor and steamed back to the West Coast of the United States under their own power for repairs. *West Virginia*, which had taken an incredible seven torpedo hits in addition to dive-bomber-delivered armor-piercing direct hits, was evidence of what a trained and dedicated crew could do to keep a dreadnought from capsizing while under air attack. She, too, settled on Pearl Harbor's shallow bottom, but her damage was more severe and she was not refloated until six months later. Then she too was repaired, wreaking her revenge on Japan at the Surigao Strait in 1944. Obviously, Mitchell's proclamation of the "death of the battleship" was premature. However, as with all things, perhaps in 1921 the battleship, if she could be presumed to have a consciousness, became aware of her own mortality.[94]

As the Washington Naval Conference was about to conclude, the lingering disputes over the General Board's role during World War I and after was articulated by the former naval insurgent and aide for operations, RADM Richard Wainwright (Ret.), in an article about the General Board for the February 1922 *Proceedings*. Wainwright wrote in conclusion that "with a real General Staff [CNO] established, a General Board, untrammeled by executive duties, considering and reporting on larger questions of naval policies would be of assistance to any Chief of Staff and would help to protect him from the annoying assaults of Galley Yarns."[95] With the ratification of the Washington Naval Treaty, Wainwright and the General Board soon saw that the unintended consequence of that event vaulted the board into a position of even more influence and power, exceeding that which it had wielded as merely an operational war-planning body. Now it became a component of the highest levels of national policy-making while continuing its efforts to match the construction of those means—submarines, aircraft and aircraft carriers, cruisers, and, after ten years, battleships—with the policy ends it hoped to shape.

CHAPTER 7

The Heyday of the General Board
From Washington to London and After, 1922–31

Sea Power is not made of ships, or of ships and men, but of ships and men and bases far and wide. . . . Manifestly the provisions of the Treaty presented a naval problem of the first magnitude that demanded immediate solution. A new policy had to be formulated which would make the best possible use of the new conditions.
—CAPT Frank H. Schofield, 1923

I have always been a great advocate of a real entente between us [the United States and Great Britain] *but do not believe in written alliances. As I think I have told you in the past, Great Britain makes me pretty hot under the collar sometimes, but I admire the nationalism that is always manifest in all that they do. If ever we could get them really at heart to recognise that the U.S. must be treated as a co-equal and must march in international affairs shoulder to shoulder with her, it would go a long way to straightening out questions between us.*
—RADM Hilary Jones to RADM W. V. Pratt, February 1926

The naval treaty system adopted at Washington in 1922 strengthened the evolved role the General Board had assumed in Navy policy and strategy after World War I. Its policy role interacted with its strategy role. The roles reinforced each other, leading the board to retain responsibility for "questions of naval policy, the size and composition of the fleet, the military characteristics of the various types, the numbers, etc.," as ADM Wainwright noted in 1922.[1] Quite simply, the board's job had become how to match the ends, ways, and means of U.S. maritime strategy as shaped by two contexts: the treaty system and War Plan Orange. The treaty system had two components of interest to the board: its existing limitations on types and numbers of warships and its evolution in a series of follow-on conferences. The General Board became the foremost executor, along with personnel from the Department of State, in preparing and attending the conferences. As such it became a virtual partner with State in the execution of foreign policy—and a not always agreeable one, either. The board then took what the treaties permitted, or portended, and turned them around in its ship characteristic recommendations to SecNav.

The Orange plan shaped strategic and operational contexts, but in 1922 the plan was in flux between what Edward Miller has characterized as the "thrusters" and the "cautionaries."[2] Washington had foreclosed both a Western Pacific bastion as well as any naval buildup in the Philippines. This had hurt the thrusting school strategy as manifested in Orange, and the 1924 version of Orange (WPL-9) included the first cut at what became the cautionary step-by-step strategy with its revolutionary mobile base project.[3] However, the results of the Washington Naval Conference had wounded but not killed the grandiose plan for a single-season naval campaign to defeat Japan at sea. This would take another twelve years.[4] The impact of this on the board is seen in its other primary responsibility of matching fleet design to the existing strategy. As we shall see, despite the ascendancy of the thrusters into the 1930s, the General Board prefigured the adoption of the step-by-step plan with the increasing emphasis in its design hearings upon warships of a scouting fleet with great range and endurance, in addition to its continued plans to build a mobile base to establish somewhere in the central Pacific.[5] The division of the seagoing U.S. fleet into four functional components—battle fleet, scouting fleet, control fleet, and the fleet base force (logistics or "fleet train")—was also an unintended result of Washington. By essentially foreclosing much in the way of major development of the battle fleet, the treaty system ensured that the members of the General Board would put most of their efforts into the other components, especially the scouting and logistic components.[6]

Budgets were a final contributor to the board's advice, from the Washington Naval Conference to the London Naval Conference and the election of Daniels' assistant, Franklin D. Roosevelt (FDR), as president. If the Battle of Paris in 1919 had foretold a drastic decrease in naval construction budgets, the promise of further reductions due to arms limitation drove even more parsimonious spending during what was an era of prosperity prior to the Great Depression. Finally, the Great Depression only increased the desire to restrict naval construction because of President Herbert Hoover's belief that government must set the example in wise fiscal policy. From 1922 to 1929, an era in which one might have expected healthy naval expenditures, one instead finds the General Board and leaders in the Navy watching in horror as they attempted to get presidents and Congress to build to the limits set by the naval treaties of the period. In effect, Japan viewed the treaty limits as a minimum for its naval expenditures, while the United States treated those same limits as maximums. Fiscal neglect led to new ways of thinking, not the least inside the hearings and processes of the General Board.

Josephus Daniels' departure cast a long shadow over his successors during the interwar period. Daniels subordinated the General Board to his own judgment in implementing and executing naval policy for eight years. His departure, along with the results of the Washington Naval Treaty, yielded the unintended consequence that the board dominated naval strategy and policy during this period, especially building policy.[7]

The 1922 U.S. Naval Policy

Navy strategy revolved around the successful application of sea power. Writing as senior member of the General Board, RADM Hilary Jones told Secretary of the Navy Curtis Wilbur that "sea power comprehends combatant ships plus merchant marine, plus bases." This is almost the same language that Schofield used in the epigram at the head of this chapter. Schofield later said much the same thing about the merchant marine as senior member of the executive committee of the General Board in 1928.[8] The elimination of the ability of the United States to construct new bases or to improve (fortify) existing ones in the Western Pacific struck at the heart of this view of sea power.

The General Board's first order of business in 1922 was to publish its first U.S. Naval Policy. President Harding's SecNav, Edwin Denby, directed the board to draft a detailed statement of its post-Washington policy and to link it to its naval construction recommendations.[9] Previously the board had prepared its building recommendations through its hearings process in accordance with NavyRegs. The result was an annual naval construction program summarized as a General Board serial: for example, serial 1055 was for naval construction in 1923. The board's members rightly concluded that the Washington Naval Treaty had codified the "second to none" axiom once and for all. Accordingly, they took advantage of the opportunity afforded by the treaty to support their building recommendations by tying the axiom to the treaty in the 1922 U.S. Naval Policy. It was distributed to the entire Navy to educate it with the terms of the treaty and its impact. The Naval Policy was to be reviewed on an annual basis, but the board anticipated that no substantive changes would be necessary in the short run given that the treaty was fifteen years in duration.[10]

The board's first step in crafting this policy was to canvass Navy organizations for their input. The operational fleet, the bureaus, and the NWC were among the most important organizations queried for their inputs on the "tentative draft U.S. Navy Policy." Since the CNO, ADM Coontz, was a full-time member of the board, he provided OpNav's inputs directly. This process began in late February 1922, the ink barely dry on the various Washington treaties.[11] RADM Moffett, chief of BuAer, responded to the board on 2 March. Moffett did not limit his recommendations and opinions to air matters but commented on all classes of ships. The first subparagraph of his memorandum urged highest priority for modernizing capital ships. Other bureaus responded similarly.[12]

The board applauded the sentiments that led to the success of the Washington Naval Conference, but it immediately recommended building to the absolute limits allowed by the treaty. It further recommended that this construction program be retained until "serious evidence" of a "spirit" of mutual "confidence and frankness" presented itself. Thus was established the board's new internal policy of using the Washington Naval Treaty as the basis for a new ambitious building program for everything except battleships. This was not what the cost-cutting Harding administration wanted to hear, as its strategy assumed that good faith generated by the treaty system would lead to further arms limitation across the military spectrum. The best way to maintain this momentum was to have more conferences, which in turn would result in reduced naval construction. In order to show good faith, current naval construction could be delayed or even put on hold.[13]

The General Board took the opposite position. The board wanted to build every ton permitted and build it quickly. The board's skepticism toward the treaty is exemplified by the last sentence of its U.S. Naval Policy: "The General Board recommends therefore, that steps be taken to keep the uncompleted 1916 capital ships in a state of complete preservation and that plans be in readiness immediately to resume work on this program should it become evident that the treaty will not be ratified within a reasonable period (one year from date of signature) by the signatory powers, and that meanwhile no old capital ships which are still useful be scrapped."[14] The board also recommended that the 5:5:3 ratio "be made the present basis of building effort in all classes of ships."[15] This was consistent with its goal of rectifying the failure at Washington—or perhaps good fortune—to limit auxiliary tonnage by unilaterally observing auxiliary limits and attaining these ratios by the next naval arms limitation conference. By doing this, the board had a benchmark for building auxiliary classes of ships should Japan, for example, start building large numbers of cruisers. The goal, reflected in the U.S. Naval Policy, was to achieve these ratios for modern 10,000-ton cruisers by laying down eight of this class by 1924. This move was justified as "replacement" construction to make it more palatable to the public. However, the foremost priority budget item in the 1922 recommendations for the 1924 fiscal construction plan was the modernization of the existing battleship fleet as allowed by treaty.[16]

The Washington Naval Treaty also allowed both Japan and the United States each to convert two capital ships already under construction into large aircraft carriers. This gave both nations approximate parity in aircraft carrier tonnage, not including the experimental aircraft carriers *Langley* (United States) and *Hosho* (Japan). As a result, the United States was already behind in its 5:3 ratio for carriers. To rectify this problem, the new policy recommended that construction begin at once on a 27,000-ton aircraft carrier. Here we see the genesis of what eventually became, in the late 1930s, the design for the *Essex*-class carriers, although these carriers would not be commissioned until after World War II was under way. One can see that, as predicted by Dudley Knox, naval building competition had already shifted from capital ships to cruisers and carriers. The United States also used the Five-Power Treaty as a pretext to build the most modern ships permissible.[17]

Within the General Board's final published policy was a section titled "Building and Maintenance Policy," which manifestly reflected the treaty system's direct impact on naval construction and innovation:

> To make the capital ship *ratios* the basis of building effort in all classes
>   of fighting ships.
> To make superiority of armament in their class an end in view in the design
>   of all fighting ships.

> To provide for *great radius of action* [emphasis added] in all classes of fighting ships.[18]

It is clear that the board wanted to ensure that it had a written basis for continued naval construction to keep up with Great Britain and ahead of Japan. Second, it emphasized innovation in two areas, "superiority of armament" and cruising radius. The Navy regarded superiority of armament, meaning as large a caliber of gun and as much armor as possible, a priority requirement in the design of its ships. The final general design precept of the building policy emphasized the new importance the board placed on building ships with efficient power plants and large fuel reserves given the lack of shore-based logistics support in the Pacific. This especially showed the effect of the fortification clause. Moreover, the last two items competed with one another, reflecting the tension that existed in ship design throughout the period. The efforts to maximize protection (armor) and striking power (guns and eventually aircraft) conflicted with the requirement for maximum storage space for provisions and fuel for long-range, sustained cruising. The tension between these design characteristics immediately led the Navy to advocate building to the limits of individual ship sizes: 10,000 tons for cruisers, 27,000 tons for aircraft carriers, and large "fleet" submarines. These details were spelled out immediately following the general precepts of the building policy.[19]

A final component of sea power not addressed directly by the policy involved merchant tonnage, which had been a primary source of British concern at the time of the Versailles Conference.[20] The General Board did not think a commensurate adjustment of the merchant marine could compensate for inferiority in one of the other two areas (bases and warships). Its position on an expanded merchant marine was favorable, but it felt it could not compete with Great Britain in this manner given the United States' paucity of overseas bases and the now-inferior size of American flagged commercial shipping compared to Great Britain. It wrote as much in 1925: "Great Britain, by reason of superior strength in merchant marine and bases, remains the dominant sea power. And, therefore, every bilateral limitation in combatant ships [sic] whether in numbers, or size, or power of individual ships, further weakens American sea power relative to British sea power."[21] With the inclusion of Article 19 on the status quo of fortification in the Pacific, the U.S. Navy's leadership perceived that the only factors that offered any hope of equalizing, or ameliorating, sea power were the Washington ratios that allowed it to build and maintain equality of capital ships and carriers with

Great Britain and a superiority over the Japanese. The board continued to maintain this position for the remainder of the interwar period and argued strenuously against any proposals to include merchant ship tonnages into an overall tonnage formula at the naval conferences of the period.[22]

In executing the tasks *it set for itself* in the 1922 policy, the General Board had a profound impact on the development of the U.S. Navy in the interwar period. Its actions and decisions shaped naval innovation in all areas, including naval aviation, amphibious warfare, surface warfare (especially battleships, cruisers, and destroyers), submarine warfare, merchant marine recommendations, floating dry docks, and underway replenishment. Specific programs' details are included simply to highlight the dynamics of the General Board's organizational and institutional relationships as it sought to implement the clauses of various naval treaties, influence policy for upcoming conferences, and (most important) build the most efficient and effective fleet possible to support national policy and existing war plans.

The General Board had arrived at the peak of its organizational power and influence with the publication of the 1922 policy, which had been requested by Denby. The board still included ex officio membership by the CNO, the president of NWC, and the commandant of the Marine Corps. Selection to serve as the secretary was reserved for only the most promising junior officers; for example, Robert Ghormley and Thomas Kinkaid both served in this billet during the interwar period, and the General Board studies provide abundant evidence of their talent for argument, planning, and conceptual thinking. Ghormley later commanded in the South Pacific during the early years of World War II, but after his relief in 1942 during the Guadalcanal campaign, he returned to the General Board. Kinkaid, more famously, became the commander of the Seventh Fleet, sometimes known as "MacArthur's Navy."[23] OpNav remained very much an operational planning staff, although it continued to work closely with both the General Board and the NWC.

After Washington

The General Board's ambitious plan to build a treaty fleet immediately ran afoul of presidential and congressional economizing. The first harbinger of the administration's curtailment of naval construction occurred when Secretary of the Navy Edwin Denby convened the General Board to discuss the language for the next year's (1923) U.S. Naval Policy. In particular, references that tied building to the specific tonnages of other foreign powers were deleted. Further, Denby eliminated the words "to maintain the present extent and efficiency of all naval facilities now existing in Guam and the Philippines" because he believed them to be provocative. Even more ominous was the administration's rejection of the board's strategic view of the world. On 4 December 1922, Denby "orally" informed the board members that they were to strike the following sentence from the "Allocation Policy" of the U.S. Naval Policy: "That the principal naval strategic center of interest in the world today is the Pacific." This deletion was intended to avoid provoking Japan.[24]

At this time the General Board's membership included a combination of particularly talented officers. Its chairman was now RADM William Rodgers, former Asiatic Fleet commander and one of the principal authors of the initial U.S. position for the Washington Naval Conference. Rodgers had first served on the board in 1912 and returned for his final stint there in 1920. He assumed the helm of the board from Badger in September 1921, shortly before the naval arms conference.[25] Joining Rodgers on the board were RADM Joseph Strauss, RADM S. S. Robson, Coontz, RADM Clarence Williams (NWC), MG John LeJeune (commandant of the Marine Corps), CAPT Luke NcNamee (DNI), Frank Schofield, later to take over the war planning division in OpNav, and CAPT (selected for admiral) William Pratt. Pratt had been the only supporter of the Washington Naval Treaty in its final form.[26]

The board membership believed that the United States must build to an absolute 5:3 ratio in all classes of ships. Once this policy was executed—in the form of a healthy construction program tied to the naval construction of the other powers for noncapital ships—then the United States would be in a position of strength, as it had been prior to the Washington Naval Conference. The diplomats then might affect further limitations at another conference. The Harding and Coolidge administrations held that the United States must set a good example by *restraining* naval construction. The Coolidge administration attempted to establish the basis for another arms limitation conference in Washington in 1924 in order to build on the perceived success, and rectify the shortcomings, of the first Washington Conference. Subsequent administrations of the 1920s held true to a policy that attempted to use the treaty system to justify and enact further naval limitation. Presidents Harding, Coolidge, and Hoover reasoned that moderation in U.S. naval construction would spur the other major powers to agree to another conference. Such a conference, if successful, could make unnecessary the ambitious cruiser and carrier programs being advocated by the General Board.[27]

President Harding's death in the summer of 1923 and the subsequent Teapot Dome scandal (which saw Denby forced to resign) temporarily pushed naval limitation to the back burner.[28] But in 1924 President Coolidge focused the General Board on the issue of another limitation conference. He directed his acting Secretary of the Navy, Theodore Roosevelt Jr., to query the General Board about further naval limitation "as soon as conditions in Europe justify such a move."[29] In August Roosevelt outlined four areas that he wanted the board to consider: (1) naval ratios, "if the same formula [should] be used," (2) "methods" for limiting "military or naval aircraft," (3) new "angles under which the submarine could be treated," and (4) merchant marine restrictions.[30] The board could drag its feet when it wanted to, and it was happy to leave the Washington Treaty unmodified, especially since the new initiatives implied further cuts and restrictions. There was only one study on arms limitation between August 1924 and June 1925.[31]

During this period the board also established its agenda for how to frame naval construction as mandated by Washington and the 1922 *Naval Policy*, which despite some revisions under Coolidge and the new SecNav Curtis Wilbur remained the board's primary template for fleet design. Innovative strides were taken in all areas that led to the building of the "treaty fleet."[32] Hearings occurred for all the key programs, from aircraft carriers to submarines and from battleship modernization to floating dry docks.[33]

Almost a year (1925) after Roosevelt's query, the president revived the limitation process, directing Wilbur to again ask the board for its recommendations on the topic of naval limitation. Shortly after Pratt departed the General Board in June 1923 to take command of a battleship division of the fleet, he was replaced as the board's de facto arms limitation expert by RADM Hilary P. Jones, whom historian William Braisted has called "the Navy's recognized authority in arms limitation." Jones took the helm of the board from RADM Strauss in May 1926.[34] The board's first priority was to recommend against any extension of the ten-year capital shipbuilding "holiday." Allowing the "holiday" to end in accordance with the treaty would enable the Navy to start replacing its oldest battleships with newer, more modern vessels. The board again recommended retaining the ratio method "for all types not now limited and limitation of total tonnages in each." Jones took advantage of the occasion to emphasize once again the role that the board's interpretation of sea power played in arms limitation: "As sea power comprehends *combatant ships* plus *merchant marine* plus *bases*, it follows that, in comparison with British sea power, for instance, if the United States and Great Britain arrive at an equality of combatant ships, Great Britain, by reason of superior strength in merchant marine and bases remains the dominant sea power [emphases added]."[35] Wilbur was less than pleased with this advice and brusquely annotated the study with the instruction to "please reconsider this recommendation."[36]

The board's recommendations reflected a deepening pessimism each subsequent year after 1922 about the prospects for building a full-strength treaty navy. In December 1926 the board emphasized the need to build to treaty limits because it was "the only fleet that will provide adequate national defense." However, its assessment of the status of the existing fleet was blunt: "We have not such a fleet at the present time."[37] By the next year, as building continued to be delayed by both parsimony and hopes for further arms reductions, the board's tone became more urgent: "We have fallen behind and continue to fall behind the treaty ratio of 5:5:3 in certain classes of auxiliary combatant craft [cruisers, carriers, and submarines]."[38] Faced with no additional authorizations for new naval construction, the board was forced to trim its fiscal year 1929 building program to what it viewed as absolutely essential. The following list illustrates how the board identified and prioritized the most important programs:

1. Modernize five oil-burning battleships in accordance with previous recommendations of the General Board.
2. Lay down eight 10,000-ton modern cruisers.
3. Lay down three fleet submarines.
4. Lay down one aircraft carrier not to exceed 23,000 tons.
5. Construct aircraft in accordance with five-year building program recommended in reference (e).
6. Lay down one floating dry dock.[39]

Only the most fuel-efficient battleships were chosen for modernization in the following year.[40] Thus the longest "radius of action" ships received the first gun turret modifications and other combat efficiency upgrades needed for battle in the Western Pacific. Likewise, large cruisers and submarines were given priority in order to support the battle fleet and provide long-range reconnaissance.

Floating dry docks for deployment to either the central Pacific or the Philippines reflected the work of the Orange planners and were first identified in the 1923 board serial on naval building policy. The 1924 Orange war plan had included a plan for a "mobile base" as a secret annex. This plan included an ambitious program to build large floating dry docks that could be deployed to undeveloped but promising locations in the Marshall, Caroline, or even Philippine Islands in order to ameliorate the effects of the fortification clause.[41] Up to that time the General Board had not included floating dry docks among the warship programs. Their retention in the pared-down priority list above gave it an equivalency with the warship programs that was remarkable for that day and age.[42]

An emphasis on aviation also reflects the innovative mindset of the members of the General Board. However, the board, desperate to build an aircraft carrier, scaled back the carrier's size to 23,000 tons (from 27,000) in hopes that the smaller cost would meet the aims of Congress and the administration "to keep down appropriations . . . avoiding excessive peaks in expenditure in ensuing years." By November 1927 the board had held another round of hearings and decided that a small 13,800-ton carrier was better than nothing. Subsequent tactical justifications for the smaller carrier size from three organizations—the board, OpNav, and the NWC—read like rationalizations only made after the acceptance of the reality that they could not get a bigger carrier.[43]

Carrier construction illustrates the effect of the interaction of the budget process with the hopes generated by the treaty system for more naval limitation. For example, the language in House Resolution (H.R.) 8687, which authorized naval construction in 1924, clarified the relationship between construction and the treaty system: "That in the event of an international conference for the limitation of naval armaments the President is hereby empowered, in his discretion, to suspend in whole or in part any or all alterations or construction authorized in this Act."[44] The president's budget submissions could also be scaled back during the allocation process by Congress, whose membership included arms-reduction advocates. Legislators often saw no sense in building ships that might be scrapped by a new treaty, as had been the case after Washington.

Ranger, the first carrier built after the conversion of the battlecruisers *Lexington* and *Saratoga*, reflected the attempts by the board to develop a successful budget strategy. Carrier tonnage recommendations show how the budget process—influenced by the administration's plans for more arms limitation—caused the board's members to compromise over time in order to get at least one carrier of any size built.[45] These factors contributed to the extremely small size of the first U.S. aircraft carrier built from the keel up for that purpose—the 13,800-ton *Ranger*. Even so, *Ranger* was not commissioned until 1934, twelve years after the first proposal to build her. These issues also played a role in the construction of key auxiliaries such as destroyers, patrol aircraft (both heavier and lighter than air), and submarines.

The General Board and the Morrow Board

In September 1925 Billy Mitchell again entered into the deliberations of the General Board in a very public way due to tragedy. Mitchell, no longer a general after being reduced to the permanent grade of colonel after World War I, and his allies in Congress and the Army aviation branch still agitated for the creation of an independent air force with control over all aviation, as was the case in Britain.[46] The first episode involved breaking news of a missing flying boat piloted by "aviation pioneer" CDR John Rodgers on 2 September.[47] Ironically, the board was to have held a hearing that day with CDR John "Jack" Towers on naval aviation developments in Britain as a subordinate component to the RAF. Earlier that year the ONI had catalogued the problems of subordinating naval aviation to an air ministry dominated by the RAF, noting that the "anomaly of a service 70% manned by the Navy being directed by [the Air Ministry] is self-apparent."[48] Towers had just returned from naval attaché duty at the American embassy in London and reported for temporary duty with BuAer en route to California to become the executive officer of *Langley*, the Navy's only active carrier. RADM Strauss, chairman of the board, delayed the hearing for one day because of the news about Rodgers' flying boat. The following day brought worse news: the dirigible *Shenandoah* had crashed, killing her pilot and thirteen crewmen at Lakehurst, New Jersey. Despite Rodgers' later showing up safe in Hawaii, these high-profile events caused Mitchell to accuse the Navy and War Department leadership of "incompetency, criminal negligence, and almost treasonable administration of the National Defense."[49]

These incidents served as a catalyst for three developments involving the General Board. First were the ongoing hearings about how naval aviation had fared in Britain with the creation of the RAF. In addition to his testimony to the board, Towers was appointed as an associate board member, delaying his departure for *Langley*. Additionally, Hilary Jones, after Strauss the second-most senior member of the executive committee of the board, was assigned with Towers to a special board investigating the *Shenandoah* accident. Finally, President Coolidge, in addition to initiating court-martial proceedings against Mitchell, also appointed a board to be headed by his friend, banker Dwight Morrow, to look into all aspects of military aviation, including creating an independent air force and a higher-level ministry of defense along British lines to coordinate the actions of the Army, Navy, and a new air force. This last effort tied defense unification to the creation of an independent air force. It was a movement that appeared again after World War II and that again involved the General Board. In 1925 Moffett assigned Towers, with the collusion of the board, to serve as a technical adviser to the Morrow Board. He was a very busy man indeed.[50]

The first order of business was Towers' testimony to Strauss and the board on 3 September. In it, he made it clear that the creation of an independent RAF had had a negative effect on Britain's naval aviation, supporting earlier testimony after World War I that had recommended the Navy keep naval aviation under its control rather than become part of an independent air force.[51] Once the *Shenandoah* board was complete, Towers traveled from Lakehurst, New Jersey, back to Washington to attend the Morrow Board meetings in early October. Initially he served as an expert witness, although he was really an agent for both the General Board and for Moffett.[52] The board, in the meantime, virtually ceased its normal routine for the remainder of 1925 while it supported the department in providing information and witnesses for the Morrow Board. One of the few experts it did hear in October, while the Morrow Board met, was Captain McNamee, the senior naval attaché from London. McNamee also emphasized for the board the difficult situation for naval aviation in Britain due to the very proposals the Morrow Board, at the instigation of Mitchell, was now considering.[53]

Towers ably defended Navy interests, and his recommendations were adopted in toto because Morrow had asked Towers write up the Morrow Board's final position, keeping naval aviation under the Navy.[54] The Morrow Board's final report also repudiated the idea of a separate air force and a unified military establishment under a ministry of defense. It strengthened naval aviation by confirming Towers' recommendations to the General Board to keep aviation units under command of naval aviators; however, this position was Moffett's and most of the General Board's, too. It also created a second assistant secretary of the Navy for aeronautics to ensure air policy received the proper attention.[55]

RADM Hilary Jones and the London Naval Conference

As we have seen, the General Board inherited two mechanisms, fleet design and naval arms limitation, which conferred upon it the primary agency to execute and uphold the Washington Naval Treaty system.[56] Its members influenced Navy policy and programs in a way that was meant to wring every advantage possible allowed under the treaty system. These habits informed its approach to naval conferences at Geneva in 1927 and London in 1930. Board members crafted advice meant to shape future treaty negotiations to the advantage of the United States. They came to perceive themselves as a group of subject matter experts on the clauses of the naval treaties.

By the time of the Geneva Naval Conference in 1927, the internal organization of the General Board had been relatively stable for quite some time. It was composed of an executive committee of twelve officers, up to seven of them admirals, either coming from or going to sea duty. Among these were the four significant ex officio members—the CNO, commandant of the Marine Corps, president of the NWC, and DNI (usually a captain). Also assigned was a secretary (usually a senior commander or a captain), and other officers could be temporarily attached as needed by SecNav. In this period the entire board, ex officio members inclusive, met regularly on the last Tuesday of every month and as directed by SecNav, whereas the executive committee met at 10 a.m. every day Monday through Friday throughout the year except on national holidays.[57]

Despite the existence and increasing influence of the CNO, the General Board remained *authoritative* in the sense that other Navy entities, and often SecNav, considered its advice "the last word" on a particular issue.[58] For example, the correspondence of the interwar period is full of references to "the opinion of the Board" or "the judgment of the Board." These opinions and judgments were reference points that the Secretary of the Navy, CNO, NWC, and the bureaus used in making decisions, initiating programs, and spending money.[59] At the time of the London Naval Treaty, the General Board also perceived itself as an important entity in the formulation of plans, policy, and strategy: "Although the General Board is not established by [congressional] Statute, it has long been recognized in legislation by Congress. In the organization of the Navy Department it has a very definite standing as a personal advisory board to the Secretary of the Navy. Its membership being composed of officers of long experience and special qualification, its advice is available to the Secretary on broad questions of naval policy and specific questions referred to him from time to time."[60]

The hearing process in use since World War I remained a pillar for how the board continued to develop its advice. The board's secretary in 1929, CAPT Robert Ghormley, explained the purpose and initiation of its hearings:

> When the General Board has a subject before it for consideration on which the advice or recommendation of materiel bureaus, other officers of the Department, or civilian experts, is desired, a hearing is held at which these various representatives are requested to be present and present such information as they may have for consideration by the Board. These hearings are recorded, bound kept in the General Board offices, and form an excellent set of reference papers for further use. From such hearings and personal knowledge of the members, the General Board formulates its recommendations to the Secretary.[61]

The board could use the transcribed hearings to either draft a new study or make changes to an existing one. After World War I, the process for the production of the studies differed only slightly from that under Dewey, with transcription of hearings being the major change. Once a draft study had been revised, it was submitted as a numbered "serial" to the Secretary of the Navy. The General Board assigned the numbers in chronological fashion based on when the topic was received by the board. For example, serial 1427 on "The Reduction and Limitation of Armaments" was referred to the board on 31 May 1929. On 8 June 1929, the board spent the entire morning discussing this serial after being briefed by RADM Jones, member at large, concerning his attendance at the Sixth Session of the Preparatory Commission (for naval armaments) at the League of Nations in Geneva. On 8 June the finalized serial was forwarded to SecNav, who directed further action in preparation for the upcoming London Naval Conference in 1930. These numbered serials were retained for reference. Sometimes serials were referred to other Navy organizations (typically the bureaus) for work, or in the Navy terminology of the time "for action."[62]

At the time of the Geneva Conference (1927), the General Board was still organized into the four sections it had developed from committees during World War I. The board's records delineate and detail assignment to those committees of the various members. CDR H. C. Train and RADM Jehu V. Chase constituted the "Fourth Section," which presumably had been the former fourth subcommittee that oversaw base security. Since Train was regularly detached to Geneva as the assistant to Hugh S. Gibson (the civilian chairman of the American delegation) for most of the period, and he was assigned to this section, it stands to reason that this section's duties now included naval arms limitation.[63] There were also technical experts in the bureaus, such as CDR Van Keuren from BuC&R and RADM Moffett, chief of BuAer, who participated routinely in work with the board. In fact, Moffett and Van Keuren can be considered as de facto members of the General Board given their frequent testimony at hearings.[64]

After Washington, the political leaders of the naval powers planned for another conference to address the "unfinished business" from that conference. This was because naval competition had moved to other categories of warships, especially cruisers. The failure to cap cruiser construction had worked in Japan's favor because of the paucity of U.S. construction during the Harding, then Coolidge administration, as we have seen. Japan built as much as she could to further ameliorate the inferior position conferred by the ratio for capital ships, although she too was restrained by her government. Nevertheless, her auxiliary warship construction exceeded that of the United States during the same period (1924–29), especially for submarines and cruisers.[65] The General Board desired to build as many heavy cruisers as possible, a desire that stemmed from its need for long-range ships that could operate independently of their bases for extended periods in the opening phases of operations as outlined in War Plan Orange. However, lagging naval construction—especially for scouting fleet ships such as submarines, cruisers, and aircraft carriers—jeopardized this part of the plan.

Jones' assignment to the leadership of the General Board capped a very successful career in the Navy that included commander in chief of the U.S. Fleet. Jones' personality has often been the subject of historians' invective and used as an explanation for the failure of the United States and Great Britain to come to terms at the Geneva Naval Conference in 1927. However, as both the epigraph to this chapter and more recent scholarship clarify, Jones was not the instinctive or reactionary anglophobe that some have portrayed him.[66] His correspondence prior to the Geneva Conference with another of the experts on naval arms limitation, Pratt of the NWC, reflects an emerging consensus among the senior Navy leadership on the need for a rapprochement and a good working relationship between the two English-speaking maritime powers. Responding to Jones' letter of 1 February 1926, Pratt wrote, "For so long as she [Britain] maintains equality or preponderance *with us* and preponderance of sea strength against any possible European combination of naval powers, she can remain secure in what is to her vital—the economic factor [emphasis added]." Pratt continues in a far more self-interested and realpolitik vein than does Jones in emphasizing that Britain "should never make the mistake of 1776 with America again. Hence equality in cruisers and all else."[67]

Jones attended the League of Nations Preparatory Commission for Disarmament in Geneva as the senior observer of the United States. The league had established this commission to discuss the basis for a comprehensive arms-reduction conference tentatively scheduled in 1927. Jones was assigned despite his and the board's clear differences over naval construction with Secretary of the Navy Wilbur. Jones took with him an agenda Wilbur had asked him to "reconsider" the previous year. Prior to leaving for Geneva, Jones had reflected the frustration of the board in a response to a query from Pratt: "No one has been able to get any information regarding the reasons why the Secretary declines to sign such a precept, nor have any specific modifications to it been suggested."[68]

Jones ably defended U.S. interests at the commission meetings. Forewarned by the U.S. naval attaché in London about British proposals for the conference, Jones emphasized the opposition of his country to any initiatives to abolish the battleship or the submarine.[69] The retention of the battleship has been viewed as evidence of the interwar Navy's obsession with this vessel. If one looks at this issue from the perspective of the General Board at the time, one finds instead that the battleship was viewed as the one element of the fleet that the United States had managed to maintain at close to parity with Great Britain in the wake of the treaty. More important, this ratio gave the United States a 40 percent advantage over the Imperial Japanese Navy in this category of warship. As for the submarine, the board viewed it as essential to strategy in the Pacific based on the courses of action in the Orange plan. Jones had been a party to the extensive board hearings on the topic of fleet submarines in 1924–25 and regarded the submarine as an essential reconnaissance and screening asset for the fleet.[70]

Jones' primary purpose at the 1926 Geneva meetings was to maintain the primacy of the Washington formula in the face of French proposals to limit navies by using a "global tonnage approach." This method simply gave nations a maximum tonnage figure, and they could build as they saw fit within it; a variation on this theme added merchant tonnages to that of the warships. Jones found willing allies in the Japanese and the British naval delegations for maintaining the Washington formula as the correct basis for future conferences—tonnages and ratios by class. He judged seeking a universal consensus from these meetings to be a "hopeless task." However, Jones and the administration held out hope for a successful effort in 1927 outside of the aegis of the League. The State Department called for a three-power conference to meet the next year at Geneva "independent of the League," in part due to Jones' recommendations. Jones was detached from his General Board duties again to visit his British Admiralty counterparts in November 1926. He and the British ended up talking past each other on the issue of cruiser tonnages and ratios due to a British reluctance to reveal their overall cruiser requirements, which were substantially higher than the United States was willing to accept.[71]

The cruiser issue was critical. The British wanted to build large numbers of cruisers to secure the sea lines of communication for their empire. They wanted a cruiser ceiling that was double (600,000 tons) what the General Board had recommended. The board knew they would never get Congress or the president to approve a building program to reach 600,000 tons, calculating that 300,000 tons was probably the maximum they could get authorized for cruisers built and building. Jones continued his shuttle diplomacy and met with British naval representatives again in March 1927 to ascertain if they had become more flexible on the cruiser issue. The British led him to believe they were.[72] The truth of the matter was that the Japanese were the board's, and Jones', real concern. If a much higher cruiser tonnage cap was adopted to accommodate the British, then the Japanese could build to 60 percent of that total figure. The problem was that the Republican administration had no intention to build up to 400,000 tons, never mind 600,000 tons. This meant that the Japanese might actually be able to exceed the United States in cruiser tonnage. It was not Jones' anglophobia driving this position—it was War Plan Orange and the threat posed by the Japanese fleet (Kaigun).[73] It was no accident that Jones' primary aide at the 1928 Geneva Conference was none other than RADM Frank Schofield, fresh from a tour as the chief of the OpNav War Plans Division, which had produced the latest update of War Plan Orange.[74]

The real question, often obscured by the focus on Jones' presumed anglophobia, is why the British seemed so intent on limiting the U.S. Navy's acquisition of 10,000-ton 8-inch-gun cruisers. They had no Japan-like naval threat in the wings as the most likely adversary. Versailles had limited (or more truthfully eliminated) the German navy, and the Washington system limited the French and Italians. So the question remains: who was really the more phobic naval institution, the U.S. Navy or the Royal Navy? Might Jones, as historian William Braisted suggests, have been merely responding to a British animosity—an animosity that made no sense given his regard for the British Empire as one of "two main pillars of civilization" alongside the United States?[75]

Article 19 of the Washington Treaty exacerbated the American position because it established a status quo on building up the U.S. naval bases in the Western Pacific. These bases were barely adequate to maintain the small Asiatic Fleet.[76] The "nonfortification" clause caused the board to build to the treaty limit of 10,000 tons, thereby giving its cruisers as large an operational radius of action as possible in the absence of bases. The British, on the other hand, had less need of these largest cruisers given their mature and extensive system of imperial bases. The Americans could not afford to build to match overall British tonnages.[77] The difference between the U.S. and British positions was profound, as the gap separating the extremes of the two positions was 300,000 tons. Jones and his civilian counterpart, Ambassador Hugh S. Gibson, proceeded to the Geneva Naval Conference in June 1927 with no idea that the difference was so great.[78]

The hope of the U.S. delegation was that a treaty agreement would restrict the other powers' cruiser construction programs. At the same time, the General Board's members regretted the negotiating position their country's anemic construction program had placed them in vis-à-vis Japan and Great Britain. At the time of the Geneva Conference, the United States had begun construction on only two of the eight cruisers first authorized in 1924.[79] Great Britain, on the other hand, had laid down thirteen new cruisers and Japan eight. Clearly, U.S. construction was lagging in this category, as the General Board had repeatedly emphasized in its annual building policy studies. The U.S. plan proposed a cruiser limitation of 300,000 tons for the United States and Great Britain and restricted Japanese to 60 percent or less of this total (180,000 to 150,000 tons). However, the context for the Geneva Conference was completely different from that at Washington in 1921–22. At the first conference, the United States had negotiated from a position of strength—capital ships built and building. However, at Geneva it was in a position of relative inferiority on the numbers of cruisers, both commissioned and under construction. It was thus less likely that either Great Britain or Japan would agree to any substantial limits without significant concessions from the U.S. delegation.[80]

A complete breakdown occurred over the cruiser issue between the U.S. and British delegations. Even if this issue had been resolved, the Japanese delegation, ably led by Admiral Saito Makoto, was already engaged behind the scenes in negotiations with the British over the "inferior" 60 percent cruiser ratio. Vice Navy Minister Osumi Mineo remained "intransigent" and committed to a 70 percent cruiser ratio for Japan and vetoed all compromises proposed by Saito. The Geneva Conference might still have faltered on the Japanese position regarding cruiser tonnages even if the British and Americans had worked out their disagreement.[81]

The breakdown of the naval arms limitation process at Geneva prompted the Coolidge administration to take decisive action. Taking advantage of the impression of bad faith projected by the British, Coolidge proposed, and the House passed, a second "cruiser bill" shortly after the end of the conference. The Senate rejected this bill due to fierce lobbying by powerful peace groups. However, a modified "cruiser bill" was submitted in 1928. This new bill authorized the construction of fifteen additional cruisers and a small aircraft carrier. Even so, the Senate delayed approving the bill until after the 1928 fall elections.[82] This legislation was the first substantial demonstration in more than four years that the United States might build to match its rhetoric about treaty ratios. As such, it constituted a positive step, albeit a stormy one, on the path toward British and American rapprochement. The Americans had real concerns and intended to act on them. They would not be bullied into a position of inferiority vis-à-vis the primary threat—Japan.

Despite the setback at Geneva, the governments of Japan, the United States, and Great Britain remained interested in naval limitation as a means to cut spending. Jones, now retired, was dispatched to Geneva again on behalf of the board—this time for the third meeting of the Preparatory Commission on the Reduction and Limitation of Armaments in early 1928. This forum evolved into the organizational agency through which British and American positions on naval limitation slowly improved. Discussions with the British resolved ship classes and types for the next naval limitation conference, now scheduled for 1930 at London. On the issue of setting ratios for naval "effectives" and trained reserves, the "British Empire and the United States" stood together in mandating that personnel limitation would only be implemented if concurrent tonnage ratios on ships were also agreed to. The two powers also made common cause on the issue of reserve stock and material, the British in the lead while the "American delegation [headed by Jones] viewed with sympathy the British attitude." These sorts of agreements on the peripheral issues boded well for a continuing thaw in the relationship between the American and British naval delegations and occurred before Herbert Hoover's election as president.[83]

Acting in his capacity as an ex officio member of the board, the CNO, ADM C. F. Hughes, endorsed Jones' letter reporting this agreement as the basis for further discussion. This letter also mentioned a French proposal to separate cruisers and destroyers into two separate classes for the purposes of tonnage limitations.[84] The General Board minutes for this period are full of references to Jones as well as to members of the board detached to support him in his ongoing discussions.[85]

Later that year (1928), the board denounced a separate draft Anglo-French proposal that established limits on the 8-inch-gun, 10,000-ton cruisers but left smaller 6-inch-gun cruisers and below unrestricted. This seeming reversal of course by the British can be explained as a move by British diplomats without reference to their naval representatives, since the idea had come out of the British Foreign Office. The board opined that using this proposal as the basis for further limitation would make U.S. participation "fruitless."[86] However, the Anglo-French proposal may have served as the motivation for a new means of measuring cruiser equivalencies nicknamed the "yardstick." The yardstick was a formula developed in the United States, initially by Jones according to one account, to calculate "equivalent" cruiser tonnages. It used "tonnage, age, and gun power" as factors.[87] The sixth meeting of the Preparatory Commission met in April–May 1929 at Geneva with Jones as the U.S. naval representative to diplomat Hugh S. Gibson. Commander Train of the General Board was detached to serve as Gibson's technical adviser. Jones and Train both returned that June with Jones briefing a meeting of board on 4 June 1929. It was at this session that Jones acceded to, and perhaps refined, the idea of the yardstick.[88] All of this high-flying international diplomacy included the board's experts at the forefront; the board had become a virtual appendage of the State Department for such purposes.

Shortly after the meeting, while Jones was briefing the General Board, Secretary of State Henry Stimson notified the U.S. ambassador to Great Britain, Charles G. Dawes, that he had been contacted by the British ambassador about the positive outcome of the meeting in Geneva. The British were proposing a head-to-head meeting between the new prime minister, Ramsay MacDonald, and President Hoover in the fall. Perhaps Stimson was alluding to the General Board when he wrote, "While it was of course impossible that [Hoover and MacDonald] could settle all the details of the naval disarmament matter they might announce that they had reached an agreement in principle leaving the details *to be worked out by others*" [emphasis added]."[89] The "others" had already started working the details and would do so right up until the moment that the prime minister arrived in October.

The change in the willingness of Jones and members of the board (including the CNO) to reach a modus vivendi with Great Britain was given more momentum by President Hoover, one-time delegate to the original Washington Conference and advocate for worldwide disarmament. Hoover wanted to bring the British back into negotiations while accommodating the board's desire to build no fewer than twenty-three 8-inch-gun cruisers. This only makes sense if one identifies the board's motivation as building with Japan in mind as the adversary, not Great Britain. Secretary of State Stimson relayed the utility of the yardstick to the new Secretary of the Navy, Charles F. Adams, in July 1929: "At the moment I am interested only in the results vis-à-vis Great Britain." However, Stimson had alarmed the General Board in the same letter by proposing to include destroyers in yardstick calculations. Britain and the United States had no disagreements over destroyer numbers. The board cited an earlier opinion about the impracticability "to commute combatant value of one class of ships into combatant value of another." They reminded both secretaries that the Anglo-French proposal of the third Preparatory Commission meeting was the basis for naval limitations on which everyone had agreed, that is, that destroyers and cruisers would be limited separately and in no way linked for the upcoming London Naval Conference.[90] The American naval and diplomatic polity wanted a consensus on the cruiser issue in a way acceptable to only the British.

To this end, Hoover presided over a marathon meeting of the General Board, his secretaries for State and Navy, Stimson and Adams, as well as the CNO and Navy undersecretary in the White House on 11 September 1929. Notably absent was anyone from the War Department. The meeting lasted until past midnight as the president and the board attempted to draft a telegram to Prime Minister MacDonald that proposed a yardstick acceptable as a basis for negotiation. The meeting convened again the following day and lasted until past 8:00 p.m. before the final wording laying out the U.S. position on cruisers was approved by the president. The United States proposed to limit itself to twenty-one 8-inch-gun (heavy) cruisers, ten older *Omaha*-class light cruisers, and five new 6-inch-gun (light) cruisers.[91] These light cruisers would eventually include an experimental new type of cruiser with a substantial complement of aircraft that came to be known as the flying deck cruiser. The results were captured in a subsequent presidential memorandum to the General Board on 24 September 1929. The memo included a series of questions as to why the board had modified certain yardstick components in Jones' formula, especially as regarded "gun factor." Jones and Hoover were more closely aligned than Hoover and the General Board as a whole.[92]

A variation on the formula agreed to by the president, Jones, and the board was eventually adopted for use at the London Naval Conference in 1930. It limited both classes of cruisers (8- and 6-inch guns) separately but linked them by the yardstick.[93] This formula, whose technical details need not concern us here, led to rapprochement on the cruiser issue between the United States and Great Britain and laid the ground for success of the London conference. It was an elegant way for the British and Americans to have their cake and eat it too. The British could have more absolute cruiser tonnage but of the smaller light cruiser type, and the United States would have less overall tonnage but more of the heavy cruiser type. Both navies would have the optimal cruiser inventory for what they perceived as their most critical strategic needs. For the British this meant patrolling the sea lanes of the empire; in the U.S. case, it meant screening the fleet for the decisive battle outlined in War Plan Orange.

When MacDonald arrived that October to visit the president, Hoover went to great lengths to ensure that the British and American positions remained aligned by an agreement between the two political heads of state. A series of meetings with MacDonald and their diplomatic advisers from 5–11

October 1929 finalized the joint stance on cruisers by the two great maritime powers. Stimson highlighted the importance of the General Board's role in this process:

> The President presented our proposition to divide the world into two hemispheres in the western one of which the British will not maintain naval or military stations which are a menace to us and in the eastern one of which we shall not maintain such bases which are a menace to them. ... They were willing that the armament should extend only the ability to stand off raids of privateers and to do ordinary police work against internal troubles. Finally, it was decided *that the best way was to have our General Board advise us as to the truth of the British statement* [emphasis added] that their bases are thus innocuous and then to have them agree not to increase them so that they would not become a menace to us.[94]

Stimson also emphasized that any joint statement would reassure the Japanese that Article 19 (the nonfortification clause) of the Washington Naval Treaty remained germane, as did the Four-Power Pact. Stimson later emphasized that the goal was to reduce armaments and to seek a "moral influence and not a military one." In other words, he did not wish to establish a bilateral grand naval alliance that divided the maritime world between Great Britain and the United States.[95] This tortured conciliatory language was aimed at Japan.

For reasons discussed below, the final cruiser numbers agreed to at the London Naval Conference were very similar to the British revised proposal that October: eighteen heavy cruisers and 119,500 tons of light cruiser tonnage of varying ages. At the upcoming conference, the United States would gain more than 20,000 tons extra for its light cruiser tonnage in compensation for the reduction of the three heavy cruisers. A proposal the previous October during Macdonald's visit had outlined much of what would become the American-British compromise.[96] Prior to Macdonald's departure, the General Board delivered its opinion on the "menace" posed by British bases. The memo signed by the president stated, "With the further view to reducing fear and the friction that comes from fear, we have obtained the opinion of our General Board of the navy, that the existing military and naval stations of Great Britain in the Western Hemisphere are not in a condition to be a menace to the U.S." The initial input of the president for the joint statement of the two political heads of state emphasized the hard work of "the past three months [resulting] in such an approximation of views as has warranted the calling of a conference of the naval powers in the belief that at such a conference all views can be reconciled. (Between ourselves we have agreed upon parity, category by category as a great instrument for removing competition between us.)"[97] The language of the British was similarly positive: "The exchange of views on naval reduction has brought the two nations so close to agreement *that the obstacles in the previous conferences . . .* seem now substantially removed [emphasis added]."[98] There is no mention of the yardstick in these formal papers, but it is in the fine print, so to speak. The date for the London conference was set for 21 January 1930.[99]

Despite Jones' good work to date, Hoover hedged his bets by including other personnel in the delegation in order to ensure that compromise would occur. Jones' presence on the delegation was balanced by the inclusion of the former president of the War College, ADM Pratt, still nominally the commander in chief of the U.S. Fleet. Pratt, a known supporter of the treaty system, had the confidence of the head of the delegation, Stimson. Stimson had also consulted with Theodore Roosevelt Jr. Roosevelt had worked closely with Pratt at Washington in 1922 and recommended him as the senior technical adviser. Pratt then handpicked a veritable "dream team" of innovators and leaders to assist him, including:

RADM William Moffett, chief of BuAer
RADM J. R. P. Pringle, president of the NWC and regular attendee at Preparatory Commission meetings from 1928
RADM Harry Yarnell, former chief of BuEng
RADM Arthur J. Hepburn, chief of BuEng and a former and future General Board chairman
CAPT A. H. Van Keuren, from BuC&R
CAPT W. W. Smyth, from BuOrd
CDR H. C. Train, from the General Board
LCDR Jimmy Campbell, Pratt's flag aide[100]

Pratt effectively became the key senior Navy adviser for the conference, and Jones' role in the conference became muted, although he was not without influence. The British representative, Craigie—later Britain's ambassador to Japan—recognized Jones' influence in the U.S. Senate might be an obstacle to ratification as well as noting that Stimson still listened closely to Jones.[101] However, Pratt, a man who could more readily compromise, departed from Jones on the issue of the American delegation's tentative position to accept fewer than twenty-one 8-inch-gun heavy cruisers. Pratt put in writing his disagreement with Jones, arguing to return to the baseline proposal. In this manner Pratt went on the record of siding with the civilian diplomats. Health problems eventually prompted Jones return to the United States before the conclusion of the conference.[102] Jones later opposed the London Naval Treaty for the compromises adopted regarding 14-inch guns for battleship replacements, the extension of the capital shipbuilding holiday, and naval ratios vis-à-vis the Japanese, though not because of anglophobia.[103]

In contrast to the Geneva conference, the London conference almost foundered on the rocks of the hard-line attitude of the Japanese over an inferior ratio to the American fleet, especially the proposed ratio for treaty cruisers.[104] They now had a much larger number of auxiliaries built than the 10:6 ratio proposed by the Americans. The Japanese delegation regarded 70 percent as the absolute minimum for any ratio because they already had 80 percent equivalence to the United States in cruisers, and these were mostly heavy cruisers. When it appeared that the conference might break up with a Japanese withdrawal, Stimson notified Washington that he was fully prepared to proceed, as he had denied earlier in October, with a "two-power" agreement with Great Britain.[105]

At the eleventh hour a compromise was brokered by Senator David Reed of the American delegation with Japan's Ambassador Matsudaira Tsuneo. Under this compromise, the Japanese were given the 70 percent ratio for all auxiliaries except heavy cruisers (which would be 60 percent) and parity in submarines (although not for the higher tonnages they requested). In order to make this bitter pill easier to swallow for the Japanese, the Americans promised not to build three of their heavy cruisers until at least 1936, the year the London Naval Treaty was to expire along with the original Washington Naval Treaty.[106] Perhaps as important in the long run, Great Britain, Japan, and the United States agreed to extend the capital shipbuilding "holiday" to 1936.[107] This last element had been opposed from the start by the General Board but accorded well with President Hoover's commitment to both fiscal restraint and disarmament.[108] The General Board now had to delay its plans to begin building replacements for its battleships until after 1936. This in turn kept the focus of innovation on those classes which could be built, including carriers, submarines, cruisers, and other auxiliaries.

The General Board and the Flying Deck Cruiser

One major result of the Reed-Matsudaira compromise at London involved the increase in the importance of the new class known as "light cruisers." They could be laid down prior to 1936 and still displace as much as 10,000 tons. Not so well known were some interesting codicils about light cruisers in the language of the treaty. The focus on cruisers generated by the treaty system offered the Navy a means to address another problem involving its dearth of naval aviation for Pacific operations.[109]

At Moffett's suggestion, the Navy came to see the smaller class of cruisers in a new light. The still-anemic pace of carrier construction in the United States due to costs had suggested to Moffett that perhaps cruisers were another way to get more aviation into the fleet. Moffett, in reference to light cruiser design, testified two months prior to the London Naval Conference to the board, "I would say briefly that Aeronautics thinks that we should carry as many planes on cruisers as can be done without interfering with the proper mission of the ship." He further recommended these light cruisers carry at least six aircraft, to be launched by catapult.[110] The idea of putting as many airplanes as possible on cruisers was not new. A 1925 War Plans Division study had recommended installing flying decks on all light cruisers.[111] The Navy's plan "to build aircraft carriers at such a rate that the United States shall not fall behind treaty ratios" had been put on hold by the expectations generated by the treaty system.[112] However, because of the London conference, there was an opportunity to redress this paucity of naval aviation in the fleet with a cruiser. A treaty allowance opened the door for long-range 10,000-ton *light* cruisers equipped with as many aircraft as possible—the flying deck cruisers.

Moffett had grown frantic on the issue of carrier introduction by the late 1920s. He had asked the SecNav to recommend that five carriers of the smaller size be built and had only gotten funds approved for one. SecNav duly forwarded Moffett's correspondence to the board. Moffett was coming to believe that spreading aviation around on smaller decks would allow the Navy more operational flexibility in using aircraft carriers. They would not only support the battle fleet but also provide air cover for the increasingly important fleet train, ferry aircraft, and act as principal elements of the scouting fleet. The General Board concurred with most of this reasoning, although it was loath to abandon the big carriers until more evidence was available after experience was gained with the new smaller carrier (*Ranger*) authorized in the Butler "cruiser bill" for the fleet.[113] With only the *Saratoga*, *Lexington*, and the old, slow *Langley*, there were hardly enough carriers to support the battle line. Even with every ton built, Pratt while at the Naval War College was convinced there were not enough carriers to do everything that needed to be done. According to a 1927 annual fleet report, "In a Pacific War, Navy control of the air cannot be attained by any arrangement of tonnage of aircraft carriers within the allotment of 135,000 tons, whether all were of 10,000 tons, or all of 27,000 tons displacement, and that in order to secure this, quantity production will have to be resorted to."[114]

ADM Mark Bristol (as commander in chief, Asiatic Fleet) and Moffett had emphasized the urgent situation of the Asiatic Fleet and its bearing on strategy and were supported in their views by Pratt: "One of the outstanding lessons of the overseas problem played each year is that to advance into a hostile zone the fleet must carry with it an air force that will ensure, *beyond a doubt*, command of the air. This means not only superiority to enemy fleet aircraft but also to his fleet and shore based aircraft combined."[115] A few months after Moffett's memorandum to the Secretary of the Navy, Schofield of the War Plans Division added his voice to the clamor for more carriers. In a memorandum addressing the aircraft-building program, Schofield used the occasion to bluntly state, "I consider the greatest need of naval aviation today is more carriers."[116]

Moffett's memorandum showed that he was not alone in identifying the critical need for naval aviation as an operational means to enable the strategy of the Orange plan by ameliorating the prohibition against basing aviation ashore in the Western Pacific. Buried in Moffett's memo was the following recommendation: "Within 10,000 tons displacement it is practicable to build an aircraft carrying cruiser which can operate upward of 40 planes of the intermediate or smaller types. Such a complement of planes can be used alternately on gunnery observation, tactical scouting, fighting [air defense], smoke laying or bombing missions with bombs carrying at least 400 pounds of explosive."[117] Here was the outline for a new type of naval vessel—a hybrid cruiser/aircraft carrier. Moffett was clearly worried that the Japanese might take this path given their ambitious cruiser construction programs.

Moffett's solution was a new vessel with the 10,000-ton displacement of a cruiser that carried substantial numbers of aircraft. After the extreme disappointments and delays of the late 1920s, the board held hearings on light cruiser design in November 1929 prior to the London conference. ADM Moffett was asked for his views on how many planes the new light cruisers recently authorized in the Butler cruiser bill should have. He responded that the "minimum number should be six." Interestingly, after an extended discussion of how these planes were to be positioned on board the ship, the transcript noted, "At this point a discussion took place not for the record." Moffett, who was to be a member of the London conference delegation, may have shared his flying deck cruiser ideas with the board. The board certainly had access to these views via Moffett's secret correspondence of the previous year, in which he first broached the idea. The nature of the topic, and the plan to propose a new class of ship at London, may have been viewed as too sensitive to commit to the hearing transcript.[118]

At the same time, Moffett lobbied the General Board to recommend formally that the London delegation propose "transferring these carriers [*Lexington* and *Saratoga*] to the experimental class" of carriers allowed by the Five-Power Treaty. In this way the United States could replace these two carriers with four "16,500-ton carriers" that had "several advantages over" the larger carriers. Moffett's purpose here was to try to retain the large ships while building even more of the smaller ones. The board forwarded Moffett's advice and endorsed it by recommending that should the naval conference in London advocate a reduction in overall carrier tonnage "below 135,000, the General Board is of the opinion that the United States should insist that the *Saratoga* and *Lexington* be placed in the experimental class as a necessary provision for agreement." However, their bottom line was that treaty allowances for carrier tonnage should not be decreased under any circumstances since the "United States must conduct any naval war at greater distance from home than would be the case of other Powers signatory to the Washington Treaty."[119]

Fleet aviation needs could be augmented by cruisers with up to twelve aircraft on board. In later hearings before the General Board, the numbers went as high as forty aircraft. Additionally, Fleet Problem IX in 1929 had emphasized a need for more aviation vessels. Limited to two large aircraft carriers, the fleet could lose most of its aviation support if either of these ships were sunk or damaged. All the eggs were in two baskets. Flying deck cruisers would spread the risk across the fleet and ensure that it was not so vulnerable to the loss of its aviation due to the sinking of the precious carriers.[120] With all this in mind, Moffett inserted the idea for a flying deck cruiser into the language of the 1930 London Naval Treaty. Such a ship could serve multiple purposes. First, it would get naval aviation into the fleet by employing a different class of ship—ships that could carry more than just two or three planes but not as many as the larger carriers. Such ships promised operational flexibility because aviation would be distributed more evenly throughout the fleet. Moffett jotted off a note to the design engineer, Van Keuren from the Bureau of Construction and Repair, who was also at the conference: "Aircraft will settle next war. Don't care how many surface vessels we build. The more the other nations build, the less money they will have for aircraft. Friday Mar 21st proposed to Captain VanKeuren [sic] he get up a design for a 6-inch-gun cruiser that would have a landing deck for aircraft."[121]

Using this opportunity, Moffett proposed treaty language that created a new "loophole" using two separate articles. Article 3 of the London Naval Treaty prevented the counting of "landing-on or flying-off platforms" against a nation's overall carrier tonnage "provided such vessel was not designed or adapted exclusively as an aircraft carrier." Also, Article 16, Part 3 of the treaty stipulated that "not more than twenty-five percent of the allowed total tonnage in the cruiser category may be fitted with a landing-on platform or deck for aircraft."[122]

This loophole may have in fact been the key to agreement by the U.S. naval delegates, especially ADM Hepburn, ADM Pringle, ADM Yarnell, and CNO Pratt, to accept the lower heavy cruiser number (eighteen) proposed by the British. This was because they believed the flying deck cruiser (which could be counted as a light cruiser) was probably superior in what they called "combat power." Certainly Moffett believed as much, as the quotation above makes clear. Later, Pratt and many other naval officers, if they were not yet convinced the design to have more "combat power," came to believe it did after the ratification of the London Naval Treaty. This happened through the mechanism of a series of hearings by the General Board. By 1932 a design had been approved and money to build it allocated by Congress.[123] At the same time, the British were unconvinced (or maybe oblivious) to the potential of the concept.[124] They and the Japanese allowed the Americans to insert the language allowing for conversion of heavy cruiser tonnage to light cruiser tonnage in Article 18 and language in Article 16 allowing the Americans to convert that tonnage to the flying deck type.[125]

The aviation situation as perceived by Navy leaders in 1930 was urgent. The Navy had only just begun to experiment with the big carriers *Saratoga* and *Lexington*. The General Board was still undecided as to the utility of large carriers versus small carriers. Also, the one thing everyone in the Navy did agree on was that there were not enough aviation ships in the fleet, be they carriers, aircraft tenders, or flying deck cruisers. Moffett's purpose was congruent with the consensus in the Navy. Although the Navy could no longer purposefully build carriers under 10,000 tons because of the London Naval Treaty, it could build flying deck ships as long as they looked like, and were armed as, light cruisers. Moffett's view carried with it certain risks. First and foremost was the risk that in building flying deck ships other aviation ships might not get built. Clearly, Moffett wanted aircraft carriers as well. In addition, the concept, however promising, remained unproven until one of these ships could be built and tested with the fleet.[126] Pratt, addressing the General Board after the London Naval Conference, warned, "We have to be very careful. This ship is a cruiser first according to the treaty. Otherwise you will have Japan and every other country on your neck."[127]

Because the light cruiser was smaller and cheaper per unit, it was hoped more of them could be built than had been the case with aircraft carriers. More cruisers meant that they could be assigned to provide, or at least dispute, command of the air in the remote areas of the Pacific and provide air cover for those assets for which larger carriers were considered inappropriate (such as the fleet train or portions of the scouting forces). As a cruiser, the ship could also perform all those functions—screening, reconnaissance, and commerce raiding—at which cruisers excelled. And it could do these missions, and new ones such as convoy protection and antisubmarine warfare, in ways that aviation would only enhance because of its operational reach.[128] Finally, it would be a "treaty" ship, one that naval officers could point to in the language of a naval limitation treaty in order to justify construction. It stood a good chance of being constructed by stingy administrations and Congress because it was relatively inexpensive. As it turned out, Congress authorized the construction of the flying deck cruiser before the Navy was ready to build it.[129] It was only by the "slimmest of circumstances" that the United States did not build the prototypes for the flying deck class codified and allowed for by the London Naval Treaty. The great irony is that this concept—never built—*convinced* the U.S. naval delegation to some degree to accept the cruiser compromises at London.[130]

The Japanese, however, did lay down scouting cruisers with an increased floatplane complement beginning in 1934—the *Tone* class.[131] This they did as a direct result of the London Naval Treaty flying-deck language. However, the *Tones* were eventually armed with 8-inch rather than 6-inch guns.

In the United States, the treaty was roundly criticized and the ratification process was not nearly as smooth as it had been for the Washington Naval Treaty. The General Board and many in the Navy publicly opposed it. Many in the Navy blamed ADM Pratt, and when Pratt became CNO, his predecessor, ADM C. F. Hughes, reputedly refused to shake hands with him at the change of command ceremony. However, some historians identify a new spirit of cooperation between the United States and Great Britain as emerging from the London conference. Certainly the pre-London level of effort for accord between the two nations on the part of the Hoover administration, as well as the installation of the anglophilic and treaty-friendly Pratt as CNO after, did much to pave the way for increased U.S.-British amity.

The following exchange between Admiral Sir Roger J. B. Keyes and a confidant of Franklin Delano Roosevelt over lunch in March 1934 captures the new spirit in all its complexity:

> [ADM Keyes said,] "I agree that you are not a prospective enemy, but (and he smiled) you are a prospective bully." We all laughed and the Admiral continued, "You know you did object to some of our naval policies at the beginning of the last war and greater naval strength gives weight to such objections"—" to answer your question I think we should approve of your building what you like so long as we may do the same." ... The net impression which I gained from this conversation was one of great friendliness toward the U.S.A., which this letter has not fully expressed."[132]

Shortly thereafter, following naval conversations in June and July with British officials in London, the General Board reported to the Secretary of the Navy: "The British officials were most cordial and friendly and on every occasion evidenced their desire for cooperation with the United States, both in matters affecting the 1935 Conference [on naval armaments in London] and, so far as might be practicable, in general political affairs, such as a common understanding with reference to the Orient."[133]

Many observers identify the London Naval Treaty as the key turning point in Japan's path to aggressive militarism in the 1930s.[134] Far fewer have noticed that it was also, perhaps, the high point in the influence of the cadre of General Board diplomat-officers before World War II. The board's role in improving Anglo-American relations in this period can now be seen as beneficial—in contrast to the supposed anglophobia of earlier narratives.

The period immediately after London, as Pratt took over as CNO with his fellow travelers such as Mark Bristol (see chapter 5) as chairman of the General Board and Harris Laning at the NWC, proved among the most innovative periods in U.S. naval history. Fundamental decisions were made, ironically not supported by the parsimonious Hoover administration, that would have to wait until 1933 and the return of Franklin Roosevelt to a position of influence over the Navy. Hoover's administration, always waiting for one more arms conference to reduce warship tonnage and construction, did not lay down one keel for a warship. It did, however, build a small floating dry dock for submarines and destroyers, one that had been conceived and deliberated in the many board hearings in the 1920s and early 1930s.[135] Parsimony had forced the board, and soon most of the Navy, to consider how to sustain a long naval campaign in the Pacific should war come. This temporal poverty of resources enabled new thinking that soon bore rich fruit.

CHAPTER 8

Innovation and Decline, 1932–41

I think myself that it is rather immaterial whether the Chief of Naval Operations is on the General Board or whether he is out of the General Board. I haven't given the matter much thought, but there are many who think that he is stronger out of it. . . . His position is a stronger position if he is not on the General Board, and I dare say that is correct.

—ADM William V. Pratt, 1931

We might technically date the decline of the General Board in the period from the influence imparted to it by the treaty system to 1931, when the Chief of Naval Operations, ADM William V. Pratt, moved to abolish the board's ex officio memberships.[1] Pratt did not have the authority to make this decision; such an action was the prerogative of the Secretary of the Navy, at the time Charles F. Adams. However, it is an indication of the growth in the power and influence of the CNO, and Pratt's own immense prestige, that he did instigate this reorganization of the board in the last year of the Hoover administration. After his inauguration, President Franklin D. Roosevelt turned on the spigot for naval construction, which led to a continuing expansion of the CNO's power commensurate with the growth of the treaty fleet.[2] Too, with the CNO now "out of the loop" as to the deliberations of the board (unless invited to offer testimony at a hearing), subsequent CNOs became more remote in their loyalty and understanding of the board and its value. Finally, FDR acted as his own SecNav for much of this period, using his appointee, Claude A. Swanson, as a cipher of sorts. Swanson was one of the more forgettable, but long-serving, SecNavs, and under him, CNOs grew in power while the General Board's influence waned, albeit slowly. When world war arrived again in 1941, just as in World

War I, the board saw its primary functions subordinated and delegated to other agencies for the duration of the conflict, this time for almost four years, not eighteen months. This chapter will recount that trajectory of decline and conclude with a discussion of the overall impact of the General Board on innovation in the interwar period.

The Board and the Treaty System after London

After the 1930 London Naval Conference, the prospects for naval construction in the United States only worsened. This was due to two related factors. Foremost was the deepening economic depression that so bedeviled Herbert Hoover's presidency. Hoover adopted a policy of government "economy" involving across-the-board cuts, including the Navy. Hoover had proposed "laying up" (temporarily inactivating) either one or both of the expensive-to-operate U.S. carriers *Saratoga* and *Lexington* before the stock market crash. Things only got worse after 1929.[3] Related to this was Hoover's sincere desire for disarmament through arms reductions. It was an article of faith for Hoover that arms reductions led to peace. Thus arms reductions and cuts in naval expenditures were mutually supporting policies. A memorandum from the office of the SecNav to the president captured the mood and the lingering resentment over the London Naval Treaty ratification fight: "The Navy is facing the most critical situation in its history. Upon the decision reached within the next few weeks depends the entire future of the naval defense. Formulation of a national naval policy in lieu of the one scrapped by the London Conference is irrevocably included in the building program now under consideration.... The bitterness of the fight against the London Treaty is not forgotten."[4]

The memorandum further proposed that a "special board" be convened. Pratt and the General Board were specifically rejected as the forum for a fresh look at this problem. In the meantime, Secretary of the Navy Adams directed the General Board to write a new U.S. Naval Policy based on the London Naval Treaty. Instead, the board submitted its recommendations to build the Navy up to allowed limits by the end of 1936 based on "the Limitation of Armaments of 1922 and 1930." The board also emphasized the now-limited role of the battleships in its considerations—battleship modernization was a funded program, and the focus had switched to aircraft carriers, cruisers, and submarines. However, fiscal realities also played a negative role. The General Board dropped the large floating dry dock from its building plan priority list so it could spend its limited funds on building warships and combat aircraft.[5]

In the meantime, the administration pressed on with its policies, further delaying construction of the new ships allowed under the London Naval Treaty and authorized by Congress until after the League of Nations disarmament conference in Geneva in 1932. One initiative proposed by Hoover and Secretary of State Stimson offered not to increase naval construction for a year from November 1931. The General Board felt that this agreement need not prevent the construction of already approved ships. However, Hoover disagreed and interpreted the agreement as preventing "new" construction, even if already authorized prior to the agreement. To make things worse, the Hoover administration extended the building "truce" another four months. Hoover laid down no new ships, as a result of this last extension, during his entire term.[6]

The board's great fear was that the 1932 Geneva Disarmament Conference would reduce the 35,000-ton limit for battleships codified at Washington and reaffirmed at London. It had already seen battleship gun size reduced successfully from 16 inches to 14 at London (see chapter 7). World events, set in motion in part by Japan's invasion and conquest of Manchuria, undermined the 1932 conference. Hoover's sweeping proposals were meaningless in the face of Japan's flouting of international opinion. The conference was eventually stalemated, not only due to Japanese defiance and intransigence but also over the increasingly disruptive issue of how to accommodate Germany, which was intent on repudiating the naval restrictions of the Treaty of Versailles and rearming.[7] Hoover sought the board's advice for a naval arms-limitation meeting in late 1932. A formal conference was tentatively scheduled for London in 1935, on the eve of the expiration of both the Washington and London treaties. This request was yet another attempt by Hoover to try to get the arms-reduction movement and the treaty system back on track. Hoover's policies, especially his response to the Great Depression, were repudiated at the polls with the election of Franklin D. Roosevelt.[8]

The General Board did not deliver its opinion on further naval arms limitation until after the election of FDR. The timing of the delivery of the thirty-three-page response—verbose by General Board standards—suggests much. Perhaps the newly elected president would heed the board in a way that his predecessor had not about the necessity of building the fleet up to allowed treaty limits. To this end the board reviewed in laborious detail the advent and course of the treaty system to 1932. The study closed ominously: "Present preparedness must not be sacrificed to an illusory future readiness. National emergencies cannot be foreseen and must be met by existing forces." These words were for Roosevelt, not Hoover.[9]

The new president did not disappoint the board's members, but neither did he meet all of their expectations. FDR had been a very active assistant secretary under Daniels and shared a common understanding of sea power with the board's members. He made no secret of his preference for the Navy, even "unofficially" saying he "loved the United States Navy more than any other branch of our government" in his closing for a commencement speech at Annapolis in 1933.[10] However, Roosevelt was also serious about continuing the process of arms limitation. He believed he could have both sea power and the political rewards that came with arms limitation by adopting a program to build the fleet to treaty limits. Nonetheless, he wrote the Navy no "blank checks" and held out great hopes for the 1935 conference in London.

Roosevelt also brought new attitudes to the equation: friendship, even partnership, with Great Britain, and a willingness to build ships. Two key pieces of legislation in 1934 marked a turning point as the Japanese were withdrawing from the League of Nations: the implementation of the National Industrial Recovery Act (NIRA), which included $238 million for naval construction, and the first Vinson-Trammel naval bill.[11] The Vinson legislation committed Congress toward a program that would achieve the Navy's targets for numbers and classes of ships for a treaty navy over the next ten years. Roosevelt was able to address two problems with one solution—providing much-needed jobs and building a treaty navy that could both deter Japanese aggression in the Pacific and defend U.S. territory in the event of war. Ironically, the admiral who had been most criticized within the service for his perceived part in stunting the treaty navy's growth—William V. Pratt—oversaw building the recommendations these events funded, though they came to fruition only after he had retired.[12]

Pratt and the 1932 Reorganization of the General Board

In March 1932 the Secretary of the Navy reorganized the General Board via the tried-and-true method of a change to U.S. Navy Regulations.[13] The change eliminated the ex officio memberships—those of the CNO, president of the NWC, commandant of the Marine Corps, and DNI. The executive committee became the standing membership of the board. CNO Pratt requested that the board continue to forward its advice to the CNO as well as to the Secretary of the Navy.[14]

The push toward this move began with Pratt, shortly after he had assumed the office of CNO on 17 September 1930.[15] At the key board hearing that first broached the topic in June 1931, RADM F. H. Clark (chief of OpNav's Training Division) made it clear that Pratt had "been left off for the [past] year" in the deliberations of the board. This meant that the CNO had not attended the monthly meetings specified in NavyRegs. RADM Mark Bristol, the chairman of the executive committee, made it clear that he, the SecNav, Pratt, and the commandant of the Marine Corps, MajGen Ben Fuller, had previously discussed this issue and decided to eliminate the ex officio memberships. In a subsequent meeting, it was decided to leave the CNO on the General Board. Evidently this decision was not final, however, and the board was directed to hold a hearing on the topic with Pratt as the primary witness.[16]

The hearing held on 30 June 1931 soon brought to light Pratt's role more completely in advocating the change. The importance of the meeting was underscored by the fact that all the major bureau chiefs attended the meeting, along with representatives from SecNav, the Assistant CNO, RADM William Sexton, and the admirals, such as Clark, who were senior division heads under the CNO. Pratt outlined the issue at stake best in his opening comments for the board and all assembled: "This is a rather important subject . . . because it treats of the relations which should exist between the Chief of Naval Operations and the General Board, the General Board and the Secretary, and, incidentally, the position of the Chief of Naval Operations relative to the General Board, the Secretary, and the President [of the United States]."[17] Pratt then cut to the heart of the matter, proposing a change to remove the CNO along with the other ex officio memberships. He argued this would make his a "stronger position if he is not on the General Board" and went on to emphasize that the board, too, "must be safeguarded," adding that the "General Board is the Secretary's board and should act as a balance wheel for the Navy." Bristol subsequently agreed with this position.[18]

Pratt's action in instigating this change has sometimes been regarded as an action taken to reduce the influence of the board.[19] As Pratt's testimony

ADM Hilary P. Jones on the deck of the battleship USS *Pennsylvania*, c. 1923. Jones was an expert on naval arms limitation and served as the de facto leader of the General Board during the difficult period of the 1920s. His last hurrah was the London Naval Conference of 1930, by which time he had lost much of his influence on the board and in the Navy to the rising star of ADM William V. Pratt. *Naval Historical Foundation, Naval History and Heritage Command*

makes clear, the reorganization of the board was not intended so much to give additional power to the CNO and OpNav as it was to ensure that the board's advice was not unduly influenced by a powerful CNO, nor the CNO in turn constrained by the board. It also meant the CNO could freely give his advice and comment without contradicting the opinion of a body he also served on.

Following Bristol's lead, the board as well as SecNav must have agreed, because in March 1932 the ex officio members departed per a change to NavyRegs. Even after these changes, the former ex officio members could, and did, provide testimony and written input to the board.[20] However, on balance, this was to be a key factor in the slow decline of the influence of the board. Lost, too, were the direct inputs and participation of the Naval War College, the commandant of the Marine Corps, and ONI. The NWC migrated further away from its war-planning function and roots in 1934 as it passed from CNO control to that of the Bureau of Navigation. The long-term impact on the college must be judged as negative. By 1940 we find the NWC's president writing to the senior member of the board asking to be placed "on the mailing list" for copies of the board's "military requirements" for various new construction warships. His goal was to use the best available data in war gaming at the college. The board gladly acceded to this request, but it would not have been necessary in the first place had someone from the NWC retained membership on the board.[21] Meanwhile, the CNO's staff continued to grow in size, so that by 1937 it included eleven different divisions. The coming of war in Europe would only accelerate this growth. During the same period, the size of the General Board remained static at its new smaller size (an average of about seven members), about the size it had been prior to the aide system.[22]

The End of the Treaty System

By the end of 1934, the handwriting was on the wall for the treaty system. The Japanese insisted that the basis for any future naval limitation be parity with the United States and Great Britain. When the United States refused to give this assurance in informal preconference discussions, the Japanese gave a formal two-year notification, as specified in the Washington and London Treaties, of their repudiation of these treaties on 1 January 1937. The Vinson-Trammel Act and NIRA had also contributed to the Japanese resolve to leave the system.[23] President Roosevelt hoped the Japanese could be convinced to rejoin the system at the upcoming London Conference, now scheduled for December 1935.

The Japanese did return to the table, but with their position fixed at naval parity. Great Britain was willing to compromise, but the U.S. delegation was firm and the Japanese withdrew from the conference early, in January 1936. France, Great Britain, and the United States signed a treaty of naval limitation; however, the treaty offered numerous waivers for building in excess of limits by leaving intact the "escalator" functions of the original naval treaties.[24] If Japan exceeded tonnage or gun-caliber limits, the other powers were authorized to exceed treaty limits. In 1936 the United States did precisely this, as advised by the General Board, in its design for the *North Carolina*-class battleships. The 1935 London Naval Treaty had limited new battleships to 14-inch guns. However, the president delayed approval of the 16-inch guns allowed by the "escalator clause" until July 1937, when the Japanese confirmed their intent to build 16-inch-gun battleships. This action effectively ended U.S. participation in the treaty system.[25]

The end of the treaty system in 1936 spelled the demise of the increased power and influence the General Board had held since the Washington Naval Treaty in 1922. Again, the irony that the board had opposed a system of naval limitations that actually worked to the board's advantage during the interwar period must be pointed out. With the end of the treaty system, the board's foreign policy influence did not disappear, but it diminished greatly.

As an aside about the analytical habits encouraged by the arms limitation process in the General Board during this period, a particularly telling example can be found in meeting notes prepared for the Secretary of the Navy prior to the second London Naval Conference in 1935 by the board on the civilian members of the delegation. Secretary of the Board Thomas Kinkaid (later commander of Seventh Fleet in World War II) prepared an addendum for the SecNav on serial 1640 in late 1934 with vitae for the various members of the delegation. For example, of member Allan Dulles, later inaugural director of the Central Intelligence Agency, Kinkaid wrote:

> Often called in by State Department for conference work, ostensibly as Legal Adviser but actually does most of the drafting.... Has the complete confidence of Norman Davis; an extremely hard worker of the aggressive belligerent type; very ambitious; takes charge on all occasions; internationally minded; ... frequently publishes articles in ... *Foreign Affairs*; tries without success to understand the point of view

of military and naval advisers; will cooperate up to a certain point, then breaks off completely and nothing can turn him from his purposes; sympathizes with British demand for smaller capital ships; will not support the Navy Department against British contentions regarding cruisers; dangerous.[26]

This tells one much about Kinkaid's powers of analysis, and perhaps prescience, in this particular case, but it also highlights the analytical depth and range of the board and the sort of advice it forwarded to civilian SecNavs.

The General Board and Naval Innovation in the Interwar Period

After the Washington Conference, the General Board was forced to think in terms of fighting a distant naval war in the absence of any significant bases in the projected theater of operations. The London Conference only reaffirmed this paradigm. The Navy's traditional concept of sea power, and the challenge posed to it by the nonfortification clause of the Washington Naval Treaty, determined the way in which innovation occurred in the interwar Navy. This caused the General Board to channel its efforts into emphasizing the seagoing fleet as the basis of U.S. sea power in the Western Pacific. However, once a battleship modernization program was authorized, the board's focus—and that of the other major Navy organizations, such as the NWC and OpNav—came to center on the construction of other classes of ships and aircraft.[27] These designs in turn were maximized to compensate for a lack of overseas bases.

As discussed in chapter 6, the General Board submitted a comprehensive plan reflected in the 1922 U.S. Naval Policy for a new kind of fleet suited to the treaty system that reflected these design considerations. In addition to battleship modernization, the treaty fleet included long-range heavy (and later light) cruisers, new destroyer designs, large fleet submarines, a one-thousand-plane naval air force, and aircraft carriers. The air programs spurred on by the efforts of RADM Moffett, the head of BuAer, emphasized embarking as much aviation as possible on all the ships of the fleet. This in turn led to creative exploratory hearings and innovative designs.[28]

The Navy had a standard method for strategic and operational problem solving that it taught to its officer corps and practiced at the NWC. As outlined by RADM Sims in his speech at the reopening of the college after World War I, the method focused on war gaming abetted by a system derived from the Prussians involving analyses with a view to producing an "estimate of the situation." This estimate was followed by development of courses of action that were then war-gamed "in-house." These war games were always followed by rigorous after-action reviews that included comments by both umpires (often senior faculty) as well as representatives from outside the college, such as BuAer (after 1922). In the 1927 records of a NWC game, one finds extensive critiques of student performance, including remarks by CAPT Harry Yarnell and a critique of air operations by LT Forrest P. Sherman.[29]

The War Plans Division of OpNav used the fortification clause as an integral consideration in its planning process for Orange courses of action. These plans were then forwarded to the fleet, the Joint Army-Navy Board, and the Naval War College for testing and refinement. The General Board received copies for its records as well and referenced them in its studies and hearings. The Navy also used the fleet to practice and test courses of action developed by the college, the OpNav planners, and on occasion the General Board, as well as those the fleet developed on its own. Officially called "fleet problems," these were annual fleet exercises that addressed a specific set of operational and strategic problems, usually those associated with War Plan Orange. The exercises were often held during the summer and addressed new tactics, techniques, and platforms. For example, Fleet Problem IX (1929) addressed the tactical and operational use of the new large carriers *Lexington* and *Saratoga* within the strategic context of a defense of the Panama Canal.[30]

The chairmen of the executive committee of the board also attempted to achieve advantages within the treaty system by altering or adding language to proposals for arms limitation that were favorable to the strategic situation of the United States. This was the case with the flying deck cruiser (see chapter 7). The board was often frustrated in its efforts to leverage the treaty system as a building rationale for most of the period, tending to lose rather than gain ground in naval construction, but designs proceeded apace. This in turn contributed to innovation by forcing the members of the board to address problems differently than they had in the past. Building more battleships (as in 1916) and enhancing or expanding overseas bases (the attempt to build up Guam in 1919) were no longer options. Even the money to maintain the existing facilities was cut back during the fiscal crises of 1931 and 1932. What follows are summations of innovative influence by the General Board for specific programs during the interwar period.

The Mobile Base, Fleet Train, and Amphibious Warfare

The Navy planned to build a mobile base to support War Plan Orange, which had evolved from the earliest work of the board (under Taylor) on advanced bases in immature theaters. The latest plans devised in the 1920s included massive dry docks that could be floated in separate pieces through the Panama Canal and deployed to the far reaches of the Pacific. The fleet would bring its bases with it. The mobile base plan included not only floating dry docks but identification of the necessary, and huge, shipping needs for logistics and troops movements. This plan was a readiness plan for peacetime versus an operational plan for off-the-shelf execution in wartime. Once war began, the mobile base was to be incorporated into the U.S. Fleet Train as a full-fledged member of the operational Navy.[31]

The area of greatest neglect in the board's work in this area involved oilers and underway replenishment. As early as 1924, the criticality of underway replenishment of fuel had been demonstrated during the annual fleet problem, as well as the first demonstration of the abeam (alongside) method for doing this.[32] However, the board held no direct hearings on this vital component of fleet operations and design, deferring to the fleet commanders and CNO. The explanation may be that limited funds were perceived as more necessary for the tooth than the tail, a problem that still afflicts military professionals today. It may also reflect how naval line officers often had more interest in operational planning but tended to neglect or waive certain logistical requirements.[33] Despite ADM Chester Nimitz's famous quotation that acknowledges naval leaders' awareness of these issues in the fleet problems and war games, these organizations did little better than the board, at least until 1938, in getting need matched to naval construction.[34]

Also reflective of the General Board's plan to address the lack of Pacific bases was the Marine Corps' simultaneous development of amphibious warfare doctrine to seize bases for the Navy as it fought its way across the Pacific. This doctrine was finally published as the *Tentative Landing Operations Manual* in 1934.[35] These measures reflect the influence of the treaty, the fortification clause, and the policy recommendations of the General Board. As important to seizing advanced bases in this doctrine was their defense. For example, more than half of Maj Earl H. Ellis' famous "Advanced Base Operations in Micronesia" was devoted to defense and not offense. This doctrine also supported the new view of sea power, which used Marines for

VADM William V. Pratt, shown here in a portrait taken on board ship and inscribed by Pratt to his son, Billy, January 1928. Pratt was one of the most progressive and "air-minded" admirals in the Navy, and in 1932 he removed the ex officio members (such as the CNO and the commandant of the Marine Corps) from the General Board in an attempt to make its advice more independent. The result was a slow decline in the board's influence. *Naval Historical Foundation, Admiral William V. Pratt Collection, Naval History and Heritage Command*

defense, as at Guadalcanal (1942) and Bougainville (1943), to protect both undefended and seized terrain from the enemy and thereby enable further power projection by sea and air. The weakness in this area involved the lack of development and experimentation with specialized assault shipping and landing craft of the type that became common during World War II.[36]

Battleships

Because of the capital-ship-building "holiday" of ten years (later extended to fifteen), the Navy was forced to focus on how to improve its retained battleships as much as possible. It combined lessons the General Board and Navy learned by exploiting the German navy's damage-control doctrine with those learned in tests after World War I to yield the battleship modernization program. Liberally interpreting the Washington Naval Treaty, board members believed improving propulsion systems on battleships did not constitute "reconstruction" as defined in the original document. Thus the board was able to upgrade both propulsion and damage-control systems on U.S. battleships during the building holiday established by the treaty system.[37]

In 1931, the board commissioned a special study by CDR E. M. Williams that argued against any modification of the Washington capital-ship limits in anticipation of the aforementioned Geneva talks in 1932. In the section of the study titled "Arguments in Support of Reasons for the Decision," primacy was given to the 35,000-ton displacement, which in turn was due to the fortification clause: "A reduction in the unit size of capital ships would emphasize the value of a chain of naval bases to the disadvantage of the United States. Bases of operation are essential to the use of a navy." Lacking bases the Navy needed these larger ships. After extensive further arguments, including a complete review of the terms of Article 19, the study continued, "The reduction of the size of ships, which tends to lessen the mobility of the ships . . . , would operate in two ways to the advantage of Japan; i.e., (1) expose our own vital lines of communication, and (2) secure the Japanese lines of communication from attack by the United States."[38]

Williams' study also emphasized the board's role in ship design characteristics and how they represented innovation. Tradeoffs between endurance and range, speed, and weight due to weapons and armor would always have to be made, and the board freely acknowledged this design calculus. How to realize the most efficient balance between these factors was often determined during the board's hearings. Further, Williams' report highlighted how the fortification clause influenced these factors, making size all-important due to range and endurance required by the Orange strategy. Williams' study is among the first commissioned by the board during the interwar period to especially emphasize the critical role that the battleship's main battery would *play in seizing bases* as outlined in the Orange war plans. Williams argued that the larger size of the battleships and their gun caliber were needed to both better protect U.S. lines of communication and support seizure of bases with naval gunfire. This proved especially true since Williams predicted that the Japanese would install as many large-caliber shore guns as they could should war break out. Williams' study must have been familiar to the U.S. Marine Corps since the General Board membership at this time still included the commandant of the Marine Corps and he was on the distribution list for the board's studies. Battleships were now being considered for use as an integral part of newer operational concepts, in this case how to use the fleet to support amphibious warfare.[39]

One other area of innovation brought together the thinking within OpNav, the NWC, and the board: naval gunnery and gun size. These factors had to do with forecasts early in the interwar period of an increased range of engagement for capital ships because of new technology such as the Ford Rangefinder and long-distance spotting using aircraft.[40] As we have seen, gun size was frozen by the building holiday and then a reduction confirmed—with escalator caveats—to the maximum 14-inch caliber at London in 1930. However, the board used the loophole in the reconstruction clause of the Washington Naval Treaty to further modify its existing battleships so that they could elevate their guns to get a higher trajectory, and thus greater range, to match the promise of the new technology. With the exception of the Navy's six oldest battleships (as of 1922), this program was implemented along with the other battleship modernization modifications discussed and owed its impetus almost entirely to the General Board.[41] After 1937, the board became unconstrained and no longer had to work around the restrictions of the treaty with the end of the battleship building holiday.

Aircraft Carriers

The notion that the General Board was slow to adopt naval aviation and especially carrier aviation has been completely discredited in recent (and not so recent) scholarship.[42] From the beginning, the board realized the potential of aircraft carriers and recognized that, from a design viewpoint, bigger was better. In September 1918, while the war in Europe still raged, the board identified the "need for airplane carriers of high speed to accompany the fleet.... The General Board recommends that the design and construction of such vessels not be delayed." When it came to number, the board recommended that "the Department request Congress to include in new construction six (6) Airplane Carriers."[43] The cancellation of this building request occurred because of the agreement at Paris to set aside the huge building program approved during the war (see chapter 6). By 1921, Charles Badger, Dewey's successor and an admiral regarded as long in the tooth, was in favor of the largest carriers possible: "We don't want to go back to the 25,000 ton [aircraft carrier]. We want the very best we can get and that is a ship of about 35,000 tons, with about 35 knots speed."[44] The *Essex* class of World War II came in fully loaded at 33,000 tons with a speed of 33 knots.[45] The smaller carriers built prior to the *Essex*, especially the *Ranger* and later *Wasp*, were not what the board wanted.[46] In a 1930 U.S. Naval Institute *Proceedings* article about the General Board, Jarvis Butler, secretary of the Joint Board and a senior clerk in the Navy Department, highlighted the board's progressive attitude toward aviation. Butler dismissed as ignorant those critics who had accused it of "hampering the development of naval aviation, of fogyism [*sic*], and downright indifference." He pointed to its "published recommendations ... [that] show its real conception and advocacy of aviation."[47]

At the time Jarvis wrote his article, ADM Pratt was serving as CINCUS. He and the board were already discussing a sophisticated organization, advocating ship ratios for the carrier groups that became the standard operational unit for the Navy in 1942. Pratt attended a hearing of the entire board on 27 May 1930 after being invited by then-chairman Bristol to come talk about his vision for the fleet. Pratt adhered to the Taylor-Mahan model, advocating that the battle fleet (battleships) be concentrated entirely in the Pacific. He additionally recommended against having any battleships in the scouting fleet, the fleet component that would fight the Japanese in the "approach phase" of War Plan Orange.[48] Pratt then outlined his vision for the scouting fleet consisting of "sufficient carrier tonnage and sufficient ... cruisers to accompany these carriers in order to form what I think to be a really effective scouting force." Note that Pratt's reference to tonnage reflects how the treaty system shaped his thinking, since he knew that carriers were a limited asset. Pratt then reemphasized that "slow moving battleships" should not be a part of this force. When pressed for the actual makeup of these carrier forces, he specified four heavy cruisers and five to six destroyers for every carrier.[49]

At Midway in 1942, the *Yorktown* carrier group consisted of two cruisers and six destroyers, so Pratt was not far off in his assessment of what might be needed. When queried by Bristol as to how many of these he thought he should have, Pratt responded, "Three divisions," meaning three carrier groups of one carrier each. This was precisely what was present at Midway in 1942. It is evident from the back-and-forth between Pratt and the board that they were more concerned about how to build the carriers to do this, rather than questioning the soundness of Pratt's conception of the organization. The only notes of discord had to do with concern from some members about the *Lexington* and *Saratoga* being unavailable for use to protect the battle fleet, leaving only *Langley* or possibly the new carrier (*Ranger*, not yet built) to do this. However, Pratt emphasized that the battle fleet would be held in reserve, and out of danger from enemy air, again forecasting almost exactly what happened after Pearl Harbor.[50] Thus was forged a common understanding of how the Navy might actually fight if war occurred suddenly and in the future.[51]

On the eve of World War II, with RADM Ernest King as a member prior to his appointment in command of the Atlantic Fleet, the board recommended conversion of the light cruiser hulls of the *Princeton* class into light aircraft carriers. Ironically, one of these hulls had been one that King had lobbied be built as a flying deck cruiser less than a year earlier. Again, the decision, incorporated into the 1940 Two-Ocean Navy Act, paid handsome dividends in World War II as the bloodied treaty fleet was replaced by the new ships, including the *Princeton* light carriers and *Essex* fleet carriers conceived of, discussed, and supported by the General Board during the interwar period. Carriers of the *Princeton* class were more rapidly built because their hulls had already been laid.[52]

Cruisers and Destroyers

The idea of the role of cruisers in the scouting force was discussed in the previous section. The General Board's involvement overall in cruiser design was ubiquitous and constant during the interwar period, a carryover from its conceptions for the scout cruiser prior to World War I (see chapter 4). Additionally, the paucity of construction of carriers that had influenced how the board developed and designed aviation tenders played the same role in bringing the flying deck cruiser idea into vogue at London and after, even though it was never built (see chapter 7).[53]

Too, one must recall that after Washington, the naval arms race shifted from capital ships to the cruiser classes, thus the General Board naturally spent a lot of time talking about ships it could actually build, as noted earlier. The cruisers designed and built to the board's specifications, both before London and after, reflected the heavy influence of that body. Although tactics and torpedoes for these ships have been criticized, nonetheless it was these designs, especially their antiaircraft armament, which became critical once World War II began. With the carriers they held the line as the closest thing to capital ships that the treaty navy had until 1943 when the flood of new, modern warships arrived. The designs, for example, of the *Brooklyn* light cruiser class proved adaptable enough so that as war brought lessons learned, especially regarding needs for antiaircraft armament, these ships could be modified to meet the emergent requirements.[54]

In the case of destroyers, a similar dynamic applies. Unlimited at Washington and then virtually so after London due to the paucity of building in all classes, destroyers could be designed and built during the interwar and thus received a healthy scrutiny in the design hearings before the General Board during this period. Additionally, the board brought the sensibilities of the "frozen" lessons learned from World War I to its deliberations after Washington.[55] However, there were some missteps. One was a direct result of the World War I. Because of the urgency of the submarine threat, construction of the new *Clemson*-class destroyers took precedence. Their construction continued without significant modification after the war ended, saddling the Navy with a slower destroyer than might have been the case had the board adopted a redesign policy.[56]

In addition, the board's prioritization of ship classes delayed destroyer innovation when it came to the destroyer leader class. Originally classified as a "flotilla leader," this class ship was another lesson learned from the war about the difficulty of commanding and controlling destroyers in a complex and diffuse combat environment at sea and the existence of similar ship types in the navies of the other major powers: "The destroyer leader retained the same qualities as a standard destroyer, but would also have more speed, bigger guns, centerline torpedo and gun arrangements, separate plotting and larger communication rooms, and a range finder for accurate information on the enemy."[57] This idea had great merit and may have served as an early stepping-stone to the later *Fletcher* class of World War II fame, but despite the board's interest after 1918, it assigned destroyer leaders as sixth in priority behind aircraft carriers, submarines, and cruisers. In effect, this terminated the idea of new large-type destroyer until the 1930s.[58]

With the infusion of money again into naval construction after 1934, the General Board resurrected the idea of the large destroyer-destroyer leader. Whereas Japan decided to use light cruisers to perform this function, the board continued to build on the idea of this type of vessel as a destroyer.[59] The design process and characteristics for these bigger destroyers, and the earlier leader type, led to excellent *Fletcher* class of destroyers, named after one-time board senior member ADM Frank F. Fletcher. The board's process for doing this can be labeled as "evolutionary" versus some of the more revolutionary concepts it espoused (e.g., flight deck cruiser) during the interwar period.[60] Nonetheless, with the arrival of the war in European and Atlantic waters in 1939, the reemergence of the German submarine threat, and the highlighting (by the Luftwaffe) of the air threat, the board and the Navy found they had the requisite designs on the books to generate rather rapidly the winning design of the *Fletcher* destroyer as a premier, multimission class, readily modified.[61]

Submarines

As for the submarine, the board viewed it as essential to strategy in the Pacific based on the courses of action in the Orange plan. Between 1919 and 1940, the General Board held forty-six separate hearings on submarines' characteristics and design.[62] As we have seen, it even ranked ahead of the destroyer in the postwar priority lists for new construction. CAPT Frank Schofield, member of the General Board and later chief of OpNav's War Plans Division, recommended using submarines as the "eyes" for a fleet denied sanctuaries in the Western Pacific.[63]

RADM Hilary Jones had been a party to the extensive board hearings on the topic of fleet submarines in 1924–25 and regarded the submarine as an essential reconnaissance and screening asset for the fleet. This principle was now a component of the U.S. Naval Policy and reflected in tactical practice. During hearings, Jones and the board had focused on how to get as much "radius of action" as possible from these vessels, including holding hearings on a "submersible fuel tender." The board's hearings on the submersible fuel tender highlight the intersection of new technology with innovative operational approaches in response to the geography of the Pacific and the constraints of the fortification clause. It also highlights the use of the General Board hearings as the preferred forum for the initial discussion of new concepts. Jones chaired the 10 April 1925 meeting attended by Captain Pye, one of the authors of the then-current plan Orange, where they discussed a proposal by OpNav for using submersible fuel tenders to increase the range of the Navy's S-class submarines in the Pacific. The tenders would carry not only fuel but also spare parts and personnel for augmentation. The General Board produced no less than seven studies on the topic of increasing submarine operational ranges in 1924–25. The fact that the Germans, without distant bases of any sort in the Atlantic during World War II, adopted the same concept ("milch cows") to support their submarine fleet further supports this design's innovative merit.[64]

The submersible fuel tender also provides an interesting example of the influence of the budget process on innovation during the 1920s. This hybrid vessel was never built, even as a test bed, principally due to limited funds, which were recommended and programmed for the most urgent priorities—battleship modernization, cruisers, aircraft carriers, and so on. The submersible fuel tender example highlights a shortcoming in the Navy's methods. A promising concept was proposed—it was clear from the transcripts of the hearings on the submersible fuel tender that the General Board's members thought as much.[65] However, without a prototype vessel, the concept could not be tested in the fleet and the idea might be shelved or even forgotten. In the case of the submersible fuel tender, the Navy decided to address the operational radius of its submarine fleet by simply building larger, more fuel-efficient, and more habitable submarines. However, money was slow in coming to construct these vessels, whereas the construction of even one submersible fuel tender would have immediately increased the operational range of the submarines already in the fleet as well as provided valuable design data through actual experimentation. In this case the budget process had adversely affected innovation instead of encouraging it as some historians claim.[66]

The topic of using submarines as logistics vessels did not go away. In a harbinger of their use at Guadalcanal in 1942, the final hearing of 1940 looked at the issue of designing a submarine specifically to carry aviation gasoline, although the intent here was more likely to fuel long-range PBY seaplanes at remote stations rather than to get much-needed aviation gas ashore for land-based air.[67] Nonetheless, this type of discussion shows that the board remained a forum for innovative and creative thinking about the challenges of a long-range war in the Pacific, and it perhaps planted seeds recalled during the exigencies of war.

As for the design of the long-range fleet submarines, the process again emphasizes the impact of the budget, the driving considerations of the approach phase of the Orange plan, which depended on large "cruiser submarines," and the serendipity in the final phases that led to the famous fleet boats of the *Tambor* and *Gato* classes, which did such extreme damage to the Japanese merchant fleet once U.S. torpedo problems were fixed.[68] The General Board oversaw the entire process, and the personality of Thomas C. Hart, commander of the U.S. Asiatic Fleet upon the outbreak of war with Japan, looms large throughout. Hart ended up using the General Board hearing process to fine-tune the concepts and designs, and even to discuss behind closed doors the sensitive issue of using submarines against Japan in a fashion similar to that of Germany.[69] As it turned out, the "accidental" commerce raiders, which destroyed much of the Japanese merchant fleet in World War II, were not as accidental as some have portrayed; however, the primary design characteristic for submarines in the interwar period remained the long-range scouting role as outlined in War Plan Orange.[70]

A fascinating aspect of the board's role in development of fleet submarines concerns the Submarine Officers Conference (SOC), an advisory body to OpNav that "acted like a sub-committee to the Board."[71] As the board developed submarine designs, it tended to defer to the SOC in technical matters and opinions. However, once more senior submarine admirals like Hart became members of the board, they tended to question more critically the SOC recommendations, which overall was good for the process. The treaty system and War Plan Orange, as with the other systems discussed, shaped the story of submarine innovation as relates to the board. Serendipity played a role here. Initially unlimited by treaty, the board sought the largest possible submarines, initiating the V-class program, which ended up building some of the largest submarines then in existence. Three design characteristics drove this development: speed, endurance, and propulsion. A speed of 21 knots was recommended by the board to be able to keep pace with the fleet, endurance drove the large size initially, and propulsion forced the board to abandon the idea of a steam-driven cruiser submarine in favor of a diesel electric.[72]

All these factors played out in the V-class, with each new unit of this class differing significantly from its predecessors as lessons learned were incorporated. By the time submarine tonnage was limited at London in 1930, the impact drove the size of these submarines down. However, by this time the board had decided on the right propulsion (diesel electric) and come to the conclusion that high speed was not as essential as range and endurance. Additionally, Hart's influence was not always beneficial, with a smaller submarine design temporarily adopted before the board went back to a larger submarine. By the time World War II arrived, the board had a submarine with a robust propulsion, better torpedo magazines and firing ability, air conditioning (something the General Board insisted on), as well as the 21-knot speed initially sought in 1920. All of these capabilities stemmed directly from the influence of the board as advised by the SOC. The board also insisted on mountings for heavier 5-inch guns, although the fleet submarines of the newer classes after the V-class went to sea with 3-inch guns. Once problems with the infamous Mark XIV torpedoes occurred in the war, it was a relatively easy matter to refit the 5-inch guns to the submarines for use to sink smaller Japanese merchant vessels, saving torpedoes for larger, more lucrative targets. Although the General Board did not catch the design flaws of the Mark XIV, neither did any other organization in the Navy prior to the war, and the delay in fixing this problem once the war began is better laid at the door of the Bureau of Ordnance.[73] Overall, the story of the General Board and submarine design is one of innovation and success, contrary to narratives that claim the opposite.[74]

Aircraft

The creation of Bureau of Aeronautics and the fights over naval aviation had given BuAer immense credibility in the design of combat aircraft. The General Board, accordingly, deferred even more to the positions of BuAer and the aviators than it did with submarines and the SOC.[75] Although senior "aviator" officers such as RADM Mason Reeves did serve on the board, they too tended to defer to the "experts," including Moffett, Whiting, Towers, and King. The case of aviation tenders for long-range patrol aircraft reinforces this view, with the board getting involved as a budget advocate for a system—the aviation tender—that BuAer and the fleet had deemed essential. The board leveraged experts such as Captain Van Keuren for ship designs, and here it tended to exercise a more hands-on approach, but as to the platforms themselves, the story of aircraft innovation and the General Board is more one of setting priorities and advocating the BuAer "party line."[76]

A possible exception to this story was the rocky development of patrol aviation during the interwar era. We now know that the story had a successful ending with the development of the long-range PBY Catalina flying boat, but the board's involvement with the concept of long-range aviation patrol for the fleet is supportive of several themes already discussed. The key problem here had to do with whether to go with a lighter-than-air (LTA) long-range dirigible platform or with a heavier-than-air seaplane. The idea of using a long-range land-based platform was foreclosed by the Pratt-MacArthur agreement of 1931, by which the two services prevented the Navy from developing land-based aircraft that looked like a strategic bomber, limiting it to seaplane, carrier, and LTA options. This was in part due to the increasing promise of long-range flying boats.[77]

The board ended up serving as a counterweight to Moffett's influence, and after his death it lent the bulk of its support to the long-range seaplane alternative, which along with fleet submarines were to serve as the scouting fleet's "eyes and ears" for the early phases of an Orange campaign. The General Board consistently encouraged the development of this option, and in collaboration with the fleet, OpNav, and BuAer, again managed an innovative trajectory during the lean years of budgets, treaty limitations, and the false promise of Moffett's obsession with LTA.[78] The role of the treaty system in this process was, once more, counterintuitive. With the new limitations on the long-range submarines and cruisers the board intended as critical to the opening phases of Orange, the unlimited and relatively cheap long-range flying boat became an even more attractive option for the CNO, the fleet, and the General Board. Naval War College war gaming enforced this utility, but LTA development, immature technology, and limited money all delayed the emergence of a feasible solution until the mid-1930s. The General Board's chief contribution in this regard was to serve as a forum for all the stakeholders. At the individual level, with Moffett's death, the personality of Ernest King looms large in his command of the Base Force, inputs to the gaming at the NWC, and then the ironing out of technological needs and operational employment of the seaplanes in the annual Fleet Problems. Finally, King's terms of service as chief of BuAer and on the General Board itself provided venues for his advocacy of this approach. King was one of those rare people who seemed to be in the right place at the right time, able to see clearly how to use these Navy organizations to their best advantage to attain the right results, except (as noted in chapter 7) with the flying deck cruiser. Before World War II, in late 1941, the Navy had a superb weapon in the PBY, and due credit must go to the General Board for this being the case.[79] PBYs would strike the first blow against the Japanese fleet at Midway.[80]

The interwar period often found the General Board at loggerheads with the various administrations until that system ended. Even Franklin Roosevelt desired—as did his predecessors—the reduction of arms expenditures through the mechanism of the treaty system. The board members of the period felt strongly that the nation needed to be prepared with the ships it had on hand to meet national emergencies, and this could not be done without a full-strength treaty fleet. The fundamental issue, which raised its ugly head over and over again, concerned the Navy's ability to exercise long-range sea power given the constraints of the fortification clause of the original Washington Naval Treaty. The board's arguments constantly returned to its lack of bases in the Pacific: sea power that had been "traded away" at Washington.

The intersection of Navy leaders' conception of sea power with the constraining effects imposed upon it by the treaties forced the Navy to seek solutions elsewhere—submarines, cruisers, and long-range flying boats, for example. A combination of technological and operational innovation was the means for pursuing strategic goals in the midst of new political and material conditions after 1922.

Stymied in its efforts to effect change by modifying the treaty system, the General Board sought solutions through a combination of technology, ship design, and operational concepts. In the process the board's attitudes about sea power and it relationship to bases, battleships, and aviation gradually changed, and with it the attitudes of the Navy at large. Although the battleship remained the primary measure of naval power, its importance was less than what it was prior to the Washington Conference.[81] The battleship still represented power and dominated naval minds, but Navy officers had wrestled with its limitation and diminution for so long that a fundamental change in attitude had occurred, one that would only be fully exposed by the Japanese success against American battleships at Pearl Harbor. Recall that the entire Pacific Fleet battle line, eight battleships in all, had been sunk or damaged in the attack at Pearl Harbor in December 1941.[82] Yet the fate of the battleships at Pearl Harbor was not the occasion for a revolutionary change in attitude. This is best understood by a priority list that ADM King, then in command of the Atlantic Fleet, sent to the General Board in July 1941. King's number one priority for building were submarines, followed by destroyers, with aircraft carriers third in priority. Battleships were last in priority of construction. Attitudes certainly had changed.[83] The Navy fought the first year and a half of the war with the treaty fleet it had built—mostly the "scouting fleet" for the Orange approach phase—and the attitudes toward sea power it had developed as a result of building the treaty fleet.

The General Board's membership had been at the center of innovation as Pratt's "balance wheel." Its initiatives and programs changed the way the Navy thought about overseas bases and the projection of sea power, especially in the vast reaches of the Pacific. With the end of the treaty system, it had thrown itself back into its role as the arbiter of general ship characteristics and overall fleet design, working with the CNO, the bureaus, and the fleet. Because of the board's subtle "behind the scenes influence," Navy officers began to conceive of supporting the fleet at the advent of war without preexisting bases. Amphibious warfare, mobile bases, underway replenishment, submarine warfare, and embarked air power were concepts that matured during World War II, but they were conceived and embedded in the Navy's collective consciousness in the interwar period, in part due to the General Board. The board still wielded considerable influence in 1941, but its (until now) slowly declining influence was about to be accelerated by a global naval war of unprecedented proportions.

CHAPTER 9

Phoenix or Icarus?
The Resurgence and Death of the General Board, 1941–51

The phoenix was a mythical, fiery bird rising from its own ashes, whereas Icarus, in his hubris, flew too close to the ultimate source of power and light, the sun, and then crashed disastrously to earth. Both figures can be said to symbolize the evolution of the General Board in the decade from 1941 to 1951. The period from 1940 to 1947 saw the General Board sink to its lowest level of esteem within the Navy as an institution. Yet even so, the CNO, ADM Ernest King, did not abolish it and even had a hand in maintaining its existence when he might easily have gotten it disestablished due to the war's pressing need for flag officers in the greatly expanded Navy. During these lean years, the General Board seemed to have become something of a leper colony for discredited admirals. (The term "leper colony" here refers to a way station for "screw ups," as made famous in the film *Twelve O'Clock High*.)[1]

However, after the war a move to abolish the board created a backlash, led in part by Secretary James Forrestal and ADM John Towers, to restore its prestige. The board was rejuvenated and ended up including not just the savvy bureaucratic infighter Towers but also the brilliant CAPT Arleigh Burke, who later became one of the most important CNOs in the last half of the twentieth century. In less than nine months, the board reestablished its prominence as the Secretary of the Navy's personal policy advisory group and regained its control of the general aspects of ship design and characteristics. The days of significant influence seemed to have returned, with the board fulfilling a role similar to today's think tanks, such as the RAND Corporation and the Center for Naval Analysis.[2]

However, like Icarus, the board perhaps rose too high and too fast within the context of a renewed unification fight in 1948-49, known to history as the "Revolt of the Admirals." This episode involved the move to greatly curtail, if not eliminate, naval aviation in the aftermath of the creation of an independent U.S. Air Force and secretary of defense in 1947.[3] One by the one the advocates for a General Board went by the wayside. Its talented members were retired, moved to other jobs, and in one case was pulled to investigate his fellow naval officers. By the time the dust had settled, the board was like Joseph in the biblical story: "Now there arose a new king over Egypt, who knew not Joseph."[4] That king was actually two men, Louis Johnson as the SecDef and his handpicked SecNav, Francis Matthews. Too, the board still had powerful enemies inside the enlarged postwar OpNav staff who had little utility for an organization they regarded as a relic from prewar days. Its ship characteristics and policy functions migrated to OpNav. With many enemies and almost no friends, the board died a lingering death in late 1950, quietly disappearing in the same way it was born, by secretarial fiat.

The Leper Colony?

At the beginning of the period, the General Board was still a vibrant and valued organization inside the Navy. The SecNav and CNO valued both its policy recommendations and guidance on ship characteristics, which came from the mature hearings-study process. Its annual building policy recommendations remained the coin of the realm inside the Navy concerning the way ahead for the fleet and priorities of construction. However, two items more than any other accelerated its transformation into something of a backwater for admirals: the advent of World War II and the accession of Ernest King as commander in chief of the Navy as well as CNO. These developments tipped the scales of influence and power vis-à-vis policy and ship characteristics to the CNO and OpNav at the expense of the General Board. The creation of the Joint Chiefs of Staff (JCS) and a general order making King the president's primary military adviser on naval affairs also diminished the influence of the General Board.[5]

To understand the role of the outbreak of World War II in the diminution of the General Board, one need only recall the similar dynamic in World War I (see chapter 5). Recall that the board had been sidelined to a degree in that war as the new CNO (Benson), commander in Europe (Sims), and Atlantic Fleet Commander (Mayo) had moved to the fore in advising

Josephus Daniels. The key differences between how the two wars shaped views of the utility of General Board by both the civilian and senior uniformed leadership involved personality, time, institutional memory, and talent (who was assigned to the board).

The first sign that FDR might have come to see the General Board as a place to assign troublesome admirals still on active duty occurred in 1940 shortly after the president and CNO, Admiral "Betty" Stark, decided to leave the U.S. Fleet forward based at Pearl Harbor, Hawaii, after the annual fleet problem that summer.[6] They wanted to send a deterrence message to Japan in response to its decision to join the Axis Tripartite Pact. The fleet commander, ADM James O. Richardson, protested this move as being risky, exposing the fleet to a possible attack far from its repair and logistics bases on the West Coast of the United States. Richardson also argued that the readiness of the fleet for war was inadequate. Franklin Roosevelt relieved Richardson in February 1941 but retained him on active duty and sent him to the General Board the following month. The U.S. Fleet was renamed the Pacific Fleet. King, who had departed the General Board in December 1940, commanded the new Atlantic Fleet created from the former Atlantic Squadron, performing the Neutrality Patrol in defense against German submarines.[7]

Roosevelt appointed King as the overall U.S. Fleet commander to coordinate the activities of the three major U.S. fleets—Asiatic, Pacific, and Atlantic—after Pearl Harbor. For a time King served in that capacity, with Stark remaining as the CNO. However, Roosevelt solved the problem of having more than one senior officer running the fleet in March 1942, replacing Stark with King as CNO, with King retaining the title of COMINCH. He also gained control over the functioning of the bureaus—a longtime goal of the line-officer community. King superseded SecNav in the business of running the Navy in achieving these milestones. He additionally represented the Navy on the new JCS, the body that advised Roosevelt. King had become the most powerful admiral in American history. By contrast, the General Board merely advised a SecNav who had been marginalized by King in cahoots with Roosevelt as justified by "the requirements and rapid developments of war." At the same time, the power and influence of King translated itself to the OpNav organization, which grew larger with every day.[8]

Postwar memories played an important role in all of this. Up through 1941, the General Board had not only continued its important function in

ADM John Towers replaced Fleet Admiral Chester Nimitz as commander, Pacific Fleet when Nimitz "fleeted up" to become the CNO. Towers later was able to stay on and serve in the Navy when Secretary of the Navy James Forrestal moved him into position as chairman of the General Board, giving him talented officers such as "Soc" McMorris and Arleigh Burke in a postwar attempt to reinvigorate the board as an independent policy-advising body. *National Archives, Naval History and Heritage Command*

determining building policy and design but also had been asked every year from 1939 to address the question "Are We Ready[?]" by the SecNav and president. It had uniformly said no all three times. At the same time, it had supported a move toward a unified strategy that favored a "Europe First" strategy, declaring that "the issues of the Orient will largely be decided in Europe."[9] However, this role became moot once war started. A smaller board with a more limited scope, as in World War I, contributed to a dynamic of "memory loss" as recollections of the board's utility began to fade. Because World War II was much longer, and much bigger in scope for the United States, the institutional loss of memory had more time to percolate and on a broader scale inside the officer corps, especially with those officers who came of age during the war and led the Navy after the war. Unlike the war in 1917, after 1939 the demand for senior officers for a rapidly expanding fleet grew exponentially. The fall of France in the spring of 1940 stimulated passage of the Two-Ocean Navy Act for hemispheric defense of the United States should Britain also fall. This created a pressing need for experienced officers at all ranks, but especially for senior officers to handle the immense complexities of a naval mobilization that dwarfed what had happened in 1917–18.[10] The U.S. Navy grew in size from a fleet of several hundred warships (to say nothing of the merchant marine) to several thousand. By late 1944, the Navy had more than 300,000 commissioned officers.[11]

Thus, as the fleet and staffs grew, the General Board shrank and the character of its membership changed. At the outbreak of hostilities with Japan in December 1941, the board consisted of eight voting members of the executive committee, including RADM Walton Sexton as chairman, and six other active-duty line rear admirals, plus a captain serving as the secretary. By the end of December, three of these admirals had departed to serve in urgent billets elsewhere. For example, FDR selected RADM James L. Kauffman to establish a naval base in Iceland.[12] The crisis came in the summer of 1942, when the board shrank to five members and the load could not be taken up by captains because there was even more need for officers of that rank than for admirals. Admiral King, writing as COMINCH in July, stressed these problems to SecNav: "Officers on the active list . . . having appropriate qualification for assignment to duty as members of the General Board are almost all employed in active commands, from which they cannot be spared." He noted that four candidates, ADM Hepburn, ADM Hart, ADM Yarnell, and ADM Reeves, were all serving in other important duties and unavailable. King added that Hepburn might be available soon and that Sexton could be retained for continuity until Hepburn, soon to be in a retired status, could relieve him. He also mentioned assigning ADM Claude Bloch to the board.[13] Even the discredited but still active-duty RADM J. O. Richardson left the board to serve with the Navy Relief Society and on the expanding staff of the Joint Chiefs.[14] During the crisis that summer—with U-boats rampaging in the Atlantic and the Japanese navy surging southeast in the Solomon Islands—King seemed to want to keep the board manned with the appropriate talent.

Secretary of the Navy Frank Knox adopted King's recommendations in August by the expedient of using recently retired admirals to serve on the board. By November 1942 the board consisted four retired admirals, including Hepburn, serving as chairman, Hart, Bloch, and Edward Kalbfus (three names from King's July list). Only three members were active-duty officers, including Sexton, now outranked by Hepburn. Until November of 1944, this membership of the board was remarkably static, with only the secretary position changing hands. Hart, too, had the stigma of defeat after his Asiatic Fleet had been virtually annihilated by the Japanese in the first four months of the war in the Far East.[15] Thus the General Board, which had long served as a stepping-stone to higher command, had become a place to which officers went after high command (possibly if that command had not gone well) and even returned to after retirement. It no longer seemed a place, as in Pratt's day, from which to advance one's career as a senior captain or junior "lower half" rear admiral.

This wartime legacy of the board began to reverse course after the war as more active-duty admirals became available service on the board, allowing the retired admirals to actually retire. VADM Fletcher reported to the board in late 1945. Fletcher, the nominal victor at both Coral Sea and Midway, had been under a cloud since leaving command in September 1942 after being on board USS *Saratoga* when it was torpedoed in waters around Guadalcanal. King did not have a high opinion of him and later moved him to a command ashore. However, the story that King never employed him again in a seagoing capacity (reputedly because of his jealousy that Fletcher, a "blackshoe," or surface line officer, had commanded at the two most important naval air engagements in 1942) has little to support it. Fletcher did command at sea again during the war, albeit in the secondary theater of the North Pacific.[16]

The technique of having admirals on the verge of retirement serve on the board for short periods reappeared after the war. ADM Richmond Kelly Turner served for less than a month on the board in late 1945. In January 1946, Robert Ghormley, relieved of command at Guadalcanal by Nimitz, the board's chairman, effectively served as Fletcher's boss since he was more senior by date of rank as a vice admiral. This, too, was a change due to the war; vice and full admiral ranks were no longer temporary, and General Board members retained the rank they had held prior to coming to the board. They no longer reverted to rear admiral as in the prewar days. Rank thus played a role, albeit minor, in the rejuvenation of the board after the war.[17]

The notion that the General Board became something of a leper colony is tenuous. Urgent times required expedient measures, and for the bulk of World War II the admirals who served on the board were, for the most part, well-regarded officers, especially Sexton, Bloch, Kalbfus, and Hepburn. Hart had not been so much incompetent as unlucky in having to face the full brunt of the Imperial Japanese Navy after Pearl Harbor. Perhaps a better explanation is that King, despite his sometimes harsh judgments of officers such as Fletcher, did not let good talent go to waste when it could be of use somewhere in the huge entity the U.S. Navy had become by 1942.

World War II lasted longer than World War I, and as the conflict dragged on, the General Board became more marginalized for the reasons mentioned above. The proliferation of agencies and organizations inside the Navy matched that of FDR's New Deal "ABC" organizations, and to some degree the General Board became lost in the mix, but it did not disappear. More and more it focused its efforts on the future of the fleet and how to cycle the lessons of a war under way into the designs of the warships and fleets of the future. By 1944 these designs began to contemplate what was needed in the postwar world.[18] This brought the board into conflict with the Ships Characteristics Board of OpNav, and thus indirectly into conflict with the CNO and powerful OpNav staff.

The General Board and the Ships Characteristics Board
In 1940 the Bureau of Ships (BuShips) was created by combining Bureau of Construction and Repair with the Bureau of Engineering.[19] Because of the war, the Interior Control Board was established inside BuShips to bring some semblance of order to the rapidly proliferating requirements

for an increasing number of ship designs and types. The General Board still had oversight of ships' characteristics; however, the detailed work was done inside BuShips by the Interior Control Board. In March 1945 this organization changed its name to the Ship Characteristics Board (SCB), and its composition and charter were formalized that November.[20] Interestingly, the SCB functioned much as the General Board did, holding hearings on characteristics and forwarding its results to the General Board. It did this at a much more detailed level than the General Board, as one would expect from a design bureau. However, in performing this function, the SCB came to be seen as an organization that made the General Board superfluous.[21] It often produced its results before the General Board, which then had to turn them around rapidly with recommended approval. The reverse process was supposed to have been the case, with the General Board providing the SCB the general characteristics desired and then the SCB incorporating this broad guidance into its process. Formerly this function had occurred at the General Board hearings, when design bureau members such as Van Keuren from BuC&R had attended the meetings and then returned for later hearings with options and results (as in the case of the flying deck cruiser). But the war had made this process too cumbersome, even though two organizations, the General Board and SCB, existed to resolve it. This situation was exacerbated in November 1945, when the General Board became an informational participant in the SCB process rather than its recommendations serving as the basis for that process.[22]

The CNO's "ownership" of the bureaus brought the General Board into conflict with him and his staff, and it was at this point that dissolution of the board was first proposed. Prior to November 1945, Secretary of the Navy James Forrestal had made it clear that he wanted the board intimately involved in making recommendations for ships characteristics. In May 1945, for example, he sent the General Board as well as BuShips, BuOrd, and BuAer guidance on the most urgent needs for wartime "combatant ships" as aircraft carrier, light cruiser, submarine, and destroyer classes. The board was first in priority of memorandum addressees. Forrestal stated his "purpose" in doing this as profiting from "the experience of this war and [to] keep alive the arts of combatant design and construction."[23] To ensure OpNav's awareness, he added both the CNO and the vice chief of Naval Operations on information distribution for the memo.

The following month Forrestal made more explicit his desire to rejuvenate the board's role in this process for the task of postwar building policy, one of the General Board's bread-and-butter tasks prior to the war: "It is desired that the General Board prepare as a matter of urgency a continuing postwar building program giving types, numbers, rate of building and approximate annual cost so as best to sustain the post-war fleet. . . . Since the program is required at an early date it will not be necessary at this time to determine detailed characteristics of ships involved." This time the only action recipient was the General Board, but Forrestal included as information addressees all the bureaus mentioned above as well as the CNO and VCNO so that they would know his charter for the functioning of the General Board in the postwar period.[24] This correspondence practically returned to the board to its previous position of authority, emphasizing that "detailed characteristics" could come later, presumably after the board's study was done and sent to the SCB. The move to a new SCB precept in November by OpNav can be seen as an attempt to marginalize the board by the OpNav staff. Too, the actions of OpNav, using the SCB as a vehicle, might be understood as something of a civil-military dispute between CNO and SecNav because Forrestal was moving to make the board a major policy organization in the affairs of the Navy again.

And where did King stand in all of this? He was leaving the Navy (December 1945) as the reaction to Forrestal's moves unfolded. Perhaps King's imminent departure explains why the OpNav staff waited until November to release its new precept for the SCB. The new CNO (and no longer COMINCH), Fleet Admiral Chester Nimitz, had never served on the board, although he must have known something of it given its importance in the prewar Navy.[25] This may have been a factor in his attitude toward the utility of the General Board, as well as the its low visibility for him as a wartime commander as opposed to that of COMINCH, OpNav, and JCS, to say nothing of the operations that Nimitz oversaw in the Pacific. Whatever the case, Nimitz came to actively support those under him who viewed the General Board as a superfluous organization whose former utility had been transferred to OpNav and the SCB. Nearly simultaneous with King's retirement was an odd query from a "management engineer" with the Executive Office of the Secretary of the Navy (EXOS). EXOS was something of a competing organization inside the SecNav's personal staff (which included the General Board), and its query might have presaged a move against the board by OpNav allies under the cover of a scientific management initiative for more efficiency. These initiatives always seemed to occur in lean budget times or after wars concluded.[26]

King, on the other hand, came out strongly for the board once he retired, in contrast to his impact on diluting its influence and institutional value during the war. This probably resulted from a personal request by Forrestal. Conflict with the SCB had continued, and the opponents of the board inside OpNav and, possibly EXOS, used a revision of NavyRegs as the vehicle to propose eliminating the board. The situation finally boiled over in April 1946, bringing King and other retired admirals back into the debate inside the Navy Department. The importance of this conflict is highlighted by how busy a time this was, with demobilization requiring a great deal of effort and time by all parties, General Board included. That Forrestal expended so much correspondence at the secretarial level in such a busy period shows the importance that the principals at the time ascribed to the issue. Forrestal had established the separate Navy Regulations Board to examine the issue of changing the charter for the General Board. The president of this board asked the General Board for its position on including staff corps officers as members. The General Board, led by Ghormley, saw no need to change the line officer membership requirement at the time. In April 1946 the board had grown again, as it always seemed to do after a war, to five vice admirals (including Ghormley and Fletcher), two rear admirals, and a lieutenant commander as secretary.[27]

However, at the end of the month, CNO Nimitz asked Fletcher, now chairman, "why it [General Board] should not be eliminated." Fletcher notified Forrestal and recommended the General Board make a study of the proposal for its own dissolution, opining that it would take about two weeks to do the study. He also recommended that Forrestal query former members of the board for their opinion on the matter. Forrestal agreed.[28] Two weeks later to the day, Fletcher forwarded the results of this study to Forrestal, including the accomplishments of the board over the previous fifteen years. The study also identified the war as the reason for the board coming to its "current state."[29] Two days later, King, a former member and retired fleet admiral, sent a personal memorandum to Forrestal, stating, "It is, of course, obvious that the General Board should not go on it is half-alive state." He then proposed an expansion of the board's influence, thus revealing his view of the board's utility in peacetime, despite the curtailment of its powers during the recent war.[30]

Preceding King's memorandum by a week was a 10 May CNO draft memorandum prepared by the Vice Chief of Naval Operations, VADM Dewitt "Duke" Ramsey, for Nimitz's signature to "abolish the board." Nimitz's name was written in pencil under that of Ramsey. The main argument posed involved the CNO and his OpNav staff's perception of the board's inability to perform its ship-characteristics function duties during war. In a section called "historical background" in one of the memos, the authors referred to the board in demeaning terms, calling it a "vestigial appendage" and thus implying that it must be amputated.[31] Ramsey was another naval aviator who had had little contact with the board during his career and had come into his own in various aviation commands during the war, including as skipper of the *Saratoga* while Fletcher was embarked. This last may have factored into his low regard for the board, since Fletcher was the second-ranking member of the board at that time. King had evidently seen this Ramsey-Nimitz memorandum, thus stimulating his outburst in favor of the board and its utility in the postwar security environment.[32]

The Resurgence of the General Board, 1947

Forrestal had no intention of amputating the General Board from the naval body, but he had to be careful because of the ongoing move toward defense unification; any perception of bitter infighting inside the Navy could give advocates for the elimination of naval aviation—especially those in the soon to be independent Army Air Force—ammunition to criticize the Navy.[33] King, ironically, solved Forrestal's problem by having the Secretary of the Navy reduce the mandatory retirement age for admirals when King retired as CNO. This meant that John Towers, in command of the Pacific Fleet and heir presumptive to Nimitz as CNO, would be unable to serve in that capacity due to the new rule. However, because SecNav could keep admirals slated for retirement on active duty in service on the General Board, it offered a means to use Towers. Forrestal wanted the most influential and prestigious senior naval aviator to take charge of the General Board and replace the unassuming Fletcher. This move also gave Forrestal a counterweight to OpNav, the organization he felt had become too powerful during the war. Towers had four stars (as commander, Pacific Fleet) as opposed to Fletcher's three. Forrestal ran the proposal by Towers in early 1947, and Towers agreed on the condition that he be allowed to choose the members himself.[34]

Towers' picks reflected both his keen judgment of talent and experience in high command as well as the large scope of action Forrestal intended for a new and rejuvenated General Board. Towers brought the Marine Corps back into the fold for the first time since 1932, choosing Guadalcanal combat hero Col Randolph M. Pate, who later served as the twenty-first Commandant of the Marine Corps in the 1950s. On the Navy side, he picked RADM Charles "Soc" McMorris, a blackshoe officer and victor of the Battle of the Komandorski Islands in World War II. Towers also chose the brilliant destroyerman CAPT Arleigh "30-Knot" Burke (later CNO under Eisenhower and Kennedy). He retained RADM P. Bellinger (a naval aviator) and CAPT S. M. DuBois as the secretary. By May, Towers had added one more rear admiral and another Navy captain, thus making the board's composition four flag officers, three captains, and a colonel. In June he added another rear admiral (C. E. Momsen) and another navy captain, bringing the total to ten members. His choice of surface officers of high esteem for the board proved wise, although somewhat counter to the prevailing mood and preference in OpNav for naval aviator dominance. He explained to Nimitz, "In my nominations for members of the reconstituted board I have been very careful to select officers of recent active Fleet experience in the various types of vessels and aircraft that can be expected to comprise the postwar navy of the foreseeable future."[35] Nimitz and Towers may not have had the best relationship, having been on opposite sides of the unification fight in 1946, although Nimitz had ranked Towers with an excellent fitness report for his job in the Pacific Command. Towers' new job as chairman of the General Board continued to stress this relationship.[36]

While these changes occurred, the General Board worked through a complete revision of NavyRegs instigated the previous year by Nimitz as a result of the dispute over the SCB (which remained unresolved). This effort extended through Fletcher's, Towers', and McMorris' (Towers' successor) tutelage of the board. Although the revision might have been a "busy work" strategy employed by Nimitz, the result was a complete and professional recasting by the General Board leading to the first post–World War II revision and promulgation of NavyRegs in 1948. Interestingly, the final version of the 1948 NavyRegs omitted specific mention of the General Board, leaving it as the unspecified board allowed for under article 103.3. This would have the effect, perhaps unintended, of making the board much easier to disestablish because no revision of NavyRegs would be required to do so. It could simply be dissolved at the Secretary of the Navy's whim.[37]

During the Towers period, which only lasted nine months (March–December 1947), several issues were resolved and the board again resumed its position of seniority in the area of general ships' characteristics over the SCB, although this was not accomplished smoothly. Towers had reclaimed its role as the premier policy advisory unit for SecNav as opposed to the OpNav and CNO, although this may have had as much to do with the OpNav staff's shrinkage after World War II and its commensurate increased workload for fewer people. This left the luxury of undertaking higher level strategic and political policy studies something better done by others higher up the chain, either the emerging entities in a new unified national security system, such as the JCS and the National Security Council, or, in this case, a rejuvenated General Board.[38]

The first order of business was to resolve the ongoing conflict with the SCB over ship design. Towers took the issue to task using the ongoing NavyRegs hearings and studies by the board as his vehicle.[39] In May he wrote to Nimitz on the topic, proposing that the November 1945 SCB precept be "replaced." He also recommended that the General Board be given the ship program ideas generated out of Op-03, hold its hearings, and then have the SCB more narrowly work within the board's guidance.[40] Towers articulated his vision of the role of the General Board in terms similar to those of Pratt fifteen years earlier: "Psychologically, I see a great advantage in having a detached body such as the General Board handle [general ships' characteristics] for there is inherent in the present procedure for the agency of one division of C.N.O. to support the recommendations of another division."

Nimitz responded via a series of memoranda authored for him by the senior member of the SCB and the deputy CNO for Material, VADM Robert "Mick" Carney. Carney recognized that the "current composition of the General Board has revived its potentialities," but the first memorandum reviewed in laborious detail the various modifications of NavyRegs, citing that the real problem lay there. Further, Carney proposed that the General Board essentially become an additional advisory body to the CNO and not independent of it.[41] Towers had no problem with the CNO forwarding topics to the board for consideration, however, he responded with a point-by-point discussion of Carney's paragraphs, often "agreeing in principle" and then gently rebutting the point. For example, he responded to Carney's proposal that the board have no authority to disagree with the CNO's recommendations to SecNav: "Here again I agree in principle, but the fact that *impartial* recommendations might be different from those of the Chief of Naval Operations should not stop the General Board from presenting them to the Secretary for consideration. *Herein lies one of the chief values of the Board* [emphases added]."[42] At the end of the memo, Towers highlighted that the revised SCB–General Board precept Carney had written for Nimitz "is not in accord with [Forrestal's] ideas." This ended the matter, and the next communication issued by the SCB emphasized this resolution and the return to the submission of future general building plans and ships characteristics programs to the General Board, either by the SCB or by Op-03.

The ship-construction program referred to the General Board in July 1947 by the SCB tells much about the way the Navy viewed both the future and role of the General Board. It reflected Nimitz's own vision of a sea-control type of fleet, emphasizing logistics ships, new antisubmarine destroyers, submarines, and only one "new type" aircraft carrier. It also recommended modification of several submarines and surface ships for service in the Arctic (perhaps in response to Soviet threats) as well as the conversion of two *Essex*-class carriers "to operate new heavier type aircraft." Presumably these would be aircraft that could carry atomic weapons.[43]

Meanwhile the secretary tasked the board with a more active role in looking at areas for efficiency in the shore infrastructure of the Navy, tasking it to survey these activities. Arleigh Burke helped produce the initial draft. Burke made it clear that he believed that there was too much centralization inside the SecNav office and the CNO with the implication that more authority should be decentralized to the shore activities.[44] Under Towers the board gained in power and influence, although occasionally it was still tasked with "busy work," such as a study late in 1947 on dress uniforms requested by Nimitz—recall that the CNO, as well as SecNav, could request General Board studies. Towers may have taken this on because of his desire to avoid further conflict and perhaps because of his impending retirement at the end of the year. The passage of the 1947 National Security Act and Forrestal's subsequent appointment as the first secretary of defense saw two defenders of the board's newly reestablished prestige and prerogatives leave the scene.[45]

The Revolt of the Admirals

The General Board might easily have then faded again into insignificance. That it did not is due to several factors: the new Chief of Naval Operations,

The rejuvenated General Board with ADM Towers as its chairman, 1947. The brilliant CAPT Burke is at the far right, seated. VADM McMorris is sitting next to Towers (*third from left*). The Marines had returned to membership of the board with Col R. M. Pate, later the twenty-first commandant of the Marine Corps (*far left*). Note also that members now wore their military uniforms at meetings. *Naval History and Heritage Command*

the new Secretary of the Navy, and the continuing service of Towers' hand-picked lieutenants (especially McMorris and Burke). Nimitz retired nearly at the same time as Towers. His replacement, ADM Louis Denfield, had been serving as chief of the Bureau of Naval Personnel. Denfield might have reflected his position on the value of the General Board in a report in late 1945 for Forrestal delineating flag officer billets for the postwar Navy. Denfield recommended retention of the General Board with a complement of seven admirals. In another sign of his probable esteem and empathy for the board, Denfield recommended upgrading the chairman's rank from vice admiral to full admiral. This was precisely what Forrestal had done when he brought Towers in to serve as chairman. The tone of the communications between the board and the CNO became more cordial. The board was to carry out some of its most interesting work under Denfield until the fight over naval aviation in 1949 witnessed the departure of Secretary of the Navy John Sullivan (formerly the assistant SecNav) and removal of Denfield.[46] At the same time, the General Board decreased in size slightly, shrinking down to seven members (including only three admirals) with Towers' departure.

A scan of the subjects assigned for the board to study in 1948 reveals its new scope and charter. Beginning in January, Sullivan referred to it several very important policy topics, including "Functions of the Navy in Support of a National War Effort," "Composition and Cost of Reserve Fleets," and a revision of the U.S. Naval Policy.[47] Just as in 1922, the Secretary of the Navy had turned to the General Board for an overall policy document under the new defense regime instituted by the 1947 National Security Act. The idea of a potential war, too, was very much on the minds of naval leaders at the highest levels, although it was at odds with the continuing demobilization and costs for maintaining some of the ships of the huge World War II legacy fleet in various states of readiness.

That summer, the Secretary of the Navy ordered another naval policy review, but more important, Sullivan turned to the General Board for a long-range recommendation for the design of the Navy for the next decade (1951–60). Burke also undertook the task for overseeing this study. The process had actually started the previous November under Towers with a top-secret memorandum to the CNO that in turn had been stimulated by the Joint Strategic Plans Committee seeking the board's "views ... as to the Naval Operating Forces which will be required in Fiscal Year 1955, particularly as such information pertains to naval aviation."[48] Thus the board became involved in two of the most important naval issues of the day—the Navy of the future and the role of naval aviation in that future.

The initial report by Burke in November 1947 emphasized that the "only major war likely to occur between now and fiscal 1955 is a war instigated by the USSR against the United States." Burke went on to emphasize his (and presumably the other board members') view as to the kind of navy for which that threat should be designed: "The USSR will not intentionally risk such a war until she is fully prepared to fight with, in addition to her land forces, an air force, a submarine force, and possibly a guided missile force capable of delivering an effective surprise attack on industrial and military centers within the continental United States, our principal advance bases, and our lines of communications as the initial, hostile act." The report also emphasized that the board should use "history as a guide," especially recent history—thus the notion that a Pearl Harbor–type attack using new modern missiles, possibly on submarines or other ships, must be considered in construction and building decisions. It makes sense that naval aviation figured prominently as one means to keep this threat as far as possible from vital targets overseas as well as in the continental heartland. Just as important, however, were U.S. submarines, both in the attack and as radar pickets. This view of future warfare helps understand better the selection of Denfield, a submariner, as CNO and the alignment of Burke and the board in this matter.[49] At the same time, the board was receiving updates from JCS staff papers (presumably those of the Joint Strategic Plans Committee) "each Friday."[50]

By June 1948 the analysis had expanded and included political and economic factors as well as military, each area getting its own enclosure. The study's scope reminds one of George Kennan's work. Indeed, possibly Burke or other members had read Kennan's famous 1947 article, "The Sources of Soviet Conduct" in *Foreign Affairs*.[51] The study emphasized the ongoing concern over defense unification as a means to highlight the need to resolve these disputes to better formulate strategy: "The controversy which accompanied the attempts to merge the armed forces has not died out. The paramount interests of national security demand an atmosphere of harmony and unanimity of purpose in the military establishment and allow no room for unhealthy service jealousies and for bickering and jockeying for favored position." The authors found that Europe and the Middle East were the two most "critical points of contact in a war with Russia."[52]

Enclosure D of the study discussed the Navy's "contribution" inside a "harmonious" military establishment. The study made several predictions, including an estimate that the USSR would have atomic bombs by no later than 1952 ready for use in war and that the United States would not initiate a "preventative war."[53] In a later section, it discussed the most urgent threats to aircraft carrier–centered forces as aircraft and submarines. It also emphasized the need for a large, flush deck carrier to allow for operation of larger aircraft to carry atomic bombs as well as to intercept attacking aircraft at better stand-off ranges (presumably due to atomic bomb–equipped aircraft from the USSR). Other "lessons learned" from World War II appeared in the form of an emphasis on antisubmarine warfare to counter a Soviet unrestricted submarine war similar to that of the Germans in World War II as well as the seizure of advanced bases on the periphery of the USSR to project power against the Soviet industrial base.[54]

The completed top-secret report was then forwarded to Secretary of the Navy Sullivan with the recommendation to provide copies to the secretaries of Defense (Forrestal), Army, and Air Force. At the same time, it included a withering critique of the readiness of all U.S. military forces to engage in a war with the USSR, focusing in particular on the poor readiness as a result of budget economies that had left the U.S. Navy bereft of antisubmarine warfare craft, submarines, aircraft, and with only eleven attack aircraft carriers. It also emphasized that the delineation of "roles and missions" at Key West the year before had done little to solve the problem of interservice rivalries and disunity of command.[55] Forrestal undoubtedly agreed with almost everything in the report, but one can see how these positions, especially the board's assessment of abysmal military readiness (among other things), might rub members of the Truman administration the wrong way.

Forrestal's demise, and his protection as SecDef of the General Board, was not long in coming. During the 1948 presidential campaign, it leaked out that he was willing to serve in a subsequent democratic administration. His principled opposition to further cuts and subordination of the Navy to a centralized Army and Air Force–controlled defense establishment further alienated him from those services and the president. In March 1949, Truman replaced Forrestal with Louis Johnson as secretary of defense.[56] Johnson believed in economy via reliance on air power to justify cuts. With Forrestal out of the way and an election mandate from the American people for Truman, Johnson adopted the attitude of the Army and Air Force vis-à-vis naval aviation and the Marine Corps. During the civil-military conflict known to history as the Revolt of the Admirals, Johnson informed ADM Richard Connolly that "the Navy is on its way out. Now, take amphibious operations. There's no reason for having a Navy and a Marine Corps. General Bradley . . . tells me that amphibious operations are a thing of the past. We'll never have any more amphibious operations. That does away with the Marine Corps. And the Air Force can do anything the Navy can do nowadays, so that does away with the Navy."[57]

However, the General Board was not the lightning rod at the center of this major policy dispute in peacetime in the Navy, even though it supported Denfield and a strong role for naval aviation in the current defense structure. Shortly after helping write the "ten-year" study, Burke left the board for command of the cruiser *Huntington*. McMorris, the chairman, had left the month prior. The board was now under the leadership of a two-star admiral (Shafroth) again, although his heir apparent, RADM Allan McCann, could be categorized as an "up and comer."[58] Because of the perceived shortcomings in the original ten-year study, another was commissioned for the board shortly after Burke's departure in an effort to come up with a compromise. The resulting study had no more effect outside the Navy than its predecessor and might be regarded as the last national policy study the board carried out.[59]

Burke's work for the General Board attracted high-level attention, and in late 1948 Denfield decided to use his policy expertise inside CNO, moving him from command and making him head of a new organization, OP-23, devoted exclusively to unification policy issues.[60] Burke's OP-23 became the lightning rod instead of the General Board during the Revolt of the Admirals in the summer and fall of 1949. This episode in naval history has been dealt with at length elsewhere, but its impact on the existence of the General Board, which was not heavily involved, was significant. For Secretary of Defense Johnson, the Navy's resistance to a strategy that relied almost entirely on air power for power projection in a possible nuclear war with the USSR had created a deep rift. Additionally, conflict over use of the B-36 bomber versus a "super carrier," or both, also underlay the conflict.[61]

The chain of events characterized as "revolt" started not long after Johnson took over from Forrestal. Johnson initiated a series of actions that caused an eventual housecleaning of the top leadership of the Navy, both civilian and senior officers, although it is unlikely that this is exactly what Johnson intended. The first to go was Secretary of the Navy Sullivan, who resigned shortly after Johnson cancelled the contract to finish building the supercarrier *United States*—capable of launching nuclear-armed Navy bombers—in April 1949.[62] Sullivan's replacement, Francis P. Matthews, was a political appointee with no experience with the Navy. He shared Johnson's policy views on defense and the Navy's subordinate role to the Air Force in strategy.[63] Matthews took charge during a period when congressional opinion of the Navy had been damaged by the perception of official Navy misbehavior, if not misconduct, in a spate of hearings on the B-36 before Congress. Burke and Vice Chief of Naval Operations Arthur Radford worried about this perception and organized the hearings that fall (1949) to try to redeem the situation. At the same time, Burke worked under increasingly difficult conditions when McCann was pulled from the General Board in June and assigned as naval inspector general, his charter being to investigate Burke, among others.[64]

The crisis came to a head when Radford and others began testifying to Congress early in October. Their reasoned testimony, supported by Burke's office despite the seizure of its files, impressed congressional observers and did much to retrieve the Navy's reputation with the branch of government that could hurt it most. The climax came on 13 October, ironically the day celebrated as the U.S. Navy's birthday, with Denfield's testimony. The CNO made an impassioned appeal for a robust defense policy not based solely on the "self-sufficiency of air power."[65] Johnson and Matthews interpreted this as disloyalty and removed Denfield as CNO not long after, although Denfield remained on active service. Forrest Sherman, who had stayed in the background on the unification debates, became the CNO. It has been argued by some historians that Radford's, Burke's, and finally Denfield's actions saved naval aviation. However, at the time this was far from certain. By June 1950 the Navy's component of aircraft carriers was on the blocks to go as low as six on active duty, with only one on station in the Western Pacific when the forces of North Korea invaded South Korea. This war, which confirmed predictions made in the board's 1948 study, had as big a role in saving naval aviation (and the Marine Corps), and a large conventional Navy for sea control, as did the actions of Navy officers during the "revolt."[66]

The General Board might be regarded as collateral damage due to the revolt. However, it is not completely clear if the revolt was anything more than a contributing factor rather than the proximate cause of the board's disestablishment at the beginning of 1951, more than a year later. Little in the minutes and hearings of its activities references the momentous events in Congress, Burke's OP-23, and the testimony by the CNO. During August 1949 the board did look at two potentially controversial topics—one on the Army's "General Staff System Applicability to the Navy." COL Kilbourne Johnston, USA, of the Office of the Army Comptroller and the "leading expert" on the Army system, testified to the board on 9 August. In his opening comments, he said of the board, "In my organization studies extending over a period of seventeen years, the Navy General Board has always appeared to me to be the epitome of the pure general staff theory. I think you will see as I develop my subject that in my own mind at least there is a grave doubt whether or not the Navy does not have a General Staff much closer to that conceived of by the Germans in the early part of the nineteenth century [than the Army]."[67]

Unfortunately, Secretary Matthews was not present to hear this rather astonishing judgment by an Army officer on the value of the General Board. The board recommended that a specialized and centralized general staff corps not be adopted, and that the current OpNav organization be retained without major changes "until the full impact of the implementation of the National Security Act Amendments of 1949 . . . on the Department of the Navy is known." It also emphasized that this system resulted in "a high degree of civilian participation" but neglected its own significant role in assisting that participation.[68] Better reflecting Matthews' concerns was another hearing two days later on the "Organization of the Navy Department," featuring testimony by two "management engineers," although it was clear that this hearing was closely related to whatever findings might emerge from the general staff discussions. Most of this discussion centered on how general staff functions and operations of the fleet had been concentrated under ADM King as an expedient measure in wartime.[69]

However, as the crisis of the revolt came to a head in September, the General Board record was silent. It turned in its report on the General Staff on 19 August, and the next set of minutes does not appear until 19 September 1949, after Denfield's testimony was complete. The record simply picks up at the point with "business as usual," announcing that VADM

Harry W. Hill had reported as chairman. Hill had extensive combat experience in command of amphibious operations in World War II, from Tarawa to Okinawa, and had recently stepped down as the first commandant of the newly founded National War College in Washington. His first order of business was to have the board consider questions submitted to it by the Secretary of the Navy, although the record is silent about what these questions were. Perhaps they involved the recent unpleasantness with the Chief of Naval Operations.[70] These questions might be the reason that at the same time the board began to plan for various field trips to naval bases and facilities from Key West to the West Coast in October. The record never specifies what its answers were, or even if they were forwarded to the Secretary of the Navy, but if they were about recent events, they did not cause Matthews to dissolve the board. The hearings reflect no perturbations in routine either; on 4 October, a secret hearing was held about integrating guided missiles onto surface ships, and much of the remainder of the month was spent on the aforementioned field trip.[71] In mid-November the board picked up its routine again, looking at the "Relationship of the Importance of the Various Budgetary Programs to Maintain the Most Effective Navy." It would work this project until March of the following year. At this time the General Board consisted of Hill, two rear admirals, two captains (one as secretary), and one Marine colonel.[72]

The Last Year

The records for the hearings of the board list a change in serial nomenclature for 1949. The board went from numbered serials—the last serial of 1948 was number 348—to "project numbers." These were used for both 1949 and 1950, with the last set listed in the overall serial list being Project 8–49. However, if one consults the index for the hearings for 1950, one finds an additional six project numbers for which the board held forty-five separate hearings in 1950. Most of these hearings involved the "military characteristics" of ships and aircraft, although several of the first hearings in 1950 from January to March actually covered the final project of 1949, which examined important programs in the budget. The board looked at everything from individual attack aircraft to nuclear-powered submarines (in March). Ironically, its final hearings in October 1950 considered the new-construction "Attack Carrier" based on the designs of USS *United States,* which had been cancelled by Johnson the year before. The Korean

War had changed the SecNav's and SecDef's minds about the need for a new large carrier.[73] The SCB provided attendees for many of the hearings in 1950, just as it had done in 1949 for the hearings related to ship designs and numbers.[74] Keeping all these factors in mind, it appeared that the General Board was in little danger of being disestablished at the end of 1949 and into the spring of 1950. Hill was a strong leader, but his departure on 14 April 1950 to become the superintendent of the Naval Academy with no commensurate replacement of his stature might be another possible indicator that the board was living on borrowed time.[75]

The board did address one nonship-characteristics topic in July 1950: flag officer "employment" in the Navy. These hearings examined the flag officer numbers for rear admiral and higher in all of the nonfleet (shore) establishments, including the office of the CNO. Significantly, the board did not address its own admirals in this report. Another notable change that occurred during the last year of the General Board had to do with the intended consumer for its products. On 10 August 1950, it submitted Project 7–50, a study on admiral "employment" to the Secretary of the Navy. In the minutes for its meeting five days later, it simply listed forwarding "The General Board's Report on Project No. 8–50, 'Shipbuilding and Conversion Program FY 1951 Increment, Second Supplementary,' . . . to the Chief of Naval Operations." The CNO had finally achieved oversight over the board's products, probably due to Matthews' direction.[76] This is a much bigger sign that Matthews and the CNO were considering, or even cooperating, to eliminate the board, especially since ADM William Fechteler had replaced ADM Forrest Sherman, who had died in July, as CNO.[77]

The General Board held its last hearing on 31 October but met two more times in November, once to turn in its report on the new carrier and for the last time, on 6 November 1950, to begin discussions on new catapult designs. Earlier that October conflict with the SCB had resurfaced when the board's chairman, Rear Admiral Fort, responded to criticism from the CNO over the old issue of ship characteristics. Apparently the board had been castigated inside OpNav for delays on its characteristics hearings and its lack of awareness about the recommendations and actions of the SCB. Fort recommended that the current way of doing business, as ironed out by Towers nearly two years earlier, be retained.[78] This may have proved the proximate cause for both the CNO and SecNav to reexamine the necessity for the board. Its policy work could be done by RADM Burke's Strategic

Plans Division inside OpNav, the SCB could handle its ships' characteristics function, and the reconciliation of materiel ends, ways, and means was now the province of a new Material Review Board, created in December 1950.[79]

After 6 November, the archival records are opaque about what precisely caused the dissolution of the General Board. The member list for 1950 fails to list detachments as it did for all previous board personnel changes. The membership remained at seven, consisting from August until dissolution: RADM G. H. Fort (chair), RADM W. K. Harrill, RADM E. W. Burrough, RADM H. H. Goodwin, Col S. G. Taxis, CAPT G. W. Stott, and CAPT Gifford Scull (secretary). Appropriately, the Marines were with the board at both its creation and end.[80] The records simply stop, with no discussion or announcement that the board was being dissolved or disestablished in accordance with Navy Regulations. What one finds in the board's own 401 files, which catalogue its organizational history, is also sparse until 16 January 1951. On that day the CNO informed Fort of the "dissolution" of the board by "appropriate changes to U.S. Navy Regulations, 1948." No reason was provided.[81] Secretary of the Navy Matthews apparently did not even tell the board directly of his decision, although perhaps he had delegated the CNO to make this decision in the previous August.

Historian George Baer claims that Matthews thought the board had "outlived its usefulness" but also laments its dissolution as "a loss to the service."[82] Several months later, Hanson Baldwin of the *New York Times* bemoaned the quiet "death" of the General Board.[83] Fort, perhaps writing for the last time on behalf of the board in late January 1951, penned the following epitaph: "The General Board enjoyed a long and honored existence, and its files are fraught with historical interest. It is believed that this fact is appreciated in the Office of Naval Records and History and that the files will be appropriately employed."[84]

EPILOGUE

America's First General Staff

On 1 October 1919 the executive committee of the General Board of the Navy met in the old Army-Navy Building in Washington, D.C., not far from Constitution Hall, site of the future Washington Naval Conference and of today's Vietnam War Memorial at the western end of the National Mall. That day the discussion was led by RADM Frank Friday Fletcher, former commander in chief of the U.S. Fleet and the uncle of Frank Jack Fletcher of World War II fame. The board's witness that day was Maj W. L. Redles, USMC, who had served as an attaché in Japan, having just returned from that nation. The interest of the board was more than curiosity. Japan had recently been involved in World War I as first a British and then a U.S. ally, as well as a somewhat unlikely "ally" against the Russian Bolsheviks in the recent intervention in Siberia.[1] More important, the board's interest lay in the concern that Japan's Imperial Navy might be the U.S. Navy's most likely future adversary. To that end, it wanted to understand the Japanese strategic psyche as much as possible. Redles held the members' interest, recounting Japan's recent history and its structure as a society and state. After discussing the role of the emperor, he moved to a topic many board members had likely never heard before:

> Next to the Emperor are the "Genro," called "Elder Statesmen." They were composed of certain of the former feudal lords who had remained faithful to him. Only two survive of the original number, Yamagato [Yamagata Aritomo] and Matsukata [Toshitane]. Saionji [Kinmochi] has been made a member. Okuma [Shigenobu] is at times included informally. They have no legal status. "They are not recognized in either the Japanese Constitution or in the laws of Japan." They are a group of old men of high rank who are trusted advisers of the Emperor.[2]

One wonders if not a few of the members, especially the five admirals and one general (the commandant of the Marine Corps) present, saw in the Genro concept something of themselves and the role of the General Board in advising the Secretary of the Navy. Many of them were "past their prime," especially Fletcher, Winterhalter, and Chairman Charles Badger, who had replaced Admiral of the Fleet George Dewey—America's first naval Genro. However, as with the Genro and the Japanese emperor, their nation still trusted them to provide advice. Too, their organization had not been established by law or in the Constitution. The situation was rich with irony.

The General Board as a Model for an Innovative Organization

If there is an "American Way of War," perhaps part of such a way is a distinctive American way of problem solving.[3] If so, then the General Board represents one case study reflecting this characterization. We might further define this approach as collaborative, but with healthy doses of good old American individualism. Directed, but with a consensus; collegial yet impassioned; eschewing the language of militarism while retaining the efficiency of military professionalism; controlled by the civilian sector but allowing a respected team of military advisers a "voice"; small in size but big in influence; and, above all, interested in the greater good of the Republic (as the participants envisioned that good).

A wise friend once informed me that "those who innovate least often innovate best" (or more successfully).[4] His example was the German army after World War I and its development of the blitzkrieg concept of warfare. The Germans had innovated successfully at the operational level because they had improved upon an existing system called Bewegungskrieg, translated as "maneuver warfare."[5] This is perhaps why the Navy reformers' adoption and adaptation of the German system functioned so efficaciously prior to World War II and delivered such stunning results in design of the fleet and operations in the total war environments of World War I and World War II. They were only adapting and improving on a previously tested general staff *system* to their own particular, maritime circumstances.

Naval officers of the period, especially the generation prior to World War I, but World War II as well, read and wrote military history. The historical knowledge of officers such as Mahan, Luce, Taylor, Fiske, Wainwright, Sims, Frost, Knox, Pratt, Lanning, and King might put today's technocratic admirals to shame.[6] They modeled themselves to some degree on Mahan, but many of them already had the habit being "historical-minded" before Mahan ever published his first and most influential book in 1890.[7]

Final Thoughts

The General Board started out as an "experiment," as a means to the ultimate end of a naval and American version of the German General Staff of Scharnhorst and Moltke the Elder. It ended as something a bit different—a group of esteemed Genro policy advisers, elder statesmen in a sort of senior-officer think tank. Its evolution from one to the other is instructive, and this book has spilt much ink (or electrons) narrating that evolution. Certainly it started out as a "stealth" general staff, although Taylor and Dewey had no doubts about its main functions of war planning, oversight of warship construction (both large and small), and strategy. In these early years, one can characterize it as a *naval general staff system* that encompassed the Naval War College, Bureau of Navigation, Marine Corps (until 1904), and General Board. The board acted as the "balance wheel" of the whole enterprise.

The tireless efforts of the reformers and the war in Europe combined to bring about changes to this system, removing the direct war-planning function from the board and giving this system a new *operational* staff entity: CNO-OpNav. The American naval general staff system now consisted of the NWC, General Board, and OpNav (replacing BuNav) organizations in 1915 and brought the leadership of the Marine Corps back into the system. This general staff construct existed in relative harmony until ADM Pratt's reforms in 1932. Although Pratt intended a more cohesive and effective system, the long-term result of his action to eliminate the ex officio memberships compartmentalized and desynchronized the system. The Naval War College and Marines effectively left the system, and the Office of the Chief of Naval Operations gathered more of the functions of a general staff unto itself, although the board still reigned supreme on fleet construction and design and occasionally in the policy area. By the end of World War II, though, it had lost much of its former influence.

As we saw in the last chapter, Forrestal deliberately attempted to recapture the goodness of the board, almost to a pre-Pratt system, although he did not manage to bring the NWC back into the main workings of the system other than as a place to educate and train officers in strategy and naval staff and planning procedures. Forrestal wanted to turn the General Board into a counterweight to the too-powerful CNO-OpNav staff, if not a counterweight to the JCS. Eminent Japanese historian Sadao Asada has termed this mechanism "civilian control by proxy" in referring to the Navy Ministry of Japan's internecine battles with the naval general staff at the time of the Washington Naval Conference.[8] However, the board did not succumb to a power grab by militarists as in the Japanese case; rather, it became a collateral casualty because of national defense reforms of 1947–49 and the interservice conflict that resulted from defense unification.

An emerging civilian-dominated national security state, a supersecretary of defense, the Joint Chiefs of Staff, and the new National Security Council all seemed to obviate the policy functions Forrestal had tried to reclaim for the General Board. Moreover, its ships-characteristics function continued for decades after in the SCB inside the Bureau of Ships and its successor, the Naval Sea Systems Command. In the continuing search for efficiencies by the Truman administration, there seemed no reason for any redundancy, no matter how vital as a "second opinion," within a Navy that had been cut down to size after the Revolt of the Admirals. The Korean War, which erupted during the last year of the board's existence, did not save it, although it may have saved naval aviation and the Marines. The board had done its best work in peacetime, not war, preparing the nation for crises. The pattern of the past had always been for war to diminish the role of the board relative to the CNO. This seemed the case by late 1950, except this time the diminution was fatal.

What does it all mean? Is this tale simply a story without a moral? God forbid. The case of the General Board has much to teach us about ourselves and how we got here, especially if the pronoun "we" applies to naval professionals. Yet it also applies to American leaders in general, who see themselves solving problems today that are just as complex and daunting as those faced by the General Boards of yesteryear. All the new technology, such a troubled world, visions of the Republic in dire danger—their policy serial summaries breathe the familiar phobias that we worry about today to varying degrees. May this story inform our efforts to solve problems of strategy and policy collaboratively and collegially. Three cheers for the General Board. May its service to our nation be remembered with gratitude.

APPENDIX 1

General Orders Relating to the Establishment and Reorganization of the General Board of the Navy

General Order 544, March 13, 1900
A General Board is hereby established, to be composed of the following named officers: The Admiral of the Navy, the Chief of the Bureau of Navigation, the Chief Intelligence Officer and his principal assistant, the president [*sic*] of the Naval War College and his principal assistant, and three other officers of or above the grade of lieutenant commander.[1]

Should the principal of assistant of the chief Intelligence Officer, or the principal assistant of the President of the Naval War College be below the rank of lieutenant commander, an officer or officers of the grade of lieutenant commander or above will be designated to fill such place or places on the Board.

The purpose of the Department in establishing this Board is to ensure efficient preparation of the fleet in case of war and for the naval defense of the coast.

The chief of the Bureau of Navigation will be the custodian of the plans of campaign and war preparations. He will indicate to the War College and the Intelligence Officer the information required from them by the General Board, and in the absence of the Admiral of the Navy, he will preside at meetings of the Board, and exercise the functions of president of the Board.

The Board will meet at least once a month, five of its members constituting a quorum and two of its sessions every year shall extend over a period of not less than one week each, during which time the Board shall meet daily.

General Order 43, April 16, 1901
General Order No. 544, of March 12, 1900, republished in General Order No. 1 of June 30, 1900, is so far modified that the General Board will be composed of the following named officers:

---

1. General Order 544 is cited in Wainwright, "General Board," 189–201.

Admiral George Dewey, President
The Chief of the Bureau of Navigation
The Chief Intelligence Officer
The President of the Naval War College, and
Such other officer of or above the grade of lieutenant commander as the Department may designate.

APPENDIX 2

Secretaries of the Navy, 1900–1951

John D. Long, 6 March 1897–30 April 1902

William H. Moody, 1 May 1902–30 June 1904

Paul Morton, 1 July 1904–30 June 1905

Charles J. Bonaparte, 1 July 1905–16 December 1906

Victor H. Metcalf, 17 December 1906–30 November 1908

Truman H. Newberry, 1 December 1908–5 March 1909

George von L. Meyer, 6 March 1909–4 March 1913

Josephus Daniels, 5 March 1913–5 March 1921

Edwin Denby, 6 March 1921–10 March 1924

Curtis D. Wilbur, 19 March 1924–4 March 1929

Charles F. Adams, 5 March 1929–4 March 1933

Claude A. Swanson, 4 March 1933–7 July 1939

Charles Edison, 2 January 1940–24 June 1940

Frank Knox, 11 July 1940–28 April 1944

James Forrestal, 19 May 1944–17 September 1947

John L. Sullivan, 18 September 1947–24 May 1949

Francis P. Matthews, 25 May 1949–31 July 1951

Source. This list is from "Secretaries of the Navy," Naval History and Heritage Command, https://www.history.navy.mil/research/library/research-guides/lists-of-senior-officers-and-civilian-officials-of-the-us-navy/secretaries-of-the-navy.html.

APPENDIX 3

General Board Studies Produced in 1901

No.	Serial Subject	Submitted
1-01	Special stowage of war plans aboard ship	7 Feb 01
2-01	Proposed naval bases at Guantanamo and Cienfuegos	7 Feb 01
3-01	Survey of USS BLAKE in locality of Dry Tortugas	8 Feb 01
4-01	Guns for defense of Asiatic Advanced Bases	18 Feb 01
5-01	Use of torpedoes for defense of an advanced base	18 Feb 01
6-01	Mines and mining outfits for battleships and cruisers	18 Feb 01
7-01	Maneuvers North Atlantic Fleet	11 Mar 01
8-01	Ordinance material for Cavite	24 Apr 01
9-01	Furnishing steam to run air compressors for torpedo batteries on shore	24 Apr 01
10-01	Proposed naval bases at Guantanamo and Cienfuegos	24 Apr 01
11-01	Survey of Magarita Straits and vicinity recommended	24 Apr 01
12-01	Defense of Haiti from enemy attack	23 Apr 01
13-01	Sphere of U.S. naval control in South America	25 Apr 01
14-01	Harbor in vicinity of Puerto Rico to be used as naval base	27 Jun 01
15-01	Fresh water basins on the Pacific Coast	28 Jun 01
16-01	Congressional legislation re General Board	28 Jun 01
17-01	Extension of Naval War College	29 Jun 01
18-01	Characteristics of Picket [sic] boats	29 Jun 01
19-01	Culebra as naval base in West Indies	21 Aug 01
20-01	Surveys of waters of Puerto Rico and Nantucket Sound	23 Aug 01
21-01	Organization of Naval reserve [sic]	25 Sep 01

No.	Serial Subject	Submitted
22-01	Naval station in the Philippines	26 Sep 01
23-01	Culebra as naval base in West Indies	26 Sep 01
24-01	Characteristics of picket boats	30 Oct 01
25-01	Additional ships recommended for Navy	30 Oct 01
26-01	Coaling stations in the Philippines	31 Oct 01
27-01	Naval and coaling stations on Coast of Cuba	1 Nov 01
38-01	Organization of 4 Marine companies for expeditionary field service	1 Nov 01
29-01	Assignment of reservation for Subig [sic] Bay Naval Station	1 Nov 01
30-01	Preparedness of Marine Corps for war	1 Nov 01
31-01	Acquisition of Danish islands in West Indies	12 Nov 01
32-01	Assignment of reservation for Subig [sic] Bay Naval Station	26 Nov 01
33-01	Use of Naval Port in China	27 Nov 01
34-01	Winter maneuvers of North Atlantic Fleet and Asiatic Fleet	25 Nov 01
35-01	Culebra as Naval Base in West Indies	27 Nov 01

Source. This list is from the list of the studies of the General Board, 1900–1950, Roll 1, PHGB.

NOTES

Preface and Acknowledgments

1. See John T. Kuehn, "The Influence of Naval Arms Limitation on U.S. Naval Innovation during the Interwar Period, 1921–1937" (PhD diss., Kansas State University, 2007), especially chapter 2 and the bibliography. See also Daniel J. Costello, "Planning for War: A History of the General Board of the Navy, 1900–1914" (PhD diss., Fletcher School of Law and Diplomacy, 1968).
2. Albert A. Nofi, *To Train the Fleet for War: The U.S. Navy Fleet Problems, 1923–1940* (Newport, RI: Naval War College Press, 2010), 16n10. Nofi characterizes the board's duties as "somewhere between a general staff and those of a board of trustees" (10).

Chapter 1. What Was the General Board of the Navy?

Epigraph, Jarvis Butler, "The General Board of the Navy," U.S. Naval Institute *Proceedings* 56, no. 8 (August 1930): 700; emphasis added.

1. Two recent excellent works that emphasize the strategic focus of the planners within the Admiralty of Great Britain are Nicholas Lambert's *Planning Armageddon: British Economic Warfare and the First World War* (Cambridge: Harvard University Press, 2012) and Phillip Pattee's *At War in Distant Waters: British Colonial Defense in the Great War* (Annapolis: Naval Institute Press, 2013).
2. Butler, "General Board of the Navy," 700.
3. Philip L. Semsch, "Elihu Root and the General Staff," *Military Affairs* 27, no. 1 (Spring 1963): 16–27; Ronald H. Spector, *Professors at War: The Naval War College and the Development of the Naval Profession* (Newport, RI: Naval War College Press, 1977). Spector makes a direct link between organizational reform in the Navy as a subset of the larger societal trends and developments, especially the Navy's quest for "efficiency" and the Navy's "business approach to war."

4. Williamson Murray and Alan Millett, "Innovation: Past and Future," in *Military Innovation in the Interwar Period*, ed. Williamson Murray and Alan Millett (New York: Cambridge University Press, 1996), 313–314. The authors dispel the axiom that we should not study to fight the last war and replace it with one that proposes an honest study of conflict, including "the last war."
5. See John T. Kuehn, "The Martial Spirit—Naval Style: The Naval Reform Movement and the Establishment of the General Board of the Navy, 1873–1900," *Northern Mariner/Le marin du nord* 22, no. 2 (April 2012): 121–140.
6. See appendix 1 in this book.
7. Costello, "Planning for War," 22.
8. John T. Kuehn, *Agents of Innovation: The General Board and the Design of the Fleet that Defeated the Japanese Navy* (Annapolis: Naval Institute Press, 2008), chapter 2.
9. Norman Friedman, "The South Carolina Sisters: America's First Dreadnoughts," *Naval History Magazine* 24, no. 1 (February 2010).
10. Butler, "General Board of the Navy," 703.
11. Henry P. Beers, "The Development of the Office of the Chief of Naval Operations," pt. 1, *Military Affairs* 2 (Spring 1946), 55, and Henry P. Beers, "The Development of the Office of the Chief of Naval Operations," pt. 3, *Military Affairs* 11, no. 2 (Summer 1947): 3, 89, implies as much but does not say so specifically. Beers also aligns the General Board's character as one of "conservatism," which recent scholarship has revised considerably; see Kuehn, *Agents of Innovation*. See also Robert W. Love Jr., *History of the U.S. Navy*, vol. 1, *1775–1941* (Harrisburg, PA: Stackpole Books, 1992), 458–460, 534. Love does not identify the creation of OpNav and CNO so much as Dewey's declining health as the reason for the decline of the influence of the General Board, but he notes its rise again to great influence at the time of the Washington Conference.
12. Butler, "General Board of the Navy," 703. The quotation from the 1930 U.S. Navy Regulations is from Butler. Although written in 1930, this language absolutely conveys the role of the General Board in 1922 and after. Kuehn, *Agents of Innovation*, chapter 3.
13. See John T. Kuehn, "Abolish the Secretary of Defense?" *Joint Force Quarterly* 47 (4th Quarter 2007): 114–116.
14. For case studies on most of these programs and the General Board's involvement, see Kuehn, *Agents of Innovation*, chapters 5, 6, and 7; Jeffrey K. Juergens, "The Impact of the General Board of the Navy on Interwar Submarine Design" (master's thesis, USA Command and General Staff College, 2009); Jason H. Davis, "The Influence of the General Board of the Navy on Interwar Destroyer Design" (master's thesis, USA Command and General Staff College, 2011); and Christopher J. Mergen, "Development of Maritime Patrol Aviation

in the Interwar Period, 1918 to 1941" (master's thesis, USA Command and General Staff College, 2015).
15. Kuehn, *Agents of Innovation*, chapters 3 and 4, and Appendix 2, "U.S. Naval Policy 1922." The authoritative work on Orange is Edward S. Miller, *War Plan Orange* (Annapolis: Naval Institute Press, 1991).
16. For a complete discussion of Pratt's influence on the board, see John T. Kuehn, "The Influence of Naval Arms limitation on U.S. Naval Innovation during the Interwar Period, 1921–1937" (PhD diss., Kansas State University, 2007), 51–52.
17. Ibid. See also Kuehn, *Agents of Innovation*, chapter 2 and 175–177. Membership of the General Board, Roll 1 (microfilm), Proceedings and Hearings of the General Board of the Navy, RG 80, National Archives and Records Administration (hereafter cited as PHGB).
18. Kuehn, *Agents of Innovation*, chapter 2 and 175–177; and Jeffrey G. Barlow, *From Hot War to Cold: The U.S. Navy and National Security Affairs, 1945–1955* (Stanford, CA: Stanford University Press, 2009), 61–69.
19. For an interesting account of the Morrow Board and the first unification fight, see Clark G. Reynolds, "John H. Towers, the Morrow Board, and the Reform of the Navy's Aviation," *Military Affairs* 52, no. 2 (April 1988): 78–84.
20. Members of the General Board, 1945–1947, Roll 1, PHGB.
21. Kuehn, *Agents of Innovation*, 175–177; and Members of the General Board, 1945–1947, Roll 1, PHGB. See also Jeffrey G. Barlow, *The Revolt of the Admirals: The Fight for Naval Aviation, 1945–1950* (Washington, DC: Naval Historical Center, 1994), 277–289; and George W. Baer, *One Hundred Years of Sea Power: The U.S. Navy, 1890–1990* (Stanford, CA: Stanford University Press, 1994), 299–301.

Chapter 2. The Naval Reform Movement and the Creation of the General Board

Epigraph, Costello, "Planning for War," 21. This chapter is in part based on John T. Kuehn, "The Martial Spirit—Naval Style: The Naval Reform Movement and the Establishment of the General Board of the Navy, 1873–1900," *Northern Mariner/ Le marin du nord* 22, no. 2 (April 2012): 121–140; it has been updated and adapted for this book.
1. For a recent discussion of the Fisher Revolution, see Holger H. Herwig, "The Battlefleet Revolution, 1885–1914," in *The Dynamics of Military Revolution, 1300–2050*, ed. Macgregor Knox and Williamson Murray (Cambridge: Cambridge University Press, 2001), 114–131.
2. This best exposition on the antimilitary tradition of Americans can be found in Samuel Huntington, *The Soldier and the State* (Cambridge: Harvard University Press, 1957), chapter 4, especially 97–98; for the bad attitude of

British professional officers toward North American colonists, see Douglas Leech, *Roots of Conflict: British Armed Forces and Colonial Americans, 1677–1763* (Chapel Hill: University of North Carolina Press, 1988).
3. See Article 1, Section 8 of the Constitution of the United States of America.
4. Walter Millis, *The Martial Spirit: A Study of Our War with Spain* (Boston: Houghton Mifflin, 1931), especially 407–410. For navalism, see especially Peter Karsten, *The Naval Aristocracy: The Golden Age of Annapolis and the Emergence of Modern American Navalism* (New York: Free Press, 1972); for the classic exposition after World War I, see Harold Sprout and Margaret Sprout, *Toward a New Order of Sea Power: American Naval Policy and the World Scene, 1918–1922* (Princeton, NJ: Princeton University Press, 1940); for a more recent synthesis, see Lisle Rose, *Power at Sea: The Age of Navalism, 1890–1981* (Columbia: University of Missouri Press, 2006).
5. Senate, "Address of the President of the United States at the Opening of the Conference on the Limitation of Armament at Washington, November 21, 1921," S. Doc. 77 (Washington, DC: Government Printing Office, 1921), 6–7. Indirect evidence existed prior to the war's end in point four of Woodrow Wilson's famous "Fourteen Points" speech to Congress; see http://www.firstworldwar.com/source/fourteenpoints.htm.
6. See Robert H. Wiebe, *The Search for Order, 1877–1920* (New York: Hill and Wang, 1967), for a concise history of the Progressive Era.
7. My arguments here follow almost entirely from Beers' seminal and still-useful article "Development of the Office," pt. 1, 40–68.
8. Williamson Murray and Alan Millett, "Innovation: Past and Future," in *Military Innovation in the Interwar Period*, ed. Williamson Murray and Alan Millet (New York: Cambridge University Press, 1996), 313–314. The authors dispel the axiom that we should not study to fight the last war and replace it with one that proposes an honest study of conflict, including "the last war."
9. Beers, "Development of the Office," pt. 1, 41–42.
10. Ibid., 44. For assessments of Fox as a proto-chief of naval operations, see Ari Hoogenboom, *Gustavus Vasa Fox of the Union Navy: A Biography* (Baltimore: Johns Hopkins University Press, 2009), ix; and Craig L. Symonds, *Lincoln and His Admirals: Abraham Lincoln, the U.S. Navy, and the Civil War* (New York: Oxford University Press, 2008), xiv.
11. The Navy decreased from seven hundred warships to just forty-eight. Beers, "Development of the Office," pt. 1, 44–45.
12. For the famous "Frontier Thesis," see Frederick Jackson Turner, "The Significance of the Frontier in American History," in *Frederick Jackson Turner: Wisconsin's Historian of the Frontier*, ed. Martin Ridge (Madison: State Historical Society of Wisconsin, 1986).
13. *History of the U.S. Navy* 1:327–330.

14. From U.S. Naval Institute Constitution and By-Laws, 27 April 2010, https://www.usni.org/pdf/bylaws.pdf; for the stages of professionalization, see Ronald Spector's discussion, *Professors at War: The Naval War College and the Development of the Naval Profession* (Newport, RI: Naval War College Press, 1977), 152n11.
15. Arlington National Cemetery, http://www.arlingtoncemetery.net/dammen.htm.
16. Daniel Ammen, "The Purposes of a Navy, and the Best Methods of Rendering It Efficient," *Record of the United States Naval Institute* 5, no. 4, 119–130 (journal hereafter titled U.S. Naval Institute *Proceedings*).
17. A. T. Mahan to Samuel A. Ashe, 9 May 1879, in *Letters and Papers of Alfred Thayer Mahan*, vol. 1, ed. Robert Seager II and Doris D. Maguire (Annapolis: Naval Institute Press, 1975), 474–476 (hereafter cited as *Mahan Papers*, followed by volume number). Mahan wrote, "Last year as the Institute was growing feeble we determined as a last resort to offer a money prize for an Essay on the subject of Naval Education." See also Robert W. Love, *History of the U.S. Navy*, vol. 1, *1775–1941* (Harrisburg, PA: Stackpole, 1992), 330; and Jon T. Sumida, *Inventing Grand Strategy and Teaching Command: The Classic Works of Alfred Thayer Mahan Reconsidered* (Washington, D.C.: Woodrow Wilson Center Press/Johns Hopkins University Press, 1997), 16–18.
18. U.S. Naval Institute *Proceedings* 5 (1879): 323, 377. Volume numbers were not listed between numbers 4 and 9 and mostly encompassed the first-prize essays as well as the extended discussion of them facilitated by Soley.
19. Beers, "Development of the Office," pt. 1, 45–48.
20. Love, *History of the U.S. Navy* 1:350–352. "ABCD" stood for the names of the ships appropriated for by Congress due to the Rodgers Board: the unarmored cruisers *Atlanta, Boston,* and *Chicago* and the dispatch boat *Dolphin* (*Dolphin* later served as the presidential yacht). See also Daniel Ammen and A. T. Mahan, "Naval Education," U.S. Naval Institute *Proceedings* 5 (1879): 345–376.
21. CAPT Henry C. Taylor, "Memorandum on General Staff for the U.S. Navy," U.S. Naval Institute *Proceedings* 26, no. 3 (September 1900): 441–445; see also Spector, *Professors at War*, 14–17. Taylor discusses the German influence in this famous memorandum he wrote for the Secretary of Navy in the winter of 1899–1900. See also Beers, "Development of the Office," pt. 1, 45–4; Sumida, *Inventing Grand Strategy*, 19–21; Spector, *Professors at War*, 27–29.
22. Navy Department, General Order 292, 23 March 1882, from M. S. Thompson, *General Orders and Circulars Issued by the Navy Department from 1863 to 1887* (Washington, DC, 1887), 208.
23. A. T. Mahan, *The Gulf and Inland Waters*, vol. 3 (New York: Charles Scribner's Sons, 1883), 269. Soley wrote on the blockade and the cruisers and

Ammen addressed the Atlantic theater; Beers, "Development of the Office," pt. 1, 47–48; for more on Ammen, see Spector, *Professors at War*, 19.
24. Beers, "Development of the Office," pt. 1, 48–50. See also Spector, *Professors at War*, 27–29. Spector gives Bliss the credit for passing on to his naval colleagues the comparative method of historical analysis. Bliss was later a founder and first president of the Army War College. See also note 19 above.
25. Love, *History of the U.S. Navy* 1:368–369.
26. For a concise discussion of Mahan's influence, see Sumida, *Inventing Grand Strategy*, 1–8; Beers, "Development of the Office," pt. 1, 48–51.
27. Michael W. Wever, "The Influence of Captain Alfred Thayer Mahan upon the United States Navy through the United States Naval Institute's *Proceedings*" (master's thesis, U.S. Army Command and General Staff College, 2012), 67–70.
28. Mahan to Luce, 26 December 1891, *Mahan Papers* 2:60–61; Beers, "Development of the Office," pt. 1, 50–51.
29. Mahan to Luce, 26 December 1891, in *Mahan Papers* 2:60–61. Mahan alludes to this in his letter to Luce and emphasizes that the college is about developing a "group of officers" to practice and prepare for war, not a launching pad for his own fame.
30. See especially the discussion by Williamson Murray and Barry Watts, "Military Innovation in Peacetime," in *Military Innovation in the Interwar Period*, ed. Williamson Murray and Barry Watts (New York: Cambridge University Press, 1996), 383–405; and Kuehn, *Agents of Innovation*, 3–6.
31. Spector, *Professors at War*, 27. Taylor paid his own way to Newport in order to teach the inaugural class at the college.
32. F. E. Chadwick, "Naval Department Reorganization," U.S. Naval Institute *Proceedings* 20, no. 3 (1894): 493–525, discussion of the paper by institute members passim. See also Charles O. Paullin, *Paullin's History of Naval Administration, 1775–1911* (Annapolis: Naval Institute Press, 1968), 371, essay originally published in U.S. Naval Institute *Proceedings*, 1905–14); see also *Mahan Papers* 2:60, wherein Mahan confides his thoughts on the NWC with Chadwick on a train ride to New York. For NWC presidents, see http://www.usnwc.edu/About/History.aspx.
33. Chadwick, "Naval Department Reorganization," 493–499.
34. Formal noun usage is retained here from ibid., 500–501, and his accompanying diagram (it was a foldout insert in that issue).
35. Ibid., 493–506 and diagram.
36. See discussion in Kuehn, *Agents of Innovation*, 15–21.
37. Chadwick, "Naval Department Reorganization," 502.
38. Ibid., 506, 524.
39. Ibid., 510–515.
40. Ibid., 515–523.

41. Ibid., 524–525.
42. H. C. Taylor, introduction to "The War in the East," by Capt Richard Wallach, USMC, U.S. Naval Institute *Proceedings* 21, no. 76 (1895): 691.
43. Solution to the Problem of 1894, UNOpP, RG 12, Naval War College Archives, Newport, RI; Solution to the Problem of 1895, UNOpP, RG 12, Naval War College Archives, Newport, RI. I am indebted for this information to both Michael Crawford and Kenneth Wenzer of the Naval Historical and Heritage Command, who used the papers at the Naval War College to present scholarship based on these war plans at the most recent Society of Military History Conference in April 2016 in Ottawa, Kansas. This reference is used with their permission.
44. Henry C. Taylor to Stephen B. Luce, 22 January 1896, DLC-MSS, Reel 9, Stephen B. Luce Papers. Thanks to Kenneth Wenzer for pointing out this quotation and correspondence to me.
45. A. T. Mahan, *The Influence of Sea Power Upon History, 1660–1783* (Boston: Little Brown, 1890), 28–29, 50–51.
46. Love, *History of the U.S. Navy* 1:365–368.
47. *Mahan Papers* 2:60–61. See also Mahan to Luce, 24 November 1891, *Mahan Papers* 2:56–57, which mentions Chadwick's work on the board as well as Mahan's recommendation that he replace Mahan should Mahan be ordered to sea pursuant to a war with Chile. Mahan's overriding concern in these letters was the future of the Naval War College. See also Beers, "Development of the Office," pt. 1, 53.
48. For a concise discussion of the Jeune École, see Martin N. Murphy and Toshi Yoshihara, "Fighting the Naval Hegemon: Evolution in French, Soviet, and Chinese Naval Thought," *Naval War College Review* 68, no. 3 (Summer 2015): 12–19.
49. For an overview of the transformation of the Pax Britannica, see Peter Padfield, *Maritime Dominion and the Triumph of the Free World: Naval Campaigns that Shaped the Modern World 1852–2001* (New York: Overlook Press, 2009), chapter 5. For British attempts to reconcile new technology, see Alan H. Burgoyne, "The Future of the Submarine Boat," paper presented to the Royal United Services Institution, 8 June 1904. Also in *RUSI Journal* 48 (July–December 1904): 1288–1311, discussion with institute members included, including Admiral Sir E. R. Fremantle.
50. Cited in Millis, *Martial Spirit*, 33; for the Melian Dialogue, see Thucydides, *The Peloponnesian War*, trans. Thomas Hobbes, with notes and editing by David Gree (Chicago: University of Chicago Press, 1989), 89:365.
51. Millis, *Martial Spirit*, 107–145.
52. Ibid., 112–113, 121.
53. Beers, "Development of the Office," pt. 1, 53.
54. Mahan to Long, 9 May 1898, in *Mahan Papers* 2:551–552.

55. RADM Albert Gleaves, ed., *Life and Letters of Rear Admiral Stephen B. Luce, U.S. Navy* (New York: G. P. Putnam's Sons, 1925), 234–235.
56. Lodge, cited in Gleaves, *Life and Letters*, 27 May 1898, 235.
57. Beers, "Development of the Office," pt. 1, 54; see also Kenneth C. Wenzer, "The Naval War Board of 1898," *Canadian Military History* 25, no. 1, article 1 (March 2016), at http://scholars.wlu.ca/cmh/vol25/iss1/1/.
58. "The Work of the Naval War Board of 1898: A Report to the General Board of the Navy," 29 October 1906, *Mahan Papers* 3:627–643.
59. Costello, "Planning for War," 18–19.
60. Henry C. Taylor, "Memorandum on General Staff for the U.S. Navy," republished in U.S. Naval Institute *Proceedings* 26, no. 3 (September 1900) with an introduction of the background by the author, 441–448. The reference to Clausewitz is on page 443.
61. Ibid., 446–447. For a discussion of the Root reforms, see also Philip L. Semsch, "Elihu Root and the General Staff," *Military Affairs* 27, no. 1 (Spring 1963): 16–27; see also John Keilers, "Soldier and Statesman: Tasker H. Bliss," http://www.army.mil/article/26498/Soldier_and_Statesman_Tasker_H_Bliss. The Army reformers were employing the same tactic and the example of the Naval War College to get their own general staff.
62. Perhaps the best work in English to consult on how Taylor and others understood the German General Staff and its organization is Spenser Wilkinson, *The Brain of an Army: A Popular Account of the German General Staff*, 2nd ed. (London: Constable, 1913), especially part 3, where Wilkinson discusses the Great General Staff's organization.
63. Taylor, "Memorandum on General Staff," 447–448.
64. Ibid.
65. Costello, "Planning for War," 19.
66. From the establishing general order cited in the memorandum from General Board (GB) to Assistant Secretary of the Navy, 14 December 1929, Box 156, Hoover Library (HL) (hereafter cited as HL GB). Soon after his election, President Herbert Hoover called on the members of the board to explain the genesis of their organization and to describe its role in naval policymaking. See also Love, *History of the U.S. Navy* 1:417; and Costello, "Planning for War," 22.
67. Costello "Planning for War," 29. See also members of the General Board, 1900, Roll 1, PHGB (hereafter cited as GB ML, preceded by the year).
68. Baer, *One Hundred Years of Sea Power*, 11.
69. Herwig, "Battlefleet Revolution," 114–131; see also Nicholas A. Lambert, "Admiral Sir John Fisher and the Concept of Flotilla Defence, 1904–1909," *Journal of Military History* 59 (October 1995): 639–660.
70. Herwig, "Battlefleet Revolution," 124.

71. Paul E. Pedisich, *Congress Buys a Navy: Politics, Economics, and the Rise of American Naval Power, 1881–1921* (Annapolis: Naval Institute Press, 2016), chapter 6.
72. Ammen, "Purposes of a Navy," 119.
73. Chadwick, "Naval Department Reorganization," 494.
74. Mahan to Luce, 7 May 1890, *Mahan Papers* 2:10. Mahan writes, "My principal aim has been to write a critical military history of the naval past," as he explains to Luce his progress on *The Influence of Sea Power Upon History, 1660–1783*. As for the already existing method, see Carl von Clausewitz, *On War*, ed. and trans. Peter Paret and Michael Howard (Princeton, NJ: Princeton University Press, 1984), bk. 2.
75. A. T. Mahan, *Naval Strategy* (Newport, RI: Department of the Navy, 1909), reprinted in 1991 as Fleet Marine Force Reference Publication (FMFRP) 12-32, 19.
76. The reference here is to the essential rallying cry of the Navy during World War I on the need for a "Navy second to none." See George T. Davis, *A Navy Second to None: The Development of American Naval Policy* (New York: Harcourt Brace, 1940); and "U.S. Naval Policy," 17 January 1925, PHGB. The 1922 "U.S. Naval Policy" is attached to the 1925 General Board hearing transcript.

Chapter 3. In the Shadows of Nelson and Scharnhorst, 1900–1904

1. Kuehn, "Martial Spirit," 124–128.
2. George Dewey, "Needed—A Powerful Navy," 7 December 1912, Dewey Papers, Library of Congress (hereafter cited as DP/LOC).
3. Ronald W. Knisely, "The General Board of the United States Navy—Its Influence on Naval Policy and National Policy" (master's thesis, University of Delaware, 1967), 54.
4. Cited in ibid., 53.
5. Ibid., 53–53; Costello, "Planning for War," 22.
6. Miller, *War Plan Orange*, 15–16; and, to a lesser degree, Knisely, "General Board of the United States Navy," 52–54.
7. RADM Bradley A. Fiske, *From Midshipman to Rear-Admiral* (New York: Century, 1919), 478.
8. For a discussion of Scharnhorst and his reforms, see John T. Kuehn, *Napoleonic Warfare: The Operational Art of the Great Campaigns* (Santa Barbara, CA: Praeger, 2015), 106, 174–175.
9. Henry C. Taylor, "The Fleet," U.S. Naval Institute *Proceedings* 29 (December 1903): 802–804.
10. Fiske, *From Midshipman to Rear-Admiral*, 476–478.
11. Members of the General Board, 1910, Roll 1, GB ML.

12. Costello, "Planning for War," 33–34
13. Proceedings and Hearings of the General Board, Minutes, 16 April 1900 (hereafter cited as GB minutes, followed by the date).
14. Costello, "Planning for War," 34n32.
15. GB minutes, 17 April, 21 May 1900.
16. Proceedings and Hearings of the General Board, serial list for 1900, PHGB.
17. Costello, "Planning for War," 35.
18. Memo, 2, HL GB.
19. GB minutes, 21 May 1900.
20. Kuehn, *Napoleonic Warfare*, 174–176.
21. Costello, "Planning for War," 35–37.
22. See http://www.arlingtoncemetery.net/hctaylor.htm.
23. French E. Chadwick, "The Naval War College," *Papers of the Military Historical Society*, vol. 14 (Wilmington, NC: Broadfoot, 1997), 355.
24. Taylor to Sampson, 23 April 1898, http://www.history.navy.mil/research/publications/documentary-histories/ united-states-navy-s/coal/captain-henry-c-tayl/_jcr_content.html#page2; Anonymous, "Obituary," U.S. Naval Institute *Proceedings* 30, no. 3 (1904): 687.
25. Thomas C. Hone, "A WWI Naval Officer's Story," in *War on the Rocks*, 6 September 2013, http://warontherocks.com.
26. Costello, "Planning for War," 28.
27. Beers, "Development of the Office," pt. 1, 54.
28. Members of the General Board, 1904, GB ML. Wainwright first joined the board in October 1904; Costello, "Planning for War," 27. By 1922 Wainwright was singing the praises of the board in "The General Board: A Sketch," U.S. Naval Institute *Proceedings* 48, no. 2 (February 1922): 189–201.
29. Luce to Mahan, 25 August 1898, in Gleaves, *Life and Letters*, 237; Costello, "Planning for War," 49–50. Costello refers to Luce as a "revolutionist" (as opposed to Taylor's "evolutionary philosophy").
30. Rose, *Power at Sea*, 20–22.
31. Cited in Knisely, "General Board of the United States Navy," 89–90.
32. GB minutes, 16 April 1900; Costello, "Planning for War," 27.
33. GB minutes, 17 April, 21 May 1900.
34. Members of the General Board, 1900, GB ML; Kenneth Wenzer, "The First Naval War College Plan against Spain by Lt. Cmdr. Charles H. Stockton," *International Journal of Naval History*, April 2016, http://www.ijnhonline.org/ 2016/05/26/the-first-naval-war-college-plan-against-spain-by-lt-cmdr-charles-h-stockton; and Michael Crawford, "U.S. Naval Plans for War with the United Kingdom in the 1890s: A Compromise between Pragmatism and Theory," paper given at the Society of Military History conference, 2016. The author obtained Crawford's permission to use his scholarship in this work.

35. GB minutes, 23 May 1900. For a reference in U.S. policy to the term "human capital," see Anonymous, "Force of the Future: Maintaining our Competitive Edge in Human Capital," 18 November 2015, memorandum of the Secretary of Defense, U.S. Department of Defense.
36. GB minutes, 21 May, 26 June 1900.
37. Andrew J. Birtle, *U.S. Army Counterinsurgency and Contingency Operations Doctrine, 1860–1941* (Washington, DC: Center of Military History, 2003), 108–110 and 147–148.
38. GB minutes, 26 June 1900; General Board studies, 1900, Roll 1, PHGB (hereafter cited as GB study/studies followed by the study number and, where applicable, the year).
39. GB minutes, 21 May, 26–29 June 1900.
40. GB minutes, 29 June, 28–31 August 1900; Birtle, *U.S. Army Counterinsurgency and Contingency,* 148–149. Captain Stockton had broached the issue of avoiding an alliance with Japan in the 29 June meeting.
41. GB minutes, 28 August 1900; John T. Kuehn, *A Military History of Japan* (Santa Barbara, CA: Praeger, 2014), 153–154.
42. GB minutes, 9 October 1900.
43. See https://history.state.gov/milestones/1899–1913/hay-and-china; see also William R. Braisted, *Diplomats in Blue: U.S. Naval Officers in China, 1922–1933* (Gainesville: University of Florida Press, 2009), 2–3, for a short discussion of the Open Door policy and U.S. naval involvement in China.
44. GB studies, 1900. See also "Light Draft Gunboats for Service in Chinese Waters," 30 October 1903, GB study 27-03.
45. Cited in Costello, "Planning for War," 29.
46. LT John Hood, USN, "Naval Administration and Organization," U.S. Naval Institute *Proceedings* 27, no. 97 (March 1901): 5.
47. CAPT French Chadwick, USN, "Naval Administration and Organization," U.S. Naval Institute *Proceedings* 27, no. 97 (March 1901): 28.
48. CAPT Caspar F. Goodrich, USN, "Naval Administration and Organization," U.S. Naval Institute *Proceedings* 27, no. 97 (March 1901): 30; Costello, "Planning for War," 29–30.
49. GB minutes, 23 April 1901. Records the changes effected by General Order 43.
50. Long to Dewey, 10 July 1901, DP/LOC.
51. CAPT French Chadwick, USN, "Opening Address Delivered by the President of War College, June 4, 1902," U.S. Naval Institute *Proceedings* 18, no. 102 (1902): 258.
52. Members of the General Board, 1901, GB ML; GB minutes, 28–31 August 1900; Costello, "Planning for War," 47.

53. GB studies, 1901, especially 4-01, "Guns for Asiatic Advanced Bases," 18 February 1901 (the studies always included an associated date for their approval by vote of the board), 28-01, and 30-01.
54. Capt H. C. Taylor, USMC, introduction, and Capt Richard Wallach, USMC, "The War in the East," U.S. Naval Institute *Proceedings* 21, no. 76 (1895): 691-740. For the current Marine Expeditionary Units concept, see http://www.globalsecurity.org/military/agency/usmc/meu.htm.
55. "Congressional Legislation re: General Board," 28 June 1901, GB study 16-01.
56. Beers, "Development of the Office," pt. 1, 50-51.
57. Henry J. Hendrix, *Theodore Roosevelt's Naval Diplomacy: The U.S. Navy and the Birth of the American Century* (Annapolis: Naval Institute Press, 2009), 23.
58. Members of the General Board, 1902, GB ML; see also http://www.arlingtoncemetery.net/ascrowninshield.htm.
59. Beers, "Development of the Office," pt. 1, 57; "Obituary," U.S. Naval Institute *Proceedings*, 1904.
60. Knisely, "General Board of the United States Navy," 132.
61. "Proposed Joint Maneuvers with [U.S.] Army and Militia," 26 March 1902, GB study 5-02; Navy Department General Order 136, 18 July 1903, cited in Beers, "Development of the Office," pt. 1, 55n70.
62. Hendrix, *Theodore Roosevelt's Naval Diplomacy*, 25-29.
63. GB studies 11-01, 13-01, 19-01, 23-01, and 35-01.
64. GB studies, 1900-1902; see also Baer, *100 Years of Sea Power*, 37-38.
65. See GB study 25-01 for additional ships and studies 7-01 and 34-01 for fleet maneuvers; Hendrix, *Theodore Roosevelt's Naval Diplomacy*, 30-31. The forty-eight-battleship program was first proposed in GB study 420-2, 17 October 1903, cited in GB study 420-2, 18 November 1914, RG 80, NARA. See also Fiske, *From Midshipman to Rear Admiral*, 350.
66. See GB study 25-01 for additional ships, and GB studies 7-01 and 34-01 for fleet maneuvers; Hendrix, *Theodore Roosevelt's Naval Diplomacy*, 30-31; the forty-eight-battleship program first proposed in GB study 420-2, 17 October 1903, cited in GB study 420-2, 18 November 1914.
67. Hendrix, *Theodore Roosevelt's Naval Diplomacy*, 32-33; "Harry" was how Taylor signed his intimate correspondence, in this case to ADM Luce. Taylor to Luce, 29 June 1904, in Gleaves, *Life and Letters*, 240.
68. Hendrix, *Theodore Roosevelt's Naval Diplomacy*, 37, 46.
69. Ibid., 33; Proceedings and Hearings of the General Board, list of studies, 1900-1912, PHGB. It can be no accident that the written proposal prepared by the General Board then became actual orders by Moody. In other words, Taylor and Dewey drafted proposals for what they wanted to do, gave them to Moody, and then Moody ordered them or the bureaus to do the ones

applicable at the moment. This very much reflects how Long and the War Board of 1898 had worked. See Wenzer, "Naval War Board of 1898," article 1.
70. Members of the General Board, 1902, and list of studies, 1902, GB ML; Hendrix, *Theodore Roosevelt's Naval Diplomacy*, 36.
71. "Rear Admirals Are Unfriendly," *San Francisco Call* 87, no. 115 (23 September 1902).
72. Fiske, *From Midshipman to Rear Admiral*, 350.
73. Hendrix, *Theodore Roosevelt's Naval Diplomacy*, 32, 37–40.
74. Ibid., 39–41.
75. Fiske, *From Midshipman to Rear Admiral*, 350.
76. Ibid., 350–352.
77. Hendrix, *Theodore Roosevelt's Naval Diplomacy*, 40–48.
78. Baer, *100 Years of Sea Power*, 38–39; Hendrix, *Theodore Roosevelt's Naval Diplomacy*, 48.
79. Cited in Baer, *100 Years of Sea Power*, 38; Hendrix, *Theodore Roosevelt's Naval Diplomacy*, 49.
80. Anonymous, "Crowninshield Retires," *New York Times*, 4 March 1903.
81. Fiske, *From Midshipman to Rear Admiral*, 350–352.
82. GB study 420-2, 17 October 1903, cited in GB study 420-2, 18 November 1914.
83. Kuehn, *Agents of Innovation*, chapter 7.
84. Taylor, "Fleet," 806.
85. Costello, "Planning for War," 37–39, emphasizes the integral nature of the work of the NWC and ONI to the board and as adjuncts to it by virtue of their leaders' membership on it.
86. Luce to Taylor, 29 June 1904, in Gleaves, *Life and Letters*, 240; Costello, "Planning for War," 47, addresses his early concerns about Long abolishing the board.
87. Costello, "Planning for War," 49–52.
88. Ibid., 62.
89. Ibid., 52–54.
90. Ibid., 56.
91. GB minutes, 7 May 1903–25 June 1903. The first unscheduled session was on 29 May.
92. GB minutes, 19 May 1903; see also appendix 1 in this book.
93. GB minutes, 22 May 1903.
94. GB minutes, 11–25 June 1903.
95. Costello, "Planning for War," 39–40.
96. Semsch, "Elihu Root and the General Staff," 27.
97. GB minutes, 22 June and 11, 28 July 1903; Costello, "Planning for War," 40.
98. GB minutes, 11 July 1903: Costello, "Planning for War," 56. One sign of this turbulence might be reflected in the minutes themselves, which are barely

readable in some sections, as if they had been soaked in water. Perhaps they had not fared so well in the trip to Newport and back to Washington in the humid summer heat.
99. Taylor, "Fleet," 806.
100. Ibid.
101. Costello, "Planning for War," 58–59.
102. Cited in Gleaves, *Life and Letters*, 238.
103. Luce to Taylor, 25 June 1904, in Gleaves, *Life and Letters*, 238–239.
104. Moody's testimony cited in Costello, "Planning for War," 61.
105. See appendix 4 in this book.
106. Luce to Taylor, 25 June 1904, in Gleaves, *Life and Letters*, 238–239.
107. Ibid., 239.
108. Taylor to Luce, 29 June 1904, in Gleaves, *Life and Letters*, 240.
109. Anonymous, "Obituary," 687; http://www.arlingtoncemetery.net/hctaylor.htm.
110. Taylor to Luce, 13 February 1903, cited in Costello, "Planning for War," 64.

Chapter 4. From Taylor to Fiske
Epigraph, Costello, "Planning for War," 65.
1. Taylor to Luce, 29 June 1904, in Gleaves, *Life and Letters*, 240; Costello, "Planning for War," 65.
2. Kuehn, *Napoleonic Warfare*, 181.
3. Gleaves, *Life and Letters*, implies in his editorial comments on Luce's letters that Luce and his confederates were merely awaiting the departure of Bonaparte to agitate anew for a more formal general staff, 243.
4. See appendix 4 in this book.
5. Members of the General Board, 1905–1906, GB ML.
6. Members of the General Board, 1904, GB ML; Wainwright reported on 27 October 1904.
7. Members of the General Board, 1904, GB ML.
8. See http://www.arlingtoncemetery.net/gaconverse.htm.
9. Costello, "Planning for War," 59–60.
10. See Katherine C. Epstein, *Torpedo: Inventing the Military-Industrial Complex in the United States and Great Britain* (Cambridge: Harvard University Press, 2014), 20–25, 70–73; and http://www.arlingtoncemetery.net/gaconverse.htm.
11. GB serial list, 1904.
12. Regulations for the Government of the U.S. Navy, 1905 (Washington DC: Department of Navy, 1905), 19; Costello, "Planning for War," 66–67.
13. General Board members list, 1904–1907.
14. 1905 U.S. Navy Regulations, 19.
15. Beers, "Development of the Office," pt. 1, 52–53; Costello, "Planning for War," 76.

16. General Board member list, 1904, 1915; *Army and Navy Register*, 2 July 1904; Costello, "Planning for War," 60.
17. Luce to General Board, 1905, cited in Gleaves, *Life and Letters*, 242; Costello, "Planning for War," 71–72.
18. Costello, "Planning for War," 72.
19. Members of the General Board, 1904–1906, GB ML.
20. Memos dated 25 and 27 January 1906, GB study 401.
21. GB minutes, 26 September 1904.
22. Proceedings and Hearings of the General Board, serial lists, 1904 and 1905, PHGB; In 1904 there were forty-three completed studies, whereas in 1905 the total number increased to sixty-four.
23. Costello, "Planning for War," 72.
24. Ibid., 72–74.
25. Barnette to Luce, 15 October 1905, cited in Costello, "Planning for War," 73; Gleaves, *Life and Letters*. Gleaves had an active history as a reformer and had served as an editor for the Naval Institute during the 1890s. See John T. Kuehn, "Grudging Respect? Kaigun through the Lens of the U.S. Navy at the Time of the Sino Japanese War," *Northern Mariner* 26, no. 3 (July 2016): 266–267.
26. See Gleaves, *Life and Letters*, 242–244. In fact, there is no correspondence between 29 June 1904 and 18 April 1906 other than some edited excerpts from Luce's March 1905 letter to the board.
27. Members of the General Board, 1906, GB ML; Costello, "Planning for War," 74.
28. Costello, "Planning for War," 107–109; Proceedings and Hearings of the General Board, serial list, 1905, PHGB.
29. Proceedings and Hearings of the General Board, serial list, 1905, especially GB study 2-05, 24 January 1905, PHGB; Hendrix, *Roosevelt's Naval Diplomacy*, 99–103; Rose, *Power at Sea* 1:43–44.
30. Cited in Costello, "Planning for War," 80–81.
31. Ibid., 79.
32. Dewey to SecNav in attachment "B," 28 May 1906, GB study 420; Suzanne Geissler, *God and Sea Power: The Influence of Religion on Alfred Thayer Mahan* (Annapolis: Naval Institute Press, 2015), 77.
33. Edward S. Miller, *War Plan Orange*, 21–24; Hendrix, *Theodore Roosevelt's Naval Diplomacy*, chapter 5.
34. Costello, "Planning for War," 109; members of the General Board, 1906, GB ML.
35. Hendrix, *Theodore Roosevelt's Naval Diplomacy*, xiii–xv.
36. Miller, *War Plan Orange*, 21–22; Costello, "Planning for War," chapter 4; Hendrix, *Theodore Roosevelt's Naval Diplomacy*, 160–161. Of the three historians cited, only Hendrix directly links the General Board's planning function

to the decision to send the Great White Fleet across the Pacific. Miller characterized as "a goodwill visit," which it became, but it began as a concentration and movement of the entire fleet in response to a crisis.
37. A. T. Mahan, "Reflection Historic and Other, Suggested by the Battle of the Japan Sea," U.S. Naval Institute *Proceedings* (June 1906): 452; for a more recent account of the battle, see Constantine Pleshakov, *The Tsar's Last Armada: The Epic Voyage to the Battle of Tsushima* (New York: Basic Books, 2002), chapters 11 and 12.
38. Cited in Costello, "Planning for War," 81. For a recent discussion of Bonaparte's lackluster performance as SecNav, see also Andrew C. S. Jampoler, "The American Bonaparte," *Naval History* 27, no. 6 (December 2013): 40–45.
39. Luce to Hollingsworth, 27 April 1906, in Gleaves, *Life and Letters*, 245–246.
40. See Costello, "Planning for War," 112–117.
41. Ibid., 122–126; Miller, *War Plan Orange*, 24.
42. LCDR Ridley McLean, September 1910, cited in Costello, "Planning for War," 119.
43. Costello, "Planning for War," 127.
44. Most histories refer to the system as the "aid system"—for example, Beers, "Development of the Office," pt. 1, 60—but in the General Board member list the actual title of the various officers assigned was spelled "aide"; see members of the General Board, December 1909, GB ML, where RADM Richard Wainwright was first formally listed as "Aide for Operations" and RADM William Swift as "Aide for Material." The spelling "aide" is used throughout this book, except in quotations.
45. See http://millercenter.org/president/essays/metcalf-1904-secretary-of-commerce-and-labor.
46. Cited in Costello, "Planning for War," 82.
47. Henry Reuterdahl, "The Needs of Our Navy," *McClure's Magazine* 30 (January 1908): 251–263; Beers, "Development of the Office," pt. 1, 59.
48. Costello, "Planning for War," 85; members of the General Board, 1907–1908, GB ML.
49. Costello, "Planning for War," 86–87; Beers, "Development of the Office," pt. 1, 59.
50. Members of the General Board, 1908, GB ML; Proceedings and Hearings of the General Board, serial lists, 1907 and 1908, PHGB.
51. Proceedings and Hearings of the General Board, serial list, 1908, PHGB; members of the General Board, 1908, GB ML; CAPT Seven E. Maffeo, *U.S. Navy Codebreakers, Linguists, and Intelligence Officers against Japan, 1910–1941* (Colorado Springs: Rowman & Littlefield, 2016).
52. Beers, "Development of the Office," pt. 1, 59–60; Costello, "Planning for War," 87.

53. Costello, "Planning for War," 87–89.
54. Dewey to SecNav, 11 November 1908, GB study 420-2.
55. Luce to Roosevelt, 14 July 1908, and Roosevelt to Luce, 16 July 1908, in Gleaves, *Life and Letters*, 247–248.
56. Friedman, "South Carolina Sisters," 17–19; Katherine Epstein, "No One Can Afford to Say 'Damn the Torpedoes': Battle Tactics and U.S. Naval History before World War I," *Journal of Military History* 77, no. 2 (April 2013): 492–498; Beers, "Development of the Office," pt. 1, 55–56.
57. Friedman, "South Carolina Sisters," 20–23.
58. Beers, "Development of the Office," pt. 1, 59–60; Hendrix, *Theodore Roosevelt's Naval Diplomacy*, 148–149; Costello, "Planning for War," 87–88; Friedman, "South Carolina Sisters," 23. Friedman also discusses the conference in *U.S. Cruisers: An Illustrated Design History* (Annapolis: Naval Institute Press, 1984), 8. If any works need be referenced as proof of the importance of the General Board to ship design prior to World War II, then first on that list are Friedman's, whose references to the impact of the General Board are ubiquitous in all these volumes.
59. Beers, "Development of the Office," pt. 1, 60.
60. Congress, House, Naval Affairs Committee, *Hearings on Appropriations Bill Subjects for Fiscal Year 1910*, 60th Cong., 2nd sess. (Washington, DC, 1909), 879.
61. Beers, "Development of the Office," pt. 1, 60–61; Costello, "Planning for War," 90.
62. Beers, "Development of the Office," pt. 1, 61; Costello, "Planning for War," 91, 92n92.
63. See Geissler, *God and Sea Power*, 126–128, and Mahan, *Influence of Sea Power*, 289–291, for the tragic story of ADM John Byng, shot for his failure at Minorca during the Seven Years' War.
64. Beers, "Development of the Office," pt. 1, 60–62; Costello, "Planning for War," 90–92; A. T. Mahan, *Naval Administration and Warfare* (Boston: Little, Brown, 1908), 5.
65. Beers, "Development of the Office," pt. 1, 62.
66. Costello, "Planning for War," 90; Beers, "Development of the Office," pt. 1, 62.
67. "Skip echelon" is a term meaning going above one's superiors to their superiors. Sims had no compulsion about taking advantage of his friendship with TR to get his way. As Tom Hone has noted, Sims was first a reformer and only secondly a naval officer loyal to the larger institution. See "A WWI Naval Officer's Story," *War on the Rocks*, 6 September 2013, http://warontherocks.com/2013/09/a-wwi-naval-officers-story.
68. Beers, "Development of the Office," pt. 1, 63; members of the General Board, 1902–1906, GB ML.

69. Beers, "Development of the Office," pt. 1, 63–66; Costello, "Planning for War," 95–96.
70. Cited in Costello, "Planning for War," 95–96.
71. *Regulations for the Government of the U.S. Navy 1909*, change number 9 (Washington DC, 1909); Beers, "Development of the Office," pt. 1, 64.
72. See John Byron, "Three Great Apes," U.S. Naval Institute *Proceedings* (May 2005): 50–53.
73. Beers, "Development of the Office," pt. 1, 64; Costello, "Planning for War," 95–97.
74. Fiske, *From Midshipman to Rear Admiral*, 478; Beers, "Development of the Office," 64; members of the General Board, 1900–1910, GB ML.
75. Beers, "Development of the Office," pt. 1, 64, 66n99; Costello, "Planning for War," 97; members of the General Board, 1909, GB ML.
76. Costello, "Planning for War," 97–98.
77. *Annual Reports of the Navy Department for the Fiscal Year 1910* (Washington, DC: U.S. Government Printing Office, 1910), 5 (hereafter cited as SecNav Annual Report, followed by the year).
78. Ibid., 6–7.
79. "Rules for Aids [sic] in their Relations with the General Board," SecNav Meyer to Aids (copy provided to General Board), 13 February 1915, GB study 401, 1913.
80. Henry C. Beers, "The Development of the Office of the Chief of Naval Operations," pt. 2, in *Military Affairs* 10, no. 3 (Autumn 1946): 10.
81. Beers, "Development of the Office," pt. 1, 55.
82. Members of the General Board, 1909, GB ML.
83. H. S. Knapp to General Board, 10 February 1910, endorsements by RADM Rodgers (20 May), CAPT R. C. Smith (20 May), RADM Luce (11 May), RADM Chadwick (12 May), RADM Sperry (12 May), and, finally, Mahan (17 May), GB study 401.
84. Members of the General Board, 1910, GB ML; Fiske, *From Midshipman to Rear Admiral*, 462, 475.
85. Costello, "Planning for War," 99.
86. Knisely, "General Board of the United States Navy," 57.
87. Costello, "Planning for War," 99; Knisely, "General Board of the United States Navy," 57.
88. Fiske, *From Midshipman to Rear Admiral*, 478.
89. Ibid., 477.
90. Ibid., 479.
91. Miller, *War Plan Orange*, 66–68; SecNav Annual Report, 1910.
92. GB serial lists, 1908–1909.
93. Fiske, *From Midshipman to Rear Admiral*, chapter 31.
94. Ibid., 480.

95. Ibid., 480–481; Miller, *War Plan Orange*, 77–78; "Authority Requested to Make Requisition for Airplane for CHESTER," 14 October 1910, GB study 115-10.
96. Norman Friedman, *U.S. Cruisers: An Illustrated Design History* (Annapolis: Naval Institute Press, 1984), 67–68. The need for scout cruisers had come from Dewey's exercises with the fleet during the Venezuelan Crisis of 1902.
97. SecNav Annual Report, 1910, 23.
98. Beers, "Development of the Office," pt. 1, 67.
99. GB serial list, 1910, PHGB; SecNav Annual Report, 1911, 26–27.
100. See http://militarynews.com/app/fleetweeknewyork/ships.html.
101. SecNav Annual Report, 1912, 5–27, 25–28.
102. David W. Holden, "Managing Men and Machines: U.S. Military Officers and the Intellectual Origins of Scientific Management in the Early Twentieth Century" (PhD diss., University of Kansas, 2016), 114–115, 118.
103. See 4 May 1912, GB study 401.
104. Fiske, *From Midshipman to Rear Admiral*, 491–492; Costello, "Planning for War," 31. For the term "fleet ladder," see Gerald A. Wheeler, *Admiral William Veazie Pratt, U.S. Navy: A Sailor's Life* (Washington, DC: Naval History Division, Department of the Navy, 1974), xiii, chapter 8.
105. Members of the General Board, 1910–1913, GB ML.
106. Holden, "Managing Men and Machines," 91–92; Bradley A Fiske, *The Navy as a Fighting Machine* (New York: Scribner's Sons, 1916); Fiske telegram, 1930. Fiske was complaining about the Senate hearings considering the London Naval Treaty (see chapter 7).

Chapter 5. The General Board in Peace and War, 1913-18

1. See, for example, Baer, *100 Years of Sea Power*, 54–61. In all fairness, Baer does emphasize the role of the board more than other historians, for example, Paul G. Halpern, *A Naval History of World War I* (Annapolis: Naval Institute Press, 1994), index, passim.
2. Fiske, *From Midshipman to Rear-Admiral*, chapter 35, "The Unpreparedness of the Navy."
3. See Beers, "Development of the Office," pt. 2, 10–38; see also Love, *History of the U.S. Navy*, vol. 1, chapters 29 and 30; and Knisely, "General Board of the United States Navy," 113–114.
4. Love, *History of the U.S. Navy* 1:473–476; Costello, "Planning for War"; Knisely, "General Board of the United States Navy," 44–47.
5. Love, *History of the U.S. Navy* 1:481–489; Baer, *100 Years of Sea Power*, chapters 29 and 30; Halpern, *Naval History of World War I*, 356–359; Dennis Conrad, "Were They So Unprepared? Josephus Daniels and the United States Navy's Entry into World War I," in *U.S. Military History Review* 1, no. 3 (December 2016): 5–19.

6. Louis Auchincloss, *Woodrow Wilson* (New York: Viking Books, Penguin Lives Series, 2000), 43, 46, 48.
7. As of the writing of this book (2016), the U.S. Navy of World War II, with more than two thousand warships and the third largest air force in the world at the time (behind the U.S. Army Air Force and Royal Air Force), remains the most powerful force afloat that human history has ever seen.
8. Fiske, *From Midshipman to Rear-Admiral*, 541–542.
9. For a more sympathetic rendering of this decision and story, see Lee A. Craig, *Josephus Daniels: His Life and Times* (Chapel Hill: University of North Carolina Press, 2013), 244–245. The story about "cup of Joe" remains apocryphal but has its basis in increased coffee purchases after General Order 99 (1 June 1914) was issued by Daniels.
10. Cited in E. David Cronon, ed., *The Cabinet Diaries of Josephus Daniels, 1913–1921* (Lincoln: University of Nebraska Press, 1962), v.
11. Ibid., 4 and 4n11.
12. Beers, "Development of the Office," pt. 2, 10.
13. Fiske, *From Midshipman to Rear-Admiral*, 526–527.
14. SecNav to Dewey, 10 February 1913, GB study 401; members of the General Board, 1913, GB ML (Fiske reported on 11 February).
15. Fiske, *From Midshipman to Rear-Admiral*, 530.
16. Beers, "Development of the Office," pt. 2, 10–11; Costello, "Planning for War," 99–100; Fiske, *From Midshipman to Rear-Admiral*, 533.
17. Fiske, *From Midshipman to Rear-Admiral*, 532–533.
18. Costello, "Planning for War," 315–319.
19. Fiske, *From Midshipman to Rear-Admiral*, 529.
20. Ibid., 538–539; Beers, "Development of the Office," pt. 1, 67.
21. Fiske, *From Midshipman to Rear-Admiral*, 539; Thomas A. Bryson, "Mark L. Bristol, an Open-Door Diplomat in Turkey," *International Journal of Middle East Studies* 5, no. 4 (1974): 450–467; Braisted, *Diplomats in Blue*, 166–167.
22. See, for example, Kenneth J. Hagan, *This People's Navy: The Making of American Seapower* (New York: Collier Macmillan, 1991), and William M. McBride, *Technological Change and the United States Navy, 1865–1945* (Baltimore: Johns Hopkins University Press, 2000), 127; Costello, "Planning for War," 271–272; Corbin Williamson, "Keeping Up with the Times: The General Board of the Navy on Airpower at Sea, 1917–1925," 2011, unpublished paper, 2, provides evidence in support of the board's cautious progressive stance toward aviation.
23. GB study 449, 20 August 1913, cited in GB study 420, 17 November 1914.
24. Costello, "Planning for War," 273–276; see John T. Kuehn, "Air-Sea Battle and Its Discontents," *U.S. Naval Institute Proceedings* 139, no. 10 (October 2013): 42–47.

25. Costello, "Planning for War," 266–267; SecNav Annual Report, 1912, and SecNav Annual Report, 1913.
26. Auchincloss, *Woodrow Wilson*, 57–59; Andrew J. Birtle, "Military Interventions during the Wilson Administration, 1914–1920," in *U.S. Army Counterinsurgency and Contingency Operations Doctrine, 1860–1941* (Washington, DC: Center of Military History, 2003), 191–193.
27. Dewey to Fletcher, 18 June 1914, Folder 2, Box 38, DP/LOC.
28. Fiske, *From Midshipman to Rear-Admiral*, 543.
29. Beers, "Development of the Office," pt. 2, 12–13.
30. Folders 1 and 2 (1913–1914), Box 38, DP/LOC.
31. Dewey to Fletcher, 18 June 1914, Box 38, DP/LOC. Fletcher was the uncle of ADM Frank Jack Fletcher, victor of the battles of the Coral Sea and Midway in World War II.
32. Cited in Knisely, "General Board of the United States Navy," 89–90.
33. Costello, "Planning for War," 249–250, 272, 316–317; Knisely, "General Board of the United States Navy," 55 (for reference to Daniels).
34. Badger to Dewey, 28 June 1914, Box 38, DP/LOC.
35. Senior Member Present (Fiske) to Secretary of the Navy, 1 August 1914, DP/LOC. This serial was signed by Austin McKnight, the board's secretary.
36. Dewey to Fullam, 26 May 1914, DP/LOC.
37. Members of the General Board, 1914, GB ML (Badger reported on 18 September 1914).
38. See 21 May 1914, GB study 420-1.
39. Ibid., 3.
40. McKnight to Dewey, 10 August 1914, Fiske to Dewey, 17 August 1914, and Fiske to Dewey, 24 August 1914, DP/LOC.
41. For an authoritative discussion of the Rainbow plans, see Stetson Conn and Byron Fairchild, *The Framework of Hemispheric Defense, from United States Army in World War II* (Washington, DC: Center of Military History, 1960), 30–67.
42. Knisely, "General Board of the United States Navy," 110.
43. See 17 November 1914, GB study 420-2; for destroyers and torpedoes, see Epstein, "No One Can Afford to Say," 491–520.
44. See Halpern, *Naval History of World War I*, 24; Miller, *War Plan Orange*, chapter 8.
45. See 17 November 1914, GB study 420-2.
46. Daniels to Dewey, 25 January 1915, and Dewey to Daniels, 25 January 1915, DP/LOC.
47. Fiske, *From Midshipman to Rear-Admiral*, 537–538.
48. Beers, "Development of the Office," pt. 2, 11–12; members of the General Board, 1914–1915, GB ML.

49. Cited in Beers, "Development of the Office," pt. 2, 12.
50. Ibid., 12–13; Love, *History of the U.S. Navy* 1:460.
51. Beers, "Development of the Office," pt. 2, 12, 19.
52. Daniels to Dewey, 4 March 1915, handwritten note with press notice attached, DP/LOC; Dewey to Daniels, 5 March 1915, DP/LOC.
53. Beers, "Development of the Office," pt. 2, 21–22.
54. Members of the General Board, 1915, GB ML.
55. CNO legislative language cited from Beers, "Development of the Office," pt. 2, 12–13.
56. See 23 April 15, GB study 420.
57. See, for example, correspondence in Boxes 39 and 40, for example, Hudson Maxim, "Defenseless America," 5 June 1915, DP/LOC.
58. "An Effective Navy," memorandum read by CAPT H. S. Knapp, chief of the Bureau of Yards and Docks, at the 28 July 1915 General Board meeting; ADM Knight's and ADM Rogers' memoranda were also read at same meeting.
59. See May 1916, Boxes 126 and 127, GB study 425.
60. Marine report signed by John Lejeune, 11 July 1916, Box 126, GB studies 425 and 425-5.
61. "Fleet Organization," 29 December 1915, in second endorsement to GB study 420.
62. Thomas C. Hone and Trent Hone, *Battle Line: The United States Navy, 1919–1939* (Annapolis: Naval Institute Press, 2006), 128.
63. "Fires in Action," 19 May 1915, GB study 420. For the U.S. Navy's adoption of German damage-control doctrine, see Jeremy P. Schaub, "U.S. Navy Shipboard Damage Control: Innovation and Implementation during the Interwar Period" (master's thesis, U.S. Army Command and General Staff College, 2014).
64. Dewey to Robert M. McCracken, 6 December 1915, DP/LOC; see also the correspondence in Boxes 39–43.
65. The act and the numbers of ships it authorized is cited in "Naval Policy: Building Program, 1920," 10 September 1918, GB study 420-2. Box 61, from which this report came, was not declassified until 1986. Beers, "Development of the Office," pt. 2, 17–19; Wheeler, *Admiral William Veazie Pratt*, 66.
66. "Mobilization Plan for a War in the Atlantic," 16 May 1916, GB study 425; see also 14 December 1929, HL GB, which discusses the General Board's advisory role in war planning. Also, remember that the CNO was an ex officio member of the board until 1933, which further integrated war planning with the CNO in deliberations by the board.
67. See the discussion in Baer, *One Hundred Years of Sea Power*, 59–63. For the General Board's assessment of submarine threat, see 9 November 1915, GB study 429. See John Terraine, *The U-Boat Wars* (New York: Putnam, 1989),

chapter 2, for a discussion of German operations in 1916 and the British navy's ongoing failure to effectively protect its commerce from legal submarine operations.
68. Naval History and Heritage Command, http://www.history.navy.mil/research/histories/bios/dewey-george.html; Rose, *Power at Sea*, 256–257; members of the General Board, 1917–1920, GB ML.
69. Cronon, *Cabinet Diaries*, 101n11, 131, 192; Beers, "Development of the Office," pt. 2, 17–26; Baer, *100 Years of Sea Power*, 57–58.
70. Members of the General Board, 1917, GB ML; see also 24 October 1917, GB study 425-5 (778); 14 December 1929, 3, HL GB.
71. Cronon, *Cabinet Diaries*, 122. Sims quotation cited in Conrad. "Were They So Unprepared?" 2, 17–20. Author permission granted to use. Conrad relies heavily on ADM William Sims' own words and correspondence to prove his case in contradiction to Sims postwar congressional testimony, which practically accused Daniels (and by implication the General Board) of criminal neglect. See also Barbara Tuchman, *The Zimmermann Telegram* (New York: Bantam, 1971), 179–194.
72. Wheeler, *Admiral William Veazie Pratt*, 67, 69–72, 88; Beers, "Development of the Office," pt. 2, 23.
73. Beers, "Development of the Office," pt. 2, 23; Wheeler, *Admiral William Veazie Pratt*, 88–92.
74. Wheeler, *Admiral William Veazie Pratt*, 95; members of the General Board, 1921, GB ML.
75. Proceedings and Hearings of the General Board, various hearings, August–September 1917, Roll 11, PHGB.
76. Proceedings and Hearings of the General Board, 6 September 1917, 1, PHGB.
77. Proceedings and Hearings of the General Board, 6 September 1917, 1–24, PHGB.
78. See GB study 42515.
79. See Terraine, *U-Boat Wars*, chapter 2, for this discussion.
80. Kuehn, *Agents of Innovation*, Appendix 2, "U.S. Naval Policy 1922."
81. Josephus Daniels to Bureau of Navigation for retransmission, ALNAV message, 2 August 1917, GB study 425-5.
82. See 27 October 1917, GB study 425-5.
83. Secretary of the Navy, 14 November 1917, and CNO, 18 December 1917, both in GB study 425-5.
84. Enclosure A, Tabular Statement, 27 October 1917, GB study 425-5.
85. Ibid., 7.
86. From Geoffrey L. Rossano and Thomas Wildenberg, *Striking the Hornet's Nest: Naval Aviation and the Origins of Strategic Bombing in World War I* (Annapolis: Naval Institute Press, 2015), 4, 209–212.

87. Sir Michael Howard, "Military Science in an Age of Peace," *RUSI: Journal of the Royal United Services Institute for Defense Studies* 119 (March 1974): 3–9.

Chapter 6. The Challenges of Peace

Epigraph, Wainwright, "General Board," 201.

1. See Kuehn, *Agents of Innovation*; and John T. Kuehn, "The Influence of Naval Arms Limitation on U.S. Naval Innovation during the Interwar Period, 1921–1937" (PhD diss., Kansas State University, 2007).
2. Excellent short essays on the aftermath of World War I can be found in *The Cambridge History of Warfare*, ed. Geoffrey Parker (New York: Cambridge University Press, 2005), 314–320, and Hew Strachan, *The First World War* (New York: Penguin Books, 2005), chapter 10.
3. Interestingly, Benson was listed as the "senior member" of the General Board in both 1919 and 1918, so seniority of rank applied when he attended the meetings, even though the officer with the most senior date of rank always acted as the chairman of the executive committee. Proceedings and Hearings of the General Board, 18 December 1918, PHGB; see also the cover page for Proceedings and Hearings of the General Board, vol. 11, 1919, Roll 4, PHGB.
4. The Washington Naval Treaty was signed in February 1922. See Kuehn, *Agents of Innovation*, Appendix 1.
5. See Michael Simpson, ed., *Anglo-American Naval Relations, 1919–1939* (Surrey, UK: Naval Records Society, 2010), 4–5.
6. General Board, "Building Policy for the Fiscal Year 1922," 24 September 1920, in Simpson, *Anglo-American Naval Relations*, 29–30.
7. Memorandum for the Board of the Admiralty, 17 July 1919 (probably from First Sea Lord), in Simpson, *Anglo-American Naval Relations*, 12–13; see Norman Friedman, Thomas C. Hone, and Mark Mandeles, *America and British Aircraft Carrier Development, 1919–1941* (Annapolis: Naval Institute Press, 1999), 21–24.
8. Norman Friedman, *U.S. Cruisers: An Illustrated Design History* (Annapolis: Naval Institute Press, 1984), 94.
9. See Love, *History of the U.S. Navy*, 475–476.
10. The two battlecruisers were *Lexington* and *Saratoga*, about which we will hear more later. Friedman, *U.S. Cruisers*, 85–103.
11. Jerry W. Jones, "The Naval Battle of Paris," in *Naval War College Review* (Spring 2009): 77–89.
12. Simpson, *Anglo-American Naval Relations*, 5; Jones, "Naval Battle of Paris," 77–89. For the ends-ways-means approach to strategy, see Arthur F. Lykke Jr., "Toward and Understanding of Military Strategy," in *Military Strategy: Theory and Application* (Carlisle Barracks, PA: U.S. Government Printing Office, 1989).

13. Sadao Asada, "The Revolt against the Washington Treaty: The Imperial Japanese Navy and Naval Limitation, 1921–1927," *Naval War College Review* (Summer 1993): 82–85.
14. Jones, "Naval Battle of Paris," 79–81.
15. Cronon, *Cabinet Diaries*, 379n13 and 387n12; members of the General Board, 1920–1921, GB ML. Long joined the board as director, ONI, in 1920, and Schofield and McNamee joined in 1921, McNamee as Long's replacement.
16. Memorandum by the First Lord, 25 March 1919, in Simpson, *Anglo-American Naval Relations*, 12; Cronon, *Cabinet Diaries*, 379; Jones, "Naval Battle of Paris," 81–82.
17. Cronon, *Cabinet Diaries*, 379–381; Jones, "Naval Battle of Paris," 81.
18. Cronon, *Cabinet Diaries*, 380; Jones, "Naval Battle of Paris," 82.
19. Cronon, *Cabinet Diaries*, 380–381.
20. Cited in Jones, "Naval Battle of Paris," 82.
21. Cronon, *Cabinet Diaries*, 380–382; Jones, "Naval Battle of Paris," 83.
22. Cronon, *Cabinet Diaries*, 384–385.
23. "Protocol Signed on Behalf of Germany Upon the Deposit of Ratifications of the Treaty of Versailles," *American Journal of International Law* 16, no. 41, Supplement: Official Document (October 1922): 193.
24. Jones, "Naval Battle of Paris," 81.
25. Both Jones and the editor of Daniels' diaries, Cronon, seem to forget Benson's role as representative of the General Board in this "battle." Jones, "Naval Battle of Paris," 80–84; Cronon, *Cabinet Diaries*, 384n8.
26. From Miller, *War Plan Orange*, 65, and chapter 7, "The Great Western Base."
27. See, for example, "Naval Policy: Building Program for the fiscal year 1923," 1, paragraph 3, 15 July 1921, GB study 420-2, 1083.
28. See Kuehn, *Agents of Innovation*, 154.
29. Miller, *War Plan Orange*, 68–69.
30. For example, see Adam Ashton, "Quietly, Guam Is Slated to Become Massive New U.S. Military Base," http://www.mcclatchydc.com/news/nation-world/world/article45241053.html.
31. GB, serial list, 1907; see study 63-07, "Development of Olongapo, Pearl Harbor, and Guam," 3 October 1907.
32. Miller, *War Plan Orange*, 70.
33. Cited in Costello, "Planning for War," 223; "Defense of Guam," 4 December 1912, GB study 158-12 (422).
34. Miller, *War Plan Orange*, 70–71.
35. LCDR H. H. Frost, CDR W. S. Pye, and CAPT H. W. Yarnell, "The Conduct of an Oversea Naval Campaign" October 1920, Papers of the Strategic Plans Division, Office of the Chief of Naval Operations, RG 38, NARA; Miller, *War Plan Orange*, 73. See also Kuehn, *Agents of Innovation*, 130–131.

36. Fiske telegram, 1930. Although Fiske does not refer to Guam directly, he references the board's 1921 plan and the island's adequacy.
37. Miller, *War Plan Orange*, 73; "WW II Era Dry Dock Moving from Guam to Philippines," *Stars and Stripes*, http://www.stripes.com/news/wwii-era-drydock-moving-from-guam-to-philippines-1.391147; see also http://blogs.scientificamerican.com/expeditions/dreading-the-dredging-military-buildup-on-guam-and-implications-for-marine-biodiversity-in-apra-harbor.
38. Miller, *War Plan Orange*, 111–113; Kuehn, *Agents of Innovation*, 127–129.
39. Proceedings and Hearings of the General Board, hearings, 1919, Roll 1, Rolls 13–15, PHGB. February, March, April, and May 1919 were almost entirely devoted to hearings on naval aviation developments and naval aviation policy (serial topic 449).
40. Proceedings and Hearings of the General Board, hearings, 1919, Roll 1, Rolls 13–15, PHGB.
41. Proceedings and Hearings of the General Board, hearings and attached correspondence, 1918–1919, Rolls 11–13, PHGB. See also Proceedings and Hearings of the General Board, serial list, 1918, Roll 4, PHGB; LT Robert A. Lovett, USNRF, "Report on Marine Fighting Squadrons to Protect Navy Bombing Seaplanes on Anti-Submarine Patrol," 19 March 1918. This report was attached to a General Board hearing following up on this idea.
42. Maj. A. C. Cunningham, 7 April 1919, PHBG; "Naval Aviation Policy in Connection with Coast Guard Aviation," 20 May 1919, PHGB.
43. CAPT W. R. Gherardi, USN, "Conditions in Germany," 11 March 1919, PHGB; Maj W. L. Redles, USMC, "Conditions in Japan," 1 October 1919, PHGB.
44. GB minutes, 29 May, 19 June, and 29 July 1919, PHGB.
45. "Development of Naval Aviation Policy," 1–2, 27 March 1919, PHGB. This hearing included testimony by Towers and Whiting and was conducted by RADM Winterhalter; the 18 March 1919 hearing included, among others, Mustin, and King first testified on 15 May 1919; Captain J. W. W. Ashworth, RAF, "Developments in Aviation," 5 December 1918, PHGB.
46. Williamson, "Keeping Up with the Times," 1–2.
47. "Characteristics of Airplane Carriers," 21 February 1921, 3–4, PHGB; Friedman, Hone, and Mandeles, *American and British Aircraft Carrier Development*, 23–24.
48. Some components of this section come from John T. Kuehn, "The Ostfriesland, the Washington Naval Treaty, and the General Board of the Navy: A Relook at a Historic Sinking," in *New Interpretations in Naval History: Selected Papers from the Sixteenth Naval History Symposium*, ed. Craig C. Felker and Marcus O. Jones (Newport, RI: Naval War College Press, 2012), 73–86.
49. Love, *History of the U.S. Navy* 1:528.
50. Miller, *War Plan Orange*, 75.

51. Alan Stephens, "The True Believers: Airpower between the Wars," in *The War in the Air, 1914–1994*, ed. Alan Stephens (Maxwell AFB, AL: Air University Press), 29–43.
52. William D. O'Neil, "Transformation Billy Mitchell Style," U.S. Naval Institute *Proceedings* (March 2002): 101; Stephens, "True Believers," 39–42.
53. O'Neil, "Transformation Billy Mitchell Style," 101–103.
54. "Development of Naval Aviation Policy," 2, 27 March 1919, PHGB.
55. "Developments in Aviation," 2, 10 March 1919, PHGB.
56. Hon. Newton Baker to the Secretary of the Navy, 21 October 1919, War Department Correspondence, GB study 449.
57. See 27 March and 3 April 1919, PHGB. See also Kuehn, *Agents of Innovation*, 15–21.
58. See 3 April 1919, PHGB; see also Kuehn, *Agents of Innovation*, chapter 3, for a detailed discussion of hearing procedures and dynamics. Both Badger and Winterhalter were the most senior officers in the Navy at that time according to date of rank. Also, the General Board routinely provided prospective witnesses questions on the topic they intended to cover; see General Board to LCDR A. C. Read, memo, 25 March 1919, attached to transcript page 29 for that date, PHGB.
59. See 3 April 1919, PHGB.
60. Hearing, 1–10, final page of hearing, 3 April 1919, PHGB.
61. Murray and Watts, "Military Innovation in Peacetime," 390–392.
62. Ibid., 392; see also Richard Hough, *Death of the Battleship* (New York: Macmillan, 1963), 22.
63. Murray and Watts, "Military Innovation in Peacetime," 393–396.
64. See http://wwi.lib.byu.edu/index.php/Conditions_of_an_Armistice_with_Germany; see also Williamson Murray, "Versailles: The Peace without a Chance," in *The Making of Peace*, ed. Williamson Murray and James Lacy (Cambridge: Cambridge University Press, 2009), 221.
65. Van Keuren Report.
66. See http://www.homeofheroes.com/wings/part1/6_survival.html; O'Neil, "Transformation Billy Mitchell Style," 100; Harry H. Ransom, "The Battleship Meets the Airplane," *Military Affairs* 1 (Spring 1959): 21–27.
67. O'Neil, "Transformation Billy Mitchell Style," 101. For a concise discussion of the British system, see Geoffrey Till, "Adopting the Aircraft Carrier: The British, American, and Japanese Case Studies," in *Military Innovation in the Interwar Period*, ed. Williamson Murray and Allan R. Millett (New York: Cambridge University Press, 1996), 191–226.
68. Van Keuren Report.
69. For an objective short description of Mitchell's preparations unencumbered by air-power hype, see Rose, *Power at Sea*, 26–27. See also Hough, *Death of the Battleship*, 30–31.

70. Gene T. Zimmerman, "More Fiction than Fact: The Sinking of the Ostfriesland," in *Warship International* 12, no. 2 (1975): 142–154; Herwig, "Battlefleet Revolution," chapter 7. For Jutland, see John Keegan, *The Price of Admiralty* (London: Penguin, 1988), 176.
71. See Kuehn, *Agents of Innovation*, index, 263, and chapters 6 and 7; see also Juergens, "Impact of the General Board," 80–81.
72. Van Keuren Report.
73. Ibid.
74. Ibid. Arthur Hezlet, *Aircraft and Sea Power* (New York: Stein and Day, 1970), 109–110. See also Rose, *Power at Sea*. This otherwise excellent account states a boarding party was sent aboard *Ostfriesland* to "keep it afloat" (27), but he does not cite the authoritative Van Keuren Report, which in this author's opinion clarifies just what the boarding party was doing.
75. Van Keuren Report; Hough, *Death of the Battleship*, 32–33.
76. Hough, *Death of the Battleship*, 33–34. For the photo, see http://www.bobhenneman.info/photos%20for%20website/Diving/SMS_Ostfriesland_sinkings.jpg. The photo clearly shows *Ostfriesland's* port list and how that accelerated her sinking.
77. Hough, *Death of the Battleship*, 34–35; *Congressional Record* 61 (5 August 1921): 4708.
78. Van Keuren Report; "Characteristics of Airplane Carriers," February 21, 1921, PHGB.
79. "Developments in Naval Aviation," 3 April 3 1919, PHGB. For disruptive technology, see Gautam Mukunda, "We Cannot Go On: Disruptive Innovation and the First World War Royal Navy," *Security Studies* 19, no. 1 (January 2010): 127.
80. Ransom, "Battleship Meets the Airplane," 22; O'Neil, "Transformation Billy Mitchell Style," 101–104. For the Washington Naval Conference, see Kuehn, *Agents of Innovation*, 2, 3, 25–27. For the definitive account of Towers and the Morrow Board, see Clark G. Reynolds, "John H. Towers, the Morrow Board, and the Reform of the Navy's Aviation," *Military Affairs* 52, no. 2 (April 1988): 78–84. Joint Board, "Report on the Results of Aviation and Ordnance Test," (Washington, DC, 18 August 1921), 7.
81. Members of the General Board, 1921–1922, GB ML; "Interpretation of Treaty re: Modernizing Capital Ships," 17 April 1922, PHGB. Pratt testified on this occasion in his capacity as a recent Washington Naval Conference adviser. See also Harold Sprout and Margaret Sprout, *Toward a New Order Sea Power: American Naval Policy and the World Scene, 1918–1922* (Princeton, NJ: Princeton University Press, 1940), 146, 242. "Lower Navy Morale Forecast from Cut," *New York Times*, 1 December 1921, 2, mentions Rodgers' role in drafting the submarine report for adoption by the Washington Naval Conference.

82. George Baer, *One Hundred Years of Sea Power*, 93–96; Kuehn, "Influence of Naval Arms Limitation," 77–80; Sprouts, *New Order of Sea Power*, 146–148.
83. H. S. Knapp, "The Limitation of Armament at the Conference of Washington," to the American Society of International Law, 17 April 1922, GB study 438-1. Knapp's address in its entirety resided in the board's working papers for naval arms conferences, the 438-1 series. See also Sprout and Sprout, *New Order of Sea Power*, 266–271; and Kuehn, *Agents of Innovation*, chapter 3.
84. Van Keuren Report; "Characteristics of Airplane Carriers," 1–7, 21 February 1921, PHGB. See also Appendix 1 in Kuehn, *Agents of Innovation*, 185.
85. "Interpretation of Treaty re: Modernizing Capital Ships," 17 April 1922, PHGB. The details of modernization allowed under the treaty was contained in the "reconstruction clause," which can be found in Article 20, Chapter 2, Part 3, paragraph (d); see again Kuehn, *Agents of Innovation*, Appendix 1, 193–194. See also Kuehn, "Influence of Naval Arms Limitation," 143–145 and 147–149.
86. Sprout and Sprout, *New Order of Sea Power*, 266–271.
87. See 4 November 1921, GB study 449. ADM Taylor of the Bureau of Construction and Repair had in fact made this very recommendation in a letter to the General Board before the Washington Naval Conference had even convened: "If the opportunity should be had to carry out such experiments on fairly modern ships, this . . . would be of great value."
88. ADM Rodgers to Colonel Lucas, 22 April 1922, GB study 438-1.
89. H. B. Grow, "Bombing Tests on the 'Virginia' and 'New Jersey,'" *U.S. Naval Institute Proceedings* 49, no. 12 (December 1923). Grow emphasized that the battleship remained "the first line," but that the "officers in the fleet aid the progress of Naval Aviation in every way possible."
90. Norman Friedman, *U.S. Battleships: An Illustrated Design History* (Annapolis: Naval Institute Press, 1985), 186.
91. Secretary of the Navy to the president, 17 November 1924, GB study 438-1. Presidential approval was attached and dated with the same date.
92. Kuehn, *Agents of Innovation*, 75.
93. Alan D. Zimm, "The U.S.N.'s Flight Deck Cruiser," *Warship International* 3 (1979): 231. Zimm argues that this dedication, at least in 1930, was perfectly understandable given the defensive power of battleships versus the capabilities of the aircraft of that day.
94. Samuel Eliot Morison, *The Two-Ocean War* (New York: Little Brown, 1963), 60–62, 446; see http://www.usswestvirginia.org/uss_west_virginia_history.htm.
95. Wainwright, "General Board," 201.

Chapter 7. The Heyday of the General Board

Epigraph, CAPT F. H. Schofield, "Some Effects of the Washington Conference on American Naval Strategy," lecture delivered at the Army War College, Washington Barracks, 22 September 1923, GB study 438. Portions of this chapter were developed from John T. Kuehn, "The U.S. Navy General Board and Naval Arms Limitation: 1922-1937," *Journal of Military History* 74, no. 4 (October 2010): 1129-1160. The Hilary Jones epigraph is cited in Simpson, *Anglo-American Naval Relations*, 70, and Wheeler, *Admiral William Veazie Pratt*, 240-244.

1. Wainwright, "General Board," 1922.
2. Miller, *War Plan Orange*, 77-79.
3. Kuehn, *Agents of Innovation*, 125-127.
4. Miller, *War Plan Orange*, 36.
5. Kuehn, *Agents of Innovation*, chapter 7.
6. Ibid., 128-129, 168-173.
7. Friedman, *U.S. Cruisers*, 110, also makes this point.
8. See 3 June 1925, serial 1239, GB study 438-1, and the 5 April 1928 response attached to a congressional inquiry, GB study 438.
9. U.S. Naval Policy, 17 January 1925, signed 1 December 1922 by Edwin Denby, Secretary of the Navy, attached to General Board hearing transcripts, PHGB (hereafter cited as USNP 1922). See also Kuehn, *Agents of Innovation*, Appendix 2, 198-205, for a partial reproduction of this policy.
10. Serials 1022, 1055, and 1130 for 1922 (GB study 420-2). Serial 1130, 31 May 1922, discusses these issues and then lays out justification for the design "blueprint" for the fleet. USNP 1922, first promulgated in December 1922.
11. Recall that in addition to the Naval Arms Limitation Treaty, there were many other treaties signed at Washington, the most important among them the Four-Power Pact, which replaced the Anglo-Japanese naval alliance and a nine-power pact that was supposed to protect everyone's interests in China (including the Chinese). See Kuehn, *Agents of Innovation*, 2-3.
12. BuAer letter, 2 March 1922, GB study 420-2.
13. See 31 May 1922, GB serial 1130.
14. See GB serial 1130, 10. It appears the authors of this serial were RADM Rodgers and CAPT Schofield.
15. GB serial 1130, 1-4.
16. Ibid., 1, 4-5. The Harding administration planned on hosting another conference in 1924.
17. Ibid., 4-6. See also Philip T. Rosen, "The Treaty Navy, 1919-1937," in *In Peace and War: Interpretations of American Naval History, 1775-1984*, 2nd ed., ed. Kenneth J. Hagan (Westport, CT: Greenwood Press, 1984), 223.
18. USNP 1922.

19. Ibid. Aircraft carrier tonnage varies because the Navy had already expended 66,000 tons of its 135,000 tons of allowed carrier tonnage in the conversion of *Lexington* and *Saratoga*. This left 69,000 tons for additional carriers, so the Navy could build at most two 27,000-ton carriers. The first carrier size recommended by the General Board was 27,000 tons. See also "Second Endorsement to Naval Aeronautic Policy," 3, 18 November 1922, GB study 449.
20. Memo to First Lord, 25 March 1919, in Simpson, *Anglo-American Naval Relations*, 12.
21. See 3 June 1925, serial 1239, GB study 438-1.
22. GB study 438 response attached to a congressional inquiry, 5 April 1928, and signed by RADM Schofield.
23. See Morison, *Two-Ocean War*, 423–424.
24. "Memorandum from the General Board for File, Subject: Evolution of U.S. Naval Policy," 5 December 1922, GB study 420-2. This document catalogues the changes to the 1922 policy that were published as the 1923 policy.
25. Members of the General Board, 1921–1923, GB ML; see also http://www.findagrave.com/cgi-bin/fg.cgi?page=gr&GRid=79845005.
26. Members of the General Board, 1922–1923, GB ML; Miller, *War Plan Orange*, 27, 374–375.
27. Letter from the London naval attaché forwarded to General Board referring to the machinations by the United States for another conference, 10 December 1923, GB study 438-1. The attaché claimed that the British wanted to include limits on aviation and lock in their superiority in cruiser tonnage.
28. It is worth noting, as a measure of the Harding administration's attitude toward the Navy, that the Teapot Dome scandal revolved around the transfer of strategic Navy oil reserves and fields to the Interior Department and Secretary Fall, under whose administration the scandal occurred.
29. Acting Secretary of the Navy letter, 18 August 1924, serial 1239, GB study 438-1.
30. Ibid., 1.
31. Index to General Board serials, Roll 1, PHGB.
32. Hone and Hone, *Battle Line*, 1, 2, 17.
33. See Kuehn, *Agents of Innovation*, chapters 5–7, for discussions of aviation, battleships, and floating dry docks. For additional information on the hearings on patrol aviation, see Christopher J. Mergen, "Development of Maritime Patrol Aviation in the Interwar Period, 1918 to 1941" (master's thesis, USA Command and General Staff College, 2015); for the influence of the board on damage control doctrine, see Jeremy P. Schaub, "U.S. Navy Shipboard Damage Control: Innovation and Implementation during the Interwar Period" (master's thesis, 2014); for its influence on submarine design, see Juergens,

"Impact of the General Board"; and on destroyer design, see Jason H. Davis, "The Influence of the General Board of the Navy on Interwar Destroyer Design" (master's thesis, USA Command and General Staff College, 2011). All the above theses are held at the U.S. Army Command and General Staff College in Fort Leavenworth, Kansas.

34. William R. Braisted, "On the General Board of the Navy, ADM Hilary P. Jones, and Naval Arms Limitation, 1921–1931," in *The Dwight D. Eisenhower Lectures in War and Peace, No. 5* (Manhattan: Department of History, Kansas State University, 1993); members of the General Board, 1923–1926, GB ML; Wheeler, *Admiral William Veazie Pratt*, 215.
35. See 3 June 1925, 1–3, serial 1239, GB study 438.
36. Ibid., 3. The secretary's response occurred almost a month after the General Board's finalized serial had been forwarded.
37. See 11 December 1926, serial 1338, GB study 420-2.
38. See 5 April 1927, serial 1345, GB study 420-2. This serial was signed by Jones.
39. See 1927, GB serial 1345. Reference (e) was serial 1315 of the previous year.
40. See Kuehn, *Agents of Innovation*, 70–75.
41. 1923 Appendix F (originally classified secret) to WPL-9 War Plan Orange, Mobile Base Project, Correspondence of the Chief of Naval Operations 198-1 (microfilm), 30 December, RG 80, NARA.
42. "Naval Policy/Building Policy for 1926," 7 April 1923, serial 1162, GB study 420-2.
43. GB serial 1345. See also Norman Friedman, *U.S. Aircraft Carriers: An Illustrated Design History* (Annapolis: Naval Institute Press 1983), 67–71. Friedman gives great weight to the inputs of BuAer and the War Plans Division in getting the General Board to agree to the smaller size. The board record indicates that up to April 1927, it still very much wanted a 23,000-ton carrier.
44. H.R. 8687, 26 May 1924, attached to serial 1271, GB study 420-2.
45. See 1927, serial 1345, GB study 449.
46. O'Neil, "Transformation Billy Mitchell Style," 101.
47. Anonymous, "Life of John Rodgers: Adds to Lustre of U.S. Navy's Record," *Hawaii Honolulu Star Bulletin*, 21 March 1927, http://aviation.hawaii.gov/aviation-pioneers/john-rodgers/life-of-john-rodgers.
48. ONI to General Board, memo, 14 January 1925, attached to 449 series, GB studies, 1925.
49. Cited in Reynolds, "John H. Towers," 77–78.
50. O'Neil, "Transformation Billy Mitchell Style," 101; Reynolds, "John H. Towers," 78; members of the General Board, 1925, GB ML.
51. See "Development of Naval Aviation Policy," 27 March 1919; "Characteristics of Airplane Carriers," 21 February 1921; and "Naval Aviation Developments," 3 September 25, all in PHGB.

52. Reynolds, "John H. Towers," 79.
53. Proceedings and Hearings of the General Board, 10 October 1925, 1–23, especially 22–23, PHGB.
54. Reynolds, "John H. Towers," 82.
55. Morrow Board Report, 30 November 1925, attached to serial 1250, GB study 449, 24 November 1924; "Naval Aviation Developments," 3 September 1925, PHGB.
56. This section is in part derived from material used in John T. Kuehn, "A Turning Point in Anglo-American Relations? The General Board of the Navy and the London Naval Treaty," in *At the Crossroads between Peace and War: The London Naval Conference of 1930*, ed. John Maurer and Christopher Bell (Annapolis: Naval Institute Press, 2014): 7–47.
57. Ghormley memorandum, 14 December 1929, 2, HL GB.
58. "Naval Air Operating Policy," CNO memorandum, 27 January 1931, GB study 449. Pratt uses the term "authoritative" in referring to the promulgated policy, which had been written by the General Board.
59. War Department, 21 October 1919, GB study 449; Secretary of the Navy, 7 September 1928, GB study 420-2; Curtis D. Wilbur, "To Authorize Major Alterations to Certain Vessels" (H.R. 8353), 27 March 1924; SecNav, 18 January 1927, GB study 438; Correspondence of the CNO, 11 July 1936, 9 September 1941, GB study 420-2. These are representative examples of correspondence that refer to the authoritative nature of the General Board's advice.
60. Ghormley memorandum, 2.
61. Ibid., 4.
62. Index of General Board serials and archivist comments, Roll 1, PHGB. Information for serial 1427 comes from Roll 7, including the index of serials, i–v.
63. Proceedings and Hearings of the General Board, 81 and 209, Roll 7, PHGB. Chase had just come from a major fleet command and later testified before Congress against the London Naval Treaty after taking over command of the fleet from ADM Pratt (who became Chief of Naval Operations). Chase became chairman of the General Board in 1932.
64. See Kuehn, *Agents of Innovation*, especially chapters 5–7, for examples of the ubiquity of presence at hearings by these two officers.
65. See Thomas Buckley, "The Washington Naval Limitation System: 1921–1939," in *Encyclopedia of Arms Control and Disarmament*, vol. 2, ed. Richard Dean Burns (New York: Charles Scribner's Sons, 1993); and Emily Goldman, *Sunken Treaties: Naval Arms Control between the Wars* (University Park: Pennsylvania State University Press, 1994), 31. For Japanese cruiser construction programs, see Dave Evans and Mark Peattie, *Kaigun* (Annapolis: Naval Institute Press, 1997), chapter 7, especially page 224.

66. For the anglophobe position, see W. F. Trimble, "Admiral Hilary P. Jones and the 1927 Geneva Naval Conference," *Military Affairs* 48, no. 3 (February 1979): 1–3. Trimble in this article wholeheartedly agrees with Stephen Roskill that Jones was "the most difficult character" for the British to deal with. See also Braisted, "On the General Board of the Navy," for a more balanced portrayal. Interestingly, Trimble cites the same letter this author cites in the epigram.
67. Pratt to Jones, 3 February 1926, in Simpson, *Anglo-American Naval Relations,* 71–72.
68. See 23 January 1926, GB study 438-1. Letter from the General Board to RADM Pratt, president of the Naval War College. The "precept" was the board's recommended guidance on the subject.
69. London naval attaché's report, 4, 8, 2 March 1926, GB study 438-1.
70. Juergens, "Impact of the General Board," 53–54.
71. London naval attaché's report, 8; Trimble, "Admiral Hilary P. Jones," 2; Braisted, "On the General Board of the Navy."
72. Trimble, "Admiral Hilary P. Jones," 2–3.
73. See ibid., 4, for the role of War Plan Orange; see Miller, *War Plan Orange;* and William R. Braisted, "The Evolution of the United States Navy's Strategic Assessments in the Pacific, 1919–31," in *The Washington Conference, 1921–22: Naval Rivalry, East Asian Stability and the Road to Pearl Harbor,* ed. Erik Goldstein and John Maurer (UK: Frank Cass, 1994), 110–118.
74. See http://www.arlingtoncemetery.net/fhschofield.htm.
75. For the British and American attitudes, see Braisted, "On the General Board of the Navy."
76. See Kuehn, *Agents of Innovation,* chapter 6, and the discussion regarding aviation tenders for the Asiatic Fleet.
77. See Baer, *One Hundred Years of Sea Power,* 109; Buckley. "Washington Naval Limitation System," 645; and Love, *History of the U.S. Navy* 1:554–555. All cite a fight without bases as the reason for the Navy's commitment to the 10,000-ton cruiser.
78. Trimble, "Admiral Hilary P. Jones," 2.
79. H.R. 8686, 26 May 1924 (copy attached to serial 1271, GB study 420-2).
80. Braisted, "On the General Board of the Navy." See also the discussion in Kuehn, "U.S. Navy General Board and Naval Arms Limitation," 1147–1150.
81. Sadao Asada, *From Mahan to Pearl Harbor: The Imperial Japanese Navy and the United States* (Annapolis: Naval Institute Press, 2006), 112–119.
82. B. J. C. McKercher, "From Enmity to Cooperation," in *Arms Limitation and Disarmament: Restraints on War, 1899–1939* (Westport, CT: Praeger, 1992), 75. The original bill had called for five aircraft carriers and twenty-five new cruisers to be constructed in the next nine years. This bill is also known as the Butler bill after its congressional sponsor.

83. Papers used for serial 1371, including 20 February 1928, from Jones to SecNav Curtis Wilbur, and 28 February 1928, from Wilbur to Jones, GB study 438-1. Since this letter was in serial 4381-1, it means the board was cognizant of it after using it to write the 1371 serial.
84. Members of the General Board, 1926–1930, and the minutes for this period, GB ML, reveal that Jones retired on 14 November 1927 but spent considerable time meeting with the board throughout 1928 and 1929.
85. See especially Proceedings and Hearings of the General Board, vol. 20, Roll 7, PHGB. Members detached included the president of the NWC, RADM Pringle, and CDR H. C. Train.
86. See 21 September 1928, serial 1390, GB study 438-1. The General Board rejected this pact "even as a basis for discussion."
87. Braisted, "On the General Board of the Navy."
88. Proceedings and Hearings of the General Board, vol. 21, 1929, PHGB; see also Braisted, "On the General Board of the Navy." Recall that the entire board, including the CNO and other ex officio members, met at least once a month.
89. Stimson to Dawes, *Papers Relating to the Foreign Relations of the United States* (hereafter cited as FRUS), 1929, 3:1.
90. Letter, 9 July 1929, attached to serial 1437, approved 13 July 1929, GB study 438-1.
91. Memo, 11 September 1929, serial 1444-A, GB study 438-1. This memo was attached to the serial and shows the lengths the new president went to in order to accommodate both the British as well as the General Board.
92. Letter, 24 September 1929, attached to serial 1449, GB study 438-1.
93. This final formula is referenced in serial 1430 of August 1, 1930.
94. FRUS, 1929, 3:6-7.
95. Stimson's Statement on Comment in the Press, 11 October 1929, FRUS, 1929, 3:3.
96. FRUS, 1929, 3:25-31; see also Goldman, *Sunken Treaties*, Appendix 2, Article 16, for the final cruiser tonnages after the Reed-Matsudaira compromise. Robert Craigie's was from the head of the Foreign Office's American section, and he proposed three solutions, one of which was to "transfer American 8" tonnage to "6 tonnage."
97. FRUS, 1929, 3:9.
98. From the Joint Statement also signed by Hoover, FRUS, 1929, 3:34
99. See Sadao Asada, "From Mahan to Pearl Harbor," chapter 3 in *At the Crossroads between Peace and War: The London Naval Conference of 1930*, ed. Christopher Bell and John Maurer (Annapolis: Naval Institute Press, 2014), for the pre-conference negotiations after the Hoover-MacDonald October meetings.

100. Wheeler, *Admiral William Veazie Pratt*, 297–314. All these admirals publicly supported the Treaty after the fact. Hepburn is most famous as head of the famous Hepburn Board that addressed naval preparedness in the late 1930s and was responsible for much-needed base improvements prior to World War II. He chaired the General Board from August 1942 to the end of World War II; see members of the General Board, 1920–1944, GB ML.
101. Simpson, *Anglo-American Naval Relations*, 138; from the minutes of the meeting of the British delegation, 9 February 1930.
102. Simpson, *Anglo-American Naval Relations*, 137–138. See also Braisted, "On the General Board of the Navy."
103. Jones reviews these positions in a very critical paper on naval policy he gave to the Navy League and provided to the board in 1933. Jones to Navy League, memorandum, May 1933, GB study 438.
104. See Asada, "From Mahan to Pearl Harbor," for a complete discussion of the intricacies of the Japanese cruiser ratio position.
105. FRUS, 1930, 1:171.
106. Asada, *From Mahan to Pearl Harbor*, 178–179. See also James B. Crowley, *Japan's Quest for Autonomy: National Security and Foreign Policy, 1930–1938* (Princeton, NJ: Princeton University Press, 1966), 66–71, for a retelling of the political crisis that occurred in Japan as a result of the London Naval Treaty.
107. Buckley, "Washington Naval Limitation System," 647. Italy and France were allowed to construct 70,000 tons of new capital ship construction.
108. Memo to the Secretary of the Navy, 22 November 1930, Box 34, Cabinet Papers, HL GB. See also "Reduction in Expenditures in Forces Afloat," 7 September 1930, Correspondence of the Secretary of the Navy, RG 80, NARA.
109. See 7 September 1928, 1–13, GB study 420-2. This document was a lengthy memorandum by ADM Moffett forwarded to the General Board via the CNO recounting the poor state of aircraft carrier construction vis-à-vis the Japanese.
110. Hearing, 27 November 1929, 398, PHGB.
111. Hearing, 11 March 1925, 98–104, PHGB. This Op-12C War Plans Division study was attached to testimony given by CAPT M. G. McCook before the General Board.
112. See Kuehn, *Agents of Innovation*, Appendix 2; "Building and Maintenance Policy," 1922 U.S. Naval Policy.
113. BuAer to Secretary of the Navy, 31 July 1928, attached to GB serial 1345. Moffett wrote this extremely important thirteen-page memorandum on the occasion of the development of the 1929 aircraft-building policy.
114. Ibid. Moffett included CINCUS' annual report for 1927 (A9–1/OF1[4]), ending 30 June 1927, in his memorandum as well as Pratt's endorsement.

115. Cited in BuAer to Secretary of the Navy, 31 July 1928.
116. War Plans Division to CNO and BuAer, memorandum, 8 October 1928, Op-12-CD. This correspondence was attached to GB serial 1376, the building program for 1930.
117. BuAer to Secretary of the Navy, 31 July 1928, 8.
118. "Light Cruisers Nos. 37 to 41 Authorized by the Act of 13 February 1929—General Characteristics," 27 November 1929, PHGB. Pre-conference negotiations for London had been under way for some time, and November 1929 was the "eleventh hour." The conference convened barely two months later, on 21 January 1930. See Stephen Roskill, *Naval Policy between the War*, vol. 2 (Annapolis: Naval Institute Press, 1976), 51–57.
119. See 3 January 1930, serial 1464, GB study 438–1; BuAer to Secretary of the Navy, 23 November 1929, forwarded 3 December 1929 to the General Board.
120. Kuehn, *Agents of Innovation*, chapter 6; BuAer, 28 May 1930, GB study 420–2. Moffett emphasizes all these points and recommends construction of all flying deck cruisers allowable to meet the shortage of aviation in the fleet. See also Richard Dean Burns, ed., *Encyclopedia of Arms Control and Disarmament*, vol. 4 (New York: Charles Scribner's Sons, 1993), 1177. From Article 3 and Article 16, paragraph 5 of the London Naval Treaty; Zimm, "U.S.N.'s Flight Deck Cruiser," 220–221. For Fleet Problem XI, see Till, "Adopting the Aircraft Carrier," 221; and Nofi, *To Train the Fleet for War*, 109–117.
121. From Zimm, "U.S.N.'s Flight Deck Cruiser," 221.
122. From the London Naval Treaty found in Burns, *Encyclopedia of Arms Control and Disarmament* 4:1177, 1181. Zimm, "U.S.N.'s Flight Deck Cruiser," 221, discusses Moffett's alleged subterfuge in proposing the flying deck cruiser at London.
123. See Kuehn, *Agents of Innovation*, 107–123, for the hearings after London associated with the flying deck design.
124. For British carrier and naval aviation development between the wars, see Hone, Friedman, and Mandeles, *American and British Aircraft Carrier Development*; see also Geoffrey Till's chapter on the British Fleet Air Arm in *Military Innovation in the Interwar Period*, ed. Williamson Murray and Alan Millett (New York: Cambridge University Press, 1996).
125. See Goldman, *Sunken Treaties*, Appendix 2, 314–315, for these articles. Article 16 allowed 25 percent "fitted with a landing on platform or deck for aircraft," and Article 18 allowed the conversion of 15,166 tons of heavy cruiser tonnage to light cruisers tonnage.
126. See Simpson, *Anglo-American Naval Relations*, 144–145, [1930] memorandum by RADM Moffett. Moffett states any aircraft carrier tonnage less than the Washington limit of 135,000 tons would be a "calamity."
127. "Military Characteristics of Cruisers with Landing-on Decks," 4 December 1930, PHGB.

128. At this time, and for some time to come, torpedo aircraft, because of the relatively low power of their engines, were considered too heavy for the necessarily small flight decks being proposed for the flying deck cruiser—about 325 to 350 feet. See Zimm, "U.S.N.'s Flight Deck Cruiser," 230–236.
129. "Flying Deck Cruiser," 15 February 1934, PHGB. The amount cited by 1934 was $19–20 million. See also Kuehn, *Agents of Innovation*, chapter 6, passim.
130. Zimm, "U.S.N.'s Flight Deck Cruiser," 216. See also Kuehn, *Agents of Innovation*, chapter 6.
131. Peattie and Evans, *Kaigun*, 244. These ships used float planes and catapults and played a critical role at Midway in 1942.
132. Franny Colby to President Franklin Roosevelt, 25 March 1934, found in material with 12 March 1934, serial 1640E, GB study 438-1.
133. "Participation in Naval Conversations at London, June 18–July 10, 1934," letter from the Chairman of the General Board to the Secretary of the Navy, 30 July 1934, GB study 438-1.
134. Buckley, "Washington Naval Limitation System," 646–47; Asada, *From Mahan to Pearl Harbor*, 183–184.
135. See Kuehn, *Agents of Innovation*, chapter 7, 139. The dock was ARD-1, designed for forward maintenance of destroyers and submarines.

Chapter 8. Innovation and Decline, 1932–41

Epigraph, "Recommendation of Changes in U.S. Navy Regulations 1920," 2, 20 June 1931, PHGB.

1. "Recommendation of Changes in U.S. Navy Regulations 1920," 2, 20 June 1931, PHGB.
2. See Henry P. Beers, "The Development of the Office of the Chief of Naval Operations," pt. 3, *Military Affairs* 11, no. 2 (Summer 1947): 88–99; and Henry P. Beers, "The Development of the Office of the Chief of Naval Operations," pt. 4, *Military Affairs* 11, no. 4 (Winter 1947): 229–237. Beers catalogs the growth of the CNO from World War I to World War II in these articles.
3. BuAer to CNO, 25 March 1929, memorandum, Box 38, Cabinet Papers, HL GB. Moffett argued strenuously against this initiative. See also Treasury Department memorandum, 22 May 1931, Box 39, Cabinet Papers, HL GB.
4. The memo was filed on 24 October 1930. Box 34, Cabinet Papers, HL GB.
5. "Building Program—Fiscal Year 1932," 16 October 1930, serial 1475, GB study 420-2; Norman Friedman, *U.S. Battleships: An Illustrated Design History* (Annapolis: Naval Institute Press, 1985), 202–207.
6. See 5 December 1931, 438-1.
7. James Barros, "The League of Nations and Disarmament," *Encyclopedia of Arms Control and Disarmament*, vol. 2, ed. Richard Dean Burns (New York: Charles Scribner's Sons, 1993), 618–619.

8. Wayne S. Cole, "The Role of the United States Congress and Political Parties," in *Pearl Harbor as History: Japanese-American Relations, 1931–1941*, ed. Dorothy Borg and Sumpei Okamoto (New York: Columbia University Press, 1973), 304.
9. See 18 January 1933, GB study 1521aa. "Limitation and Reduction of Armaments" was later renumbered as serial 1584.
10. See http://www.presidency.ucsb.edu/ws/index.php?pid=14655&st=Annapolis&st1; *Wings over Water*, dir. David Hoffman (Camden, ME: Varied Directions, 1986). FDR is shown making this speech in this documentary film. The transcript for FDR's June 1933 commencement address closed with the words "Keep the faith. Good luck in the days to come!" In the film, FDR continues: "Let me tell you from the bottom of my heart as one who can only say unofficially to you, but who does say unofficially to you, that he loves the United States Navy more than any other branch of our government."
11. See http://www.historycentral.com/documents/NRA.html. Quoted from section 202 of the act passed on 16 June 1933: "And if in the opinion of the President it seems desirable, the construction of naval vessels within the terms and/or limits established by the London Naval Treaty of 1930 and of aircraft required therefore."
12. Baer, *One Hundred Years of Sea Power*, 128–130; Buckley, "Washington Naval Limitation System," 649–650.
13. Members of the General Board, 1932, GB ML, specifically listed "Navy Regulations Change No. 15" as omitting all ex officio members on 10 March 1932.
14. Proceedings and Hearings of the General Board, minutes, 3 July 1931, PHGB. See Wheeler, *Admiral William Veazie Pratt*, 323–324.
15. Members of the General Board, 1930, GB ML.
16. "Recommendations of Changes in U.S. Naval Regulations 1920," 18, 30 June 1931, PHGB.
17. Ibid., 1.
18. Ibid., 2, 11.
19. See Scott T. Price, "A Study of the General Board of the U.S. Navy, 1929–1931" (master's thesis, University of Nebraska, 1989), 134.
20. Correspondence of the CNO, 11 July 1936, RG 80, NARA; CNO, 9 September 1941, GB study 420-2.
21. President, Navy War College, to senior members of the General Board, 20 July 1940, SecNav Correspondence, RG 80, NARA.
22. Beers, "Development of the Office," pt. 4, 236–237; members of the General Board, 1932–1940, GB ML.
23. Norman A. Graebner, "Hoover, Roosevelt, and the Japanese," in *Pearl Harbor as History: Japanese-American Relations, 1931–1941*, ed. Dorothy Borg and Sumpei Okamoto (New York: Columbia University Press, 1973), 34–35;

Sadao Asada, "The Japanese Navy and the United States," in *Pearl Harbor as History: Japanese-American Relations, 1931–1941,* ed. Dorothy Borg and Sumpei Okamoto (New York: Columbia University Press, 1973), 240–243. Asada claims American actions played a role, but that the trend was toward the abandonment of the treaty system principally due to the efforts of the Admiral Kato Kanji. Kato was the head of the so-called fleet faction, which had opposed the Washington Treaty from its inception.

24. Friedman, *U.S. Battleships*, 243.
25. Ibid., 270–274. The Japanese were already planning to build the 18-inch "super-battleships" *Yamato* and *Musashi*.
26. Kinkaid to Chairman for SecNav, 6 February 1934, 6, attached to serial 1640, GB study 438-1. The 1640 date of acceptance by SecNav was 1 October 1934 (GB serial list).
27. See Kuehn, *Agents of Innovation*, chapter 5.
28. See 31 May 1922, serial 1130; 8 March 1926, serial 1315, GB study 449 (Five Year Aircraft Building Program), and 5 April 1927, serial 1345, GB study 420-2. The idea for a thousand planes was initially proposed by Moffett. The final plan to acquire a one-thousand-plane force was submitted and approved in 1926. The 1927 serial summarizes the mature fiscal year 1929 plan.
29. RADM William S. Sims, "The United States Naval War College," U.S. Naval Institute *Proceedings* 45, no. 9 (September 1919): 1486–1491; see also, for this process in action, Operations Problem II—1927, 1–13, May 1927, RG 38, NARA. For more on the Naval War College process of problem solving, see Spector, *Professors at War*, and Michael Vlahos, *The Blue Sword: The Naval War College and the American Mission, 1919–1941* (Newport, RI: Naval War College Press, 1980).
30. Nofi, *To Train the Fleet for War*, 109–117.
31. Kuehn, *Agents of Innovation*, 130–135.
32. Nofi, *To Train the Fleet for War*, 61.
33. Ibid., 144–145, 203, and 214.
34. Proceedings and Hearings of the General Board, 1922–1920, PHGB; see especially the serial lists on Roll 1 as well as the indexes for the hearings. Nimitz is cited in Kuehn, *Agents of Innovation*, 162.
35. Millett in Murray and Millett, *Military Innovation in the Interwar Period*, 75.
36. "Advanced Base Operations in Micronesia," FMFRP 12-46 (Quantico, VA: U.S. Marine Corps, 1921), 59–76; see also David Ulbrich, "The Long Lost *Tentative Manual for Defense of Advanced Bases* (1936)," *Journal of Military History* 71, no. 3 (July 2007): 889–901.
37. See chapter 6 in this book. See also Kuehn, *Agents of Innovation*, chapter 5; see also Schaub, "U.S. Navy Shipboard Damage Control," 2–6, 19–22, 50.
38. CDR E. M. Williams, "Displacement and Gun Caliber of Battleships," 8, 21 May 1931, GB study 438-1.

39. Ibid.
40. Kuehn, *Agents of Innovation*, 77–78.
41. Ibid., 75–83.
42. Including that of the author, see too chapters 6 and 7. See also Williamson, "Keeping Up with the Times"; Hone, Mandeles, and Friedman, *American and British Aircraft Carrier Development*, 133–134; and Friedman, *U.S. Aircraft Carriers*.
43. See 10 September 1918, serial 874, GB study 420-2/449.
44. "Characteristics of Airplane Carriers," 7, 21 February 1921, PHGB.
45. See http://www.uss-bennington.org/essex.html (accessed 7/27/2016) for typical *Essex* specifications.
46. See also Hone, Friedman, and Mandeles, *American and British Aircraft Carrier Development*, 81–82.
47. Butler, "General Board of the Navy," 705.
48. "Testimony of the Commander-in-Chief U.S. Fleet, in Regard to Needs of the Fleet," 1–2, 27 May 1930, PHGB; for the purpose of the scouting fleet in War Plan Orange, see Thomas C. Hone with Trent C. Hone, "The Pacific Naval War as One Coherent Campaign, 1941–1945," *International Journal of Naval History* 2, no. 2 (August 2003): 1–3.
49. "Testimony of the Commander-in-Chief U.S. Fleet," 2–3.
50. Proceedings and Hearings of the General Board, 27 May 1930, 3–8, PHGB; S. E. Morison, *History of United States Naval Operations in World War II*, vol. 4, *Coral Sea, Midway, and Submarine Actions* (Boston: Little, Brown, 1949), 90–91.
51. "Limitation and Reduction of Armaments," 18 January 1933, serial 1521aa, GB study 432-1.
52. Kuehn, *Agents of Innovation*, 122–123; Members of the General Board, 1939–1940, GB ML.
53. Kuehn, *Agents of Innovation*, 101–123.
54. See especially Friedman, *U.S. Cruisers*, chapters 4–7. The photo caption on page 183 particularly makes this point.
55. See Kuehn, *Agents of Innovation*, 171–172.
56. Davis, "Influence of the General Board of the Navy," 43–44.
57. Ibid., 33–34.
58. Ibid., 34–42, 103–104, especially 43n80.
59. Peattie and Evans, *Kaigun*, 223–226; Davis, "Influence of the General Board of the Navy," 101–103.
60. Davis, "Influence of the General Board of the Navy," 45, 46, 105, 106.
61. Ibid., 91–100.
62. Juergens, "Impact of the General Board," 126.
63. Schofield, "Some Effects of the Washington Conference," 1–2, 5. Schofield first emphasized the importance of maintaining and modernizing the

battleships. His discussion of submarines emphasized their usefulness, especially the "cruiser submarine," in the absence of "outlying bases." Later, as war plans division chief, Schofield testified similarly during the 1927 board hearings on the desired characteristics for cruiser submarines.

64. Index and "Submersible Fuel Tender," 10 April 1925, Roll 1, PHGB.
65. "Submersible Fuel Tender," 10 April 1925, 219–220, Roll 1, PHGB.
66. See Waldo H. Heinrichs Jr., "The Role of the United States Navy," in *Pearl Harbor as History: Japanese-American Relations, 1931–1941*, ed. Dorothy Borg and Sumpei Okamoto (New York: Columbia University Press, 1973) 199, for the view that starving bureaucracies are more innovative.
67. Juergens, "Impact of the General Board," 126.
68. See John T. Kuehn, "Short Summary of World War II Submarine Ops," *Submarine Review* (Spring 2011): 121–124.
69. Juergens, "Impact of the General Board," 7, 35, 95, 199–120; members of the General Board, 1936–1939, GB ML. Hart had testified before the board on postwar submarines as early as February 1919. "Characteristics of Fleet Submarines," 17 February 1919, PHGB.
70. Joel Ira Holwitt, *"Execute against Japan": The U.S. Decision to Conduct Unrestricted Submarine Warfare* (College Station: Texas A&M University Press, 2009), 63–70; Juergens, "Impact of the General Board," 90–92, discusses the shift from direct fleet support to independent scouting operations within the Orange paradigm.
71. Juergens, "Impact of the General Board," 120.
72. Ibid., 113–120.
73. Ibid., 90–95, 113–121.
74. See, for example, Holger Herwig, "Innovation Ignored: The Submarine Problem—Germany, Britain, and the United States, 1919–1939," in Murray and Millett, *Military Innovation in the Interwar Period*, 252–260.
75. Mergen, "Patrol Aviation in the Interwar Period," 25.
76. For the story of the aviation tenders, see Kuehn, *Agents of Innovation*, 92–101.
77. Hone, Friedman, and Mandeles, *American and British Aircraft Carrier Development*, 59–60.
78. Mergen, "Patrol Aviation in the Interwar Period," 1–8.
79. Ibid., 151–156.
80. See John T. Kuehn with D. M. Giangreco, *Eyewitness Pacific Theater* (New York: Sterling Press, 2008), 71, for the story of the night PBY attack on the Japanese invasion component of Yamamoto's armada.
81. For example, see LCDR Melvin F. Talbot, "The Battleship: Her Evolution and Her Present Place in the Scheme of Naval War," 1938 U.S. Naval Institute Prize-winning essay, U.S. Naval Institute *Proceedings* 64, no. 5 (May 1938): 645–653. Talbot's essay is a typical defense of the battleship of the period: "She, and she alone, remains an absolute."

82. Morison, *Two-Ocean War*, 59.
83. "Priorities in 2-Ocean Navy Building Program," E. J. King memorandum to General Board, 30 July 1941, GB study 420-2.

Chapter 9. Phoenix or Icarus?

1. See "Twelve O'Clock High," *IMDb.com*, http://www.imdb.com/title/tt0041996.
2. Reynolds, *John H. Towers*, 535–539. Reynolds assessment here is wrong and slights the abundant evidence in archival records to the contrary, for example, Towers to Nimitz, 19 June 1947, 4, paragraphs 7 and 8, GB study 401.
3. The standard work on this is Barlow, *Revolt of the Admirals*.
4. Exodus 1:8 (RSE), 47.
5. "The General Board," 2, draft letter originated by VADM Robert B. Carney for CNO to SecNav, 4 June 1947, GB study 401.
6. Nofi, *To Train the Fleet*, 262.
7. Baer, *One Hundred Years of Sea Power*, 149–156; members of the General Board, 1940–41, GB ML; Asada, *From Mahan to Pearl Harbor*, 174.
8. Carney CNO Memo, 4 June 1947, GB study 401; Baer, *One Hundred Years of Sea Power*, 183–187.
9. "Are We Ready—III," 14 June 1941, GB 425.
10. "Priorities in 2-Ocean Navy Building Program."
11. Fleet Admiral Ernest J. King, *U.S. Navy at War, 1941–1945: Official Reports to the Secretary of the Navy* (Washington, DC: U.S. Navy Department, 1946), 8, 24, 147, 152.
12. Members of the General Board, 1941–42, GB ML; see also http://www.navysite.de/ffg/FFG59.htm.
13. "Composition of the General Board," COMINCH [King] to Secretary of the Navy, 30 July 1942, series 1942, GB study 401.
14. Members of the General Board, 1942–45, GB ML; see http://www.arlingtoncemetery.net/jorichardson.htm.
15. Members of the General Board, 1942–45, GB ML. For the annihilation of the Asiatic Fleet, see LCDR Steven Shepard, "American, British, Dutch, and Australian Coalition: Unsuccessful Band of Brothers" (master's thesis, U.S. Army Command and General Staff College, 2003).
16. John Lundstrom, *Black Shoe Carrier Admiral: Frank Jack Fletcher at Coral Sea, Midway, and Guadalcanal* (Annapolis: Naval Institute Press, 2006), 476–478, 488, 496–503. Members of the General Board, 1945, GB ML.
17. Members of the General Board, 1945–46, GB ML.
18. General Board serial lists for 1942–1945. These lists clearly indicate the board's dominant concern were ship designs.
19. See http://www.archives.gov/records-mgmt/rcs/schedules/departments/department-of-defense/department-of-the-navy/rg-0019/n1-019-87-001_sfl15.pdf.

20. "Appointment of Ship's Characteristics Board," SecNav to CNO, 29 November 1945, GB study 401; and untitled memorandum by John Towers (probably to SecNav), 22 May 1947, GB study 401.
21. Carney CNO Memo, 2; "Agenda for Ship Characteristics Board Meeting at 1000 8 August 1945," 6 August 1945, Ship Characteristics Board memorandum, GB study 401.
22. John Towers probably to SecNav, 28 May 1947, memorandum, GB study 401.
23. "Combatant Ships—Development and Improvement of Designs," SecNav to General Board et al., 10 May 1945, memorandum, GB study 401.
24. "Post-War Shipbuilding Program," SecNav to General Board, 29 June 1945, memorandum, GB study 401.
25. See http://www.history.navy.mil/research/library/research-guides/lists-of-senior-officers-and-civilian-officials-of-the-us-navy/chiefs-of-naval-operations.html.
26. Memo to EXOS "management engineer" from General Board, 14 December 1945, GB study 401.
27. General Board to President Navy Regulations Board, 19 April 1946, GB study 401; members of the General Board, 1946, GB ML.
28. VADM Fletcher to SecNav, 30 April 1946, GB study 401.
29. Chairman of GB to SecNav, 14 May 1946, GB study 401.
30. "Status of the General Board," King to SecNav, 16 May 1946, memo, attached to serial 300, GB study 401.
31. From Naval History and Heritage Command Arleigh Burke Papers, Boxes 5-7 (hereafter cited as Burke Papers), memo, attached to 10 May 1946 draft by CNO for SecNav, "General Board."
32. In the Burke Papers, these memorandums can be found stored next to each other. For information on Ramsey's career, see Lundstrom, *Black Shoe Carrier Admiral*, 471–472, and Barlow, *Revolt of the Admirals*, 88.
33. See Barlow, *Revolt of the Admirals*, 23–30; Reynolds, *John H. Towers*, 527–528, 535.
34. Reynolds, *John H. Towers*, 536–537; see also *Aviation Biography* and notes in the John H. Towers Papers, Naval History and Heritage Command, Washington, DC; Towers to Nimitz, 5 May 1947, paragraph 3, GB study 420-2. For Forrestal and King, see Douglass Kinnard, *The Secretary of Defense* (Lexington: University Press of Kentucky, 1980), 22–31.
35. Towers to Nimitz, 5 May 1947; members of the General Board, 1947, GB ML. For accounts of McMorris' and Burke's exploits during the war, see Ronald Spector, *Eagle against the Sun* (New York: Vintage Books, 1985), 179–180 and 148, 312.
36. See Reynolds, *John H. Towers*, 534–536.

37. GB serial list, 1946–1948, especially serial 303(A)-(T), "Final Review of Revised Navy Regs. 1920"; 1948 U.S. Navy Regulations, https://babel.hathitrust.org/cgi/pt?id=uc1.b3907814;view=1up;seq=5.
38. Members of the General Board, 1947, GB ML (Towers retired on 1 December 1947); Baer, *One Hundred Years of Sea Power*, 295–297.
39. "General Board—Certain Duties of," Towers to Nimitz, 5 May 1947, GB study 420-2; "Final Review of Revised Navy Regs," 25 October 46–19 January 48, GB serial 303.
40. "General Board—Certain Duties of"; Reynolds, *John H. Towers*, 515.
41. "The General Board," CNO to SecNav by VADM Carney (Op-04), 4 June 1947, draft memo, GB study 420-2.
42. "Proposed New Precept for the General Board," Towers to Nimitz, 19 June 1947, GB study 420-2.
43. SCB to General Board, 16 July 1947, serial 309, GB study 420-2.
44. "Survey of Shore Activities," 1–7, 31 July 1947, Burke Papers; GB serial list, 1947.
45. GB serial list, 1947, especially serial 311, "Uniforms."
46. "Flag Billets Proposal for in the Post War Navy," BuPers (Denfeld) to CNO (Nimitz), 27 March 1946, CNO Correspondence, RG 80, NARA.
47. GB serial list, 1948. These encompassed, respectively, serials 315, 316, and 317.
48. GB serial list, 1948, serial (321); "Naval Operating Forces—Fiscal 1955," 1, 21 November 1947, Burke Papers.
49. "Naval Operating Forces—Fiscal 1955," 1–2, 4–5, 21 November 1947, Burke Papers.
50. From 20 September 47 General Board Procedures, 5, Division III, Burke Papers.
51. George F. Kennan, "The Sources of Soviet Conduct," by X, *Foreign Affairs* (July 1947): 566–582.
52. "National Security and Navy Contributions Thereto for the Next Ten Years: A Study by the General Board," 25 June 1948, from Enclosure C ("Military"), 1–3, GB study 425, Burke Papers. This study was also known as serial 315.
53. Ibid., 1–3; and "Concepts of War and Navy Contributions," Enclosure D, 1–2, GB study 425, Burke Papers.
54. "Concepts of War and Navy Contributions," Enclosure D, 7, 56.
55. "Conclusions," Enclosure C, 1–9, GB study 425, Burke Papers.
56. Barlow, *Revolt of the Admirals*, 174–175.
57. Cited in Baer, *One Hundred Years of Sea Power*, 313.
58. Members of the General Board, 1948, GB ML; Barlow, *Revolt of the Admirals*, 165; Carl LaVO, *Pushing the Limits: The Remarkable Life and Times of Vice Admiral Allan Rockwell McCann* (Annapolis: Naval Institute Press, 2013),

200–202. McCann became the Navy's inspector general during the Revolt of the Admirals in 1949.
59. "Navy Contributions to National Security, Revision of 315 and Continuous Study," 6 October 1948, GB study 325.
60. Barlow, *Revolt of the Admirals*, 164–169.
61. Ibid., chapter 9.
62. Ibid., 186–191.
63. Ibid., 206.
64. Members of the General Board, 1949, GB ML; McCann was reassigned by Matthews on 20 June; see also LaVO, *Pushing the Limits*, 206–211.
65. Barlow, *Revolt of the Admirals*, 247–254.
66. Ibid., 269–273; Baer, *One Hundred Years of Sea Power*, 318–320.
67. "Organization of U.S. Army General Staff," 1, 9 August 1949, PHGB.
68. "Applicability of the General Staff System to the Navy, Study of," 1–2, 19 August 1949, GB serial 142EN2 (7-49).
69. "Organization of the Navy Department," 11 August 1949, PHGB.
70. GB minutes, 19 August 1949; for Hill, see http://www.navysite.de/dd/dd986.htm.
71. "Guided Missles," 4 October 1949, PHGB; GB minutes, September and October 1949.
72. GB minutes, November 1949–March 1950.
73. GB serial list, 1949; Proceedings and Hearings of the General Board, contents for 1950 hearings, PHGB; "Shipbuilding and Conversion Program Fiscal Year 1952 (1-50)," 1–2, 28 March 1950, PHGB. CAPT Hyman Rickover is mentioned in these hearings during discussion of a submarine powered by a nuclear reactor.
74. For example, in Proceedings and Hearings of the General Board, 28 March 1950, PHGB, there were four SCB members at the meeting, listed separately from BuShips personnel.
75. Members of the General Board, 1950, GB ML.
76. GB minutes, 10 and 15 August 1950.
77. See https://www.usna.edu/Notables//cno/1916fechteler.html.
78. "Establishment of Shipbuilding and Conversion Programs and Ship Characteristics Thereof," 1–3, G. H. Fort to VCNO, 11 October 1950, GB serial 155EN2.
79. Baer, *One Hundred Years of Sea Power*, 301; "Material Review Board," SecNav to CNO and Chief of Material, 28 December 1950, SecNav Correspondence.
80. Members of the General Board, August 1950, GB ML; GB minutes, 6 November 1950, the last minutes ever recorded by the board.
81. "General Board, dissolution of," CNO to Chairman of the General Board, 16 January 1951, GB serial 15P31; "General Board, dissolution of," Chairman of the General Board to CNO, 18 January 1951, GB serial 15EN2.

82. Baer, *One Hundred Years of Sea Power*, 301.
83. Hanson Baldwin, "General Board Is Dead," *New York Times*, 5 May 1951.
84. "General Board files, transfer of," Chairman of the General Board to Director of Naval Records and History, 29 January 1951, GB serial 22EN2.

Epilogue. America's First General Staff

1. Birtle, "Military Interventions during the Wilson Administration," 208–226.
2. "Conditions in Japan," 1–2, 1 October 1919, PHGB; the Japanese formal names in brackets come from Edward Drea, *Japan's Imperial Army* (Lawrence: University of Kansas Press, 2009), passim and index.
3. For the foundation study on this topic, see Russell Weigley, *The American Way of War: A History of United States Military Strategy and Policy* (Bloomington: Indiana University Press, 1973), xx–xxiii.
4. Conversation between author and Professor Chris Gabel at a graduate seminar on "Military Innovation in the Interwar Period," Kansas State University, Spring 2002.
5. For a discussion of this concept and its relation to blitzkrieg, see Robert M. Citino, *The German Way of War: From the Thirty Years War to the Third Reich* (Lawrence: University of Kansas Press, 2005), xiv, 240–244.
6. See the Naval Institute Press' 21st Century Foundations series, for example, David Kohnen, ed., *21st Century Knox: Influence, Sea Power, and History for the Modern Era* (Annapolis: Naval Institute Press, 2016).
7. Jay Luvaas, "Military History: Is It Still Practicable?" *Parameters* 12 (March 1982): 3.
8. Asada, "Revolt against the Washington Treaty," 86.

SELECTED BIBLIOGRAPHY

Archival Sources

Congressional Record. Microfilm held at Combined Arms Research Library, Fort Leavenworth, KS.

Hoover Library, West Branch, Iowa
- Cabinet Office Series
  - Policy messages, CNO reports, condition of the Navy, General Board, Boxes 35–36
  - Naval Conferences, Reduction, Intelligence, and Economy, Boxes 38/39
- Commerce Paper Series
  - Limitations of Armaments Conference, Box 156
  - Naval Investigation of 1920, Box 8

Library of Congress
- Papers of Admiral of the Fleet George Dewey

National Archives and Record Administration, Washington, DC, and College Park, MD
- Proceedings and Hearings of the General Board of the U.S. Navy, 1900–1950
- General Board Studies, RG 80 (microfilm)
- Formerly Classified Correspondence of the Office of Naval Intelligence, Office of Chief of Naval Operations, War Plans Division, RG 38
- Formerly Classified Correspondence of the Secretary of the Navy, Chief of Naval Operations Correspondence, RG 80 (microfilm)

Naval History and Heritage Command, Naval Warfare Division Collections and Navy Department Library, Washington, DC
- *Annual Reports of the Navy Department* (various years)
- Arleigh Burke Papers, Boxes 5–7
- *Aviation Biography* and John H. Towers Papers
- Thomas C. Kinkaid Papers

Published Primary Sources, Articles, and Memoirs

Buell, Raymond L. *The Washington Conference.* New York: D. Appleton, 1922.

Chadwick, French E. "The Naval War College." In *Papers of the Military Historical Society*, vol. 15, 343–359. Wilmington, NC: Broadfoot, 1997.

Cronon, E. David, ed. *The Cabinet Diaries of Josephus Daniels, 1913–1921.* Lincoln: University of Nebraska Press, 1962.

Davis, George T. *A Navy Second to None: The Development of American Naval Policy.* New York: Harcourt Brace, 1940.

Fiske, RADM Bradley A. *From Midshipman to Rear-Admiral.* New York: Century, 1919.

———. *The Navy as a Fighting Machine.* New York: Charles Scribner's Sons, 1916.

Gleaves, RADM Albert, ed. *Life and Letters of Rear Admiral Stephen B. Luce, U.S. Navy.* New York: G. P. Putnam's Sons, 1925.

Kennan, George F. "The Sources of Soviet Conduct," by X. *Foreign Affairs* (July 1947): 566–582.

Knox, CAPT Dudley W. *The Eclipse of American Sea Power.* New York: American Army and Navy Journal, 1922.

League of Nations. *Armaments Year-Books: General and Statistical Information.* Geneva: League of Nations, 1924–36.

Mahan, A. T. *The Gulf and Inland Waters.* Vol. 3. New York: Charles Scribner's Sons, 1883.

———. *The Influence of Sea Power upon History.* 1890. Reprint, New York: Hill and Wang, 1957.

———. *Naval Administration and Warfare.* Boston: Little, Brown, 1908.

———. *Naval Strategy.* 1909. Reprint, Newport, RI: Department of the Navy, 1991. Reprinted as FMFRP 12-32.

Seager, Robert, II, and Doris D. Maguire, eds. *Letters and Papers of Alfred Thayer Mahan.* 3 vols. Annapolis: Naval Institute Press, 1975.

Simpson, Michael, ed. *Anglo-American Naval Relations, 1919–1939.* Burlington, VT: Ashgate Publishing for the Naval Records Society, 1910.

Sprout, Harold, and Margaret Sprout. *Toward a New Order of Sea Power: American Naval Policy and the World Scene, 1918–1922.* Princeton, NJ: Princeton University Press, 1940.

U.S. Department of State. *Papers Relating to the Foreign Relations of the United States.* Washington, DC: Government Printing Office, 1929–30.

Wilkinson, Spenser. *The Brain of an Army: A Popular Account of the German General Staff.* 2nd ed. London: Constable, 1913.

Books

Asada, Sadao. *From Mahan to Pearl Harbor: The Imperial Japanese Navy and the United States*. Annapolis: Naval Institute Press, 2006.

Auchincloss, Louis. *Woodrow Wilson*. New York: Viking Books, 2000.

Baer, George W. *100 Years of Sea Power: The U.S. Navy, 1890-1990*. Stanford, CA: Stanford University Press, 1994.

Barlow, Jeffrey G. *From Hot War to Cold: The U.S. Navy and National Security Affairs, 1945-1955*. Stanford, CA: Stanford University Press, 2009.

———. *Revolt of the Admirals: The Fight for Naval Aviation, 1945-1950*. Washington, DC: Naval Historical Center, 1994.

Bell, Christopher, and John Maurer, eds. *At the Crossroads between Peace and War: The London Naval Conference of 1930*. Annapolis: Naval Institute Press, 2014.

Birtle, Andrew J. *U.S. Army Counterinsurgency and Contingency Operations Doctrine, 1860-1941*. Washington, DC: Center of Military History, 2003.

Borg, Dorothy, and Sumpei Okamoto, eds. *Pearl Harbor as History: Japanese-American Relations, 1931-1941*. New York: Columbia University Press, 1973.

Braisted, William R. *Diplomats in Blue: U.S. Naval Officers in China, 1922-1933*. Gainesville: University of Florida Press, 2009.

———. *The United States Navy in the Pacific, 1909-1922*. Austin: University of Texas Press, 1971.

Buckley, Thomas H. *The United States and the Washington Conference, 1921-1922*. Knoxville: University of Tennessee Press, 1970.

Burns, Richard Dean, ed. *Encyclopedia of Arms Control and Disarmament*. Vols. 1-3. New York: Charles Scribner's Sons, 1993.

Clausewitz, Carl von. *On War*. Edited and translated by Peter Paret and Michael Howard. Princeton, NJ: Princeton University Press, 1984.

Conn, Stetson, and Byron Fairchild. *The Framework of Hemispheric Defense, from United States Army in World War II*. Washington, DC: Center of Military History, 1960.

Craig, Lee A. *Josephus Daniels: His Life and Times*. Chapel Hill: University of North Carolina Press, 2013.

Crowley, James B. *Japan's Quest for Autonomy: National Security and Foreign Policy, 1930-1938*. Princeton, NJ: Princeton University Press, 1966.

Epstein, Katherine C. *Torpedo: Inventing the Military-Industrial Complex in the United States and Great Britain*. Cambridge, MA: Harvard University Press, 2014.

Evans, David C., and Mark R. Peattie. *Kaigun*. Annapolis: Naval Institute Press, 1997.

Friedman, Norman. *U.S. Aircraft Carriers: An Illustrated History*. Annapolis: Naval Institute Press, 1983.

———. *U.S. Battleships: An Illustrated Design History*. Annapolis: Naval Institute Press, 1985.

———. *U.S. Cruisers: An Illustrated Design History*. Annapolis: Naval Institute Press, 1984.

———. *U.S. Submarines: Design and Development*. Annapolis: Naval Institute Press, 1984.

Friedman, Norman, Thomas C. Hone, and Mark Mandeles. *American and British Aircraft Carrier Development, 1919–1941*. Annapolis: Naval Institute Press, 1999.

Geissler, Suzanne. *God and Sea Power: The Influence of Religion on Alfred Thayer Mahan*. Annapolis: Naval Institute Press, 2015.

Goldman, Emily O. *Sunken Treaties: Naval Arms Control between the Wars*. University Park: Pennsylvania State University Press, 1994.

Goldstein, Erik, and John Maurer, eds. *The Washington Conference, 1921–22: Naval Rivalry, East Asian Stability and the Road to Pearl Harbor*. London: Frank Cass, 1994.

Hagan, Kenneth J. *This People's Navy: The Making of American Seapower*. New York: Collier Macmillan, 1991.

Halpern, Paul G. *A Naval History of World War I*. Annapolis: Naval Institute Press, 1994.

Hammond, James. *The Treaty Navy: The Story of the U.S. Naval Service Between the World Wars*. Victoria, BC: Trafford, 2001.

Hendrix, Henry J. *Theodore Roosevelt's Naval Diplomacy: The U.S. Navy and the Birth of the American Century*. Annapolis: Naval Institute Press, 2009.

Hezlet, Arthur. *Aircraft and Sea Power*. New York: Stein and Day, 1970.

Holwitt, Joel. *Execute against Japan: The U.S. Decision to Conduct Unrestricted Submarine Warfare*. College Station: Texas A&M University, 2009.

Hone, Thomas C., and Trent Hone. *Battle Line: The United States Navy, 1919–1939*. Annapolis: Naval Institute Press, 2006.

Hoogenboom, Ari. *Gustavus Vasa Fox of the Union Navy: A Biography*. Baltimore: Johns Hopkins University Press, 2009.

Hough, Richard. *Death of the Battleship*. New York: Macmillan, 1963.

Howard, Michael. *War and the Liberal Conscience*. 1978. Reprint, New Brunswick, NJ: Rutgers University Press, 1994.

Huntington, Samuel. *The Soldier and the State*. Cambridge, MA: Harvard University Press, 1957.

Hyde, Harlow. *Scraps of Paper: The Disarmament Treaties between the World Wars*. Lincoln, NE: Media, 1988.

Karsten, Peter. *The Naval Aristocracy: The Golden Age of Annapolis and the Emergence of Modern American Navalism*. New York: Free Press, 1972.

Kaufman, Robert G. *Arms Control during the Pre-Nuclear Era: The United States and Naval Limitation between the Two World Wars*. New York: Columbia University Press, 1990.

Kinnard, Douglass. *The Secretary of Defense*. Lexington: University Press of Kentucky, 1980.

Knox, Macgregor, and Williamson Murray, eds. *The Dynamics of Military Revolution, 1300–2050*. Cambridge: Cambridge University Press, 2001.

Kuehn, John T. *Agents of Innovation: The General Board and the Design of the Fleet that Defeated the Japanese Navy*. Annapolis: Naval Institute Press, 2008.

———. *A Military History of Japan*. Santa Barbara, CA: Praeger, 2014.

———. *Napoleonic Warfare: The Operational Art of the Great Campaigns*. Santa Barbara, CA: Praeger, 2015.

Kuehn, John T., with D. M. Giangreco. *Eyewitness Pacific Theater*. New York: Sterling Press, 2008.

Lambert, Nicholas A. *Planning Armageddon: British Economic Warfare and the First World War*. Cambridge, MA: Harvard University Press, 2012.

LaVO, Carl. *Pushing the Limits: The Remarkable Life and Times of Vice Admiral Allan Rockwell McCann*. Annapolis: Naval Institute Press, 2013.

Leech, Douglas. *Roots of Conflict: British Armed Forces and Colonial Americans, 1677–1763*. Chapel Hill: University of North Carolina Press, 1988.

Lepore, Herbert P. *The Politics and Failure of Naval Disarmament, 1919–1939: The Phantom Peace*. Queenstown, ONT: Edward Mellen Press, 2003.

Love, Robert W. *History of the U.S. Navy*. Vol. 1, *1775–1941*. Harrisburg, PA: Stackpole, 1992.

———. *History of the U.S. Navy*. Vol. 2, *1942–1991*. Harrisburg, PA: Stackpole, 1992.

Lundstrom, John. *Black Shoe Carrier Admiral: Frank Jack Fletcher at Coral Sea, Midway, and Guadalcanal*. Annapolis: Naval Institute Press, 2006.

McBride, William M. *Technological Change and the United States Navy, 1865–1945*. Baltimore: Johns Hopkins University Press, 2000.

McKercher, B. J. C., ed. *Arms Limitation and Disarmament: Restraints on War, 1899–1939*. Westport, CT: Praeger, 1992.

Miller, Edward S. *War Plan Orange*. Annapolis: Naval Institute Press, 1991.

Millis, Walter. *The Martial Spirit: A Study of Our War with Spain*. Boston: Houghton Mifflin, 1931.

Morison, Samuel Eliot. *History of United States Naval Operations in World War II*. 15 vols. Boston: Little, Brown, 1947–62.

———. *The Two-Ocean War: A Short History of the United States Navy in the Second World War*. Boston: Little, Brown, 1963.

Murray, Williamson, and James Lacey, eds. *The Making of Peace*. New York: Cambridge University Press, 2009.

Murray, Williamson, and Allan R. Millett, eds. *Military Innovation in the Interwar Period*. New York: Cambridge University Press, 1996.

Nofi, Albert A. *To Train the Fleet for War: The U.S. Navy Fleet Problems, 1923–1940*. Newport, RI: Naval War College Press, 2010.

Padfield, Peter. *Maritime Dominion and the Triumph of the Free World: Naval Campaigns that Shaped the Modern World, 1852–2001*. New York: Overlook Press, 2009.

Pattee, Phillip G. *At War in Distant Waters: British Colonial Defense in the Great War*. Annapolis: Naval Institute Press, 2013.

Paullin, Charles O. *Paullin's History of Naval Administration, 1775–1911*. Annapolis: Naval Institute Press, 1968.

Pedisich, Paul E. *Congress Buys a Navy: Politics, Economics, and the Rise of American Naval Power, 1881–1921*. Annapolis: Naval Institute Press, 2016.

Pelz, Stephen E. *Race to Pearl Harbor: The Failure of the Second London Naval Conference and the Onset of World War II*. Cambridge, MA: Harvard University Press, 1974.

Pleshakov, Constantine. *The Tsar's Last Armada: The Epic Voyage to the Battle of Tsushima*. New York: Basic Books, 2002.

Posen, Barry R. *The Sources of Military Doctrine: France, Britain, and Germany between the World Wars*. Ithaca, NY: Cornell University Press, 1984.

Reynolds, Clark G. *John H. Towers: The Struggle for Naval Air Supremacy*. Annapolis: Naval Institute Press, 1991.

Ridge, Martin, ed. *Frederick Jackson Turner: Wisconsin's Historian of the Frontier*. Madison: State Historical Society of Wisconsin, 1986.

Rose, Lisle. *Power at Sea*. Vols. 1–3. Columbia: University of Missouri Press, 2006.

Rosen, Stephen Peter. *Winning the Next War: Innovation and the Modern Military*. Ithaca, NY: Cornell University Press, 1991.

Roskill, W. Stephen. *Naval Policy between the Wars*. Vol. 1, *The Period of Anglo-American Antagonism, 1919–1929*. New York: Walker, 1968.

———. *Naval Policy between the Wars.* Vol. 2, *The Period of Reluctant Rearmament, 1930–1939.* Annapolis: Naval Institute Press, 1976.

Rossano, Geoffrey L., and Thomas Wildenberg. *Striking the Hornet's Nest: Naval Aviation and the Origins of Strategic Bombing in World War I.* Annapolis: Naval Institute Press, 2015.

Ruge, Friedrich. *Der Seekrieg: The German Navy's Story, 1939–1945.* Annapolis: Naval Institute Press, 1957.

Spector, Ronald. *Eagle against the Sun.* New York: Vintage Books, 1985.

———. *Professors at War: The Naval War College and the Development of the Naval Profession.* Newport, RI: Naval War College Press, 1977.

Strachan, Hew. *The First World War.* New York: Penguin Books, 2005.

Sumida, Jon Tetsuro. *Inventing Grand Strategy and Teaching Command: The Classic Works of Alfred Thayer Mahan Reconsidered.* Baltimore: Johns Hopkins University Press, 1997.

Symonds, Craig L. *Lincoln and His Admirals: Abraham Lincoln, the U.S. Navy, and the Civil War.* New York: Oxford University Press, 2008.

Terraine, John. *The U-Boat Wars, 1916–1945.* New York: G. P. Putnam's Sons, 1989.

Tuchman, Barbara. *The Zimmermann Telegram.* New York: Bantam, 1971.

Vlahos, Michael. *The Blue Sword: The Naval War College and the American Mission, 1919–1941.* Newport, RI: Naval War College Press, 1980.

Weigley, Russell F. *The American Way of War: A History of United States Military Strategy and Policy.* Bloomington: Indiana University Press, 1973.

Wheeler, Gerald E. *Admiral William Veazie Pratt, U.S. Navy: A Sailor's Life.* Washington, DC: Department of the Navy, 1974.

Wiebe, Robert H. *The Search for Order, 1877–1920.* New York: Hill and Wang, 1967.

Winton, Harold R., and David R. Mets, eds. *The Challenge of Change: Military Institutions and New Realities, 1918–1941.* Lincoln: University of Nebraska Press, 2000.

Theses and Dissertations

Costello, Daniel J. "Planning for War: A History of the General Board of the Navy, 1900–1914." PhD diss., Fletcher School of Law and Diplomacy, 1968.

Davis, Jason H. "The Influence of the General Board of the Navy on Interwar Destroyer Design." Master's thesis, USA Command and General Staff College, 2011.

Holden, David. "Managing Men and Machines: U.S. Military Officers and the Intellectual Origins of Scientific Management in the Early Twentieth Century." PhD diss., University of Kansas, 2016.

Juergens, Jeffrey K. "The Impact of the General Board of the Navy on Interwar Submarine Design." Master's thesis, USA Command and General Staff College, 2009.

Knisley, Ronald William. "The General Board of the United States Navy: Its Influence on Naval Policy and National Policy." Master's thesis, University of Delaware, 1967.

Kuehn, John T. "The Influence of Naval Arms Limitation on U.S. Naval Innovation during the Interwar Period, 1921–1937." PhD diss., Kansas State University, 2007.

Mergen, Christopher J. "Development of Maritime Patrol Aviation in the Interwar Period, 1918 to 1941." Master's thesis, USA Command and General Staff College, 2015.

Price, Scott T. "A Study of the General Board of the U.S. Navy, 1929–1933." Master's thesis, University of Nebraska, 1989.

Schaub, Jeremy P. "U.S. Navy Shipboard Damage Control: Innovation and Implementation during the Interwar Period." Master's thesis, U.S. Army Command and General Staff College, 2014.

Articles and Book Chapters

Asada, Sadao. "Japan's Special Interest and the Washington Conference, 1921–1922." *American Historical Review* 67 (October 1961): 62–70.

———. "The Revolt against the Washington Treaty: The Imperial Japanese Navy and Naval Limitation, 1921–1927." *Naval War College Review*, Summer 1993, 82–96.

Beers, Henry, P. "The Development of the Office of the Chief of Naval Operations." Pt. 1. *Military Affairs* 10, no. 1 (Spring 1946): 40–68.

———. "The Development of the Office of the Chief of Naval Operations." Pt. 2. *Military Affairs* 10, no. 3 (Autumn 1946): 10–38.

———. "The Development of the Office of the Chief of Naval Operations." Pt. 3. *Military Affairs* 11, no. 2 (Summer 1947): 88–99.

———. "The Development of the Office of the Chief of Naval Operations." Pt. 4. *Military Affairs* 11, no. 4 (Winter 1947): 229–237.

Braisted, William R. "On the General Board of the Navy, Admiral Hilary P. Jones, and Naval Arms Limitation, 1921–1931." In *The Dwight D. Eisenhower Lectures in War and Peace, No. 5*. Manhattan: Department of History, Kansas State University, 1993.

Bryson, Thomas A. "Mark L. Bristol, an Open-Door Diplomat in Turkey." *International Journal of Middle East Studies* 5, no. 4 (1974): 450–467.

Buckley, Thomas H. "The Icarus Factor: The American Pursuit of Myth in Naval Arms Control, 1221–36." In *The Washington Conference, 1921–22: Naval Rivalry, East Asian Stability and the Road to Pearl Harbor*, edited by Erik Goldstein and John Maurer, 124–146. London: Frank Cass, 1994.

———. "The Washington Naval Limitation System: 1921–1939." In *Encyclopedia of Arms Control and Disarmament*, vol. 2, edited by Richard Dean Burns. New York: Charles Scribner's Sons, 1993.

Butler, Jarvis. "The General Board of the Navy." U.S. Naval Institute *Proceedings* 56, no. 8 (August 1930): 700–705.

Conrad, Dennis. "Were They So Unprepared? Josephus Daniels and the United States Navy's Entry into World War I." *U.S. Military History Review* 1, no. 3: 5–19.

Crawford, Michael. "U.S. Naval Plans for War with the United Kingdom in the 1890s: A Compromise between Pragmatism and Theory." Paper read at 2016 Society of Military History Conference. The author obtained Crawford's permission to use his scholarship in this work.

Crowl, Philip A. "Alfred Thayer Mahan: The Naval Historian." In *Makers of Modern Strategy*, edited by Peter Paret. Princeton, NJ: Princeton University Press, 1986.

Epstein, Katherine. "No One Can Afford to Say 'Damn the Torpedoes': Battle Tactics and U.S. Naval History before World War I." *Journal of Military History* 77, no. 2 (April 2013): 491–520.

Friedman, Norman. "The South Carolina Sisters: America's First Dreadnoughts." *Naval History Magazine* 24, no. 1 (February 2010): 16–23.

Hone, Thomas C. "A WWI Naval Officer's Story." *War on the Rocks*, 6 September 2013. http://warontherocks.com.

Hone, Thomas, and Mark Mandeles. "Managerial Style in the Interwar Navy: A Reappraisal." *Naval War College Review* 32 (September–October 1980): 88–101.

Hone, Trent, and Thomas C. Hone. "The Pacific Naval War as One Coherent Campaign, 1941–1945." *International Journal of Naval History* 2, no. 2 (August 2003): 1–10.

Howard, Sir Michael. "Military Science in an Age of Peace." *RUSI: Journal of the Royal United Services Institute for Defense Studies* 119 (March 1974): 3–9.

Jampoler, Andrew C. S. "The American Bonaparte." *Naval History* (December 2013).

Johnson, William S. "Naval Diplomacy and the Failure of Balanced Security in the Far East: 1921–1935." *Naval War College Review* 24, no. 6 (February 1972): 67–88.

Jones, Jerry W. "The Naval Battle of Paris." *Naval War College Review* (Spring 2009): 77–89.

Kuehn, John T. "Abolish the Secretary of Defense?" *Joint Force Quarterly* 47 (4th Quarter 2007): 114–116.

———. "Air-Sea Battle and Its Discontents." *Proceedings* 139, no. 10 (October 2013): 42–47.

———. "Grudging Respect? Kaigun through the Lens of the U.S. Navy at the Time of the Sino Japanese War." *Northern Mariner* 26, no. 3 (July 2016): 259–274.

———. "The Martial Spirit—Naval Style: The Naval Reform Movement and the Establishment of the General Board of the Navy, 1873–1900." *Northern Mariner/Le marin du nord* 22, no. 2 (April 2012): 121–140.

———. "The Ostfriesland, the Washington Naval Treaty, and the General Board of the Navy: A Relook at a Historic Sinking." In *New Interpretations in Naval History: Selected Papers from the Sixteenth Naval History Symposium*, edited by Craig C. Felker and Marcus O. Jones, 73–86. Newport, RI: Naval War College Press, 2012.

———. "Short Summary of World War II Submarine Ops." *Submarine Review* (Spring 2011): 121–124.

———. "The U.S. Navy General Board and Naval Arms Limitation: 1922–1937." *Journal of Military History* 74, no. 4 (October 2010): 1129–1160.

Lambert, Nicholas A. "Admiral Sir John Fisher and the Concept of Flotilla Defence, 1904–1909." *Journal of Military History* 59 (October 1995): 639–660.

Maffeo, CAPT Seven E. *U.S. Navy Codebreakers, Linguists, and Intelligence Officers against Japan, 1910–1941*. Colorado Springs, CO: Rowman & Littlefield, 2016.

Mukunda, Gautam. "We Cannot Go On: Disruptive Innovation and the First World War Royal Navy." *Security Studies* 19, no. 1 (January 2010): 127.

Murphy, Martin N., and Toshi Yoshihara. "Fighting the Naval Hegemon: Evolution in French, Soviet, and Chinese Naval Thought." *Naval War College Review* 68, no. 3 (Summer 2015): 12–9.

O'Neil, William D. "Transformation Billy Mitchell Style." U.S. Naval Institute *Proceedings* (March 2002): 101.

Ransom, Harry H. "The Battleship Meets the Airplane. *Military Affairs* 23, no. 1 (Spring 1959): 21–27.

Reynolds, Clark G. "John H. Towers, the Morrow Board, and the Reform of the Navy's Aviation." *Military Affairs* 52, no. 2 (April 1988): 78–84.

Rosen, Philip T. "The Treaty Navy, 1919–1937." In *In Peace and War: Interpretations of American Naval History, 1775–1984*, 2nd ed., edited by Kenneth J. Hagan, 221–236. Westport, CT: Greenwood Press, 1984.

Semsch, Philip L. "Elihu Root and the General Staff." *Military Affairs* 27, no. 1 (Spring 1963): 16–27.

Spector, Ronald H. "The Military Effectiveness of the US Armed Forces, 1919–39." In *Military Effectiveness*. Vol. 2, *The Interwar Period*, edited by Allan R. Millett and Williamson Murray, 70–97. Boston: Unwin Hyman, 1988.

Stephens, Alan, ed. *The War in the Air, 1914–1994*. Maxwell AFB, AL: Air University Press.

Trimble, W. F. "Admiral Hilary Jones and the 1927 Geneva Naval Conference." *Military Affairs* 48, no. 3 (February 1979): 1–4.

Wenzer, Kenneth C. "The First Naval War College Plan against Spain by Lt. Cmdr. Charles H. Stockton." *International Journal of Naval History*, April 2016.

———. "The Naval War Board of 1898." *Canadian Military History* 25, no. 1 (2016): article 1.

Williamson, Corbin. "Keeping Up with the Times: The General Board of the Navy on Airpower at Sea, 1917–1925." Unpublished paper, 2011. Available upon request. Author permission granted to use.

Zimm, Alan D. "The U.S.N.'s Flight Deck Cruiser." *Warship International* 3 (1979): 216–245.

Zimmerman, Gene T. "More Fiction than Fact: The Sinking of the Ostfriesland." *Warship International* 12, no. 2 (1975): 142–154.

Government Documents and Studies

Anonymous. "Force of the Future: Maintaining Our Competitive Edge in Human Capital." Memorandum of the Secretary of Defense, 18 November 2015, U.S. Department of Defense.

Congress. U.S. Senate. *Conference on the Limitation of Armament*. S. Doc. 77. Washington, DC: Government Printing Office, 1921.

———. *Conference on Limitation of Armament*. S. Doc. 126. Washington, DC: Government Printing Office, 1922.

Lykke, Arthur F., Jr. "Toward an Understanding of Military Strategy." In *Military Strategy: Theory and Application*. Carlisle Barracks, PA: Government Printing Office, 1989.

Naval Historical Center. *Dictionary of American Naval Fighting Ships*. Vols. 1–8. Edited by James L. Mooney. Washington, DC: Government Printing Office, 1991.

Contemporary Professional Journals and Newspapers
Army-Navy Journal
Army and Navy Register
Brassey's Naval Review
Hawaii Honolulu Star Bulletin
McClure's Magazine
Military Review
Naval War College Review
New York Times
Stars and Stripes
U.S. Naval Institute *Proceedings*

INDEX

ABCD ships, 13, 30, 49, 235n20. *See also Chicago*
Adams, Charles F., 160–61, 172, 173, 227
Ammen, Daniel, 12, 13, 14, 31, 236n23
Andrews, William, 66–67
Anglo-Japanese Alliance, 43, 56, 103, 120, 134, 260n11
armament limitations, 5, 132–33, 149; Butler bill, 264n82; under FDR, 269nn9,11; Geneva Disarmament Conference of 1932, 174; Geneva Naval Conference of 1927, 154–58; under Hoover, 173–74; London Naval Conference, 159–64, 169, 171; Moffett and, 267nn120,122; studies on, 147–48, 153
arms race: post WWI, 116–17, 133; pre-WWI, 10; Washington Naval Treaty of 1922 and, 188
Arthur, Chester, 13
Asada, Sadao, 224, 270n23

Badger, Charles J., 83*fig*, 95–97, 104, 106–10, 115–16, 125–26, 146, 186, 222, 257n58
Baer, George, ix, 30, 219, 249n1
Barnette, William J., 57, 65–67, 71
Beers, Henry P., 17, 232n11
Benson, William S., 89, 94*fig*, 101–2, 103, 105, 107–8, 111–12, 115, 117–20, 122, 197, 254n3
Bliss, Tasker, 14, 16, 27, 236n24

Blücher, Gebhard von, 34, 38, 62
Board of Admiralty, 10
Board of Inspection and Survey, 17, 31, 102
boards: Board of Admiralty, 10; Board of Inspection and Survey, 13, 17, 31, 102; Board of Navy Commissioners, 10; Board on Construction, 17; Board on Construction (BOC), 64, 68, 69, 73; Chapwick on, 19; Hepburn board, 266n100; Joint Army and Navy Board, 57, 66, 68, 72, 82, 87, 133, 181, 186; Joint Merchant Vessel Board, 102; Material Review Board, 219; Morrow Board, 133, 150–52; Naval Advisory Board (2nd), 13, 14, 16; Naval Advisory Board (Rodgers Board), 13, 235n20; Naval Strategy Board, 23; Naval War Board, 24–26, 29, 95, 243n69; Ships Characteristics Board (SCB), 202–5, 209; Swift's special board, 77; Taylor and, 27–28. *See also* General Board
Bonaparte, Charles J., 62, 65, 67–69, 71, 73, 227, 244n3
Bowles, Francis T., 21
Boxer Uprising, 42–43
Bristol, Mark L., 6*fig*, 7, 93, 166, 171, 176, 178, 186–87
Building and Maintenance Policy, 5, 143
Bureau of Navigation (BuNav): aide for operations and, 77, 79; Brownson and, 72; Chambers and, 85; chief

291

of, 38–39, 66–67; Converse and, 63; Crowninshield and, 24, 37, 47; General Order 23, April 16, 1901, 226; Naval War Board and, 24; Naval War College and, 16; OpNav and, 223; Potter and, 78; Taylor and, 4, 18, 45, 47–48; Walker as chief of, 14. *See also* Crowninshield, Arent S.
bureau system: beginning of, 10–11; co-opting of, 45; expansion under Fox, 11; reorganization of, 19–20; Taylor and, 21. *See also* naval bureaus
Burke, Arleigh, 8, 196, 199, 207, 209, 210*fig*, 211–12, 214–16, 218
Butler, Jarvis: attitude toward General Board, 1–2; quote, 1

Caribbean, 37, 42, 48–55, 50*map*, 59, 67, 229–30
Chadwick, French E.: General Board and, 30, 41, 44–45, 67; Mahan and, 18, 236n32, 237n47; "Naval Department Organization", 18–22; Naval War College and, 18–19, 43, 45, 74, 80; reform and, 31, 39; as reformer, 62; Taylor and, 27
Chandler, William E., 13, 14–16
Chase, Jehu V., 6*fig*, 154, 263n63
Chicago, 13, 17, 54, 235n20
Chief of Naval Operations (CNO): Benson and, 103–4; Benson as, 89, 94; creation of, 80, 83, 95, 100–102; Daniels and, 107; operational-level planning staff and, 5; reformist spirit and, 2; war planning, 54, 71, 83, 106
China, Boxer Uprising, 42–43
Civil War: Ammen during, 12; naval operations during, 14; Office of Assistant Secretary of the Navy after, 16; operational reforms during, 11
civilian attire, 3*fig*
civilian control, primacy of, 2
Cleveland, Grover, 23

Cole, Cyrus W., 6*fig*
Commander in Chief (CINC), Asiatic Fleet, 7
Commander in Chief (CINC), U.S. Fleet, 7
congressional legislation, 1882 initiatives, 13
Crowninshield, Arent S., 24, 29, 37, 47, 51, 54
Culebra. *See* Caribbean

Daniels, Josephus, 227; CNO and, 107; Dewey and, 94, 95, 105, 106; Fiske and, 87, 88, 89–91, 95, 112; General Board and, 88–102; Naval Act of 1916, 89; quote by, 88; and Roosevelt, Franklin D., 88, 90; as SecNav, 76, 87, 94*fig*
Dayton, Alston, 55, 76
defense reform/reorganization, 8
Denby, Edwin, 227
Dewey, George: aide for operations and, 63, 77–78, 81–82, 91; Badger and, 96–97, 104, 106, 186, 222; Blücher comparison, 34, 38, 62; on board membership, 44–45, 80; comparisons to, 126, 153; Daniels and, 94, 95, 105, 106; death of, 54, 89, 106–7, 115; early career of, 34; Fiske and, 34, 36–37, 80, 87–89, 91–92, 97; General Board legislation and, 45, 58; as General Board president, 4, 28–29, 35, 37, 40–41, 62, 66, 112–13, 226; Guam base and, 121–22; Hood and, 44; as incrementalist, 62; Joint Army and Navy Board, 57; Luce and, 63; Manila Bay, Battle of, 4, 24, 28, 34, 82; marital spirit of, 32; Nelson comparison, 34; Newberry and, 75; nonvoting officers and, 65–67; photos of, 3*fig*, 35*fig*; quote, 88; ship design issue, 67, 73–74, 223; Taylor and, 33, 36–40,

44, 47; Venezuelan crisis, 48–55, 50*map*; Wainwright and, 84; war planning, 223; war plans, 68–69, 82, 92, 96, 100–101, 102–4, 121–22 disarmament. *See* armament limitations
Dolphin, 49, 52, 235n20
Dreadnought Revolution, 9

Edison, Charles, 227
Evans, Robley D., 30, 34, 39, 76
ex officio memberships, eliminiation of, 7

Farragut, David, ADM, 11
Fisher, John "Jacky", 9
Fiske, Bradley A.: aide for operations and, 80, 89, 91–92; Benton and, 94; Bristol and, 93; CNO and, 89, 100–101, 102; on Crowninshield, 51, 54; Daniels and, 87, 88, 89–91, 95, 101, 112; Dewey and, 34, 36–37, 87, 91–92, 96–97; on General Board, 52, 80–87; general staff system and, 100–101; Guam base and, 121–22, 134, 256n36; influence of, 222; and insurgent reformers, 62, 75, 87, 102, 108; London Naval Treaty, 249n106; naval aviation and, 92–93; Naval War College and, 39; photo of, 83*fig*; RADM, 83*fig*; resignation of, 102; Taylor and, 39; WWI and, 97–102
fleet-building policy, General Board and, 4–5
Fletcher, Frank Friday, 79, 95–96, 106–7, 116, 189, 205–7, 222
Fletcher, Frank Jack, 7, 8, 221, 251n31; Badger and, 107; as chairman, 8; General Board and, 7; VDM, 8
foreign policy, jingoism, 10
Forrestal, James, 227; unification and, 8
Fox, Gustavus Vasa, 11, 18, 19, 21, 24, 76

France: naval organization of, 19; Washington Naval Treaty of 1922, 5
Friedman, Norman, ix, 247n58
Fullam,, 74, 76

General Board: overview of, 1–8, 221–22; conclusions, 223–24; establishment of, 28–30; General Board Studies 1901, 229–30; as innovative organization model, 222–23; meetings of, 3*fig*, 6*fig*; membership of, 210*fig*; studies, 245n22
General Board: 1900-1904: overview, 33–36; conclusions, 59–60; function of, 36–39; at sea, 47–55; Taylor and, 39–47, 55–59
General Board: 1900-1913: overview, 61–62; aide system and, 71–80; conclusions, 87; Congress and, 62–71; Fiske and, 80–87
General Board: 1913-1918: overview, 88–89; conclusions, 111–13; Dewey and, 102–11; SecNav and admirals, 89–97; WWI and CNO, 97–102
General Board: 1918-1922: overview, 114–16; conclusions, 137–38; Naval Battle of Paris, 116–20; Second Naval Battle of Hampton Roads, 124–33; Washington Naval Treaty of 1922, 133–37
General Board: 1922-1931: overview, 139–41; conclusions, 171; Flying Deck Cruiser (armament limitations), 164–70; London Naval Conference (1st), 152–64; Morrow Board (or under Morrow), 150–52; U.S. Naval Policy of 1922, 141–45; Washington Naval Treaty and, 145–50
General Board: 1932-1941: overview, 172–73; aircraft carriers, 185–87; aircrafts, 192–94; battleships, 184–85; conclusions, 194–95; cruisers and destroyers, 187–89; mobile base,

fleet train and amphibious warfare, 182–84; reorganization, 175–78; submarines, 189–92; treaty system, 173–75, 178–80

General Board: 1941-1951: overview, 196–97; admirals' revolt, 209–17; conclusions, 219; final year of, 217–19; resurgence of, 206–9; Ships Characteristics Board and, 202–6

General Orders: General Order 23, April 16, 1901, 225–26; General Order 544, March 13, 1900, 4, 225

General Staff, advocacy for, 19, 20, 21–22

Geneva Naval Conference of 1927, 154–58

Germany: military education system of, 13–14, 15*fig*; naval power of, 23, 34; Prusso-German influence, 36, 39, 235n21; Wilhelm II, 41, 76

Ghormley, Robert, General Board and, 7

Goodrich, C. F., 13, 18

Great Britain: Anglo-Japanese Alliance, 43, 56; influence of, 9, 76; Jeune École movement and, 23; as naval power, 19, 23; post WWI, 115–16; Washington Naval Treaty of 1922, 5

Greaves, Albert, 66

Greenslade, John, 6*fig*

Hart, Thomas, leadership of, 7
Heburn, A. J., leadership of, 7
Horne, Frederik, Joint General Staff, 7
Hosho (Japan), 143
Hunt, William, 13

incrementalists, 62. *See also* Chadwick, French E.; Dewey, George; Goodrich, C. F.; Taylor, Henry C.
insurgents. *See* reformers, insurent
Italy, Washington Naval Treaty of 1922, 5

Japan: Anglo-Japanese Alliance, 43, 56, 103, 241n40; Geneva Naval Conference of 1927, 154–58; Genro concept, 221–22; light cruiser use by, 189; London Naval Conference, 160, 162, 164, 169, 171; London Naval Conference of 1935, 179; Manchurian invasion, 174; naval construction, 154; naval expeditures of, 141, 143–44; naval power of, 23, 34; Pearl Harbor attack, 137, 198, 200; post WWI, 115–16, 120, 123, 133; relations with, 67, 117; Russo-Japanese War, 56, 68–69, 121; Sino-Japanese War, 22; War Plan Orange, 7, 68–71, 70*map*, 72–73, 82, 84, 92, 96, 98, 106, 120, 122–23, 140, 154, 191; Washington Naval Conference, 224; Washington Naval Treaty of 1922, 5, 133–34, 143; Williams on, 184

jingoism, 10
Johnson, Louis, 8
Joint Army and Navy Board, 66, 68, 72, 82, 87, 133, 181, 186
Joint Merchant Vessel Board, 102
Jones, Hilary P., on the *Pennsylvania*, 177*fig*

Key, Albert, 62, 66, 74, 75
King, Ernest: General Board and, 187, 200–202, 204–6; hearing testimony by, 256n45; influence of, 195–98, 222; leadership of, 7; naval aviation and, 123, 192–93
Know, Frank, 227
Korean War, 215, 217–18, 224

Langley, 143
Lincoln, Abraham, 11
Lodge, Henry Cabot, 24–25, 67
London Naval Conference (1st), 159–64, 169, 171

London Naval Conference of 1935, 140, 152–64, 173, 177, 179
London Naval Treaty, 164, 168–71, 173–74, 179, 249n106, 263n63, 269n11
Long, Andrew T., 118
Long, John D., 3, 227; base acquistions and, 37–38; Boxer Uprising and, 42–43; General Board and, 28–30, 37–38, 40, 44, 64, 255n15; Naval War Board of 1898 and, 2–4, 24–26, 95, 243n69; quote, 9; as SecNav, 37, 227; Taylor and, 26–30, 45
Long, Walter, 118–19
Love, Robert W., ix, 232n11
Lucas, Lewis C., 6*fig*
Luce, Stephen B.: Barnette and, 66–67, 71; on Bonaparte, 73; on General Staff, 24–25, 40, 57–60; influence of, 222; and insurgent reformers, 62, 65, 69, 240n29; Mahan correspondence with, 18, 23, 40, 236n29, 237n47, 239n74; Meyer and, 69, 71; Moody commission, 75–77; Naval Advisory Board (2nd) and, 16; Naval War College and, 80; photo of, 15*fig*; RADM, 15*fig*; as reformer, 14, 32, 39, 62–65; Taylor and, 22, 39, 58–60, 64, 78

Mahan, Alfred Thayer, 18, 25*fig*; Chadwick and, 18, 236n32, 237n47; *Chicago*, 13, 17; Dewey and, 34; on General Board, 25, 26, 76; geopolitical suppositions of, 22; Germany and, 41; Guam base and, 121–22; influence of, 30, 31, 76, 95, 222; Luce correspondence with, 23, 40, 236n29, 237n47, 239n74; military education and, 12–13; Moody commission, 76; Naval War Board and, 2, 24; Naval War College and, 16, 26, 46, 80, 235n17; navalism, 10; O'Neil and, 67–68; Ramsay on, 16–17, 23; as reformer, 12, 14, 25, 28, 32, 39; Roosevelt and, 24; Taylor-Mahan model, 186; Tracy and, 22; writings of, 14, 41, 239n74
Manila Bay, Battle of, 4, 24, 28, 34, 82
Marshall, George C., support for Joint General Staff idea, 8
The Martial Spirit (Millis), 10
material, organizational reforms and, 19, 21
Material Review Board, 219
Matthews, Francis P., 227
McKinley, William, 24, 47
McMorris, Charles H., VDM, 8
McVay, Charles B., Jr., 6*fig*
Metcalf, Victor H., 71, 73, 227
Meyer, George von L., 69, 71, 76–81, 86, 90–92, 95, 227
military education: German system of, 13–14; Mahan and, 12; U.S. Navy and, 9. *See also* Naval War College
Millis, Walter, *The Martial Spirit*, 10
Mitchell, Billy, unification and, 8
Mitchell, William "Billy", 124–33
Moffett, William, 133, 142, 151, 154, 163, 165–69, 180, 192–93, 266n109,113,114, 267nn120,122,126, 268n3, 270n28
Monroe Doctrine defense, 23–24, 47–55
Moody, William H., 227
Moody commission, 75–77
Morrow Board, 133, 150–52; unification and, 8
Morton, Paul, 76, 227

National Security Act of 1947, 8
National Security Council, comparison to, 5
national security reform, post WWII, 8
Naval Act of 1916, 89

296 / Index

Naval Advisory Board (2nd), 13, 14, 16; establishment of, 14–16
Naval Advisory Board (Rodgers Board), 13, 235n20
naval aviation, admirals' revolt, 8
naval bureaus: collaboration of, 7; Construction and Repair (BuC&R), 4, 8, 11, 17, 19; Engineering (BuEng), 4, 8, 19; Equipment (BuEquip), 19, 45; Medicine and Surgery (BuMed), 11; Navigation (BuNav), 11; Ordinance (BuOrd), 4, 16, 19, 24; Ordinance and Hydrography, 11; organizational innovations and, 13; organizational reforms and, 19, 21; Personnel (BuPers), 19, 22, 77–78, 211; Provisions and Clothing, 11, 19; Ships (BuShips), 8; Yards and Docks, 11. *See also* bureau system
naval construction. *See also* armament limitations; naval bureaus; Geneva Naval Conference of 1927, 154–58; London Naval Conference, 159–64, 169, 171; War Plan Orange and, 154
Naval Council, 20, 21, 27
"Naval Department Organization" (Chadwick), 18–22
naval expenditures, Depression era, 141, 143–44
Naval Institute. *See* United States Naval Institute (USNI)
Naval Policy of 1922, 5
Naval Reform Movement, 9–32; conclusions, 30–32; First Phase of Reform, 1879-1890, 11–18; General Board establishment and, 28–30; Goodrich on, 12; Interregnum period: 1891-1898, 18–28; Mahan on, 12; overview, 9–10; reformist spirit: 1812-1869, 10–11
Naval Strategy Board, 23
Naval War Board, 2, 24–26, 29, 40, 95, 243n69

Naval War College: aide system and, 77, 79–80; Chadwick and, 18–19, 43, 45, 74, 80; collaboration of, 7; establishment of, 15–16; faculty members of, 14; Fiske and, 39; General Board and, 37, 65, 72, 107, 145; Luce and, 80; Mahan and, 26, 46, 80, 235n17; Morrell and, 68; Naval War Board and, 24; Newberry and, 76; officer corps and, 13; ONI and, 21, 44–45; Pratt and, 107; presidents of, 7, 16; relocation of, 80–81; Sims and, 127; Taylor and, 19, 21, 22, 36, 46, 55, 59, 236n31; war planning and, 178; war-planning functions and, 17; warship design and, 180
navalism, 10
Nelson, Horatio, 33, 34
Newberry, Truman H., 73–76, 227
Newport, RI, Naval War College and, 16

Office of Assistant Secretary of the Navy, reestablishment of, 16
Office of Naval Intelligence (ONI): Chadwick on, 19, 21; establishment of, 14; General Order 23, April 16, 1901, 226; Naval War College and, 21; Taylor on, 54
Office of the Chief of Naval Operations (OpNav): Bureau of Ships within, 8; collaboration of, 7; establishment of, 5, 20
officer corps: during 1890s, 18; military education and, 13
operational-level planning staff: in civilian hands, 10; CNO and, 5
organizational reforms, 1880s, 13

Pearl Harbor attack, 137
Pennsylvania, Jones on, 177*fig*
Philippines: Manila Bay, Battle of, 4, 24, 28, 34, 82; naval base acquistions and, 37

Porter, David Dixon, 11–12, 13, 14, 16, 22, 34
Pratt, William V.: restructuring by, 7; structural changes by, 6*fig*; VDM, 183*fig*
Proceedings, beginning of, 12
Progressive Era, 2, 10
"The Purposes of a Navy, and the Best Methods of Rendering it Efficient" (Ammen), 12

Ramsay, Francis, 16–17, 23
Redles, W. L., 221–22
reformers, 14, 39, 62. *See also* Chadwick; Goodrich; Mahan; Porter; Robley; Rodgers; Walker
reformers, insurent, 61, 62, 64–65, 71–80, 87, 101, 108. *See also* Andrews; Barnette; Fiske; Fullam; Greaves; Key; Luce; Reuterdahl; Sims; Swift; Wainwright
Reuterdahl, Henry, 71–72
Revolt of the Admirals, 8
Richardson, J. O., 7
Rodgers, John, 14
Rodgers Board (Naval Advisory Board), 13
Roosevelt, Franklin D.: Anglo-American relations and, 170; as assistant SecNav, 88, 90–91, 99–100; General Board and, 198; influence of, 171; Joint General Staff proposal and, 7; Naval Act of 1940, 90; naval construction and, 172, 175; treaty system and, 178–79, 194
Roosevelt, Theodore: 3, 23–24; as assistant SecNav, 24; Bonaparte and, 68–69; General Board and, 58, 62–63; Japan and, 68; Naval War Board and, 2; navalism of, 10, 47; reformers (insurgents) and, 71–76; ship design issue, 4–5; Venezuelan crisis, 48–55

Roosevelt, Theodore, Jr., 134, 147
Russia, Russo-Japanese War, 56, 68–69
Russo-Japanese War, 56, 68–69, 121

Scharnhorst, Gerhard von, 33, 36, 38, 62, 223; comparison to, 36
scientific management (Taylorism), 86, 87
Secretary of Defense (SecDef): Forrestal as, 8; Johnson as, 8; RADM, 13; unification and, 8
Secretary of the Navy (SecNav): 1900-1951 list of, 227; General Board and, 2; Hunt as, 13; Naval Advisory Board (2nd) creation, 13; Sullivan as, 8; Welles, Gideon, 11
serial report system, 37, 84, 85, 141, 149, 153, 179, 217, 224, 229–30
Ships Characteristics Board (SCB), 202–5, 209
Sims, William, 36, 39, 53, 62, 69, 71–72, 74, 75; Fullam and, 76; influence of, 222; as insurgent reformer, 88–89; Naval War College and, 112, 127, 180; Pratt and, 107–8, 133; as reformer, 247n67; submarine war and, 107; testimony by, 253n71; during WWI, 197
Sino-Japanese War, 22
Soley, J. Russell, 13; Chile incident, 22–23; as librarian, 14; Office of Assistant Secretary of the Navy, 16, 17–18
Spanish-American War: contingency plans for, 22, 41; Converse during, 63; Dewey during, 34; Germany and, 41; Hobson during, 100; lessons from, 2, 9, 102; Manila Bay, Battle of, 4, 24, 28, 34, 82; militarism and, 10, 24, 27; reform and, 22, 26; Taylor during, 39
strategic planning, 8; General Board and, 5

studies: aide for operations and, 79–80; on arms limitation, 147–48, 153; on Atlantic Fleet, 67, 97; on capital-ship limits, 184–85; on flag officer employment, 218; on flying decks, 165, 267n120; on General Board's dissolution, 205; on German submarines, 109–10; hearings-study process, 197; on Japanese forces, 46; on Japanese language, 72–73; logistical studies, 84; Monroe Doctrine defense, 48–49; on naval aviation, 84–85, 93, 99, 270n28; naval base acquistions, 37–38, 42–43, 48; on naval bases, 122; naval intelligence, 104; on naval reserve, 84, 99; on new technologies, 84; on organizational innovations, 104; from *Ostfriesland* test, 128–33; on Philippine neutrality, 67; post WWII, 211–13, 215; production procedure for, 153; on treaty system, 174–75; on war and conflict, 232n4; on warships, 84–86, 98–99

Studies, General Board, General Board Studies Produced in 1901, 229–30

submarines, use of, 191

Sullivan, John L., 227; unification and, 8

Swanson, Claude A., 227

Swift, William, 65

Taft, William Howard, 3, 76–78, 86

Taylor, David W., 21, 109, 259n87

Taylor, Henry C., 3*fig*, 4, 21, 29*fig*, 259n87; Anglo-Japanese Alliance and, 56, 68; Chadwick and, 19–20, 22; comparisons to, 81, 93, 108, 126, 186, 222–23, 240n29; death of, 33, 39, 59–60, 61, 66; Dewey and, 36–38, 39; early career of, 39; General Board and, 39, 182, 242n69; General Board establishment and, 28–30; General Board legislation and, 45, 55–59, 71, 72, 243n86; as incrementalist, 62; Joint Army and Navy Board and, 56–57; Naval War College and, 19, 21, 22, 36, 236n31; Prusso-German influence, 14, 36, 39, 235n21; recommendations of, 26–28; as reformer, 14, 18, 36, 39, 62; replacement of, 62–63; Scharnhorst comparison, 33, 36, 38, 62, 223; Taylor-Mahan model, 186; Venezuelan crisis and, 47–55; on war planning, 69, 223

Towers, John, ADM, 8, 199*fig*

Tracy, Benjamin, 22

Treaty of Versailles, 120

treaty system: adoption of, 139; end of, 178–80; London Naval Conference and, 152–64; War Plan Orange and, 191

Turner, Frederick Jackson, Frontier Thesis, 11–12

United States Naval Institute (USNI): Ammen, Daniel, 12; founding of, 12; Soley, J. Russell, 14; Taylor as member of, 18

Upton, Emory, 14

U.S. Air Force, 8

U.S. Army, 7, 14

U.S. Marine Corps, 7

U.S. Naval Academy, 12–13

U.S. Navy: Constitution on, 9; Naval Library, 14, 16, 17, 27; special boards creation tradition of, 10

Versailles Peace Conference, 116–20

Wainwright, Richard, 62, 65; aide for operations and, 63, 78–79; aide system and, 246n44; General Board and, 114, 240n28; influence of, 222; as insurgent reformer, 40, 57, 62, 65–67; on naval aviation, 84; on naval treaty system, 139; Washington Naval Treaty and, 137

Walker, John G., 14(3), 17, 18, 25
war colleges, 9
War of 1812, 10
War Plan Orange, 7, 68–71, 70*map*, 72–73, 82, 84, 92, 96, 98, 106, 120, 122–23, 140, 154, 191
war-planning functions, 8; committees and, 37; Mahan on, 23; Naval Library and, 17; Naval War College and, 17; ONI and, 17; Soley and, 16
warship design: 2 battleship program, 54; battleships, 4–5; conflicts over, 4–5; new technologies of, 13, 17
warships: Board of Inspection and Survey and, 13, 17. *See also* warship design; *specific ships*
Washington Naval Conference, 110, 122, 140, 142–43, 146, 224
Washington Naval Treaty of 1922, 5, 87, 112, 133–38, 141–45, 147, 167; battleships and, 184–85, 194; cruisers and destroyers, 188–89; fortification clause, 194; London Naval Conference and, 152–64. *See also* treaty system
Washington Navy Yard, Naval Library and, 16
Welles, Gideon, Secretary of the Navy (SecNav), 11
Western Hemisphere issues: *Baltimore* incident, 22–23; Caribbean issues, 37, 67, 229–30; Venezuelan crisis, 48–55, 50*map*

Wilbur, Curtis D., 147–48, 155, 227, 265n83
Wilhelm II, German Kaiser, 41, 76
Williams, Clarence S., 122, 146
Williams, Edgar M., 6*fig*, 184–85
Wilson, Woodrow, 105; administration of, 98–99, 105; Daniels and, 88–91; declaration of war, 107; Fourteen Points speech, 234n5; Mexican civil war and, 95; Naval Act of 1916, 112; Versailles Peace Conference, 117–20
Winterhalter, 106–7, 109, 115, 126–27, 129, 222, 256n45, 257n58
World War I: postwar powers, 115–16; prewar arms race and, 10
World War II: aircraft, 194; aircraft carriers, 186–87; amphibious warfare, 182, 184, 217; cruisers and destroyers, 188–89; demobilization, 211; General Board and, 114, 195, 197, 200–202, 223; General Board during, 202; national security reform, 8; post WWII studies, 211–13, 215; ship building and, 143; submarines, 190–92; task forces, 104; unification and, 151

ABOUT THE AUTHOR

John T. Kuehn is a retired naval aviator who completed numerous cruises on board a variety of aircraft carriers. Kuehn teaches military history at the U.S. Army Command and General Staff College since July 2000. He earned his PhD in History from Kansas State University in 2007.

The Naval Institute Press is the book-publishing arm of the U.S. Naval Institute, a private, nonprofit, membership society for sea service professionals and others who share an interest in naval and maritime affairs. Established in 1873 at the U.S. Naval Academy in Annapolis, Maryland, where its offices remain today, the Naval Institute has members worldwide.

Members of the Naval Institute support the education programs of the society and receive the influential monthly magazine *Proceedings* or the colorful bimonthly magazine *Naval History* and discounts on fine nautical prints and on ship and aircraft photos. They also have access to the transcripts of the Institute's Oral History Program and get discounted admission to any of the Institute-sponsored seminars offered around the country.

The Naval Institute's book-publishing program, begun in 1898 with basic guides to naval practices, has broadened its scope to include books of more general interest. Now the Naval Institute Press publishes about seventy titles each year, ranging from how-to books on boating and navigation to battle histories, biographies, ship and aircraft guides, and novels. Institute members receive significant discounts on the Press' more than eight hundred books in print.

Full-time students are eligible for special half-price membership rates. Life memberships are also available.

For a free catalog describing Naval Institute Press books currently available, and for further information about joining the U.S. Naval Institute, please write to:

Member Services
U.S. Naval Institute
291 Wood Road
Annapolis, MD 21402-5034
Telephone: (800) 233-8764
Fax: (410) 571-1703
Web address: www.usni.org